Concepts in Urban
Transportation Planning

Concepts in Urban Transportation Planning

The Quest for Mobility, Sustainability and Quality of Life

Mintesnot G. Woldeamanuel

McFarland & Company, Inc., Publishers

Jefferson, North Carolina

LIBRARY OF CONGRESS CATALOGUING-IN-PUBLICATION DATA

Names: Woldeamanuel, Mintesnot G., 1975– author.
Title: Concepts in urban transportation planning : the quest for mobility,
sustainability and quality of life / Mintesnot G. Woldeamanuel.
Description: Jefferson, North Carolina : McFarland & Company, Inc., Publishers, 2016 |
Includes bibliographical references and index.
Identifiers: LCCN 2016000056 | ISBN 9780786499663 (softcover : acid free paper) ∞
Subjects: LCSH: Urban transportation—Planning. | Urban transportation policy. |
Urban transportation—Environmental aspects. | Local transit. | Choice of transportation.
Classification: LCC HE305 .W635 2016 | DDC 388.4—dc23
LC record available at http://lccn.loc.gov/2016000056

ISBN (print) 978-0-7864-9966-3
ISBN (ebook) 978-1-4766-2316-0

BRITISH LIBRARY CATALOGUING DATA ARE AVAILABLE

Front cover image © 2015 iStock/Thinkstock

Printed in the United States of America

*McFarland & Company, Inc., Publishers
Box 611, Jefferson, North Carolina 28640
www.mcfarlandpub.com*

To my students of the past and the future

Table of Contents

Part IV: Urban Transportation Outside the United States

Preface

Cities are at a crossroads. A choice between the widely practiced model of sprawled developments and the new models of smart growth, new urbanism, complete streets and transit-oriented developments is becoming the center of an ongoing discussion in the academic and practical world. With the concept of sustainability picking up momentum in several cities, shifting away from autocentric urban developments and focusing on alternative-to-driving options are the challenge many urban areas face today. Data shows that more and more people live in urban areas and the future is predicted to be an urban world. With that, there is an increase in travel demand, road congestion and a need to find a smart means of transport. One of the major crisis today's cities face is the complex nature of the problems associated with transportation. Safety, environmental protection and efficiency have become increasingly important in the transportation planning process. Our congested urban areas and spread-out suburban neighborhoods are a constant reminder that we need to create an efficient urban transportation system.

This book distinguishes itself as a textbook that enriches a classroom experience and at the same time serves as a reference for interested readers. Most transportation textbooks are engineering-oriented, which is sometimes intimidating for most urban planning students and students from public policy, environmental studies and political science. While transportation has long been treated as part of the civil engineering, most transportation planning courses are being offered under urban planning, geography or public policy departments/programs. Even some civil engineering programs have introductory transportation studies as a prerequisite for their transportation engineering courses. Therefore, this book is designed to deliver easy to understand yet comprehensive transportation planning content.

This book provides useful information on foundational concepts and practical tools for understanding the transportation planning process. It engages readers with the theoretical background, methodological tools and the social and environmental policies about urban transportation. Considering the rapid urban growth and increasing automobile use, this book offers a critical insight on how it is important for metropolitan planning agencies to plan on principles of sustainable transportation.

Thus, this book serves as an ideal reference for undergraduate and graduate courses as well as a resource for professionals. Drawing on critical transportation concepts, a range of case studies and practical examples, this book explores fundamental topics in the field. Historical origin and development of transportation; planning, policy and legislative initiatives;

the non-motorized and public transportation; environmental and social (in)justice issues and the concerns of safety are some of the topics covered. This book also discusses the social, health and economic impacts of autocentric developments and the possible soft and hard policy measures that address the issue. The crucial yet often forgotten policy topic of *travel behavior change* is also among the topics covered in the book.

Each chapter provides a range of resources such as case studies; chapter outlines, review questions and internet sources, making this book a user-friendly text. To enrich the learning experience of students, each chapter is designed to include class activities and project/paper ideas. PowerPoint presentations that summarize each chapter are also available upon request (urbantransportconcept@gmial.com) to assist instructors. These learning features make the book suitable for not only conventional face-to-face classes but also for the growing online instruction.

Finally, I wish to thank those individuals who played a significant role in completing this project. I especially thank Andrew Kent, Andrew Somers and Kevin Khouri for assisting me in gathering relevant information and Cody Deitz for proofreading. I am also thankful to Claude Willey for his insight and contribution to the travel behavior section of Chapter Six. Lastly, I am grateful to my students whom I not only learn from but who also have instilled in me the passion for creating this material.

Part I

History, Planning and Environmental Policy

1

Introduction: Exploring Urban Transportation

Chapter Outline

Introduction

The urban transportation system is the one that provides movement for passengers and freight in urbanized areas. The system comprises the roads, the different transportation modes, the regulation that guides the system, and the technology. The different modes that the urban transportation system supports include automobiles/private vehicles, public transportation, air transportation, water transportation and pipelines. The automobile is supported by the national, state and secondary highway systems, local and country roads and city streets while the public transportation relied on busways and railroad infrastructure. There are several commercial and general aviation airports that provide services for the air transportation. Canals, oceans and rivers provide a way for water transportation, which is heavily used for freight transportation while pipelines are used mainly to transport crude oil and refined products.

For the last several decades, the efficiency and safety of these different transportation modes have been improved with the fast-evolving technology. Ever since the creation of the horseless carriage at the turn of the 20th century, the world has experienced considerable advancements in the transportation field. These developments, especially of motorized means of transportation, have facilitated trade, increased production and made the world a closer place for everyone to live. Human civilization has transformed significantly due to the mobility and accessibility created by the transportation technology. The evolution of the different modes of transport effects the growth of societies not only at the local level, but also on the global scale. For example, with the introduction of the automobile and the innovation in the concept of interchangeable parts, motor vehicles have provided rapid, reliable and convenient transportation to society all over the world. Over the years, automobiles started to become easily available to the public and became a means of daily transportation for the majority. Statistics shows that between 1960 and 2012, the number of vehicles in the world increased from 120 million to 1.1 billion. In advanced countries such as the United States, data confirms that in 2011, there were 809 automobiles per 1,000 individuals. As developing countries grow economically, the number of vehicles in the world is increasing every year. With a combined population of 2.6 billion people, if China and India duplicated what the United States has in a distant future as ratio of vehicles to the population, we can project that there would be billions of cars on the world's street. This of course translates into various environmental, social and health issues and congestion problems. Even without the anticipated increase of vehicles from the developing and less developed countries, the impact of excessive driving is already pervasive and drastic.

To reduce or eliminate those negative consequences within the transportation system, proper transportation planning and policy is required. In fact, one of the challenges facing the growing, existing and emerging cities is how to manage the demand for travel within them. With rapid urbanization in the developed world and more so in the developing countries, the need to travel is increasing disproportionally to the supply on the transportation system. From experience, the resolution would appear to be the better direction in urban land use and transport planning, plus a greater orientation towards public transport. This can assist cities to better manage the existing and forecasted travel demand within them (Transportation Research Board 2004).

Primarily, the need for close land use and public transport integration has grown in recognition around the world over the last two decades. For example, in the United Kingdom, Planning Policy Guidelines No. 13 (PPG 13), a national planning policy guideline, provides clear direction to local councils considering town planning applications that promote non-car based travel (Department of Communities and Local Government 2001). In the United States, the Inter-modal Surface Transportation Efficiency Act (ISTEA) seeks to allocate federal funding towards transport projects that help minimize the environmental disruption of car-based trips and maximize land use and transport integration, especially where public transport can be promoted. The Dutch have a land use category system, known as the Dutch ABC policy, which gives higher development plot ratio benefits to developers that support transit-friendly land uses near or adjacent to public transport nodes (NEA Transport Research 1999). In Australia, cities like Brisbane have seen the emergence of state transport policy and guidance frameworks such as the Integrated Regional Transport Plan for South East Queensland, which promote reduced car trips and encourage residential and employment land uses around public transport nodes (Curtis 1998).

Formulating an integrated land use-transportation planning and policy is not an easy task as it encompasses multi-layered political, social, economic, engineering and environmental issues. Planners usually find themselves involved with balancing two different types of planning: short and medium-term or long-term (strategic) planning. The former is for less complex projects while the later can embroil huge expenditures, face uncertainties and involve multiple levels of government and administration.

Certainly, transportation is the most complex of human development, and it cannot be understood using a single point of view. Different chapters of this book draw different related concepts that help develop an understanding of the complexities of urban transportation including history, sociology, psychological and cultural studies, environmental science, spatial planning, geography and economics.

Historical Perspective

Transportation reflects the values, perceptions, aspirations, resources and physical environments of a society. Therefore, it is relevant to study the history of transportation as a basis for current and future planning. One of the value systems, especially in the Western world, is the concept of personal or individual freedom, including a freedom to live wherever one wants. Centuries ago, this freedom was restricted by factors such as lack of mobility and

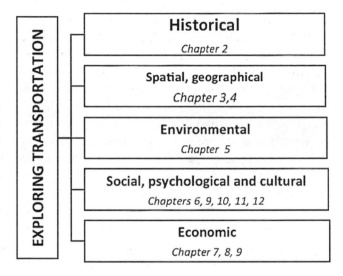

Figure 1.1 Understanding urban transportation

accessibility; distance was something to overcome. Allan Nevins, in his 1954 historical book, *Ford: the Times, the Man and The Company,* stated

> in our ever-swifter era we forget how recently men sweated, struggled, and crawled to win a few miles. A battle with distance: how great a part of American history is summed up in that phrase! To plant on three million square miles of wilderness a well-knit nation, to make pathways by water and land which would let Maine and Texas, Minnesota and California quickly exchange products, people and ideas, to fuse not merely the states but the countless local communities by efficient means of transport- these were ends toward which men struggled, using invention after invention, until they achieved victory. Each step toward success was a step in the defeat of distance and time. Modern America was built on these accomplishments and bound together them today [Nevins 1954].

The "battle with distance" has been won gradually, with horse-drawn carriages prior to the 20th century, and cheaper and lighter vehicles, fast-moving rails and airplanes during the 20th century. The automobile in particular, not only changed the distance gap, but also transformed the built and natural landscape of urban and rural areas alike. Of the many transportation developments, the automobile has played the most notable role in shaping modern culture.

With the birth of the Model T Ford, the family car became characteristically American. Like the Concord coach, it was rugged and simple. Like the buggy, it was light and cheap. European autos did not incorporate all these characteristics. Over the years, American family cars became bigger, more powerful and more luxurious, and were fueled by cheap gasoline. Even American [city] design drew further and further away from European design [The Henry Ford 2011].

The demand for driving brought the need for an efficient transportation system and there has been no national vision driving federal transportation policy in the United States like the completion of the Interstate Highway System in the 1980s. However, some argue that interstate highways create a historic shift from transit-oriented to a car-dependent society.

Learning from history, cities have recently started shifting away from complete car-reliance toward multi-modal transportation systems that balance the needs of drivers with those of bus and train riders, pedestrians, cyclists and taxi users. Bus Rapid Transit (BRT), street cars and light rail are all playing big roles in the multi-modal future of cities (Jaffe 2014), which reduces traffic and pollution and increase transportation options. Efficient public transportation systems such as intra and intercity rail and clean bus systems would make long distance travel better. Bike-share has gotten popularity in major cities; electric and hybrid cars are penetrating the market; and some cities are embracing anti-sprawl movements. Even the oldest forms of transportation, such as walking, are getting a fresh start with new focus of local governments on sidewalk improvements. This is not to mean that these alternative modes deny highways and cars, as they will still play a dominant role in the future of city mobility.

Consequently, as the agricultural and industrial revolutions are historical milestones of the past, the sustainability revolution is of the future, so smart, strategic investments in modern transportation systems are needed for creating a sustainable urban transportation system. The system needs to provide more reliability for people, goods and services to reach their destinations, boost nations' economic competiveness and enhance the quality of life for all.

Social, Psychological and Cultural Perspectives

One of the great functions of transportation for society is facilitating social interaction. However, when the transportation system gave way to the automobile, the role of transportation in creating social interaction gets in a controversial debate. While cars make it possible for people to travel greater distances to visit relatives or access important social services, the fact that people spending a lot of time behind the wheel is believed to have a detrimental effect on interaction among members of a community.

The transformation of society overtime causes a shift from a city that was concentrated at the core to an urban sprawled city that stretched far beyond the central core. Living farther from job centers and activity places causes longer hours spent traveling, especially by car, which is considered as times taken from social interaction with other individuals. In the walking era, one would interact with people on the street on the way to and from work. Even in the streetcar era, the opportunity for social interaction was very high when public transportation was the main mode of travel. But with the modern autocentric culture, commuters spend long hours going and coming to work. Studies indicate that people that rely on public transportation or people that walk or cycle have a greater opportunity for social interaction by being around other individuals (Adams 2011; Litman 2006; Leyden 2003). Also, residents that live closer to their employment locations mostly spend less time commuting and spend more time outside socially interacting with friends at restaurants or bars after work, or going to parks, beaches, shopping and other activities. They are less tired and have more energy to be socially interactive and develop a positive perception of the built environment.

On the other hand, reduced levels of walking, bicycling, and other physical activity have been associated with negative perceptions of the built environment (such as safety and traffic conditions) (Carver, Salmon and Campbell 2005; Carver, Timperio, Crawford 2008). For example, an article published in the Journal of Preventive Medicine revealed that inner-city children are engaged in less physical activity than suburban children because inner-city parents expressed much greater anxiety about neighborhood safety than suburban parents did. In the inner city population, children's physical activity levels correlated negatively with parental anxiety about traffic congestion and neighborhood safety (Weir, Etelson and Brand 2006). Indeed, the use of the streets as social and recreational gathering places was threatened and supplanted by the requirements of increasingly rapid and mounting vehicular traffic. That is the culture the car has created.

Car Culture

Around the time the car was invented, it was a luxury product exclusively for the rich and wealthy. Over time, automobile manufacturers were convinced that the future of the automobile lay with the average person, not the elite. Henry Ford was able to bring this ease of mobility to the masses by creating the Model T, and using an assembly line of production. He made it so that the car became affordable by the majority of Americans. Cities also began to invest more in automobile infrastructure in the form of newly paved roads. The car became a life style, a way of life, a culture.

Research suggest that while there is no denying that the number of cars on the road and the convenience they provide is a crucial component to car culture, the viewpoint of this culture should not simply be from a utilitarian perspective, but from a more personal and meaningful one. DeWitt (2010) holds that car travel allows for a person to separate themselves from the outside world, even as they are driving through it. "There is something intensely private about driving through public spaces in a car," he writes. "It is a time not only for travel to some place but for thinking, feeling, looking" DeWitt (2010). Sheller (2004) further expands upon the idea of more meaning in car culture, positing that the attraction to cars can be contributed to feelings and emotions that they can evoke within individuals. For instance, many derive a thrill from being able speed down an open road in a sports car, so, the car can be seen as a projection of ones interests, or as a status symbol that indicates personal achievement. Carrabine and Longhurst (2002) discuss the greater meaning within the automobile by researching how young people perceive it, finding that cars have been seen as opportunity providers for social participation, allowing them to meet and gather with friends at various locations. For these reasons alone, it should suffice to say that car culture is more than just an abundance of cars out on the road, and that cars elicit an attraction that extends beyond their utility to get people from place to place.

Public Transit Culture

Public transportation has its own culture as well, although many think that it is not the popular one (especially in many cities of the United State). However, record-breaking ridership numbers are emerging. More than 2.7 billion trips were taken on U.S. public transportation in the third quarter of 2014, according to a report released by the American Public Transportation Association (APTA). This is a 1.8 percent increase over the same quarter in 2013, and the highest third quarter ridership since 1974. APTA states that the reasons for the surge in public transit users include investment in public transportation by federal, state and local governments, increase in better transit services and a recovering economy (since most transit trips are work trips).

Within the culture of this growing mode of travel, there are clear patterns that emerge with people on a bus or a train. Generally, adult passengers tend to stay closer to the front, while youths tend to sit towards the back of the bus. Usually there are seats towards the front of the bus that are reserved for the elderly and the disabled. It is common for people to thank the bus driver as they exit the bus. Compared to private car drivers, public transportation riders are immersed in a completely different travel experience. As automobiles bring a culture of impersonality, public transportation brings about a culture of comradery. People on a bus tend to interact with one another. People who take the same bus every day and at the same time begin to see familiar faces, and these frequent bus riders begin to build a sense of community, even if they have never spoken before. Some riders are homeless or poor and routinely ask other riders for money. Although beggars can be a nuisance, there are also street performers who frequently use public transportations to collect donations. As panhandlers and street performers demonstrate, public transit is an ideal stage to perform (Fleetwood 2004). Street performers add to the culture of public transportation and can make it a "fun" and unique experience.

Another aspect of public transportation culture that goes unnoticed is the presence of vendors. It is not uncommon to see someone selling candy or drinks in a crowded metro train station at rush hour. These vendors add so much culture to the experience of taking public transportation and provide insight to the communities in which they reside. For some, having vendors at transit stations make taking public transportation more interesting.

People who rely on public transportation, especially in several cities of the United States, are considered disadvantaged when it comes to mobility. This is especially true as public transportation services are often poor or nonexistent outside central cities (Pisarski 1981). Before the automobile became commonplace, public transit worked very efficiently and the majority of city dwellers used it to get around. As the automobile became popular, public transportation ridership plummeted. Over time, people's perceptions of public transportation began to change. According to Smith (1990), poor ridership figures over the past 40 years show that mass transit has lost its public appeal and significance as a primary means of transportation for the American public as a whole. Today, the majority of people who ride public transportation in the United States are minorities and low-income people, and historically, public transportation has been related to racial and class tensions exemplified by Rosa Parks refusing to give up her seat to a white man on a Montgomery, Alabama bus. There is now a stigma attached to people who use public transportation; this stigma has also snowballed in some cases, leading to people perceiving public transportation as dangerous (Fleetwood 2004).

BICYCLE CULTURE

The bicycle has come a long way since the time it was invented, and so have its riders. Recently, riding a bike has become somewhat of a trend, changing the cultural and physical environment. In some cities, hundreds and thousands of riders even participate in "Critical Mass" events. This has spawned a culture of bike activists. Bicycle-friendly urban planning techniques that include bike parking, street striping, dedicated cyclist paths, and low-traffic "bicycle boulevards" are being introduced in many cities. In many ways, cycling puts people into the life of streets and connects them to friends, neighbors and strangers in ways that the car culture has blocked for so long (Carlsson 2011). For example, people that use a bicycle move through public space more slowly than they would if they were driving a car. Because of this, bicycles create opportunities for face-to-face contact with neighbors (Orsini 2006).

Like the car, the bicycle also has its share of devoted followers, with people all over the world using them for basic travel as well as for other activities such as mountain and cross-country treks, exercise or even competition in gigantic races such as Le Tour de France. Unlike the car, however, this culture of bike riding is considerably smaller, or at least not as pronounced, with more people preferring to drive a car than pedal a bike.

Nevertheless, there remain parts of the world where bike culture is the dominant force, more so than any other form of transportation. A perfect illustration of this point is the country of Denmark, where according to the nation's Cycling Embassy website, 9 out of 10 individuals own a bicycle, with 44 percent of all households not even owning a car. And it is within this country that one will find the city of Copenhagen, known to be one of the world's most bike-friendly cities with a count of 5 times more bikes than cars on its roads and where 4 out of every 5 people have access to a bike of their own. Bicycles have always been a major mode of travel in Copenhagen, with everyone from the general public to members of government participating. Around 1960s, the use of bicycles in the city started seeing a decline, as more and more cars became available to residents. However, in time, high accident rates, pollution, oil crises and an overall dissatisfaction about where the city was headed become prominent, prompting a shift back to focusing on tried and true bicycle culture. Now, it would seem that the city is better off having had that shift, with around 95 percent of residents happy with the city being a bike city (Cycling Embassy of Denmark 2012). Copenhagen presents an interesting question as to why the city's inhabitants, and moreover all of Denmark's, choose to stick with a bicycle culture, unlike in some countries where it seems to be primarily a form of leisure. Most Danish people associate the bicycle with positive values such as health, freedom and personal energy. To this sense of tradition, Kuipers (2013) states that condition that support cycling have also played a major part in the continued bicycle culture of the nation, noting that city planning regulations, government legislation, and even nightlife have focused on the bicycle, keeping it relevant in Danish society. Additionally, according to Lotte Ruby, from the Danish Cyclists Federation, citywide branding campaigns advertise the virtues of cycling, resulting in more cyclists and healthier and livelier city.

Environmental Perspective

The environmental aspect of transportation is the more pronounced perspective with the growing impact the transportation sector imposes on the environment. When the average person is asked about the environmental impact of motorized transportation, his common response focuses on post-production impact of an automobile such as air pollution. However, many fail to realize that even before a vehicle is driven a single mile, the environmental impacts are immense. Historian Mark Foster has estimated that "fully one-third of the total environmental damage caused by automobiles occurred before they were sold or driven." According to his findings, fabricating one car produced 29 tons of waste and 1,207 million cubic yards of polluted air (Melosi 2015). This analysis is based on the pollution caused by the extraction of iron ore, bauxite, petroleum, copper, lead, glass, rubber and other raw materials to produce steel, aluminum, plastics, and other materials. Aside from the extraction of these raw materials, the vehicle assembly plants create a lot of pollution (Melosi 2015).

Post production, the air pollution created by transportation, carries significant risks to human health and the environment. The most common form of pollutant associated with motorized transportation is Carbon Dioxide (CO_2), which is the primary greenhouse gas. It accounts for 82 percent of all greenhouse gas emissions in the United States. Particular Matter (PM) is also a pollutant that poses high risk because it penetrates into the lungs. Hydrocarbons (HC) are pollutants that react with nitrogen oxides and create ground level ozone that is a form of a photochemical smog that goes directly into the human body. Another pollutant, Carbon Monoxide (CO), is an odorless, colorless poisonous gas formed by the combustion of gasoline; it blocks oxygen to the brain, heart and other vital organs. And finally, Sulfur Dioxide (SO_2), which is caused by diesel fuel and is the leading cause of asthma in children (EPA 2015), is a product of the automobile combustion engine.

One of the significant environmental effects of transportation infrastructure is the urban runoff problem, which is a consequence of the paved roads. Rain from the paved roads causes contaminated toxic water to run into the oceans, lakes, rivers and streams. Obviously, runoff water is more severe and a bigger concern for regions that have heavy rainfall. The runoff water is toxic and affects the water supply and the wildlife that we rely upon for survival. Aside from killing the fish, the high levels of Mercury and other toxins travel through the food chain, ultimately affecting humans.

There are also other less damaging consequences of transportation, one being noise pollution. Trucks, motorcycles and airplanes all cause unbearable noise to those living near freeways, highways and airports. In some cases, transportation infrastructure creates an aesthetic nuisance. The use of asphalt, concrete, steel railings, and other materials take away from the natural environment and beauty of a neighborhood.

Of the many interventions that will be discussed in chapter 5, the adoption of land use controls to encourage compact cities and discourage urban sprawl help conserve the urban environment. This option is more of a long-term policy consideration as it is very difficult to change the landscape of a city overnight. However, as new cities are developed or urban revitalization is implemented in existing cities, land use controls could be used to create neighborhoods that reduce the demand for car travel. A recent study by The New Climate Economy indicates that sprawl (spread out development) imposes more than $400 billion dollars in external costs and $625 billion in internal costs annually in the United States, indicating that smart growth and land use control policies that encourage more efficient development can provide substantial economic, social and environmental benefits. Although these costs reflect North American conditions, the results are transferable to other countries (Litman, 2015). So, the goal of smart growth is to create a development that mixes housing, shopping and employment in a neighborhood so that residents do not always have to travel by car. Instead, transportation would be based on an affordable mass transit, bicycle or walking. In conjunction with the long-term land use planning tools, the government should adopt various strategic policies to reduce automobile use (refer to chapters 5 and 6). Since the environmental impact of transportation will remain an important issue for years to come, the key is to maintain sustainable growth by involving the public in the transportation planning process. Besides, technological companies and educational institutions need to expand their research and development of alternate means of creating energy that drive the transportation sector. Whether it's through electric vehicles or alternative fuels, technology should play a vital role in reducing transportation-related carbon footprint.

BOX 1.1 Highway removal: Harbor Drive—Portland, OR

Over thirty years ago, Portland made the decision to raze the Harbor Drive freeway and replace it with a 37-acre park, making it the first city in the United States to initiate the idea of freeway demolition. The Harbor Drive freeway was a three-mile, ground-level highway that ran alongside the Willamette River and provided a connection between an industrial neighborhood, Lake Oswego and areas south of downtown Portland. Built in 1942, the four-lane highway carried 25,000 vehicles per day. As the freeway construction movement gained momentum in the 1950s a number of additional facilities were planned for the Portland area. In 1964, the state completed the first freeway proposed under this plan, I-5, along the west bank of the Willamette River. Four years later in 1968 the State Highway Department proposed widening and relocating Harbor Drive between Front Avenue and the west bank of the Willamette River. However, by this time a movement to improve open space next to the waterfront had been initiated and the city's 1968 Downtown Waterfront Plan recommended eliminating the Harbor Drive freeway and developing the land as a park to beautify the downtown riverfront. A task force was organized to study the feasibility of removing the freeway and replacing it with a park. The nine-member task force was charged with evaluating and holding a public hearing on three alternative plans for the Harbor Drive freeway:

1. Cut and cover, which would underground the highway and place a park above the freeway on the land that the freeway once occupied
2. Widen the existing freeway and realign it to a straighter configuration
3. Relocate the Harbor Drive freeway to Front Avenue and increase capacity from four lanes to six lanes

Initially, the task force did not even consider the option of closing the freeway, based on projections that the roadway would carry 90,000 trips per day by 1990. Under increasing public pressure from the public and the governor, the task force revisited the issue and ultimately came to the conclusion that if the public were forewarned of the closure, traffic would adequately redistribute itself onto the network, and the freeway could be closed. The task force recommended closure and the proposal gained leverage when an alternate route, Interstate 405 was completed in 1973 and linked to I-5 by the Fremont Bridge. In May 1974, Harbor Drive was closed and removed to make way for construction of Tom McCall Waterfront Park. From the day of closure, no discernable congestion was recorded on surrounding surface streets.

After the removal of Harbor Drive, there were minimal negative traffic impacts partly due to the street patterns and traffic management of downtown Portland. To better manage traffic and more efficiently utilize the street grid, all the streets in the downtown were converted to one-way and the traffic lights were signalized to enable vehicles to travel across downtown without stopping. The conversion to one-way streets was also accompanied by reduced speed limits to ensure a safe and friendly pedestrian environment as well as a bike-compatible environment.

Adapted from "Case Studies in Urban Freeway Removal," Seattle Urban Mobility Plan, January 2008

Spatial and Geographical Perspective

When they began, cities were dense and compact. This condition created problems with overcrowding, housing shortage, and poor sanitation. People were forced to stay under these conditions because of the inability to travel long distances. The innovation of the horse car was a breakthrough in transportation and allowed the wealthy to move farther away from the over-crowded city centers. The electric streetcar allowed for the development of land outside of the city limits and the beginning of decentralized cities. More than this, though, the automobile was the ultimate change for the expansion and scattering of cities. It is clear that the spatial pattern and the geographical location of cities' function have been changed through time. This change indicates that it is hard to understand cities outside this spatial and geographical context.

The spatial and geographic aspects of transportation can be explained through several factors including location of residents and firms (also known as nodes), the path between different locations (also known as linkage) and the volume of traffic on the paths (also known as demand). The location of the linkage (the road networks) is determined by the forecasted travel demand (the number of trips that uses that particular road). The location choice of residents is a function of several factors such as household income, location of jobs, lifestyle and social identity. A study suggested that households place high values on travel times and costs but also value low density developments, access to high quality schools, and low noise levels in their choice of residential locations (Pagliara, Preston and Kim 2010). Where the job is located relative to residential location is becoming less of a factor for those who have better access to automobiles and freeways.

The geographic location of industries is also influenced by the availability of transportation infrastructure that connects the raw material site, the processing plant and the market. However, telecommunication and information technology is changing the spatial interaction of different locations as telecommuting and e-commerce are growing.

In this day and age, the manner in which land is used is determined by the idea that the transportation can close any gap distance creates. Cities took the form of decentralized and dispersed clusters and continued to be developed at long distances. The notion that distance is no longer a barrier allowed for the full development of the urban sprawl, where people travel everywhere by car for all their needs and services. City dwellers no longer had to sacrifice space and comfort for proximity to their jobs. The automobile makes it possible to extend to land outside of the regular city limits, giving people the ability to live outside of the densely populated city centers. This type of development created a bolder geographical division between the affluent and poor (Shore 2006), as those able to leave the deteriorating or otherwise undesirable city moved to suburban edges that were connected to their jobs in the city by highways. These factors lead to the broadening of geographic inequalities, in which those living in suburban fringes enjoy the benefits of living in livable and affordable neighborhoods while those unable to leave were forced to reside in deteriorated city centers.

Accordingly, as urban areas grow in size and road and highway construction projects are used to facilitate vehicular travel patterns, the challenge planners face is to accommodate local and regional travel demand with highway projects while not encouraging dispersed development, particularly in the urban fringe (Sanchez 2004).

To understand the spatial and geographical aspects of transportation, several spatial analysis techniques were developed. One of the techniques is Geographic Information System

(GIS) that helps analysts understand the geographical distribution and characteristics of people and structures. In a broad sense, a Geographic Information System (GIS) is an information system specializing in the input, storage, manipulation, analysis and reporting of geographical (spatially related) information. Among the wide range of potential applications GIS can be used for, transportation is one of the major ones. A specific branch of GIS applied to transportation issues has emerged, commonly labeled as GIS-T. It allows the integration of digitized drawings (maps) and rational databases for conducting efficient analysis of vast amounts of multi-attribute geographic information in a PC environment (Osegueda, *et al.*, 1999; ESRI 2001). Existing GIS data models provide an excellent foundation for supporting many GIS applications for transportation.

Economic Perspective

There is a very strong link between transportation and economic development. History shows that cities tended to be located near dependable and efficient transportation systems. This choice of location is because, without transportation, there's no linking of resources and markets, no regional specialization and resultant economies of scales, in other words, there is no economic development without transportation (Brenner 1995). While there are many different perspectives to analyze the importance of transportation, the economic perspective encompasses many parts of the perspectives discussed in the previous sections. The discussions of other perspectives such as spatial, geographical, historical and social are all economic-based. Even a basic concept of the relationship between transportation and land use is rooted in economic ideas primarily via the notions of consumer behavior (take, for example, auto ownership and suburban living) (Kelly 1994). To this end, the introduction of Ford's Model T in 1908 was a revolution in accessibility and mobility, but for Henry Ford, it was an economic success. Ford's assembly line made the car cheaper for all citizens. It was ingenuity in production practices that gave the majority access to increased accessibility and economic opportunity. The adoption of the assembly line had many monumental economic outcomes. The most notable was that it made all factory production cheaper and quicker, giving the Model T a huge consumer base to sell. For the individual consumer, life had drastically changed for the better. Cheaper production of goods and services lowered prices on all consumer products. Because of this, income per capita was higher than pre-industrialization times, and transportation costs for private and public business were lower.

At the regional and global scale, industrialization, urbanization and globalization have been the driving forces behind the upscaling and expansion of road systems as fast-moving transport are essential instruments of most economies (Garre, Meeus and Gulinck 2009). At the national level, transport investment creates improved economic and social well-being of communities by enabling economic expansion and job creation and thus improved living standards. From early cities to the modern ones, the economic success of a city was measured in terms of the efficiency of its transportation system in distribution and collection of goods and services.

There is a branch of economics called *transport economics* that deals with the demand, supply, resource allocation, etc., within the transportation sector. Within the economic study of transportation, there are also different economic models developed to understand consumer behaviors such as transportation mode choice, location preference and others. Such econometric models also study the demand of the traveler vis-a-vis the supply of transportation infrastructure. The effects of increases in supply (construction of new roads, widening of existing roads, providing railroads, etc.) are of particular interest in transport economics because of the concern of *induced demand* and potential environmental and social externalities possibly caused by the expansion of the transportation infrastructure.

As with any economic sector, transportation also imposes externalities on non-users of the system. Transportation externalities are the unintended consequences of the development of transportation infrastructure that is borne by those who are not using the system. Those externalities include air and noise pollution, accidents and traffic congestion. Traffic congestion is one important transportation-related externality that challenges urban residents. To alleviate the congestion problem, in addition to regulatory and engineering solutions, some places introduced a pricing strategy. Tolls on highways and congestion pricing in urban cores are examples of internalizing the cost of congestion to real users.

BOX 1.2 London congestion pricing

Since 17 February 2003, motorists driving in central London on weekdays between 7:00 a.m. and 6:30 p.m. are required to pay £5, increased to £8 in July 2005. There are exemptions for motorcycles; licensed taxis, vehicles used by disabled people, some alternative fuel vehicles, buses and emergency vehicles, and area residents receive a 90 percent discount on annual passes. The charging area is indicated by roadside signs and symbols on the roadway. The city expanded the zone westward in 2007, but this was reduced back to its original area the same year due to political opposition. Payments can be made at selected retail outlets, payment machines located in the area, by the internet and cellular telephone messaging, anytime during that day. Motorists can purchase weekly, monthly and annual passes with modest (15 percent) discounts. A network of video cameras records the license plate numbers of vehicles and matches it with the paid list. The owners of vehicles that have not paid as required are sent a £80 fine. This fine is reduced to £40 if paid within two weeks and increases to £120 if not paid after a month—the same policy for parking penalties in the inner London area.

The system is considered effective. Approximately 110,000 motorists a day pay the charge (98,000 individual drivers and 12,000 fleet vehicles), increasingly by mobile phone text message. Non-payment rates were high during the first few weeks, due to general confusion and errors (such as motorists confusing number 0 or 1 and the letter O or l), but these declined as users and operators gain experience. Transport for London and various academic organizations established a five-year monitoring program to evaluate the transport, economic, social and environmental impacts of congestion charging. Just over a million people enter central London during a typical weekday morning peak (7–10 a.m.). Over 85 percent of these trips are by public transport. Prior to the congestion pricing program, about 12 percent of peak-period trips were by private automobile. During the programs first few months automobile traffic declined about 20 percent (a reduction of about 20,000 vehicles per day), resulting in a 10 percent automobile mode share. Most people who change their travel patterns due to the charge transfer to public transport, particularly bus. Some motorists who would otherwise drive through Central London during peak periods shift their route, travel time or destination. Others shift mode to taxis, motorcycles, pedal cycles, or to walking. This has significantly increased traffic speeds within the zone. Average traffic speed during charging days (including time stopped at intersections) increased 37 percent, from 8 mph (13 km/hr) prior to the charge up to 11 mph (17 km/hr) after pricing was introduced. Peak period congestion delays declined about 30 percent, and bus congestion delays declined 50 percent. Bus ridership increased 14 percent, and subway ridership about 1 percent. The third-year annual report indicates that these improvements are continuing. Taxi travel costs declined significantly (by 20–

40 percent) due to reduced delays. Vehicles can cover more miles per hour, so taxi and bus service productivity (riders per day) and efficiency (cost per passenger-mile) increased substantially. There has been some increase in motorcycle, moped and bicycle travel, and vendors have promoted these modes.

Adapted from "London Congestion Pricing Implications for Other Cities" by Todd Litman from Victoria Transport Policy Institute, 2011.

TRANSPORTATION FINANCE

Another concern on the economic perspectives of transportation is the financing of transportation infrastructure for new projects as well as maintaining the old ones. The issue of financing is related to how to generate revenue and how to fairly and equitably allocate funds for different projects. Different forms of taxes and users fee are sources of revenue while the allocation of funds creates a controversial political debate in terms of social equity issues. Different federal, state and local governments use different approaches to distributing funds to short-term and long-term projects, and each approach has its supporters and opponents concerning allocation resources across neighborhoods with different socio-economic background in a fair manner.

THE HIGHWAY TRUST FUND: FINANCING IN CRISIS

Highway Trust Fund is the source of funding for most of the surface transportation programs in the United States. The fund is generated through 18.4 cents per gallon federal gas tax (and varied state taxes) from drivers and issued for maintenance and repair of federal and state highways and other roads. As electric cars start hitting the road and more efficient automobiles increase in number, coupled with inflation, there is a growing concern that there is no enough money being generated to the Highway Trust Fund. In 2008, the average fuel efficiency of new U.S. passenger cars was 31.2 miles per gallon, the highest figure ever. With more hybrid and electric vehicles in the marketplace, this efficiency is expected to continue impacting the federal gas tax. The U.S. Congress has annually compensated for the deficit by plugging funds for the general fund money. Congressional committee members proposed willingness to raise the federal fuel tax, but it didn't get the support required to get it through.

Given the federal government lack of action to solve the deficit problem, many states take their own actions. For example, the state of Utah approved a five cent increase to the state 24.5 cents per gallon gasoline tax that starts in 2016. The state of Oregon is a pioneer in looking for ways to charge users a distance-based, rather than a gallon-based fee. Under the oReGo pilot program, Oregon is seeking volunteers to pay a user charge of 1.5 cents per mile while driving on public roads instead of the 30 cents per gallon state fuel tax. This distance-based road usage charging program is believed to be a fair and sustainable revenue collection system as technology advances, and governments are shying away from fuel based economy. Iowa approved a bill that raised state's gas tax by 10 cents to 32 cents per gallon.

Review Questions

1. What are the different modes of travel and how are they supported by the transportation system?

2. Transportation is the most complex of human development. What are the different concepts that help develop an understanding of the complexity of urban transportation?
3. Discuss the relevance of the historical perspective of transportation.
4. Critically analyze the following statement: "In an autocentric culture, the contribution of transportation in facilitating social interaction is small."
5. What are some of the factors responsible for the development of a car culture?
6. What are some of the cultural displays of public transportation and bicycles?
7. What are the adverse impacts the transportation sector imposes on the environment?
8. What are some of the factors in which the spatial and geographical aspects of transportation can be understood?
9. Critically analyze the following statement: "While there are many different points of view to analyze the importance of transportation, the economic perspective encompasses many parts of other perspectives."
10. What are transportation externalities? What are some measures introduced to alleviate those externalities?

Project/Paper Ideas

1. Choose one of the perspectives discussed in this chapter. Conduct a detailed literature review and collect data specific to your city (survey, secondary data from various sources, field observation, etc.) What new insights do you develop about your city's transportation?
2. The role of transportation in creating social interaction gets in a controversial debate. While cars make it possible for people to travel greater distances to visit relatives or access necessary social services, the fact that people spending a lot of time behind the wheel is believed to have a detrimental effect on interaction among members of a community. Using data from different sources (U.S. Census, National Household Travel Survey [NHTS], etc.), prove or disprove this narrative.

Videos

Transportation by *Films Media Group, 2006 (53 min.):* In this video, Ronald E. G. Davies, curator of air transport at the National Air and Space Museum, historian Ruth Schwartz Cowan, MIT researcher Andreas Schafer and other authorities investigate the revolutionary impact of modern transportation on society and on the environment, where pollution is taking a heavy toll.

Internet Sources

Victoria Transport Policy Institute (VTPI). http://www.vtpi.org/.

Bibliography

Adams, John. 2011. "The Social Implications of Hypermobility." *RSA Lecture.*
Brenner, Charles. 1995. "Transportation and Economic Development." *Executive Speeches*, 22.
Carlsson, Chris. 2011. "King of the Road." *Boom: A Journal of California* 1 (3): 80–87.
Carrabine, E., and B. Longhurst. 2002. "Consuming the Car: Anticipation, Use and Meaning in Contemporary Youth Culture." *Sociological Review* 50 (2): 181–196.

Carver, A., J. Salmon, and K. Campbell. 2005. "How Do Perceptions of Local Neighborhood Relate to Adolescents' Walking and Cycling?" *American Journal of Health Promotion* 20 (2): 139–147.

Carver, A., A. Timperio, and D. Crawford. 2008. "Playing It Safe: The Influence of Neighborhood Safety on Children's Physical Activity – A Review." *Health Place* 14 (2): 217–227.

Curtis, Carey. 1998. "Integrated Land Use and Transport Planning Policies." A Discussion Paper for Ministry for Planning.

Cycling Embassy of Denmark. 2012. "Collection of Cycle Concepts 2012."

Department of Communities and Local Government. 2001. "Planning Policy Guideline 13, Transport." UK.

DeWitt, J. 2010. "Cars and Culture: Songs of the Open Road." *American Poetry Review* 39 (2): 38–40.

EPA. 2015. *"Carbon Dioxide Emissions."* Environmental Protection Agency.

ESRI. 2001. *Getting to Know ArcGIS Desktop, Basics of ArcView, Arceditor, and ArcGIS.* Redlands, CA: ESRI.

Fleetwood, N. 2004. "'Busing It' in the City: Black Youth, Performance, and Public Transit." *The Drama Review* 48 (2).

Garre, Sarah, Steven Meeus, and Hubert Gulinck. 2009. "The Dual Role of Roads in the Visual Landscape: A Case-Study in the Area around Mechelen (Belgium)." *Landscape and Urban Planning* 92 (2): 125–135.

The Henry Ford. 2011. "Transportation: Past, Present, and Future: From the Curators."

Jaffe, Eric. 2014. "The Future of Transportation Is Not All Flying Cars." *City Lab*, October 10.

Kelly, Eric. 1994. "The Transportation Land Use Link." *Journal of Planning Literature* 9 (2): 128–145.

Kuipers, G. 2013. "The Rise and Decline of National Habitus: Dutch Cycling Culture and the Shaping of National Similarity." *European Journal of Social Theory* 16 (1): 17–35.

Leyden, Kevin. 2003. "Social Capital and the Built Environment: The Importance of Walkable Neighborhoods." *American Journal of Public Health* 93 (9): 1546–155.

Litman, Todd. 2006. *Cities Connect: How Urbanity Helps Achieve Social Inclusion Objectives.* Victoria Transport Policy Institute.

_____. 2015. *Analysis of Public Policies that Unintentionally Encourages and Subsidize Urban Sprawl.* Victoria Transport Policy Institute.

Melosi, Martin V. 2015. "Automobile and the Environment in American History: Environmental Costs of the Auto-mobile Production Process." *Automobile and the Environment in American History.*

NEA Transport Research. 1999. "A-B-C Location Parking Policy." The Hague, Netherlands.

Nevins, Allan. 1954. *FORD: the Times, the Man and the Company.* Scribner.

Orsini, Arthur F. 2006. "Fun, Fast and Fit: Influences and Motivators for Teenagers Who Cycle to School." *Children, Youth and Environments* 16 (1): 121–132.

Osegueda, R., A. Garcia-Diaz, S. Ashur, O. Melchor, S. Chang, C. Carrasco, and A. Kuyumcu. 1999. "GIS-Based Net-work Routing Procedures for Overweight and Oversized Vehicles." *Journal of Transportation Engineering* 125 (4): 324–331.

Pagliara, Francesca, John Preston, and Jae Hong Kim. 2010. "The Impact of Transport Policy on Residential Location" In *Residential Location Choice, Advances in Spatial Science*, by Francesca Pagliara, *et al.* (eds.), Springer-Verlag Berlin Heidelberg.

Pisarski, A. 1981. "America Enters the Eighties: Some Social Indicators." *Transportation: Annals of the American Academy of Political and Social Science:* 70–95.

Sanchez, Thomas. 2004. "Land Use and Growth Impacts from Highway Capacity Increase." *Journal of Urban Planning and Development* 130 (2): 75–82.

Sheller, M. 2004. "Automotive Emotions: Feeling the Car." *Theory, Culture & Society* 21 (4/5): 221–242.

Shore, William. 2006. "Land Use, Transportation and Sustainability." *Technology and Science* 28 (1): 27–43.

Smith, M. 1990. "The Role of Marketing in Mass Transit: An Empirical Investigation." *Transportation Journal* 30 (1): 30–35.

Transportation Research Board. 2004. "Transit-Oriented Development in the United States: Experiences, Challenges, and Prospects." Washington, D.C.

Weir, L., D. Etelson, and D. Brand. 2006. "Brand Parents' Perceptions of Neighborhood Safety and Children's Physical Activity." *Preventive Medicine* 43 (3): 212–217.

2

History of Urban Transportation:
How Highways and Automobiles
Shape American Cities

Chapter Outline

- In the Beginning...
- The Advent of Motorization
- Development of U.S. Roads and Highways Systems
    - o *Traffic Control Systems*
- Getting into the Car Culture
- The Need for Planning and Policy
- Environmental Concerns
- Recent, Future and New Technologies

In the Beginning

Prior to the start of the 19th century, cities were relatively dense urban settlements in which the dominant means of getting around was a walk. People had access to locations that are within 3 to 5 miles. With reduced mobility and accessibility, almost all economic activities and residential areas were concentrated in one central place. Horse and carriage transportation enabled the wealthy to reside in the nearby countryside while the rest of the population lived in overcrowded centers with unsanitary conditions. The development of a horse cart allowed the development of transportation corridors, and railways enabled radial development adjacent to railway stations (Rodrigue 2013). Especially, the railroad was the most important transport development of the 19th century. It allowed for fast travel over great distances at relatively cheap costs, stimulating economic development. Rail is also credited with the standardization of time, which was necessary to schedule trains coming and going from local stations. Rail also came to dominate intercity transportations, gradually replacing the horse with the electric streetcar. The electric streetcar was a decentralizing force, allowing people to live farther from the urban center. Development revolved around electric street car lines produced the first suburbs, first in London and then in North America, and the rest of the world. Over the course of several decades, a number of different kinds of transportation fought for dominance in the streets. For a brief period, pedestrians, horses (and horse carts), streetcars and even the automobile were all present. But eventually, the right to the city streets was ultimately decided by the end of World War II: the automobile controlled the street.

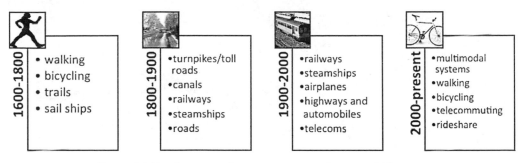

Figure 2.1 Development of transportation modes in world history.

The Advent of Motorization

The introduction of the steam engine by Thomas Newcomen in 1712 opened a door for many new capabilities for surface and water travel (Coppa and Harmond 1983). However, the pioneers of steam-driven vehicles dated back to 1770. Nicolas Joseph Cugnot was a French engineer who began to experiment with steam-driven machines. Cugnot is credited with developing the world's first self-propelled vehicle. Created based on Newcomen's engine, Cugnot's three-wheeled vehicle could carry four passengers and moved at a walking pace. While not impressive compared to latter developments in engine technology, this was a breakthrough for the time and a first major step in revolutionizing transportation. Built in 1769, Cugnot's carriage was originally designed to haul heavy artillery pieces (Georgano 1972). Intended for towing heavy cannons, its maximum speed without a load was only 4 mph (miles per hour), and it had to stop every fifteen minutes in order to build up a fresh head of steam. Eventually Cugnot overcame this problem and added further improvements to the Newcomen's engine, which employed the steam power to move pistons without condensation, significantly improving engine efficiency. Georgano (1972) explained how the engine works as follows:

> ... His (Cugnot's) engine consisted of two, 13-inch (33 cm) and 1.75-cubic-foot (50-liter), pistons connected by a rocking beam which were synchronized so that when atmospheric pressure forced one piston up, high-pressure steam forced the other piston down. The reciprocating motion was transferred to the axle, where it produced the rotary motion that turned the wheel. This arrangement is considered to be the first successful device for converting interchanging motion into rotary motion.

At the same time, British inventor James Watt made a strategic plan to use the steam power source. Watt's steam engine, developed sporadically from 1763 to 1775, was the great next step in the development of the steam engine. Offering a dramatic increase in fuel efficiency, the new design replaced Newcomen engines in areas where coal was expensive, and went on to be used in the place of most natural power sources such as wind and water. This invention was soon arguably the most important technology of the Industrial Revolution. It

Figure 2.2 Cugnot's 1771 steam-driven car.

was so significant because prior mills required water power, but by using a steam engine, a factory could be located anywhere, not just close to water.

Cornish engineer Richard Trevithick, who was a believer in "strong steam," believed he could build engine weighing no more than 2 or 3 tons that was much cheaper in first cost and also more economical to operate than a Watt's engine. Trevithick turned his attention to locomotives and in 1802 built one intended to set it on the railway of Penydarren (South Wales) to haul a 10-ton load. It was a success, and he proceeded to build two more locomotives, sparking the era of rail transportation for goods. This increased productivity as well as revenue due to being able to ship and receive products more efficiently and more rapidly (Lira 2001).

The years of 1890–1920 is considered as the electric streetcar era. During this time, the key to the first urban transport revolution was the invention of the electric traction motor by one of Thomas Edison's technicians, Frank Sprague. This innovation was ranked and remembered to be one of the most significant in U.S. history. The rapidity of this invention was enhanced by the abrupt recognition of its ability to mitigate urban transportation problems. The low-fare electric streetcars replaced the slower and less reliable horse cars, offering public transportation to a growing ridership. Streetcars, however, still relied on light-rail tracks radiating out from the central business districts into the surrounding areas and newly forming suburbs. Such development of the first forms of urban mass transportation lessened the accessibility constraint and enabled cities to expand along main tramway (streetcar) lines, creating transit corridors. In tripling the speed of urban transport, electric streetcars extended the spatial structure of cities. This permitted the emergence of specialized downtown areas with commercial and service activities. In some instances, motors could be attached to existing horse cars to convert them into self-propelled vehicles powered easily with constricted overhead wires. This allowed the development of urban activities beyond city limits and expanded emerging metropolises. The most dramatic impact of this era was the swift residential devel-

Figure 2.3 A full-size reproduction of the Penydarren locomotive, National Waterfront Museum—Swansea (Copyright© Mick Lobb, Creative Commons).

opment of those urban borders, which expanded the developing metropolis into a particularly star-shaped spatial entity. This morphological pattern was produced by trolley corridors encompassing several miles beyond the compact city limits. The quality of housing and prosperity of the street car suburb increased with distance from the central city line. This reinforced social stratification and favored the emergence of neighborhoods differentiated by socioeconomic status. Low-income people, limited in their mobility, tended to remain in central areas while the wealthier relocated to the first suburbs (Muller 2004).

In the United States, it is during this time that many cities felt the impact of industrialization in terms of factory migration to cities and the influx of thousands of European immigrants and rural American migrants. Industrial cities were focused at the core, especially for various business ventures, commerce and trade, retailing, hotel accommodations, and cultural activities. The separation between work and residence for the middle and upper classes was much more pronounced, as the well-to-do residents increasingly fled the central cities for the suburbs. The working classes, by contrast, remained near the core and close to industrial workplaces since they had little or no access to public transportation and had to live by the clock or lose their jobs (Barger 1951). Although motorized transportation, such as streetcars, radially expanded cities and lessen the accessibility constraint, never a technical innovation had a greater impact on a spatial organization than the automobile.

Initially, only wealthy classes could afford their own automobiles that were used mainly for recreational purposes (Kaszynski 2000) but it was Henry Ford with his revolutionary assembly line manufacturing techniques who first mass produced cars. Assembly line pro-

Figure 2.4 Henry Ford's 1920 Model T.

duction drove the price of the Model T down from $950 to $490 in the early1990s, making automobiles available to a majority of Americans. The private car further increased the emergence of the low-density suburbs with increased ethnic and economic segregation. With this, the decentralization of commercial and industrial activities intensified. The overall growth rate of suburban population for the first time exceeded that of the central cities.

It is during this phase that European and North American urban development started to diverge; America went into the era of decentralization while European cities remained compact and centralized (Farris 1967). In order to facilitate the diffusion of the road as a mode of urban transportation in the United States, several oil and car companies bought and dismantled tramway systems. For instance, in 1938, General Motors and Standard Oil bought the Pacific Electric Railway of Los Angeles and replaced tramway system with buses. Consequently, the influence of streetcars in the urban development of North America was removed, while it endured in many European cities (Kaszynski 2000).

Development of U.S. Roads and Highway Systems

After the Revolutionary War, in late 18th century, the government was unable to fund roads, so private parties were required to fill the void of funding and building new roads. To care for the costs of building and maintaining the roads, a toll system was used to raise funds. However, the early toll system could not keep pace with road costs, so again road construction came to a halt for some time (Kaszynski 2000).

With the introduction of new travel modes, people began to pressure state governments for better roadways along with other infrastructure improvements. At the beginning of the 20th century, when people actually started using automobiles to travel, the need for an efficient transportation system became apparent. When highway construction first began, cars were more of a pleasure vehicle. Because of this, the highways were relatively short and connected Point A to Point B with little regard to the exact path taken (Weiner, 1992). Many cities did not connect in a manner that would be very efficient; however, this was not considered a problem, as most people did not rely on a transportation system outside of the central city. However, new attitudes of an emerging progressive era began to shape demands for improved roadways, especially with the introduction of the production line automobile making private auto ownership affordable to the common man.

New Jersey was the first state, in 1891, to adopt a state aid plan where state funds were made available to local counties for new roadways and road improvements (FHWA 1976). In 1893, the federal government developed the Office of Road Inquiry that advised local governments on best practices for roadway improvements. As developments from the industrial revolution progressed, the first federal aid bill passed, creating the Bureau of Public Roads (BPR) in 1902. It marked the first time the federal government was directly involved in road building efforts through the introduction of the BPR. The bill would also administer $20 million a year in federal aid to states through the Bureau of Public Roads. Grants would be made to any state or county that agreed to pay fifty percent of construction costs. The federal government would prepare the specifications, but the state or county would administer and supervise all contracts and work.

The new demands took the forming of many newly developed organizations that established the good roads movement. The American Automobile Association (AAA) was one, which supported federal action for roadways, founded five years prior to the 1907 ruling of Wilson v. Shaw that gave Congress the power to construct interstate highways under the constitutional right to regulate interstate commerce. Shortly after that, the American Association of State Highway Officials (AASHO) was established in 1914, supporting states' advocacy for a national road improvement program (FHWA 1976).

The AASHO drafted a proposed bill to Congress that appropriated seventy-five million dollars over a five-year period for federal aid for states' roadway development. The Senate approved ten million dollars a year for ten years that both houses passed. In 1916, the Federal Aid Road Act passed requiring each state to have a highway agency for federal aid projects that improved rural post roads and enhanced socio-economic qualities of life. Also, The Federal Aid Highway Act of 1921 allocated federal aid to states for state highways. In the 1920s, many highways and roadways were constructed from advances in highway technologies that were relatively standardized. Despite construction advances, there were problems with these highways; for instance, each had their own haphazard signage, which created dangerous and confusing situations for motorists. In 1924, the Bureau of Public Roads, part of the Secretary of Agriculture's Department, was asked to investigate the creation of a system of highways with standard numerical designations. In 1925, the federal government wanted to have a continuous national system of highways, and did so by approving the Federal-Aid Highway Act of 1925 (Weiner 1992). The Federal Aid Highway Act of 1925 marked interstate highways as a response to growing needs and demand of connecting the nation.

The 1920s and 1930s marked many improvements in transportation in the U.S. This included two lane traffic roads, plantings on medians and roadways, the first transcontinental highway (Lincoln Highway), and introduction of the concept of the first formal Interstate Highway System (IHS). From 1920 to 1940, nearly a million miles of roads were surfaced, and over $40 billion was spent for construction and maintenance (Owen 1957).

The Federal-Aid Highway Act of 1934 authorized that 1.5 percent of the funds apportioned to any state annually could be used for surveys, plans, engineering, and economic analysis for future highway construction projects. The act created the cooperative arrangement between the U.S. Bureau of Public Roads, now the U.S. Federal Highway Administration, and the state highway departments, to conduct what was known as the statewide highway planning surveys. By 1940, all states were participating in this program (Holmes and Lynch 1957). The nation was primed for a formal highway system that was introduced by the Federal Aid Highway Act of 1944. It established the National System of Interstate Highways, and a federal-aid system for principal, secondary, and feeder roads. However, it was not until the Federal-Aid Highway Act of 1956 that any significant work on the system began.

The Federal-Aid Highway Act of 1962 is what actually sparked the use of comprehensive urban transportation plans. This act required that approval of any federal-aid highway project in an urbanized area of 50,000 or more in population be based on a continuing and comprehensive urban transportation planning process carried out cooperatively by states and local governments (Weiner 1992). This piece of legislation required cities to have comprehensive plans that were realistic to start receiving federal funds to support their proposed plans (Cervero 1998). It is also important to point out that this Act set in place some new rules. One of the rules was that the planning process was for all urbanized areas, not just big cities. This is important because, in order to have an efficient and successful transportation system, there needs to be cooperation between municipalities in an urban area (Weiner 1992). Because of this required cooperation, many new agencies had to be set up to efficiently meet the requirements set forth. The Bureau of Public Roads (BPR) was crucial in terms of setting up many of the agencies as BPR was the responsible government agency during the time of adoption of the 1962 Act. The Act essentially left it up to the BPR to figure out how exactly to go about setting up the requirements for the comprehensive plans.

In the late 1980s the construction of the highway system was completed, causing the extension of suburbs until the end of the 20th century. Residential and employment decentralization was thus highlighted. Also, several sub-centers emerged to serve suburbs, a process favored by the construction of roads around metropolitan areas. The development of new highways that circled urban perimeters have encouraged a collection of commercial, distribution and manufacturing activities around high accessibility clusters in suburban areas. A "suburban downtown" arose, slowly shaped by the circumferential freeway segments that embraced the central city (Muller 2004). The highways and the automobile played a significant role in the spreading out of these suburbs, heavily influencing family life, and creating a more mobile society.

TRAFFIC CONTROL SYSTEMS

Back in 1909, when the First National Conference on City Planning took place, it wasn't known to early planners what the future impacts of the motorized transportation would be. The problem they were dealing with was overcrowding in the central parts of large cities. Suburbanization was the strategy for people to escape to better quality housing and healthier lifestyles and more open space, and transportation facilities were to provide access between cities and suburbs. Planners wanted major roads to prevent distribution of traffic through smaller streets and neighborhoods in the cities, so they wanted bigger boulevards and arterials.

As automobiles became more popular, they were causing more congestion on the streets because they took up more space and were faster than other types of transportation with which they shared the space. This caused traffic congestion in downtown areas that were busy and crowded and lacked extra space. Miller McClintock and his staff did surveys to better understand traffic flow and they came up with a book (rather a manual) *"Street Traffic Control,"* in which they proposed street traffic regulations for pedestrian and motorists. Cities around the country began to carry out and implement the regulations and planners started to use signaling systems. These traffic reliefs were very brief because when McClintock had collected the data for his regulations, vehicle ownership was lower than it was by the time his book was published in 1952 (Kenworthy 1999). Because of this rising number of automobiles, planners started collecting more data to better understand traffic and the causes of the congestion. This analysis led to the development of street traffic plans. These plans advocated making the street plans rational by connecting them together and widening them, and also installing traffic signaling systems at major intersections. The plans recommended classifying streets, using speed limits and different road widths to direct traffic to main roads and away from residential roads. The plans also focused on splitting up various types of traffic to speed up the traffic flows and to minimize congestion problems.

Getting into the Car Culture

During the first two decades of the 20th century, the car became more than a machine for leisurely outings; it became the standard mode of transportation. The middle class purchased the less expensive, mass-produced autos, and the cities were transformed, to benefit and detriment, around the needs of this increasingly popular mode of transportation. The twentieth century quickly became the age of the car. Early cars provoked many negative reactions when they first appeared on the city streets. Not only did these automobiles demand a great deal of the limited road space, they also changed the nature of human interaction. As these metal machines zipped past one another and controlled the pace of street, the pedestrian was quickly demonized. Those on foot were in the way and thus slowed the flow of traffic. The street that for so long had been the center of urban life was swiftly being relinquished to the growing demands of motorists and an expanding automobile culture.

A battle for the city's streets ensued. Jaywalking became a crime; traffic regulations became the norm, and the urbanite of the new century saw the complete expulsion of all non-motorized road users. The quaintness of push carts, the chance, encounters on the street, and even stickball games played in the street had to give way to the automobile. The 1920s brought along road studies looking into the widening and straightening of urban streets; a system of concrete ribbons ushering in the expressway age was not far behind.

"We shall solve the city problem by leaving the city," wrote one of America's greatest anti-urbanists, Henry Ford, in 1922. The car would enable a complete withdraw from the congestion, vice, and slums of the central cities. Swiss architect, Le Corbusier, would imagine the city reconfigured to facilitate the rapid movement of automobiles. In his vision, the uses of the city would be kept separate, the high-rise tower block would reign supreme, and the city would be built for speed. The new obsession would be with the flow. But where Le Corbusier saw the car as rescuing the city, Frank Lloyd Wright visualized the car as the crucial tool needed to abandon the city altogether. Wright's plan for Broadacre City was based on a completely decentralized scheme, one where the rural landscape would be re-inhabited with independent homesteads (Wright 1932). Here the automobile would be the essential ingredient, and in retrospect, Wright's "Usonian" vision wasn't that far from the reality of many cities and how their built form was fast evolving into a low-density auto utopia.

Clarence Stein and Henry Wright's abandonment of the street grid and their implementation of the "cul-de-sac" in plans for a 1920s automobile suburb called Radburn offered up a new model for an age of regional growth. It was a model that synthesized the prophetic vision of H.G. Wells' piece "The Probable Diffusion of Great Cities" (Wells 1902) with the Garden City experiments envisioned by Ebenezer Howard and carried out in places like Letchworth and Welwyn in the UK.

As the automobile became more and more the focus of American life, the car was thrust into the city by a new system of roads. Robert Moses' parkways in New York City plunged through numerous urban neighborhoods. New high-speed roads allowed for swift movement from countryside to city center, but they altered the built landscape in ways that the road builders never anticipated. Thus began the fragmented metropolis. For many, the city was passed up for a carefully designed leafy suburb, one built especially for the needs of the motorist. In 1939, Norman Bel Geddes promoted General Motor's vision of the future with his Futurama exhibit at the World's Fair in New York City but it was a vision that would have to wait a few years. With World War II beginning, the brakes were put on car culture, but upon the war's conclusion, the highway age was quickly ushered in. From the start though, the relationship between the highway and the city was an uncomfortable one. In some places, when the road builders came knocking, citizens went on the defensive. Few succeeded in stopping the freeway juggernaut and the vast system of new roads that was easily superimposed on the country, and those who did stop them only postponed the inevitable.

The highway in the U.S. was intended to relieve inner-city congestion, to surgically remove slum housing, and to connect the dots or make the links between all the rising metropolitan areas that would see explosive growth in the post-war decades. As historian Kenneth Jackson (1987) put it, the U.S. became a "drive-in culture." The car, the interstate highway system, the vast oceans of single family homes, and the fast food burger joint would fit together almost as if they were part of an ingenious master plan. But the auto-utopia that had been built could not be undone. The new way of life that was quickly reshaping the United States, and to a lesser degree Europe, was seductive, fast paced, and modern.

The last few decades of the twentieth century can be defined as the age of urban sprawl. The horizontality of the United States' development became ubiquitous in the new era of cheap land and cheap oil. An autocentric environment emerged: one that can be identified by its strip development, separated land use functions, and its incoherent patchwork-quilt of land use regulated by various zoning, building codes, and other standards that reinforce the use of the car. The built environment became the full realization of a decentralized, car-dependent metropolis.

Today, getting around by foot or by bicycle in these low-density places is pretty much

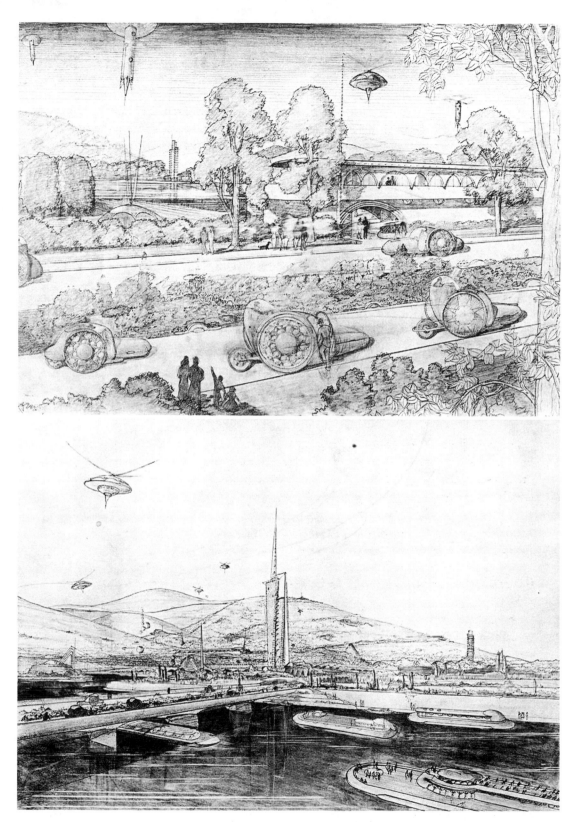

Figure 2.5 Utopias by Frank Lloyd Wright: The Broadacre City (© 2005 Kjell Olsen).

a non-issue. The "pod and collector" system present in most locations has been substituted for the flexibility of the urban grid. Mass transit options in many of these sprawling urban peripheries are incredibly inefficient due to their low-density nature and the increased distances between destinations. "Dwelling in the car," as sociologist John Urry calls it, has become commonplace (Urry 2006). Most of us move around on public roads within the confines of a private vehicle, spending increased amount of time in automobiles driving throughout the low-density regions. We pass from one transitory non-place to another, finding few places designed for us to sit and "be." Our road systems are not designed for non-motorized users. For those raised in such environments, the autocentric realm is entirely normal and changing it to suit the needs of pedestrians, cyclists, or transit riders seems almost unfathomable, for now.

Table 2.1 Estimated national VMT (Vehicle Miles Traveled) by roadway type

Year	1980	1990	2000	2010	% Change 1980–2010
Interstate	296,326,000,000	479,074,000,000	661,645,000,000	723,340,108,591	144.10%
Other freeways and expressways	79,690,000,000	127,465,000,000	177,222,000,000	240,464,722,353	201.75%
arterial	667,273,000,000	902,634,000,000	1,143,769,000,000	1,188,519,815,987	78.12%
collector	272,511,000,000	346,757,000,000	402,603,000,000	409,922,859,221	50.42%
Local	211,495,000,000	288,432,000,000	361,686,000,000	404,258,645,000	91.14%
Total	1,527,295,000,000	2,144,362,000,000	2,746,925,000,000	2,966,506,151,152	94.23%

Source: FHWA Highway Statistics 2010; (1) Data are based on State highway agency estimates reported for the various functional systems. (2) Includes the 50 States and the District of Columbia.

The Need for Planning and Policy

With the car culture well in place, transportation planning that solves problems such as growing congestion, air pollution, reliance on petroleum and unsustainable development was needed. Federal governments, state departments of transportation, and metropolitan planning organizations (MPOs) down to the local agencies are deriving short and long term plans to improve the quality and efficiency of transportation.

Transportation planning and policy has a long history that began in the late eighteenth century. Its process was and is established through laws and regulations created to develop networks that connect the country and to promote economic activity, social equity, economic development and safety. Historically, transportation planning and the building and maintenance of roadways was viewed as a state and local governmental responsibility from colonial laws patterned after British rule. The first transportation planning in U.S. history was associated with "The Society for Promoting the Improvements of Roads and Inland Navigation" in 1791. It appointed a Board of Commissioners that developed roads and waterways in the state of Pennsylvania. Many states followed similar patterns. The first National Transportation Plan was drawn up in 1807 with the first national inventory of transportation resources study. The results from this study prompted a ten year, twenty million dollar national program to complete roads and waterways (FHWA 1976).

These early plans focused on rural areas and were criticized greatly due to the lack of planning for urban areas. By the time the Federal Highway Act of 1921 was established, the concept of a continuous national system of highways was recognized. This Act required that state departments design a system of interstate and inter-county roads that was limited to 7 percent of the total mileage of the then existing rural roads (Weiner 1992). This in turn sparked a rapid growth in traffic and increasing vehicle weight. The roads at that time could not withstand the width, grade, and alignment for major traffic loads.

It was clear that a systematic approach to planning was needed to solve these problems. As mentioned before in this chapter, the Federal-Aid Act of 1934 apportioned 1.5 percent of government road funds to be used for surveys, planning, engineering, and economic analysis. These plans included complete mapping of the highway system and its physical characteristics based on traffic volume measured through surveys.

During the 1950s and 1960s, the need for a better national transportation system was promoted by President Dwight D. Eisenhower. During World War II, Eisenhower was

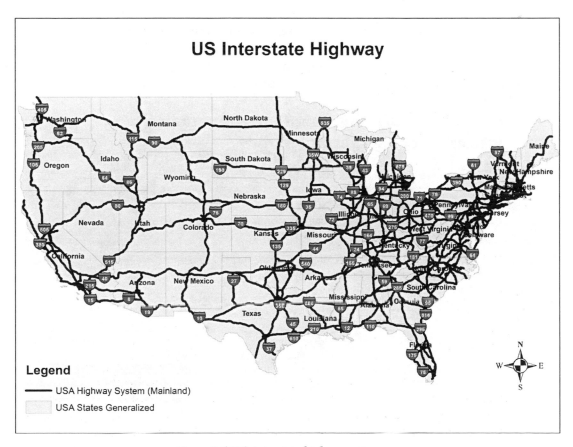

Figure 2.6 U.S. interstate highway system.

impressed by the four-lane Autobahn, which allowed U.S. forces to quickly push back the Nazi army. This divided highway system with limited access points from local roads became the model for U.S. interstates. When Eisenhower was elected President in 1952, the Bureau of Public Roads explained that 76 percent of roads were not capable of withstanding the high levels of traffic (Group 2009). Eisenhower demanded that entirely new roads were to be built instead of rebuilding the existing highways. In 1956, Congress passed the National System of Interstate and Defense Highways Act. 90 percent of the costs would be paid by the government from taxes on anything automotive. Much of the work was completed between 1956 and 1966, which then became known as the Interstate Decade. After Eisenhower signed this law and construction had begun he said, "More than any single action by government, this one would change the face of America, its impact on the American economy, the jobs it would produce in manufacturing and construction, the rural areas it would open up, was beyond calculation" (Group 2009).

In the 1960s, to adequately respond to problems of several large transportation projects, the government chose to group all transportation programs into a single government agency: the Department of Transportation (Weiner 1992). The Department of Transportation was established in 1966 to help control the old programs that did not cooperate in a seamless program (Goetz, Dempsey and Larson 2002). Prior to the development of DOT, there were programs stepping on one another's toes, and a lack of cooperation risked duplication or uncoordinated projects. Sometimes different transportation programs would each plan a new route in the same location, creating agency competition for a location. The Federal Government realized the problem in efficiency, having so many different groups responsible for the same things, just slowed progress (Goetz, Dempsey and Larson 2002; Kay 1997). Thus, DOT was a smart fix in solving some of those planning problems.

BOX 2.1 Pioneering urban transportation studies: Chicago area transportation study

Analytical methodologies began to be applied to urban transportation studies in the late 1940s. The Chicago Area Transportation Study (CATS), initiated in 1955, was a pioneering study that set the standard for the future of transportation planning. CATS used a six-step planning procedure, which is more or less maintained by transportation agencies to date:

1) Data Collection
2) Forecasting
3) Goal Formulation
4) Preparation of Network Proposals
5) Testing of Proposals
6) Evaluation of Proposals

CATS introduced another major methodology in the practice of transportation planning, the Four-Step-Model. The Four-Step-Model is a travel forecasting model that is used to simulate future travel on the transportation network based on predictions of future land use and activity patterns. The Four-Step-Model uses four sub-models, which will be further explored in the chapter on Travel Demand Forecasting. The four sub-models are:

1) Trip Generation
2) Trip Distribution

3) Modal Split
4) Network Assignment

Although more sophisticated models have been developed since CATS, the Four-Step-Model remains the standard for most transportation agencies due to its effectiveness and pragmatic nature. CATS also made major advances in the use of computers in travel forecasting. Transportation networks were developed to serve travel generated by projected land use patterns. Network effectiveness was evaluated on the basis of economic efficiency. Therefore, transportation plans were heavily based on cost and benefits factors, meaning maximum travel for least cost. This definition of effectiveness translated to maximizing automobile mobility. As a result, mass transit was given minimal consideration in transportation planning. The focus and content of transportation planning efforts to follow were largely set by this pioneering study. The CATS methodology and philosophy was later incorporated into federal urban transportation study guidelines.

Adapted from "Urban Transportation Planning in the United States A Historical Overview" (1992), U.S. Department of Transportation

Congress approved the Intermodal Surface Transportation Efficiency Act (ISTEA) of 1991, altering the overall program to allow greater elasticity in project assortment and increasing the number of programs. The Intermodal Surface Transportation Efficiency Act also established the Federal Transit Administration (formerly the Urban Mass Transit Administration). The Act also permitted transportation funds to be expended on environmental projects that enhance existing transportation facilities and created the Intelligent Vehicle and Highway System Program (Brumette 2001). Increasing transportation usage has called for new policies to be implemented so that road and transportation networks can serve the public accordingly; especially in the 2000s when transit has become even more necessary. ISTEA reinforced the policies of the Clean Air Act of 1990 by emphasizing on multimodal planning and requiring public participation and interagency consultation (Weiner 1992).

The federal government has traditionally focused on providing construction funds while states and regions are tasked with paying for the ongoing repair and operating costs. On August 10, 2005, the Safe, Accountable, Flexible, and Efficient Transportation Equity Act: A Legacy for Users became law. Signed by President George W. Bush, it authorized $286.5 billion to fund the nation's transportation network through September 2009, including $228 billion for highway programs and $53 billion for transit programs (Lang and Shoup 2011). The Act addresses many of the challenges facing the transportation system today, such as improving safety, reducing traffic congestion, improving efficiency in freight movement, increasing intermodal connectivity, and protecting the environment—as well as laying the groundwork for addressing future challenges (FHWA 2005).

The transportation technology has radically changed the way we travel and has required the continuous adaptation of policy. There has been one great tool that has been added to transportation planner's store: the computer. It has been used for collecting, organizing and computing large data. Without this improvement, today's planning systems would be very different. In particular, GIS (Geographic Information Systems) have become an essential part of the technical transportation planning process. GIS allow for data about the transportation system to be represented on the network through sophisticated mapping applications. GIS can be used to represent the network in space and across time, which is ideal for advanced planning. Without such computer software and some other statistical and spatial analysis package, it would be difficult for transportation agencies to model emissions and engage in travel demand forecasting.

Now, the remaining concern is the increasing growth of automobile travel. The constant usage of the automobile has led to policy changes in urban development, highway construction and the way pollution is mitigated. Today's policies focus on reducing emissions and promoting multimodal transportation in order to limit the use of cars. In the coming years transportation policy and planning should continue to concentrate on enhancing accessibility through integrated transportation system.

Environmental Concerns

The 1960s was the decade citizens started worrying about the environment more than ever. People became increasingly concerned about water and air quality, ecological balance, as well as socio-environmental issues such as historic preservation and how current changes, including transportation, would affect the future (Kay 1997). With growing environmental concerns, the Federal Highway Administration created (in 1969) a two-hearing process for highway approvals as opposed to the former single hearing policy. Under the original policy, people had only been able to give input toward the end of the hearing. With the change, citizens were able to have a larger say in the hearings. Under the new policy, people were given the right to be heard before a road route location was chosen (Weiner 1992). This was very helpful for conservationist and other interest groups. With groups being able to present information about how a route might impact a specialized type of tree or a species in the natural habitat, officials may be convinced to select an alternative route (Kay 1997).

In 1969, the government also passed a crucial piece of environmental legislation, the National Environmental Policy Act (NEPA). Prior to NEPA, there was no requirement of environmental consideration in terms of highway construction and route selection; as a result, highways were built through ecologically sensitive areas. Now, transportation planning organizations are required to use a systematic approach to analyzing the environmental impacts of highway construction and route selection in an Environmental Impact Statement (EIS). The EIS contains the environmental effects of a transportation project, recommended mitigation measures and potential project alternatives analysis. Before a final decision is reached, and a project can move forward, the EIS must be released to the public for review and the public must be given the opportunity to comment on the EIS at a public hearing.

The Clean Air Act Amendments of 1977 and the Highway Acts afterwards both required all regional transportation plans to show attainment of the vehicle emissions reductions specified in the State Implementation Plan, through the modeling of travel and emissions from on-road vehicles. Also, the Clean Air Act of 1990 has been the most important policy advance in transportation planning in the past few decades. It has strengthened the previous standard for air quality attainment by providing that federal transportation funds can be withheld from regions that do not show attainment by the deadlines. The conformity rule has also required that land development and regional transportation plans be accounted for in regards to severe or extreme air quality in those regions. These Acts are a testament to the government's progressive and increasingly holistic regard for the environment.

At the same time, one of the solutions for minimizing pollution from the transportation sector and maximizing equity of access was public transportation. The first real effort to provide federal assistance for mass transit development was the Urban Mass Transportation Act of 1964, promoted by President John F. Kennedy. Kennedy's message for the legislation was "to encourage the planning and establishment of area-wide urban mass transportation systems needed for economical and desirable urban development" (U.S. Department of Transportation 1979). This Act was intended to reduce personal transportation use and improve mass transit needs and service at minimum costs. Congress did not think much of this Act as they only authorized $150 million per year to carry out the legislation. So, public transportation in the U.S. declined in both passenger and service levels; total annual passenger trips fell by 69 percent from 22.3 billion in 1945 to only 8.0 billion in 1975. Transit was at its all-time high during World War II, artificially inflated by gas and tire rationing, a halt to new car production, restricted incomes and patriotic appeal to use transit to save resources needed in the war effort. However, one reason for the failure to provide service to the rapidly growing suburbs was the severe underfunding of public transportation in the three decades following World War II. Most public transit operators were privately owned companies and as such, did not receive government subsidies. As their services deteriorated and became more expensive, public transportation systems lost more and more passengers, curtailing revenues and forcing more service cutbacks (Reck 1962). Lack of government financial assistance and company bankruptcies hurt public transportation. Rising per capita incomes and urban and suburban roadway network expanded rapidly further encouraging auto use and suburban living, discouraging the use of public transit.

Another piece of legislation, the National Energy Act of 1978, was regulating all the phases of transportation, from planning to construction, to conserve fuel. The Act was needed because the 1979 oil crisis declined the availability of crude oil substantially, creating gasoline shortages and higher prices. President Nixon signed the Emergency Highway Conservation Act of 1974, which established allocations of oil to be reserved for gasoline and for heating people's homes. One of the major effects of this legislation was the creation of a nation speed limit of no more than 55 miles per hour. The speed limit was put into place, as vehicles travel the most efficiently at 55 miles per hour, thus allowing for optimum fuel economy (Kay 1997). By 1981, as authorized by President Reagan, oil pricing was to be determined by the free market. By then, energy conservation had become a major part of urban transportation planning. Reducing the use of automobiles and an emphasis on energy efficiency became more widespread by planning organizations, transit authorities and highway departments.

Another significant environmental effort was the introduction of the CAFE (Corporate Average Fuel Economy). In 1975, the CAFE standards are important for the planning of vehicles, as they require companies like Ford or Dodge to have a fleet-wide average of a certain fuel economy by certain dates or pay fines on a per vehicle scale. The problem with this system, though, is compliance with the CAFE standards. Companies like Porsche ignored standards and passed the fines onto their customer (Kay 1997). However, based on historical corporate fleet fuel economy averages, the CAFE standards have largely been successful. Data indicates that the combined average corporate fleet fuel economy for passenger cars and light trucks has risen substantially since CAFE was enacted. As well, the overall fuel economy averages have been maintained at or above the CAFE standards for the past 30 years. Looking forward, fuel economy standards for corporate fleets will rise significantly, reaching close to 40 mpg for passenger cars by 2020.

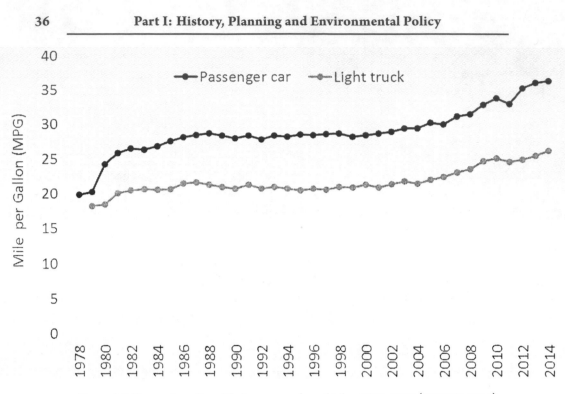

Figure 2.7 Change in national fuel economy for vehicles, 1975–2013 (USDOT, 2014).

Recent, Future and New Technologies

The completion of the Interstate Highway system shifted the focus to solving road congestion and less on building new roads. There are still new roads being built as sprawl occurs, but for the most part, United States highway planning has shifted gears towards managing the existing system (Kay 1997). Computers play a large role now that there are such advanced computing software to forecast new travel demand. Transportation agencies across the world have recently been adopting ATM (Active Traffic Management) systems. ATM is a "smart highway" concept which consists of various computer systems that collect and analyze traffic data. The information is fed to a central highway control facility where human operators can implement dynamic traffic control strategies. ATM can simulate system performance under various scenarios, evaluate strategies, provide short-term traffic predictions and select the best strategies to optimize traffic flow (Kolosz, Grant-Mulle and Djemame 2013).

Recently, local governments (and the public) have noticed that many of the roads in America are starting to age; wear and tear are clearly present. This was inevitable and planned for. However, because the planners of the past could not have known just exactly how much congestion and use the roads would generate, they could not foresee the amount of disrepair that is currently concerning the road system. Government agencies have dedicated large amounts of resources to repairing the roads. Adding to the quantity of road that needs repair, congestion prompts transportation agencies to expand highways and roads, inducing more driving. It has been suggested that the U.S. is in a cycle of traffic congestion and lane expansion that becomes progressively more expensive and environmentally damaging with time.

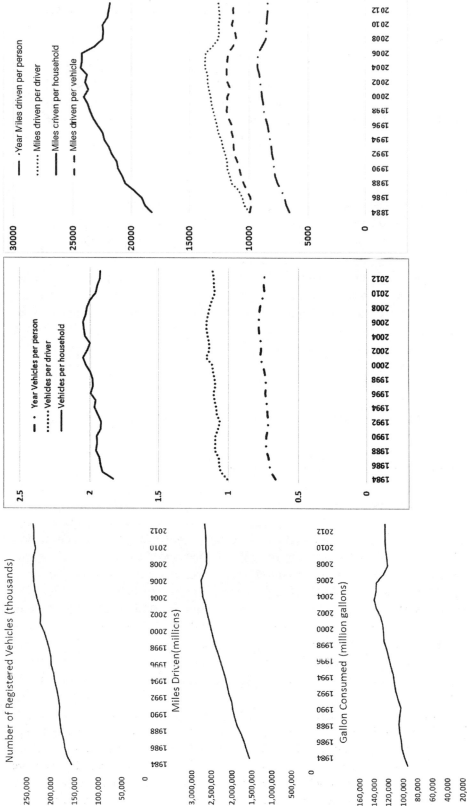

Figure 2.8 Registered light-duty vehicles, mileage and fuel consumption 1984–2013 (data: University of Michigan, TRI).

Reducing VMT (Vehicles Miles Traveled) and promoting efficient of transportation are likely solutions.

For the past 200 years, a new form of transportation has been adopted about every 50 years, and it seems that we are due for the next mode. Many believe that High-Speed Rail is the answer to efficient and environmentally sound transportation. Most High-Speed Rails use a system called Maglev (Magnetic Levitation) that uses electromagnets to suspend and propel a train to speeds of 250 km/h (155 miles/h). High-speed rail could move 100,000 passengers an hour, granting the ability to move large numbers of people using electricity. It could also be the first system to break the transportation weight rule of 1 ton of vehicle per passenger which has persisted since the use of horses and wagons. Maglev could bring the weight down to 300 kg (661lb) of vehicle per passenger (Ausubel and Marchetti 2001).

Energy efficient cars are also an option for the future. Eventually, petroleum reserves will be depleted, and alternative energy will have to be ultimately adopted. In the interim, hybrid and electric cars are becoming a popular option for energy-efficient personal transportation. Hybrid cars are powered by electric motors and run on batteries, however, are supplemented with a gas powered combustion engines to make up for the shortcomings of battery technology. Batteries suffer from low energy density and intensity, thus do not last long and need frequent recharging. The combination of gasoline and electricity offered by hybrid cars does result in substantially reduced miles per gallon of fuel consumption. A drawback of this technology is that the low mpg results in more driving and fewer road funds from gasoline taxes. Electrochemical fuel cells such as hydrogen, and natural gas are other options being explored for powering personal vehicles.

The threat of global warming and the need for economic expansion places the transport sector in the tension between maximizing efficiency and environmental preservation, which ultimately demands that both be accomplished. The most interesting idea in development is the IVHS (Intelligent Vehicle Highway System), an intelligent transportation system, in which vehicles and highways will exchange information with a two-way communication system. The automated highways will have a set of lanes on which vehicles with specialized sensors and wireless communications systems could travel under computer control at closely spaced intervals. The vehicles could continuously exchange information with other vehicles and traffic-control centers about speed, acceleration, braking, obstacles, road conditions, etc. Sensor data can be processed and sent back to each vehicle guaranteeing a continuous exchange of information (Martin 1999). It is one of the promising solutions to solving the congestion problem. With today's internet, networking, routing, and general high amounts of technology, this is a project with enormous potential. While the system would have an extremely high startup cost, it would save people many hours a year of sitting in congested traffic. It is estimated that on average, people spend sixty-five hours per year sitting in traffic due to congestion (Goetz, Dempsey and Larson 2002). A system that has complete control would, in theory, be able to optimize the traffic flow by taking the human element out of driving. IVHS is hoped to maximize the operational capacity of current highways to reduce the need for resource expenditure on highway expansion. On the other hand, some see autonomous cars as one more technology that makes driving more comfortable and convenient and thus increases the amount of people drive.

Another way the conventional transportation system is being challenged is through recent developments in smartphone technology. Uber and Lyft taxis are examples of ride sharing/taxi startup which allows anybody to become a taxi driver. Customers can download an app onto their smartphone that can be used to connect them to the Uber driver closest to their location. Uber provides smartphones, GPS and a credit card reader to drivers that provide the real-time location of customers who want to be picked up. Prices are predetermined, and the company takes a 5 percent fee. Uber drivers use their personal cars and the system is largely automated. Thus Uber cuts out the need for traditional taxi operations with a vehicle fleet and central dispatch in each city. Several of these app-based public transport services have popped up recently, raising many policy and legal issues. Similar technologies are being explored for dynamic ride-sharing, which aims to bring travelers together with similar itinerates. Ridesharing and carpooling are not new ideas for reducing energy consumption, but the ability to bring travelers together in real time and short notice is a development that could bring the practice into the mainstream (Agatz, *et al.*, 2012).

Review Questions

1) What effect did the electric street car era have on development patterns?
2) What were some of the early attempts to understand transportation from a scientific perspective?
3) How are the visions of early urban planners linked to autocentric development?
4) What act did Eisenhower say would change America more than any other single government action? Do you agree with this? Explain Why.
5) What events led to a contraction of urban mass transportation services?
6) What was the first federal action that appreciably addressed urban mass transit?
7) How did the Clean Air Act Amendments, NEPA and other legislative acts change direction and goals of urban transportation planning after the 1970s?
8) Why is transportation planning needed?
9) Explain CAFE standards?
10) What are some of the foreseeable benefits and problems of new transportation technologies looking into the future?

Project/Paper Idea

Visit your local transportation museum. Carefully observe historical milestones that have shaped the origin, growth and development of transportation in your city. Write a 2–3 page summary of your observations.

Videos

America by Design: Streets, *a PBS Video, 1987 (57 min.)*: This video traces the history of American transportation systems from rivers to railways and from simple roads to high-speed interstate highways. Architecture historian Spiro Kostof looks at such thoroughly American institutions as Main Street, Millionaire's Row, and Elm Street and shows how they reflect a city's character. The documentary also examines the effects of new technologies on land use and population growth and visits the creations of city planners.

Evolving Transportation Systems, *by Films Media Group, 2006 (20 min.)*: This video examines developments in road building and the revolutionary impact of canals and charts the rise and subsequent decline of canals as a good example of social and technological change.

Internet Sources

- New York Transit Museum: History of Public Transportation in New York City, http://www.transitmuseumeducation.org/trc/background.
- History and Politics of Transportation in the United States, www.saferoutestoschools.org/documents/Transportation_History.pdf.
- Women in Transportation: Changing America's History, https://www.fhwa.dot.gov/ohim/wmntrans2.pdf.
- UK Transportation History, http://www.historylearningsite.co.uk/transport_1750_to_1900.htm.

Bibliography

Agatz, Niels, Alan Erera, Martin Savelsbergh, and Xing Wang. 2012. "Optimization for Dynamic Ride-Sharing: A Review," *European Journal of Operational Research,* 223 (2): 295–303.

Ausubel, Jesse, and Cesare Marchetti. 2001. "The Evolution of Transport." *The Rockefeller University.*

Barger, Harold. 1951. *The Transportation Industries: 1889–1946.* New York: National Bureau of Economic Research.

Brumette, Ronald E. 2001. *Transportation History.* August. Accessed March 1, 2014. http://www.kerncog.org/transportation-history-timeline.

Cervero, Robert. 1998. *America's Suburban Centers: The Land Use-Transportation Link.* Boston: Unwin Hyman.

Coppa, Frank J., and Richard P. Harmond. 1983. *Technology in the Twentieth Century.* Dubuque, Iowa: Kendall/Hunt Pub. Co.

Farris, Martin. 1967. *Modern Transportation.* Boston: Houghton Mifflin.

FHWA. 1976. "America's Highway 1776–1976: A History of the Federal-Aid Program." Federal Highway Administration, Department of Transportation.

_____. 2005. *A Summary of Highway Provisions in SAFETEA-LU.* August 25. Accessed March 1, 2014. https://www.fhwa.dot.gov/safetealu/summary.htm.

Ford, Henry. 1922. *My Life and Work.* Fintan Books.

Georgano, George. 1972. *Transportation Through the Ages.* New York: McGraw-Hill.

Goetz, Andrew, Paul Dempsey, and Carl Larson. 2002. "Metropolitan Planning Organizations: Findings and Recommendations for Improving Transportation Planning." *Publius* 32: 87–105.

Group, Ganzel. 2009. "Transportation in Rural America." *Living History Farm.* Accessed April 23, 2014. http://www.livinghistoryfarm.org/farminginthe50s/life_14.html.

Holmes, E. H., and J. T. Lynch. 1957. "Highway Planning: Past, Present, and Future." *Journal of the Highway Division, Proceedings of the ASCE* 83 (HW3): 1–13.

Jackson, Kenneth T. 1987. *Crabgrass Frontier: The Suburbanization of the United States.* Oxford: Oxford Press.

Jeffrey R. Kenworthy, Felix B. Laube, Peter Newman. 1999. *An International Sourcebook of Automobile Dependence in Cities, 1960–1990.* Boulder: University Press of Colorado.

Kaszynski, William. 2000. *The American Highway: The History and Culture of Roads in the United States.* Jefferson: McFarland and Company.

Kay, Jane. 1997. *Asphalt Nation: How the Automobile Took Over America and How We Can Take It Back.* New York: Crown Publishers.

Kolosz, Ben, Susan Grant-Mulle, and Karim Djemame. 2013. "Modelling Uncertainty in the Sustainability of Intelligent Transport Systems for Highways using Probabilistic Data Fusion." *Environmental Modelling & Software* 2: 78–97.

Lang, Marisa, and Lilly Shoup. 2011. "Transportation 101: An Introduction to Federal Transportation Policy." Transportation for America, 1–84.

Lira, Carl. 2001. "Bibliography of James Watt," *Michigan State University.*

Martin, Alberto, Hector Marini & Sabri Tosunoglu. 1999. "Intelligent Vehicle/Highway System: A Survey (Part 1)," Florida Conference on Recent Advances in Robotics.

Muller, Peter. 2004. "Transportation and Urban Form: Stages in the Spatial Evolution of the American Metropolis" in *the Geography of Urban Transportation,* 3rd ed. By Susan Hanson and Genevieve Giuliano (eds.), Guilford Press.

Owen, Wilfred. 1957. "Transportation." *Annals of the American Academy of Political and Social Science* 314: 30–38.

Reck, Franklin. 1962. *The Romance of American Transportation.* Crowell.

Rodrigue, Jean-Paul. 2013. *The Geography of Transport Systems,* Third Edition, New York: Routledge.

U.S. Department of Transportation. 1979. *Energy Conservation in Transportation, Technology Sharing Program.* U.S. Department of Transportation.

Urry, John. 2006. *"Inhabiting the Car: Against Automobility,"* Hoboken: Blackwell.

Weiner, Edwards. 1992. "Urban Transportation Planning in the U.S.- A Historical Overview." *U.S. Department of Transportation, National Transportation Library.* Wells, H. G. 1902. *Anticipations of the Reaction of Mechanical and Scientific Progress upon Human Life and Thought.* London: Chapman & Hall, Ltd.

Wright, Frank Lloyd. 1932. *The Disappearing City.* New York: W. F. Payson.

3

Transportation Policy
and the Planning Process

Chapter Outline

- Introduction
- The Transportation Planning Process
  o *Rational vs Collaborative/Participatory Planning*
  o *Technical Nature of Transportation Planning*
- Transportation Plans
  o *The Regional Transportation Plan (RTP)*
  o *Transportation Improvement Program (TIP)*
  o *The Federal Transportation Improvement Program (FTIP)*
  o *State Transportation Improvement Programs (STIP)*
- Actors in Transportation Planning
- Transportation Policy Instruments

Introduction

Transportation provides tremendous benefits to society as well as posing many problems that involve environmental, social, and economic costs. Thus, transportation planning, policy, decision-making and legislative initiatives are involved in making rational and ethical decisions that will support the well-being of society. The justification for transportation planning and policy is inherent in the demand for maximum mobility and accessibility with minimal consequences. The two terms that will be discussed in this chapter, which are *planning* and *policy*, have slightly different meanings. Transportation policy can be defined as "a set of principles that guide decision-making or the processes of problem resolution. It deals with the development of a set of constructs and propositions that are established to achieve particular objectives relating to social, economic and environmental development, and the functioning and performance of the transport system" (Rodrigue 2013). Transportation planning, on the other hand, is the process of providing the information needed for decision-makers to choose among alternative strategies for improving transportation system performance. It is a collaborative and participatory process involving agencies, organizations and the public in a comprehensive look at national, state, regional and community need. Transportation planning also examines demographic characteristics and travel patterns for a given area, shows how these characteristics will change over a specified period of time and evaluates alternative improvements for the transportation system. It should be noted that transportation policy and transportation planning have a reciprocal effect on each other; transportation planning affects policy and transportation policy has, on numerous occasions, established the planning processes. Transportation planning, following the policy guidelines, involves looking at the past, present, and prospective problems associated with the movement of people or goods with the aim of addressing identified problems. Transportation planning has historically followed the *rational planning model* of logically sound decisions. However, planners are beginning to adapt new *participatory approaches* as people are demanding a more active role in the decision-making process. The participatory approach lends itself to the nature of planning involving demand, information and resources from many actors. The planning and operating of the transportation system requires the cooperation of all levels of government, across agencies at the same levels of government and from the many stakeholders who use the system. It is the role of these actors to technically and democratically arrange the transportation system in a way to achieve a desired outcome for the future.

The Transportation Planning Process

In metropolitan areas with a population over 50,000, the responsibility for transportation planning lies with designated Metropolitan Planning Organizations (MPOs). Metropolitan transportation planning is the process of examining travel and transportation issues and needs in metropolitan areas. It includes a demographic analysis of the community in question, as well as an examination of travel patterns and trends. The planning process includes an analysis of alternatives to meet projected future demands, and for providing a safe and efficient transportation system that meets mobility and accessibility while avoiding adverse impacts on the environment. Transportation planning consist of a comprehensive consideration of possible strategies and an evaluation process that incorporates diverse viewpoints. It also encpmpasses the collaborative participation of relevant transportation-related agencies and organization; and open, timely, and meaningful public involvement (U.S. DOT 2007).

In a simple term, transportation planning is the process of answering four basic questions: (1) Where are we now? (2) Where do we want to go? (3) What will guide us? and (4) How will we get there? (Meyer and Miller 1984). While these may seem simple enough, the reality is a complex technical and political process. Transportation planning incorporates short and long-term perspectives; involves decision making about engineering, economic, environmental and social issues; requires cooperation of varying scales; and must act in the competing interests of political officials, government agencies, business organizations, social equity groups, environmentalists, community groups, system users and the general public (Meyer and Miller 1984). The planning process, in other words, goes through a series of steps. The steps include setting the goals and objectives, identifying deficiencies and opportunities, and developing and analyzing alternatives that include (a) identification of actors, institutions, and stakeholders, (b) predicting outcomes, identifying benefits, and assessing

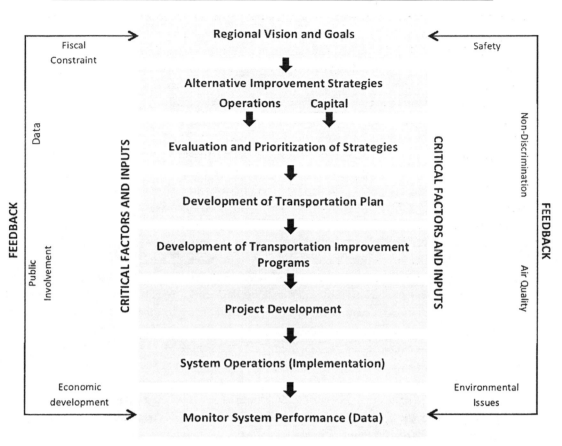

Figure 3.1 The transportation planning process (adapted from USDOT 2007).

costs, and (c) choosing a course of action. The steps also include the process of evaluating alternatives and the implementation of the plan (Johnston 2004).

RATIONAL VS. COLLABORATIVE/PARTICIPATORY PLANNING

Transportation planning has historically followed the *rational planning model* of finding the problem, defining goals and objectives, looking at alternatives, evaluating the alternatives and then developing plans. When identifying the problem, the planner must determine if the problem is seen differently by groups with different values. The planner must make sure the problem is fully understood and if the relationships between the factors that make up the problem can be quantified. When the planner is defining the goals, s/he must identify the barriers to achieving those the goals, what is needed from other agencies and the private sector, and what steps are required to achieve success (Rodrigue 2013).

The traditional rational planning model equates rationality to scientific inquiry. It is a comprehensive view and a systematic analytical approach to the planning process. The rational model encourages planners to collect a great deal of information to understand an issue, and requires they set goals about the problems. The planners must justify their recommendations in terms of the ends they are expected to serve and also to choose among alternatives on the basis of explicit criteria (Baum 1996). The *advantage* of the rational planning model is that it generates all possible solutions and objective assessment criteria. It assumes accurate and complete knowledge of all the alternatives goals and consequences. One of the *disadvantages* is that it is a group based decision making process in which it assumes a rational, non-political world. If the definition of the problem is not defined correctly, the people in the group may have differing opinions about the definition of the problem. Consequently, it can also be a time-consuming process (Jadhav, Karpe and Telang 2013).

The rational model also "encourages planners to think of themselves as living in a world of information without human beings, where the task is to organize information logically, but not to organize people (who have information, ideas, and interests) politically" (Baum 1996). A model rational planner will see situations abstractly and superficially, and will not understand the social conditions of the citizens involved. Because of this, planners may recommend interventions and goals that do not fit the actual situation of the city or its citizens. Social justice issues may effectively be ignored in a rational planning process.

Much of the classic and contemporary planning concepts follow a non-participant (rational) approach. Like any rational, comprehensive approach, the transportation planning sequence involves a survey of the area, an analysis of the results, and finally, the development of the plan. However, by the late 1960s, new models of planning began to emerge in response to criticisms of the rational-comprehensive approach. According to Innes and Booher (2000), planners, and public officials found ways to test public opinion outside of the traditional hearings or review and comment procedures. They increasingly relied on social science research methods such as public opinion polls, focus groups and other surveys. While these methods give public officials a more representative and accurate understanding of what the public wanted compared to traditional procedures, they are criticized for being detached and scientific (Innes and Booher 2000). A study shows that the rational model is workable but raises questions about whether it is effective in influencing decisions (Jadhav, Karpe and Telang 2013).

On the other hand, the *Collaborative Rational Approach* is a relatively new planning theory that emphasizes collaboration, dialogue, and consensus building. Collaborative or communicative rationality is a more inclusive and politically realistic form of transportation planning that has developed over the last two decades (Willson, Payne and Smith 2003). This plan is a decision-oriented approach where practitioners include more substantial public participation in their plans (Meyer and Miller 1984). Planners play a variety of roles in the collaborative approach, which is quite different from those of the scientific model of planning. In some cases, "planners were the initiators, providing the impetus and the ideas to establish a consensus building process, a task force, or other collaboration" (Innes 1998). The planners worked alongside the stakeholders and played an important role in designing processes and new institutions. Planners played the role of presenters of formal information and answered questions that came up. They dealt with critical challenges from participants and often had to redesign their study if participants were not in agreement (Innes 1998). Innes argues that communicative rationality is beginning to influence transportation planning (Innes 2010).

This type of planning was used in 1996 by Bay Area Rapid Transit (BART) in San Francisco. A case study by Willson, Payne and Smith (2003) shows that the BART Board of Directors launched a new strategic plan to open decision-making to greater review and participation by internal and external parties. Some of the management and improvement goals included enhancing customer satisfaction, creating access programs in partnership with communities. The results of the case study suggested "discussion enhances rationality, and it brought agreement on plans, overcame stalemates, and generated new ideas" (Willson, Payne and Smith 2003).

BOX 3.1 Case study: pedestrian plan, Oakland, CA

The City of Oakland adopted the Pedestrian Master Plan (PMP) in November 2002. The plan designates a network of pedestrian facilities and distinguishes roadway segments and intersections in particular need of safety enhancements to better serve pedestrians. The city used an innovative data analysis tool, the Space Syntax Model, to estimate pedestrian volumes throughout the city based on land use, population, and other network characteristics. These estimates were combined with crash data, traffic data, and community input to identify and prioritize areas with both safety problems and high pedestrian demand. The Master Plan establishes a Pedestrian Route Network emphasizing safe routes to school and connections to transit. The routes include streets, walkways, and trails that connect schools, libraries, parks, neighborhoods, and commercial districts throughout the City. It identifies priority street segments along these routes for targeted improvements over the next twenty years. The plan also identifies new pedestrian design elements to promote pedestrian safety and access throughout the City. Policy T4.5 of Envision Oakland, the Land Use and Transportation Element of the Oakland General Plan, recommends the creation of a Pedestrian Master Plan as part of its objective to increase the use of alternative modes of transportation. The Pedestrian Master Plan provides an essential resource for the City to prioritize the use of existing funds available for transportation improvements and secure additional grant funds for projects dedicated to pedestrian safety and livable communities. The Plan outlines infrastructure and policy improvements that address the issues of safety, sustainability, equity, vitality, and health around the city. They target specific areas with high numbers of vehicle and pedestrian collisions, poor quality infrastructure, or high estimated pedestrian volumes in an organized, efficient manner. Pedestrian volume estimates were taken from Space Syntax, which used sample pedestrian counts to model land use indicators, such as population density. To support its conclusions and recommendations, the Plan combined public input, analysis of collision data, and Space Syntax simulations.

Two key highlights of this Plan are the specific focus on pedestrian planning and the incorporation of an innovative data analysis tool. In most municipalities, if there is a focus on planning for pedestrians, it is usually incorporated into a broader transportation, or bicycle and pedestrian plan. Few plans focus only on the particular needs of pedestrians. The Space Syntax tool allows planners to estimate pedestrian volumes at an individual street level by incorporating sample pedestrian counts at key intersections with Census information and street network design. Combined with collision incident data, planners can make better decisions regarding street, sidewalk and intersection improvements, based on understanding the number of people moving through these areas.

The focal points of the Oakland pedestrian plan include a designated pedestrian network and a set of broad pedestrian policies to help identify future components of the designated pedestrian network, and improve the environmental quality of the existing network. A series of maps identifies the proposed network, which consists of primary and secondary pedestrian routes along city streets, off-street pedestrian paths, important connections between neighborhoods, and areas in need of attention due to high safety risks, or location near schools or other activity centers. Policy areas identified by the plan include safety, land use, and education. Concerning land use, the plan encourages a mix of uses and high densities to create larger volumes of pedestrians. At the same time, it recognizes that pedestrian facilities and amenities in both existing and forecasted areas of high density should be upgraded and maintained in order to sustain a desirable level of pedestrian activity. Encouraging higher densities also supports transit, which is most effective when there is good, direct pedestrian access to reach it.

The plan identifies numerous routes as part of its designated network and classifies the routes by location and land use. Land uses are defined as city, district, neighborhood, neighborhood hill, or walkway. City routes, for instance, serve "places to live, work, shop, socialize and travel," providing connections between city districts as well as transit stops. District and neighborhood routes, on the other hand, serve more local functions such as schools, while walkways serve as short-cuts and do not follow streets. To support these designations, the Plan includes a chapter on design elements. To develop the plan, planners collected crash, demographic, and geographic data. A database of crash records from the Statewide Integrated Traffic Records System (SWITRS) provided information about the number of crashes, their locations, and demographic information about the individuals involved. Other data included geographic information system (GIS) maps of the Oakland area showing all city streets, and the locations of activity centers such as schools, recreation centers, libraries, senior centers, and major transit stops.

Adapted from U.S. Department of Transportation, Federal Highway Administration, 2013

Technical Nature of Transportation Planning

The rationality of the transportation planning inherently derived from the technical nature of the process. Since early transportation studies, planning included the use of analytical methodology. For example, the Chicago Area Transportation Study in 1955 used a basic six-step procedure (refer Box 1.2.). This procedure was "data collection, forecasts, goal formulation, preparation of network proposals, testing of proposals, and evaluation of proposals" (Weiner 1987). Transportation networks were developed and tested using systems analysis, and economic costs and benefits were the primary analysis tools of the planners. In 1956, the Federal Aid Highway Act was passed for the construction of the National System of Interstate and Defense Highways. And in 1958, a conference was held at the Sagamore Center at Syracuse University where it was decided that transportation planning should be evaluated on the benefits and costs of both user and nonuser impacts. The Housing Act of 1961 gave federal planning assistance for comprehensive surveys, studies and plans involving urban development and transportation systems and in 1962, the first federal legislation to mandate transportation planning in order to receive federal funds was developed. The Federal Aid Highway Act in 1962 developed a 3-C (Continuing, Comprehensive and Cooperative) planning process for which inventories and technical analysis were required. Through the Urban Planning Division, the program developed computer programs, planning procedures, manuals and guides to aid in the planning process (Weiner 1987). The 3-C title was named for the 1962 Federal-Aid Highway Acts goals of a Continuing, Comprehensive and Cooperative (3-C) planning process. A *continuing* process called for the regular reevaluation of transportation plans. *Cooperative* referred to the need for governmental agency cooperation. A *comprehensive* planning process was a directive for transportation plans to account for all aspects of system needs and impacts. The comprehensive requirement included 10 elements for transportation plans: (1) economic factors, (2) population, (3) land use, (4) transportation and transit facilities, (5) travel patterns, (6) terminals and transfer facilities, (7) traffic control, (8) zoning, subdivision regulations and building codes (9) financial resources and (10) social, community and environmental factors (Weiner 1987). The Bureau of Public Roads or BPR included four technical phases (within the 3-C planning process). These four phases were a collection of data, analysis of data, forecasts of activity and travel, and evaluation of alternative. To date, these technical steps remain a large part of the planning process.

The major component of the technical aspect of the transportation planning process is *forecasting* (this will be discussed in chapter 4 in a great detail). To plan for the future, the travel demand in terms of population growth and travel mode needs to be measured. Traditionally, there are four steps of the travel demand forecasting.

Trip generation—This step forecasts the total number of trips that will be produced by and attracted to a given spatial unit. Typically, a metropolitan area is separated into TAZs (Traffic Analysis Zones) which serve as the spatial units for analysis. For passenger commuting, the relationship between trip production and household socio-economic factors or land use is used to forecast the number of trips produced by each TAZ. For estimating expected trip attraction to each TAZ, the model typically uses various employment data. Two methods are available for forecasting changes in a trip generation: regression analysis and cross-classification. The finished product is the number of trips originating and arriving in each TAZ.

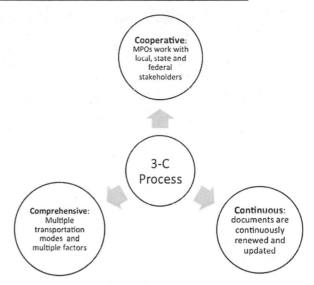

Figure 3.2 The 3-C process of transportation planning.

Trip distribution—Determines the flow of trips from each TAZ to every other TAZ. In this step, the trips produced are linked to the trips attracted so that the number of trips originating in a TAZ is disaggregated into the number of trips arriving in all other TAZ s. This is typically represented by an O-D (Origin-Destination) matrix. The common methodology used in this step is a gravity model that estimates trips between two points as a function of trip generation potential and an impedance factor, such as time or distance.

Modal split—Disaggregates the trip distribution by travel mode. In other words, this step estimates the proportion of trips originating and arriving in each TAZ that are made by passengers using personal vehicles, rail, buses, etc. Model split is usually determined using a logit model that determines the probability of mode choice as a function of utility or satisfaction. Travel by each mode can be directly estimated by applying the probability of mode choice to the trip distribution.

Trip assignment—Applies the trips between origins and destinations to the transportation network. This step predicts which routes will be taken by the forecasted trips produced to reach each destination. Traffic traveling between zones is routed on linkages (roads, highways and railways) to model the movement and impact of forecasted trips on the existing transportation system. The two most common methods are shortest path assignment or capacity constraint (incremental) assignment.

Transportation Plans

Transportation planning is a collaborative process across local, regional, state and federal agencies comprised of several interconnected transportation plans and programs which include:

THE REGIONAL TRANSPORTATION PLAN (RTP)

The Regional Transportation Plan (RTP) is a 25–30 years plan that establishes the region's vision for transportation with supporting policies and investment strategies, including a list of specific projects and programs. The Regional Transportation Plan, also called Long Range Transportation Plan is the main MPO document. It guides future transportation improvements within the region and sets goals that are developed from federal guidelines and public and stakeholder input. The Long Range Transportation Plan is designed to include all parties of interest in the regional transportation system including businesses, community groups, environmental organizations, tribal governments, the general public and local jurisdictions. The focus of the plan is at the system level that includes roads, transit, non-motorized transportation and intermodal connections. The plan documents the transportation needs for the future, lists strategies and alternatives for addressing those needs, projects available revenues, and anticipates the costs of projects. This Long Range Transportation Plan is typically updated every five years with a minimum horizon of twenty years. For a project to be funded with federal dollars, it must coincide with the goals of the Long Range Transportation Plan. All other plans and programs are linked to the Long Range Transportation Plan. The plan must be consistent with the Statewide Transportation Plan and in cases where a metropolitan area is designated a nonattainment area, the plan must conform to the SIP (State Implementation Plan) for air quality. For example, in California, the scope of the RTP has been expanded by SB 375, of 2008, which requires a Sustainable Communities Strategy for the reduction of GHG (Green House Gases) emissions from the transportation sector (CTC 2010).

TRANSPORTATION IMPROVEMENT PROGRAM (TIP)

The Transportation Improvement Program (TIP) is a six-year financial program that describes the schedule for obligating federal funds to state and local projects. The TIP contains funding information for all modes of transportation including highways and HOV, as well as transit capital and operating costs. State, regional and local transportation agencies update the program each year to reflect priority projects. While estimated completion dates are given for projects in the plan, it should be noted that the TIP is not a Capital Improvement Program (a short-range financial plan that identifies capital projects and equipment purchases). The TIP represents an agency's intent to construct or implement a specific project and the anticipated flow of federal funds and matching state or local contributions.

The first year of the TIP is called the Annual Element. Projects that have funds programmed in the Annual Element are eligible to receive federal funding for that fiscal year. TIP also serves as a schedule of accountability to the Federal Highway and Federal Transit Administrations. Annual review and certification of the TIP ensures the continuation of federal financial assistance for transportation improvements. The TIP is used as a management tool to gauge progress in achieving the goals identified in the Long Range Transportation Plan. It documents the anticipated costs of projects, and the expected revenues from all three funding sources: local, state, and federal. Basically, the TIP is the tool that allows federal funds to be effectively allocated to important projects. The TIP identifies and lists transportation projects for implementation within the next four federal fiscal years. Projects may be programmed for periods beyond the four years provided they are prioritized, and funding sources are identified; it is updated annually. To receive federal funds, projects must be included in the TIP, and in most cases must have local matching funds available. As with the Long Range Transportation Plan, the costs of the projects cannot exceed the limited amount of available revenue.

THE FEDERAL TRANSPORTATION IMPROVEMENT PROGRAM (FTIP)

The Federal Transportation Improvement Program (FTIP) is a capital listing of all transportation projects proposed over a six-year period for the MPO region. The projects include highway improvements, transit, rail and bus facilities, high occupancy vehicle lanes, signal synchronization, intersection improvements, freeway ramps, etc. In the MPO region, a biennial FTIP update is produced on an even-year cycle. The FTIP is prepared to implement projects and programs listed in the Regional Transportation Plan (RTP) and is developed in compliance with state and federal requirements. County Transportation Commissions have the responsibility under State law to propose county projects using the current RTP's policies, programs, and projects as a guide. The locally prioritized lists of projects are forwarded to MPO for review. From this list, MPO develops the FTIP based on consistency with the current RTP, inter-county connectivity, financial constraint and conformity satisfaction.

STATE TRANSPORTATION IMPROVEMENT PROGRAMS (STIP)

State Transportation Improvement Programs (STIP) includes projects such as pavement overlays, roadway widening, bridge replacement or repair, signal systems, safety enhancements, bicycle and pedestrian facilities, and transit improvements. MPOs develop the list in coordination with statewide metropolitan and rural transportation planning organizations to ensure that the proposed projects are consistent with local, regional and state plans. Projects included in the STIP are funded by a combination of federal, state and local sources. Federal-aid projects must be included in the STIP before Federal Highway Administration, or Federal Transit Administration can authorize the expenditure of federal funds.

BOX 3.2 Spending and funding for highways

The federal government's programs for highway transportation are financed, for the most part, by various taxes on users and by revenues from the Treasury's general fund that flow through the Highway Trust Fund. Under the current system, receipts from various excise taxes, most notably those on the sale of gasoline, diesel, and other motor fuels, are collected and credited to the trust fund. The fund comprises two separate accounts: one for highways and one for mass transit. The largest sources of revenues for the trust fund are excise taxes of 18.4 cents per gallon of gasoline and 24.4 cents per gallon of diesel fuel. The gas tax currently produces about two-thirds of the fund's total revenues, and the diesel tax accounts for about one-quarter. The trust fund is also credited with revenues from an excise tax on tires used by heavy trucks, a sales tax on heavy trucks and trailers, and annual tax on the ownership of heavy trucks. Together, those additional three sources provide about 10 percent of the revenues going into the fund. In the fiscal year 2009, the revenues credited to the trust fund totaled $36 billion. At their current levels, the taxes in effect are insufficient to fund fully the existing amount of federal highway spending. Because spending from the fund has exceeded its revenues for some years, on several occasions since 2008 the Highway Trust Fund has needed additional infusions of revenues from the Treasury's general fund. According to the Congressional Budget Office's (CBO's) estimates, if the historical spending and revenue patterns continued in the future, the highway account of the trust fund would be unable to meet its obligations.

Highway Funding Options

Fuel Taxes

At current tax rates, the fuel tax revenues that flow into the Highway Trust Fund are insufficient to maintain the current and likely future levels of highway spending. Fuel taxes provide incentives to reduce the social costs of driving. Vehicles that travel farther burn more fuel and, therefore, cost drivers more in fuel taxes. The resulting incentive to drive less reduces the social costs posed by greenhouse gas emissions, dependence on oil, and local air pollution. Those existing taxes on gasoline and diesel fuel are a fixed number of cents per gallon and thus do not increase with inflation. Policymakers could choose to stabilize the trust fund's purchasing power by indexing fuel taxes to account for inflation. Even so, changes to the nation's vehicle fleets that reduce gasoline use, including increased fuel efficiency and the use of hybrid vehicles, could limit the trust fund's receipts over time.

User Charges

Economic efficiency is promoted when users of highway infrastructure are charged according to the marginal (or incremental) costs of their use, including external costs that are imposed on society. A combination of fuel tax and a mileage-based tax could provide incentives for reducing the full range of driving's social costs while also generating funds for federal spending. Just as external costs of highway use are related to fuel use or miles traveled, user charges take the form of taxes on fuel and mileage-based fees. The charges differ in the administrative costs they entail and in how efficiently they match the external costs that users impose. User charges may be borne to a different extent by people in different income groups or different geographic areas.

Mileage Charges

Because about 85 percent of the external costs of driving are associated with the number of miles traveled rather than the amount of fuel consumed, paying for highways with user charges would be most economically efficient if it involved substantial mileage-based fees. A number of such fees already exist in the current financing system at the state and local levels. Greater use of those fees would provide better incentives for highway users to reduce their contribution to congestion, accident risk, and pavement damage. Mileage-based fees could take different forms, including tolls on particular roads or vehicle-miles traveled (VMT) charges.

Private Financing

Private financing of highway projects, which is currently only a small part of total financing, requires pledging future revenues to the private entities providing the funds. Whether private financing takes the form of debt or equity, private spending will typically be repaid—with a positive rate of return—through tolls, tax revenues or both. Linking private companies' opportunities for profits with their responsibility for tasks, such as construction or operations, may provide additional incentives to meet cost and schedule targets.

Adapted from "Spending and Funding for Highways." Government, Congressional Budget Office, 2011.

Actors in Transportation Planning

Transportation planning has always been conducted by state and local agencies because the road networks and transit facilities are owned and operated by the state and local agencies. The federal government set policies and provide assistance for the transportation development.

The Federal Government (U.S. DOT) oversees the transportation planning and project activities of the MPOs and state DOTs. The Federal Government also provides advice and training on transportation topics, ranging from pavement technology to design to efficient operations of highway and transit systems. The Federal Government also supplies critical

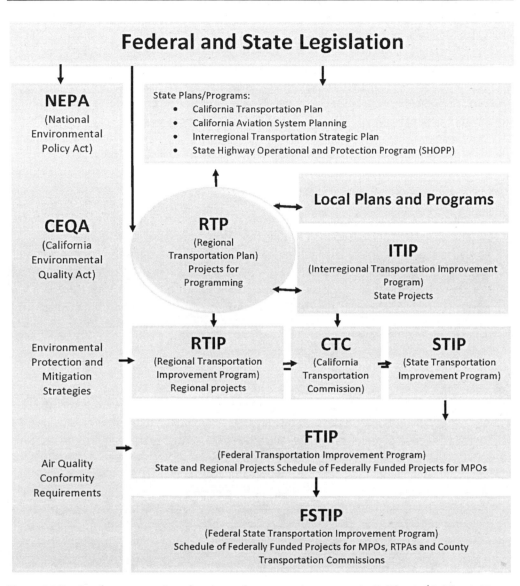

Figure 3.3 Regional transportation planning and programming process in California (California Transportation Commission, 2010).

funding needed for transportation planning and projects. At least every two years, the Federal Government approves a program of projects submitted by State DOTs that includes projects proposed for Federal Funds.

The State Department of Transportation (State DOTs) are the largest units of government that develop transportation projects and plans. They set up the transportation goals for the state. They work with the states organizations and local governments as well as other interested parties. The federal definition of interested parties includes "citizens, affected public agencies, representatives of public transportation employees, freight shippers, providers of freight transportation services, private providers of transportation, representatives of users of public transportation, representatives of users of pedestrian walkways and bicycle transportation facilities, representatives of the disabled, and other interested parties" (USDOT 2009). The state TODs handle the safe operation of the state's transportation system. Each of the U.S. states has an agency or department with official transportation planning, programming, and project implementation responsibility for that state. In addition to transportation planning responsibilities, these agencies may have responsibility for the design, construction, operation, or maintenance of state facilities for multiple modes of transportation (including air, water, and surface transportation). State departments of transportation also work cooperatively with tolling authorities, ports, local agencies, and special districts that own, operate, or maintain different portions of the transportation network, or individual facilities. Primary transportation planning functions of the state DOT:

- Prepare and maintain a Long-Range Statewide Transportation Plan: Develop and update a long-range transportation plan for the state. Plans vary from state to state and may be broad and policy-oriented, or may contain a specific list of projects.
- Develop a Statewide Transportation Improvement Program (STIP): Develop a program of transportation projects based on the state's long-range transportation plan and designed to serve the state's goals, using spending, regulating, operating, management, and financial tools. For metropolitan areas, the STIP incorporates the TIP developed by the MPO.
- Involve the public: Involve the general public and all of the other affected constituencies in the essential functions listed above.

Metropolitan Planning Organizations (MPOs) were needed to carry out the planning process cooperatively between the state and local governments as well as the various agencies within the same level of government (Weiner 1987). These are organizations that are created to carry out the metropolitan transportation planning process. According to DOT's 2007 document, a Metropolitan Planning Organization (MPO) is a transportation policy-making body made up of representatives from local government and transportation agencies with authority and responsibility in metropolitan planning areas. Federal legislation passed in the early 1970s required the formation of an MPO for any urbanized area with a population greater than 50,000. MPOs were created in order to ensure that existing and future expenditures for transportation projects and programs were based on a continuing, cooperative and comprehensive (3-C) planning process. Federal funding for transportation projects and programs is channeled through the MPO. Note that some MPO s are found within agencies such as Regional Planning Organizations (RPOs), Councils of Governments (COGs), Regional Development Councils (RDCs) and others. There are five core functions of an MPO:

- Establish a setting: Create and manage a fair and impartial setting for effective regional decision-making in the metropolitan area.
- Identify and evaluate alternative transportation improvement options: Use data and planning methods to generate and evaluate alternatives. Planning studies and evaluations are included in the Unified Planning Work Program or UPWP.
- Prepare and maintain a Metropolitan Transportation Plan (MTP): Develop and update a long-range transportation plan for the metropolitan area covering a planning horizon

of at least twenty years that fosters (1) mobility and access for people and goods, (2) efficient system performance and preservation, and (3) good quality of life.

- Develop a Transportation Improvement Program (TIP): Develop a short-range (four-year) program of transportation improvements based on the long-range transportation plan; the TIP should be designed to achieve the area's goals, using spending, regulating, operating, management, and financial tools.
- Involve the public: Involve the general public and other affected constituencies in the four essential functions listed above.

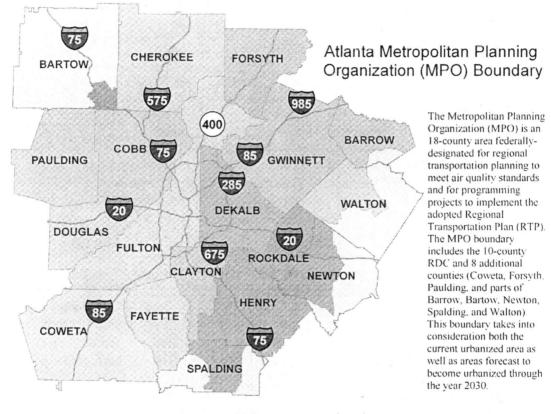

Atlanta Metropolitan Planning Organization (MPO) Boundary

The Metropolitan Planning Organization (MPO) is an 18-county area federally-designated for regional transportation planning to meet air quality standards and for programming projects to implement the adopted Regional Transportation Plan (RTP). The MPO boundary includes the 10-county RDC and 8 additional counties (Coweta, Forsyth, Paulding, and parts of Barrow, Bartow, Newton, Spalding, and Walton) This boundary takes into consideration both the current urbanized area as well as areas forecast to become urbanized through the year 2030.

Figure 3.4 MPO map of Atlanta (ARC).

In accordance with federal regulations, the MPO is required to carry out metropolitan transportation planning in cooperation with the state and with operators of publicly owned transit services. The MPO approves the metropolitan transportation plan. Both the governor and the MPO approve the TIP.

Citizens, as new actors in the planning process since the 1960s, were to becoming more aware and demanding involvement in the planning process. Citizens were concerned that changes were being made to their communities without their input. In 1969, the Federal Highway Administration established a two-hearing process, where the public could be a little more involved in the decisions about highway projects. This still did not provide adequate opportunity for community involvement and in late 1969; the guidelines for the 3-C planning process were changed. It required citizen participation in all phases of the planning process. This included the setting of the goals through analyzing the various alternatives. The planning agency is required to seek out public views on the alternatives (Weiner 1987).

Local governments—the 1980s brought decentralization of authority and responsibility in urban transportation planning. Reductions in federal regulations granted greater flexibility to local transportation agencies. The movement toward decentralization meant that time and resources could be committed to local needs rather than to

MPOs develop regional transportation plans, coordinate between state and local transportation efforts, and channel funding to transportation projects. **State DOTs** develop transportation goals for the state and, set policy and provide funding for local transportation to conform to state goals. State DOTs also construct, maintain and regulate intraregional transportation, such as rail and state highways. **The federal government** provides critical funding for transportation projects and oversees the planning of state DOTs and MPOs, as well as, provides for national highways, rail, aviation and waterways. **Stakeholders (citizens and activists)** lobby these government actors for their visions for the future. The **private sector** is another actor in the process, played a major role in addressing the needs of communities.

meeting federal requirements. It also allowed for more localized decision-making in the transportation process, however, the influence of the federal requirements had become institutionally ingrained in technocratic agencies, making it difficult to respond to local issues (Weiner 1992). Budget issues and other constraints have led to recurring debate about the level of federal involvement in local transportation. Local governments carry out many transportation planning functions such as maintenance of local streets and scheduling improvements.

Also, the *transit agencies*, the major actors in the planning process, are organizations that provide transportation to the public. Buses, subways, commuter rail, passenger ferry boats, trolleys, railways, and other people movers are all part of the local public transportation agencies.

BOX 3.3 California, Tennessee, and Washington—connecting state DOT planning and local community goals

When State Departments of Transportation (DOTs) and local governments do not coordinate with their decisions, this can result in conflicting or redundant plans, inefficient resource allocation, and tension between State DOTs and local communities, especially if State transportation planners are not aware of local priorities. Some State DOTs have addressed this challenge by creating offices for community planning. The following are examples of how State DOTs have created and used such offices.

Caltrans—Office of Community Planning

The California Department of Transportation (Caltrans) created its Office of Community Planning (OCP) in 1999 "to promote and participate in community-based planning that integrates land use, transportation, and community values." The office built on its existing Caltrans work, such as local development review, but the OCP also aimed to strengthen partnerships with local governments and to promote community participation in transportation planning processes. The OCP provides resources for public engagement, strengthening partnerships with local governments and helping Caltrans integrate community-based transportation planning into its operations. One successful project was the improvement of the Kroy Pathway, a pedestrian path near U.S. Highway 50 in Sacramento that the local community considered dangerous. The OCP brought Caltrans, the city of Sacramento, and the local community together to develop a conceptual vision for the pathway. This early planning work led to a project that improved sightlines, lighting, landscaping, and fencing to enhance multi-modal access to transit and development. The OCP supports community planning efforts through Environmental Justice and Community—Based Transportation Grants and by providing data and analysis tools to help local governments integrate land use and transportation considerations. For example, OCP-led research developed a new tool to analyze multi-modal trip—generation rates from "smart growth" development in California. This tool is especially useful for communities planning for new urban infill or transit-oriented development.

WSDOT—Community Transportation Planning Office

The Washington State Department of Transportation (WSDOT) created the Community Transportation Planning Office (CTPO) in 2010 to coordinate local, regional, and State land use and transportation planning. WSDOT had already been working with communities to review projects under the State's Growth Management Act, but the State wanted to develop a more systematic approach to local coordination as a part of how WSDOT manages the State transportation system. One of the primary goals was to use State and local resources more efficiently through greater collaboration, emphasizing additional creative solutions to meeting local needs beyond just building a new infrastructure. By coordinating with communities and communicating realistic expectations, WSDOT hopes to manage its system more efficiently. The CTPO works with municipalities during Growth Management Act, and State Environmental Policy Act reviews to foster consistency between State and local plans. The office also provides data analysis tools and training to support the local land use and transportation planning. In 2013, the office completed its new Community Planning Portal to share statewide transportation data with local and regional planners, stakeholders, and citizens.

TDOT—Office of Community Transportation

In 2013, the Tennessee Department of Transportation (TDOT) created the Office of Community Transportation (OCT) with a mission to "coordinate the State's transportation planning, local land use decisions, and community visions to guide the development of a safe and efficient statewide transportation system." The office strengthens partnerships with local agencies and ensures that State transportation planning efforts support municipalities" plans for future development. The OCT has stationed transportation planners in each of four regions of the State to facilitate local public involvement in TDOT initiatives and provide resources to local partners to develop transportation goals that support their community visions. One successful project in 2013 was in Dyersburg, where the OCT facilitated a discussion with TDOT, the city, and the advocacy group Pioneering Healthy Communities to include a bicycle lane in an upcoming road repaving project. Now Dyersburg has its first bicycle lane, increasing alternative and active transportation options for the community.

Adapted from FHWA Livability Initiative

Transportation Policy Instruments

Santosa, Behrendtb and Alexander (2011) classified transportation policy into three categories: physical policies, soft policies, and knowledge policies. All three aim to bring about changes in the transportation system. *Physical policies* include policies with a physical infrastructure element: public transport, land use, walking and cycling, road construction, and freight transport. *Soft policies*, on the other hand, are non-tangible aiming to bring about behavioral change by informing actors about the consequences of their transport choices, and potentially persuading them to change their behavior. These measures include car-sharing and carpooling, telecommuting and teleshopping, eco-driving, as well as general information and advertising campaigns about public transportation. *Knowledge policies* emphasize the important role of investment in research and development for a sustainable model of mobility for the future. The methods used by governments of different levels to implement these policies are called *policy instruments*. There are two basic types of policy instruments: regulatory and economic instruments. These policy instruments are the means by which the policy objectives can be achieved, and the problems identified overcome. Regulatory instruments include laws and regulations to encore a policy whereas economic instruments, such as tax credits, subsidy, incentives and fees are used as a way of influencing the implementation of a solution to some transportation problems.

Different levels of governments and transportation planners have available to them a wide range of transport policy instruments. Rodrigue (2013) identified several policy instruments by which governments carry out transportation policy. Of these instruments, *public ownership* is identified as a highly important instrument. Public ownership is the direct control by the state of transportation infrastructure, modes or terminals. In many countries airlines, railways, ferries and urban transit are owned and operated by public agencies. *Subsidies* represent another important instrument used to pursue policy goals. Many transport modes and services are capital intensive, and thus policies seeking to promote services or infrastructure that the private sector are unwilling or unable to provide may be made commercially viable with the aid of subsidies. *Regulatory control* is also a policy instrument by which governments can influence the entire character and performance of the industry. Air pollution control regulations are good examples. Safety and operating standards, such as speed limits, may have a profound effect in assisting the government to increase the quality of life of residents (Rodrigue 2013).

Economic policy instruments commonly used to reduce transport sector externalities. Timilsina and Dulal (2008) reviewed the literature on the effectiveness of fiscal policy instruments and found out that congestion charges would reduce vehicle traffic by 9 to 12 percent and significantly improve environmental quality. The vehicle tax literature suggests that every 1 percent increase in vehicle taxes would reduce vehicle miles by 0.22 to 0.45 percent and CO_2 emissions by 0.19 percent. The fuel tax is the most common fiscal policy instrument; however its primary objective is to raise government revenues rather than to reduce transportation externalities such as emissions and traffic congestion. Although subsidizing public transportation is a common practice, reducing externalities has not been the primary objective of such subsidies. Nevertheless, it is shown that transport sector emissions and traffic accidents would be higher in the absence of both public transportation subsidies and fuel taxation. Subsidies are also the crucial policy tool for the promotion of clean fuels and vehicles. Tax credits provided to hybrid and electric cars aims to encourage the use of vehicles powered by non-fossil fuel sources. Although some studies are very critical of biofuel subsidies, the literature is mostly supportive of clean vehicle subsidies (Timilsina and Dulal 2008).

In conclusion, transportation planning and policy has evolved over time through legislation and institutional capacity building. These changes have influenced the decision-making processes that direct transportation projects and shape the system. Where the focus of transportation policy is guiding decision making, transportation planning is the effort to provide policymakers with information. Transportation planning is highly technical in nature; the information needed to make the transportation system operate in an efficient manner traditionally includes economic analysis, travel demand forecasting, financial planning and demographic data and environmental analysis. Furthermore, the system of federal, state and local plans through which projects are linked to funding demands intimate knowledge of technocratic processes. Through recent collaborative planning approaches and legislations which encourage consideration for minority and low-income communities, the public is becoming increasingly a part of this informative process. It is from these actors that the vision for the transportation system is defined and implemented.

Besides, for the last several decades, federal funding and legislation created the conditions under which the automobile flourished and became the dominant mode in the U.S. Following this shift, the focus of much of the federal legislation to follow was confining the negative consequences of automobile use. State and federal policy have refocused with increasing consideration for multiple modes of travel, environmental awareness and social equity.

Review Questions

1) What is the difference between transportation policy and transportation planning?
2) What are the different actors in the transportation planning? Discuss their roles.
3) What was the first legislative act to address automobile emissions?
4) What are the shortcomings of the rational planning model and how can public participation benefit the transportation planning process?
5) What are the four steps of travel demand forecasting?
6) What is a Regional Transportation Plan and what is its relationship to the Federal Transportation Improvement Program?
7) What is the 3-C planning process and how did the guidelines change in 1969?
8) What is an MPO and what is its role as an actor in the transportation planning process?
9) Discuss different types of policy instruments.
10) The transportation planning process goes through a series of steps. What are these steps?

Project/Paper Idea

Do you know your local MPO? An MPO may have "council of governments" or "regional planning commission" or "area planning organization" in its official name. Each MPO is different because individual metropolitan areas are so different. Find the website of your region's MPO, and then research on the following and write a 2–3 page summary of your observation.

- What is the governing structure of the MPO?
- What are the stated responsibilities of the MPO?
- Identify the short-term and the long-term plans made by the MPO.
- Identify the funding sources and allocation of resources for different projects?

Internet Sources

- MPO maps for different States, http://regional-communities.blogspot.com/2011_03_29_archive.html.
- FHWA Transportation Planning Capacity Building, http://www.planning.dot.gov/.

- American Planning Association—Transportation Planning, https://www.planning.org/divisions/transportation/.
- Public Involvement Techniques, http://www.planning.dot.gov/publicinvolvement/pi_documents/techniques.asp.

Bibliography

Baum, Howell. 1996. "Why the Rational Paradigm Persists: Tales from the Field." *Journal of Planning Education and Research* 15: 127–135.

CTC. 2010. "2010 California Regional Transportation Guidelines." Government, California Transportation Commission. Accessed June 13, 2014. http://www.catc.ca.gov/programs/rtp/2010_RTP_Guidelines.pdf.

Dempsey, Paul Steven. 2003. "Transportation a Legal History." *University of Denver Transportation Law Journal.*

Dilger, Robert Jay. 2003. *American Transportation Policy.* Westport: Praeger Publishers.

Eutsler, Roland B. 1931. "Transportation Developments and Economic and Industrial Changes." *Annals of the American Acadamy of Political and Social Sciences.* 153. http://www.jstor.org/stable/1019123.

Innes, Judith E. 1998. "Information in Communicative Planning." *Journal of the American Planning Association* 64 (1): 52–63.

Innes, Judith. 2010. *Planning with Complexity: An Introduction to Collaborative Rationality for Public Policy.* New York: Routledge.

_____, and David E Booher. 2000. "Public Participation in Planning: New Strategies for the 21st Century." *Institute of Urban and Regional Development, UC Berkely.*

Jadhav, Jaysing, Akshata Karpe, and Saudamini Telang. 2013. *Rational Planning and Sustainability.* College of Engineering Pune.

Johnston, Robert. 2004. "The Urban Transportation Planning Process" in the *Geography of Urban Transportation,* 3rd ed. By Susan Hanson and Genevieve Giuliano (eds.), Guilford Press.

Meyer, Michael D, and Eric J Miller. 1984. *Urban Transportation Planning: A Decision-Oriented Approach.* New York: McGraw-Hill.

Owen, Wilfred. 1957. "Transportation." *Annals of the American Academy of Political and Social Science, Vol. 314, Metropolisin Ferment* 30–38.

Pikarsky, Milton, and Christine Johnson. 1978. "American Transportation in Transition." *Built Environment* 167–171.

Rodrigue, Jean-Paul. 2013. *The Geography of Transportation Systems.* New York: Routledge.

Santosa, Georgina, Hannah Behrendtb, Alexander Teytelboymb. 2010. "Road Transport Externalities, Economic Policies and Other Instruments for Sustainable Road Transport, Part II: Policy instruments for sustainable road transport," *Research in Transportation Economics,* 28 (1): 46–91.

Schiller, Preston L, Eric C Bruun, and Kenworthy R Jeffrey. 2010. *An Introduction to Sustainable Transportation.* Washington, D.C.: Earthscan Ltd, Dunstan House.

Timilsina, Govinda R. & Dulal, Hari B., 2008. "Fiscal Policy Instruments for Reducing Congestion and Atmospheric Emissions in The Transport Sector: A Review," Policy Research Working Paper Series 4652, The World Bank.

USDOT. 2007. "The Transportation Planning Process: Key Issues: A Briefing Book for Transportation Decision Makers, Officials, and Staff." Federal Highway Administration, Transportation Planning Capacity Building Program, U.S. Department of Transportation.

_____. 2009. "A Guide to Transportation Decision Making." Office of Planning and Environment, U.S. Department of Transportation, Washington, D.C.

Weiner, Edward. 1987. *Urban Transportation Planning in the United States.* New York: Praeger Publishers.

_____. 1992. "Urban Transportation Planning in the U.S.- A Historical Overview." Vers. Revised Edition. *U.S. Department of Transportation, National Transportation Library.*

Willson, Richard W, Marianne Payne, and Ellen Smith. 2003. "Does Discussion Enhance Rationality? A Report from Transportation Planning Practice." *Journal of the American Planning Association* 69 (4): 354–367.

4

Travel Demand Forecasting: The Four-Step Model

Chapter Outline

- Introduction
- Prerequisites to the Model
  - o *Segmentation Criteria*
  - o *Traffic Analysis Zones (TAZs)*
  - o *Data*
- The Four-Step Model
  - o *Trip Generation*
  - o *Trip Distribution*
  - o *Modal Split*
  - o *Trip Assignment*
- Practice Problems

Introduction

Travel Demand Forecasting (TDF) is a key component of the transportation planner's technical tasks and is essential to the future planning of the transportation system. Without TDF, planners would have to wait for a piece of the transportation system to become over-burdened or guess as to future travel demand before investing in or expanding the system. TDF allow planners to predict the volume of traffic that a given transportation system will experience in the future. For instance, if the metropolitan population will increase by 10 percent in 10 years, TDF methods can be used simulate the future travel and predict which sections of the road network will need to be expanded to accommodate extra vehicle trips. Knowing how many automobiles, transit or freight travel will be consumed in the future, where these modes will travel and which routes on the network they will travel by is necessary to make rational decisions about how to allocate transportation services and financial resources. TDF methods can also be used to model the effects of policies or for predicting how the system will respond to changes. For instance, TDF techniques could be used to predict what effect development control policies, such as smart growth, will have on transit demand.

The standard TDF method is the Four-Step-Model, developed in the 1950s, which is still widely practiced due to its practicality. There have been methodological developments in forecasting travel demand. However, this chapter will focus on Travel Demand Forecasting using the Four-Step-Model. Travel modeling is mostly performed at the regional or metropolitan planning organization level. Numerous states have their own statewide models, and various other TDF models have been developed in recent years which are more sophisticated and complex. The Four-Step-Model is four separate sub-models that are performed sequentially. The four steps are Trip Generation, Trip Distribution, Mode Choice and Network/Trip Assignment. Each step in the model requires information from the previous step(s). The Four-Step-Model is an aggregate model that estimates travel demand based on socio-economic characteristics that contribute to generating trips. The Four-Step-Model not only estimates demand for the transportation network, but does so by type of trip, mode and route. The network is characterized as a system of links and nodes. Links are roadways, bus lines, rail or other travel right-of-ways. Nodes are activity sites marked as origins and destinations, and in a wider sense intermediate travel facilities. The end product of the Four-Step-Model is the demand (the number of forecasted trips on the network) on each link of the network (Meyer and Miller 2001).

Prerequisites to the Four-Step Model

There are essential prerequisites and some considerations for Transportation Demand Forecasting within the Four-Step-Model.

SEGMENTATION CRITERIA

Segmentation criteria are one of the first things to consider in TDF. All travel and modes are part of the transportation system as a whole; however, the system needs to be broken (segmented) down into smaller pieces to accurately model travel demand. The demand for travel occurs for several different reasons at different times, so transportation is separated into several submarkets and other segments to be modeled. For instance, passenger and freight travel should be considered as distinct markets and modeled separately. Another market segmentation to consider is the trip purpose, such as work-based and non-work based trips. For example, the Southern California Association of Governments segments trip purposes as Home-Work trips, Home-Other trips, Other-Other trips, Other-Work trips and Home-Shopping trips (Fehrs and Peers TransportationConsultants 2009). Travel also occurs throughout the day at varying volumes, thus travel can be segmented into periods such as peak and non-peak travel and different time periods such as a.m. and p.m. travel or specific hours. Another common segmentation is weekday trips and weekend trips, the travel patterns of which can greatly vary (Sinha and Labi 2007).

When modeling, commute travel can be segmented as passenger travel, weekday, work-based and peak hour trips. Commuting consists of traveling from residences to employment centers and then back to residences. If we assume that passengers will take same routes home, and the traffic volume will remain constant, then the a.m. and p.m. peak travel periods will be identical, with traffic flow in opposite directions.

The segmentation criteria are parameters that define the kind of data that is put into the model. Before data is gathered or prepared for the Travel Demand Forecasting, the geographic region that is being modeled must also be broken down into smaller spatial units, called Traffic Analysis Zones (TAZs).

TRAFFIC ANALYSIS ZONES (TAZs)

The second prerequisite for the Four-Step-Model is the establishment of Traffic Analysis Zones or TAZs. TAZs are formed by dividing the study area into several geographic sub-areas. The size and shape of each TAZ are not constant though it is usually based on some criteria such as population or land use density (generally fewer than 3000 people). The geographical size of the zones typically varies, ranging from vast areas in the suburbs to as small as neighborhood blocks in the dense city center.

When traveling, trips will begin in a TAZ and end in a TAZ. Thus, these zones are used to approximate where trips originate and where they end. TAZs can be characterized by groupings of homes, shopping or employment; thus a.m. work-based trips will move from TAZs, which are dominantly residential to TAZs, which are employment centers. An alternative would be to model the flow of trips from each home to each employment destination. However, this would be extremely laborious, and any additional accuracy that could be gained is not likely to be cost-effective. The TAZ provides a practical solution from which data and travel flows can be aggregated for analysis.

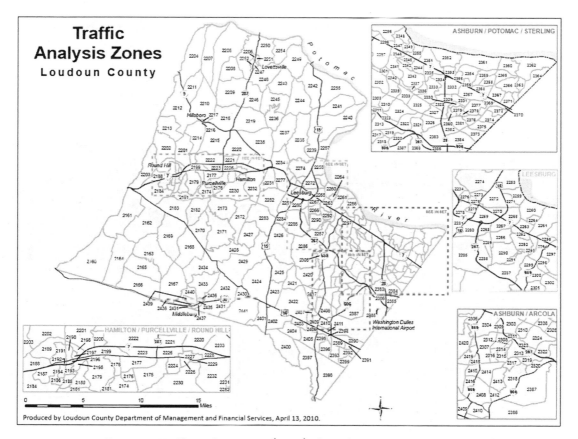

Figure 4.1 Traffic Analysis Zones (TAZs) of Loudoun County, Virginia.

DATA

Travel Demand Forecasting uses socio-economic data to estimate trips generated by each TAZ. Population, number of vehicles, land use and employment data are commonly used as predictors of trip generation and distribution in the modeling. The Four-Step-Model requires an estimation of socio-economic characteristics for each TAZ to predict the trips that will be generated in each zone. The necessary data can come from a variety of sources. However, since TAZs are unique to the area being studied, MPOs or regional transportation agencies often conduct local surveys and use other supplementary data that is locally based and up to date (NCHRP 2012).

There are many other kinds of data used in TDF methods that are beyond the basic scope of the Four-Step-Model. However, a few data requirements may be of interest as the model steps are discussed. For example, the model requires the calculation of a travel impedance matrix that is used as part of utility functions in mode choice. This chapter will go into great detail about the calculation of utility for mode choice later on, but know that utility is the satisfaction or benefits received from traveling to access an activity and from mode choice. Travel impedance refers to the costs associated with travel and can include a variety of factors such as travel time, available parking, monetary costs, etc. Travel impedance data is also the basis for calculating friction factors used in the trip distribution model. The information that is needed to calculate travel impedance is obtained through a process called "network skimming" where data on the links (highways, arterial roads, etc.) such as capacity and speed is input and modeled (Fehrs and Peers Transportation Consultants 2009). The network skimming output is required in the network assignment phase as well, where the forecasted travel demand is applied to model the effects of future trips on the network.

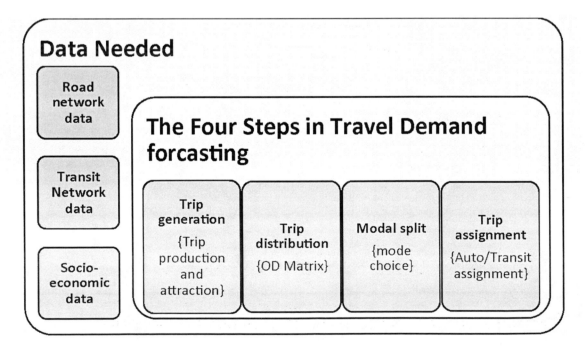

Figure 4.2 Components of the Four-Step-Model.

The Four-Step Model: Step 1—Trip Generation

The first step in the Four-Step-Model is forecasting trip generation. It predicts the number of trips originating in or destined to a particular traffic analysis zone. More specifically, the final product of this step is two forecast numbers for each TAZ: a number of trips produced and a number of trips attracted. It is based on the number of trips produced and attracted for each TAZ in the current or base year, obtained from a survey data. The goal is to calculate how many trips will be

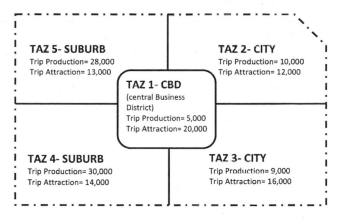

Figure 4.3 Example of trip generation.

generated (produced) in each TAZ in the forecast year. The trip generation model uses projected socio-economic data to make this forecast. Household characteristics are causally related to trip production, thus data on household characteristics can be utilized as explanatory variables to predict trip production in TAZs. For a home to work trips, the trip destinations are employment locations; therefore, trip attraction can be forecasted using employment based data.

There are two methods for calculating trips produced and trips attracted in the forecast year: regression analysis and cross-classification.

REGRESSION ANALYSIS

Regression analysis is a method of expressing a dependent variable (trips generated or trips attracted) as a function of one or more independent variables (socio-economic and employment variables) which can be computed easily in a statistics software platform. Using trip data from the base year for each TAZ and corresponding socio-economic data, regression analysis will produce an Alpha constant and Beta coefficients for an equation that will predict the expected number of trips generated by a TAZ as a function of multiple socio-economic variables. The linear regression equation is expressed as:

$$Y = \alpha + \beta_1 X_1 + \beta_2 X_2 + \ldots$$

Y= dependent variable output (trips generated or attracted in a TAZ)
α= Alpha constant
β= Beta coefficient explaining the independent variables
X= independent variable input (socio-economic or employment variable)

Two separate equations are required for trips produced and trips attracted in each TAZ. Below are two hypothetical regression equations for TAZ production and attraction:

$$\text{Production: } P_i = -48 + (3X_{a1}) + (7X_{a2})$$

$$\text{Attraction: } A_j = 29 + (6X_{b1}) + (55X_{b2})$$

P_i = number of trips produced by TAZ_i

A_j = number of trips attracted to TAZ_j

X_{a1} = number of cars in the TAZ

X_{a2} = number of residential dwelling units in the TAZ

X_{b1} = number of employed individuals in the TAZ

X_{b2} = commercial area per acre

Using the production and attraction equations generated from the base year data, projected socio-economic data for the forecast year can be input into the equations to predict the trips produced and attracted by a TAZ in the future. The calculations must be completed for every TAZ based on the projected socio-economic data in each TAZ. Using the equations above, the trips produced by and attracted to a hypothetical TAZ can be estimated for the forecast year:

X_{a1} = 150 cars

X_{a2} = 75 residential dwelling units

X_{b1} = 180 employed individuals in the TAZ

X_{b2} = 0.75 commercial area per acre

$$\text{Production: } P_i = -48 + (3 \times 150) + (7 \times 75) \qquad P_i = 927$$
$$\text{Attraction: } A_j = 29 + (6 \times 180) + (55 \times 0.75) \qquad A_j = 1151$$

CROSS-CLASSIFICATION METHOD

Regression analysis is criticized for being an aggregate model and analysts come to understand that considerable predictive power and accuracy can be gained by disaggregate analysis of influential variables. This means that the models use factors describing individual sample units (e.g., persons, households or workplaces) rather than an average value of each factor for each analysis zone.

The result is trip generation models with trip rates for sample units having specific characteristics, such as households of one, two, or more family members, owning one, two, or more vehicles. These models are based on the *trip rates* for individual sample households having those particular discrete characteristics (Edwards 1992).

This trip generation model is called cross-classification (or category analysis). Cross-classification uses a cross-tabulation matrix with two or more explanatory variables divided into several categories, such as three levels of automobile ownership by three levels of household size. The method utilizes trip rates from a base year that are cross-tabulated with socio-economic variables, and then uses forecasted household data, which is cross-tabulated with the same variables, to predict trips in the target year.

In the example below, the cross-tabulation table indicates the number of households and the number of trips for three levels of automobile ownerships and three levels of household size in the base year.

Table 4.1 Base year number of households and trips by HH size and auto ownership

| Household (HH) size | Auto ownership | | | | | |
| | 0 car | | 1 car | | 2 cars | |
	# of HHs	# of Trips	# of HHs	# of Trips	# of HHs	# of Trips
1 person	150	300	300	750	750	1050
2 persons	175	330	450	900	1500	3000
3+ persons	75	150	210	850	60	90

Dividing the number of trips in the table by the number of households yields trip rates for the base year.

Table 4.2 Base year trip rates by auto ownership and HH size

| HH size | Auto ownership | | |
	0 car	1 car	2 cars
1 person	2	2.5	1.4
2 persons	1.88	2	2
3+ persons	2	4.05	1.5

With trips per household for different levels of HH size and automobile ownership, the number of trips in a target year can be forecasted using projected households at the same levels of HH size and automobile ownership. The table below indicates forecasted households in the target year by the same explanatory variables as the trip rates.

Table 4.3 Forecasted additional households by auto ownership and HH size in target year

| HH size | Auto ownership | | |
	0 car	1 car	2 cars
1 person	40	45	97
2 persons	15	24	21
3+ persons	22	66	9

To forecast the number of additional trips generated, the trip rates from the base year are multiplied by the corresponding forecasted households in the target year.

Table 4.4 Forecasted additional trip generation for households in target year

| HH size | Auto ownership | | |
	0 car	1 car	2 cars
1 person	2*40=80	2.5*45=112.5	1.4*97=135.8
2 persons	1.88*15=28.29	2*24=48	2*21=42
3+ persons	2*22=44	4.05*66=267.14	1.5*9=13.5

For the total number of trips expected to be generated in the target year, the forecasted trips must be added to the base year trips (from Table 4.1.).

Table 4.5 Total forecasted trips in target year

HH size	Auto ownership		
	0 car	1 car	2 cars
1 person	380	863	1186
2 persons	359	948	3042
3+ persons	194	1118	104

Class Exercise: Trip Generation

1. Forecast the total number of trips based on the data given below (use a **cross-classification method**).

Table 4.6 Number of trips per household size by auto ownership (base year)

HH size	Auto ownership					
	0 car		1 car		2 cars	
	# of HHs	# of Trips	# of HHs	# of Trips	# of HHs	# of Trips
1 person	1500	3000	3050	7120	75	189
2 persons	960	2600	3945	10450	6672	20656
3 persons	523	1450	2889	9767	9143	34562
4+ persons	670	2100	1050	11213	6234	15673

Table 4.7 Forecasted number of households

HH size	Auto ownership		
	0 car	1 car	2 cars
1 person	50	250	6
2 persons	64	350	508
3 persons	20	180	1024
4+ persons	7	132	923

2. Forecast the total number of trips produced and attracted based on the following **regression formula** generated from a base year socio-economics data and the forecasted zonal socio-economic characteristics.

Production: $P_i = -20 + 4X_1 + 2X_2$,
where X_1 = number of cars and X_2 = number of households
Attraction: $A_j = -45 + 2.8X_3 + 0.08X_4$,
where X_3 = employment and X_4 = commercial areas in acres

Table 4.8 Zonal socio-economic characteristics (projected) in forecast year

Zone	Cars, X1	Households, X2	Employment, X3	Commercial area, X4
1	560	250	563	5100
2	300	200	660	1200
3	250	190	400	900
4	456	234	567	113
5	738	543	998	1145
6	289	654	417	234

The Four-Step Model: Step 2—Trip Distribution

This second step is modeling the macroscopic flow of forecasted trips from each TAZ to every other TAZ. The trip generation step estimates the number of trips produced by and attracted to each TAZ. In trip distribution, the trips produced are linked to the trips attracted so that the number of trips originating in a TAZ is disaggregated into the number of trips arriving in all other TAZs (ICPST 2010).

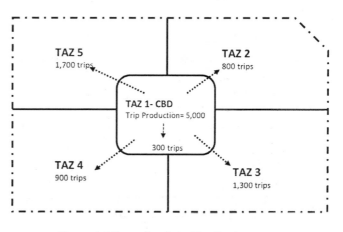

Trip distribution is commonly expressed using an O-D (Origin-Destination) matrix. An O-D matrix operates as an input-output table, where trip origins in each TAZ are inputs and trip destinations to each TAZ are outputs, which spatially expresses the interaction of trips throughout the study area. The O-D matrix is the final product of the trip distribution step (Ben-Akiva 2008).

Figure 4.4 Example of trip distribution.

Table 4.9 Origin-Destination (O-D) matrix (Ben-Akiva 2008)

				Attractions				
Generations	**1**	**2**	**3**	**...**	**j**	**...**	**J**	ΣT_{ij} j
1	T_{11}	T_{12}	T_{13}	...	T_{1j}	...	T_{1J}	O_1
2	T_{21}	T_{22}	T_{23}	...	T_{2j}	...	T_{2J}	O_2
3	T_{31}	T_{32}	T_{33}	...	T_{3j}	...	T_{3J}	O_3
.	.	.	.		.		.	.
.	.	.	.		.		.	.
i	T_{i1}	T_{i2}	T_{i3}	...	T_{ij}	...	T_{iJ}	O_i

				Attractions				
Generations	**1**	**2**	**3**	**...**	**j**	**...**	**J**	ΣT_{ij} j
.	.	.	.		.		.	.
.	.	.	.		.		.	.
I	T_{I1}	T_{I2}	T_{I3}	...	T_{Ij}	...	T_{IJ}	O_I
ΣT_{ij} i	D_1	D_2	D_3	...	D_j	...	D_J	$\Sigma\Sigma T_{ij} = T$ $i\,j$

i=TAZ generations
j=TAZ attractions
T=trips
T_{ij}=trips generated in TAZ_i and attracted to TAZ_j
D=Destination (total trips attracted to j)
O=Origin (total trips generated by i)

A widely used method for calculating trip distribution is the Gravity Model. The Gravity Model disaggregates the trips produced and attracted by each TAZ to compute the O-D matrix. The Gravity model estimates trips between two points as a function of trip generation potential and travel impedance, such as travel time or distance (Sinha and Labi 2007). Travel impedance is a measure of the resistance to the interaction between two zones. Trip interaction increases with decreased distance, time or travel costs between zones. Travel impedance is considered in the Gravity Model using a Friction Factor, which is inversely related to travel impedance (Meyer and Miller 2001). The Friction Factor is calculated through a calibration process and is obtained from a table where it is matched to the measure of travel impedance being used. An optional socio-economic adjustment factor, the K-factor, can also be applied for model calibration purposes to improve accuracy. The Gravity Model equation is calculated for every combination of TAZ trip productions and TAZ trip attractions to generate the O-D matrix.

$$T_{ij}=P_i \left(\frac{A_j F_{ij} K_{ij}}{\Sigma A_j F_{ij} K_{ij}} \right)$$

Where,
T_{ij}=trips generated in TAZ_i and attracted to TAZ_j
P_i=trips produced by TAZ_i
A_j=trips attracted by TAZ_j
F_{ij}=friction factor for impedance between TAZ_i and TAZ_j
K_{ij}=K-Factor (or the socio-economic adjustment) for interchange between TAZ_i and TAZ_j

To demonstrate how the O-D matrix is derived using the Gravity Model, each step of the calculation will be elaborated using the following two TAZ example with hypothetical data.

Step 1.
To calculate the trip distribution, the data required is the production and attractions data from the trip generation model, travel time data between each TAZ and a friction factor

reference table. For this example, the K-factor will be assumed to be equal to 1 for all TAZs. The forecasted P_i (Trips Produced) and A_j (Trips Attracted) values for each TAZ are presented in the trip generation table. Below, TAZ travel times are arranged into a 2×2 table, indicating the time in minutes a trip requires from its origin to destination for all combinations of the two TAZ areas.

Table 4.10 Trip generation

	TAZ 1	TAZ 2
Pi (Productions)	80	45
Aj (Attractions)	30	150

Table 4.11 Travel times between TAZz (min)

	TAZ 1	TAZ 2
TAZ 1	3	6
TAZ 2	6	3

Table 4.12 Friction factor vs. travel time

Travel Time	**Friction Factor**
1	92
2	69
3	62
4	51
5	49
6	36

Step 2.

After the required data is obtained, the next step is to use the friction factor reference table to attain the F_{ij} values needed for the Gravity Model equation. A new table can be made with the particular values needed for the model by replacing the travel times in the 2×2 TAZ Travel Time table with the Friction Factors from the reference table. The table below contains all the values for F_{ij} (Friction Factors between TAZ combinations).

Table 4.13 F_{ij} matrix

	TAZ 1	TAZ 2
TAZ 1	62	36
TAZ 2	36	62

Step 3.

The next step is to calculate the top half of the Gravity Model equation within the parentheses for each TAZ combination. This is done by multiplying A_j (trips attracted to each TAZ) × F_{ij} (Friction Factors between TAZ combinations) × K_{ij} (K-Factor = 1). Shown below, the

A_j data from the trip generation table for TAZ 1 and TAZ 2 is applied to F_{ij} in a new table. Note that in the new table, the A_j values are applied down both columns, corresponding with the TAZ where the trips are attracted, and that the F_{ij} values are in the same cell positions as in the F_{ij} table. When the row values are added across the table, the bottom half of the equation for TAZ 1 and TAZ 2 is completed as well.

Table 4.14 Calculation of $A_j \times F_{ij} \times K_{ij}$

	TAZ 1	TAZ 2	$\Sigma(Aj \times Fij \times Kij)$
TAZ 1	$30 \times 62 \times 1 = 1860$	$150 \times 36 \times 1 = 5400$	7260
TAZ 2	$30 \times 36 \times 1 = 1080$	$150 \times 62 \times 1 = 9300$	10380

Step 4.

The table below is an intermediate step in which a ratio is calculated for use in the subsequent step. The ratio calculated by dividing the $(A_j \times F_{ij} \times K_{ij})$ values in the cells of the previous table by the corresponding summed row values $\Sigma(A_j \times F_{ij} \times K_{ij})$.

Table 4.15 Calculation of $(A_jF_{ij}K_{ij})/(\Sigma A_jF_{ij}K_{ij})$

	TAZ 1	TAZ 2
TAZ 1	$(1860 \div 7260) = 0.26$	$(5400 \div 7260) = 0.74$
TAZ 2	$(1080 \div 10380) = 0.10$	$(9300 \div 10380) = 0.90$

Step 5.

The forecasted trips produced, P_i, from the trip generation table are then multiplied by the ratios presented in the previous table. Note that the P_i values are applied across both rows in the table and correspond with the TAZ where the trips are produced. The product of P_i and the ratio in each cell are final values for the O-D matrix.

Table 4.16 Calculation of $Pi((A_jF_{ij}K_{ij})/(\Sigma A_jF_{ij}K_{ij}))$

	Attractions		
	TAZ 1	TAZ 2	Total
Productions TAZ 1	$80 \times 0.26 = 21$	$80 \times 0.74 = 60$	81
TAZ 2	$45 \times 0.10 = 5$	$45 \times 0.90 = 41$	46
Total	26	101	127

The sum of the origins for each TAZ should equal the trip productions, and the sum of the destinations for each TAZ should equal the trip attractions in the trip generation table. In the O-D matrix, the summed trip origins for both TAZs are equal to the trip productions in trip generation table. However, the summed trip destination values are not equal to the trips attracted. To improve the accuracy of the estimated O-D values, practitioners will use a balancing method to correct for this error. When the total trip attractions calculated for each zone don't match the attractions that were given, analysts need to adjust the attraction factors. Calculate the adjusted attraction factors and repeat the trip distribution computation using the modified attraction values. Upon finishing the second iteration, if the calculated attractions are within 5 percent of the given attraction, then this is an acceptable result and the final summary of the trip distribution is presented.

Table 4.17 Final O-D Matrix

		Destinations (D)		
		TAZ 1	TAZ 2	Σ O
Origins (O)	TAZ 1	21	60	81
	TAZ 2	5	41	46
	Σ D	26	101	127

Class Exercise: Trip Distribution

Calculate the number of trips between each zone using the gravity model formula and the data given below. A study area consists of three zones. Assumtion: $K_{ij} = 1$.

Table 4.18 Number of trips produced and attracted in each zone

Zone	TAZ 1	TAZ 2	TAZ 3	Total
Trip Productions	280	660	560	1500
Trip Attractions	600	540	360	1500

Table 4.19 Travel time between zones (minute)

Zone	TAZ 1	TAZ 2	TAZ 3
TAZ 1	7	4	5
TAZ 2	4	9	8
TAZ 3	5	8	7

Table 4.20 Friction factor table

Travel time (minute)	Friction factor
1	92
2	69
3	62
4	51
5	49
6	36
7	30
8	22
9	15

The Four-Step Model: Step 3—Modal Split

The modal split model disaggregates the trip distribution by travel mode. In other words, this step estimates the proportion of trips originating and arriving in each TAZ that made by passengers using personal vehicles, rail, buses, etc. The modal split uses a choice model that predicts the probability that a trip made between a pair of origin and destination zones will be made by each mode. In the Four-Step-Model, the modal split is usually determined using a logit model, which determines the probability of mode choice as a function of utility. The logit model produces an expected proportion of the trips in the O-D matrix which will be made by each mode (ICPST 2010).

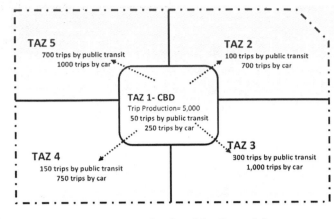

Figure 4.5 Example of modal split model.

The logit model calculates the expected proportion of trips made by a particular mode as a ratio of the expected utility a mode will provide over the sum of the expected utility of all modes.

$$P_i = \frac{e^{ui1}}{\sum \left(e^{ui1} + e^{ui2} + \dots \right)}$$

P_i= probability of choosing mode i
u= utility value ($u=f(travel\ time,\ out\text{-}of\text{-}pocket\ cost,\ etc.)$)
e= logarithmic constant$\approx$2.71828

The modal split model is premised on travelers behaving rationally, meaning that all travelers will choose the mode of travel which maximizes their utility. Utility can be thought of as happiness, satisfaction, cost, convenience or the relative benefits of choosing a mode. The utility of a transportation mode is a function of several cost factors including access time, waiting time, riding time and out of pocket cost (ICPST 2010). To calculate the modal split between automobile trips and transit trips, the estimated utility of each mode needs to be calculated within each O-D TAZ pair. Using survey data, regression analysis can be used to generate an equation that expresses utility as a function of the multiple cost factors:

$$U_i = \alpha_i - \beta_1 Ta - \beta_2 Tw - \beta_3 Tr - \beta_4 C \pm \dots$$

U_i= utility of mode i
α_i= Alpha constant for mode
β= Beta coefficient
Ta = access time

Tw = wait time

Tr= ride time

C= out of pocket cost

The values vary with each combination of origin and destination, thus modal utility using the regression equation is calculated using zonal based data in a matrix table. Once the mode utility is derived, the utility values can be input into the logit model equation. The logit equation calculates the probability of choosing a mode in each TAZ and the final product will be the number of trips for each TAZ by mode. Each step of the modal split model will be elaborated in the following hypothetical data for automobile and transit modes.

Step 1.

Calculate the utility of automobile and transit modes for travel across all TAZ O-D pairs. The utility equations for auto and transit from regression analysis are given as:

$$U_{auto} = 2 - 0.08T_t - 0.9C_t$$
$$U_{transit} = -0.03T_t - 0.7C_t$$

T_t = travel time

C_t = travel cost

Table 4.21 Trip times and travel costs for automobiles and transit

TAZ		TAZ 1		TAZ 2	
		Auto	Transit	Auto	Transit
TAZ	T_t	3.00	6.00	10.00	18.00
1	C_t	$0.50	$1.00	$2.50	$3.00
TAZ	T_t	9.00	16.00	5.00	11.00
2	C_t	$3.50	$4.00	$0.50	$2.00

The trip times and travel costs data are then applied to the utility equations to produce an O-D table for the utility of automobile and transit travel between each TAZ.

Table 4.22 Utility values by mode

	TAZ 1		TAZ 2	
	U_{Auto}	$U_{Transit}$	U_{Auto}	$U_{Transit}$
TAZ 1	1.31	0.62	-1.05	-2.14
TAZ 2	-1.87	-2.88	1.15	-0.68

Step 2.

The second step is to input the utility for each mode of travel into the logit model equation to generate an O-D table with the proportion of trips made by each mode.

$$P_{auto} = \frac{e^{u_{auto}}}{\sum \left(e^{u_{auto}} + e^{u_{transit}} \right)}$$

$$P_{transit} = \frac{e^{u_{transit}}}{\sum \left(e^{u_{auto}} + e^{u_{transit}} \right)}$$

Table 4.23 Intermediate step for e^u values

	TAZ 1			TAZ 2		
	e^u_{auto}	$e^u_{transit}$	$\sum\left(e^u_{auto} + e^u_{transit}\right)$	e^u_{auto}	$e^u_{transit}$	$\sum\left(e^u_{auto} + e^u_{transit}\right)$
TAZ 1	3.71	1.86	5.57	0.35	0.12	0.47
TAZ 2	0.15	0.06	0.21	3.16	0.51	3.67

Table 4.24 Proportion of trips by mode

	TAZ 1		TAZ 2	
	P_{auto}	$P_{transit}$	P_{Auto}	$P_{Transit}$
TAZ 1	0.67	0.33	0.75	0.25
TAZ 2	0.73	0.27	0.86	0.14

Step 3.

The final phase of the modal split model is applying the proportion of trips made by mode to the trip distribution O-D matrix (recall Table 17). This is accomplished by multiplying the mode proportions for automobiles and transit by the corresponding trips in the O-D matrix.

Table 4.25 Trip disaggregation by mode probability

	TAZ 1	TAZ 2	
TAZ 1	Trips = 21	Trips = 60	
	Auto = 21x 0.67	Auto = 60x 0.75	
	Transit = 21x 0.33	Transit = 60x 0.25	Origins
TAZ 2	Trips = 5	Trips = 41	
	Auto = 5x 0.73	Auto = 41x 0.86	
	Transit = 5x 0.27	Transit = 41x 0.14	

Destinations

The final modal split O-D matrix is presented below with the total number of automobile trips and transit trips for each O-D pair isolated from the trip distribution.

Table 4.26 Mode split O-D matrix

	TAZ 1	TAZ 2	
TAZ 1	Auto trips = 14	Auto trips = 45	
	Transit trips= 7	Transit trips = 15	Origins
TAZ 2	Auto trips = 4	Auto trips = 35	
	Transit trips = 1	Transit trips = 6	
	Destinations		

Class Exercise: Modal Split—Logit Model

The utility can be calculated using the following equation.

$$U_i = \alpha_i - 0.08\ T_a - 0.07 T_w - 0.05\ T_t - 0.03\ C$$

Where:
U_i = the utility of mode i
α_i = the constant term of mode i
T_a = the access time
T_w = the waiting time
T_t = the travel time
C = the travel cost

Based on the utility expression and using the logit model to calculate the modal split between the automobile mode (α_i = -0.001) and a mass transit mode (α_i = -0.03) based on the data given below.

Table 4.27 Data related to auto and transit

Mode of travel	T_a	T_w	T_r	C
Automobile	3	0	25	200
Public Transportation	12	20	75	100

The Four-Step Model: Step 4—Network Assignment

Network assignment or trip assignment is the final step of the Four-Step-Model. This step predicts which routes will be taken by the forecasted trips produced to reach each destination. The trip assignment involves assigning traffic to a transportation network such as roads and streets or a transit network. Network assignment applies the trip distribution O-D matrix and mode data to the transportation network. The transportation network is modeled as a series of links and nodes. Links are the main arterial roads, highways and other traffic right-of-ways, which are defined by speed and travel capacity in the model. Nodes are the origins and destinations of trips. Traffic traveling between zones is routed on links to model the movement and impact of forecasted trips on the existing transportation system. Common methods of computing trip assignment include shortest path assignment (all-or-nothing),

capacity restraint (incremental) assignment, network equilibrium models, etc. Trip assignment procedures operate on the premise of minimizing travel time or cost. Network assignment requires modeling software to make the computations and spatially represent trip flows on the network (Meyer and Miller 2001).

Traffic is assigned to available transit or roadway routes using a mathematical algorithm that determines the amount of traffic as a function of time, volume,

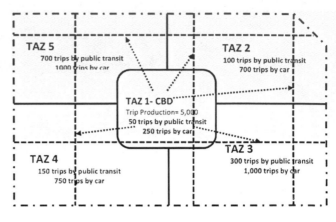

Figure 4.6 Example of trip assignment.

capacity, or impedance factor. The two commonly used methods for the trip assignment are all-or-nothing and capacity restraint.

All-or-Nothing (Shortest-Path Algorithm)

All-or-nothing is often referred to as the minimum path algorithm in which the trips from any origin zone to any destination zone are loaded onto a single, minimum travel cost path between the two zones. As volumes and travel times increase, the results of this method become more unreliable. As an example of this method, imagine that zones A and B are connected by ten separate routes. Route 3 has the shortest travel time which means that, according to this model, all trips from A to B will use route 3. This model may be reasonable in sparse and uncongested networks where there are few alternative routes and they have a large difference in travel cost. Actually, this model's most important practical application is that it acts as a basis for other types of trip assignment methods.

Capacity Restraint

Capacity Restraint is an incremental assignment and a process in which fractions of traffic volumes are assigned in iterative manner. A portion of total demand is assigned to the network, based on all-or-nothing assignment. Then, the travel times of link that connect the zones are recalculated based on link traffic volumes. After a number of iteration, the trips are assigned to the routes that yield a balanced equilibrium solution. Capacity restraint models are non-linear models and they use the volume-capacity ratio or v/c as a common factor. The underlying premise of a capacity restraint model is that the travel time on any link is related to the traffic volume on that link. This is analogous to the level of service (LOS) criterion, where LOS A corresponds to a low v/c and a higher vehicle speed and LOS E has the corresponding v/c equals or greater than one. Capacity restraint models assign traffic to possible routes in an iterative manner (Transportation Planning Handbook, 1992).

Class Exercise: Trip Assignment Model Using All-or-Nothing Method

Use in the following Origin-Destination (O-D) table to assign the trips to the network given in figure 4–7 using the all-or-nothing/shortest path method. The output will be the list of links in the network and their corresponding traffic volume.

Table 4.28 Origin-Destination matrix

From/to	TAZ 1	TAZ 2	TAZ 3	TAZ 4	TAZ 5	TAZ 6
	Trips between Traffic Analysis Zones (TAZs)					
TAZ 1	-	200	150	400	300	450
TAZ 2	500	-	175	125	650	130
TAZ 3	420	120	-	125	125	420
TAZ 4	230	225	350	-	300	250
TAZ 5	200	100	50	350	-	100
TAZ 6	420	600	150	430	260	-

Solution

As discussed earlier, in the all-or-nothing technique, all of the trips between an origin and a destination are assumed to take the shortest path (in terms of travel time). For example, all of the 420 vehicles that travel between nodes 3 and 6 will travel via nodes 3–2–5–6 (the shortest travel time). The tables shown below indicate the routes that were selected for loading, as well as the total traffic volume for each link in the system after all of the links were loaded.

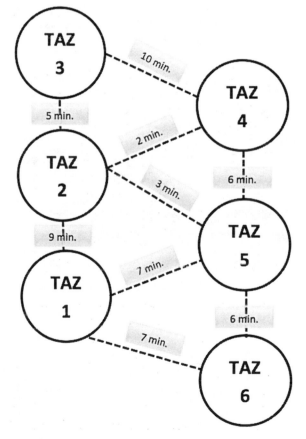

Figure 4.7 Road Network with travel time between nodes.

Table 4.29 Choosing the shortest path between Traffic Analysis Zones (TAZs)

From Node…	To Node…	Link/way	Travel time	Trip volume
1	2	1–2	9	200
	3	1–2, 2–3	14	150
	4	1–2, 2–4	11	400
	5	1–5	7	300
	6	1–6	7	430
2	1	2–1	9	500
	3	2–3	5	175
	4	2–4	2	125
	5	2–5	3	650
	6	2–5, 5–6	9	130
3	1	3–2, 2–1	14	420
	2	3–2	5	120
	4	3–2, 2–4	7	125
	5	3–2, 2–5	8	125
	6	3–2, 2–5, 5–6	14	420
4	1	4–2, 2–1	11	230
	2	4–2	2	225
	3	4–2, 2–3	7	350
	5	4–2, 2–5	5	300
	6	4–5, 5–6	12	250
5	1	5–1	7	200
	2	5–2	3	100
	3	5–2, 2–3	8	50
	4	5–2, 2–4	5	350
	6	5–6	6	100
6	1	6–1	7	420
	2	6–5, 5–2	9	600
	3	6–5, 5–2, 2–3	14	150
	4	6–5, 5–4	12	430
	5	6–5	6	260

Table 4.30 Trips assigned on the road network

Link/way	Trip volume	Trip volume added
1–2	200+150+400	650
2–3	150+175+350+50+150	875
2–4	400+125+125+350	1000
1–5	300	300
1–6	430	430

Link/way	Trip volume	Trip volume added
2–1	500+420+230	1150
2–5	650+125+130+300+420	1625
5–6	130+420+250+100	900
3–2	420+120+125+125+120	1210
4–2	230+225+350+300	1105
4–5	250	250
5–1	200	200
5–2	100+50+350+600+150	1250
6–1	420	420
6–5	600+150+430+260	1440
5–4	430	430

Practice Problems

Practice Problem 1: Trip generation model: Cross-classification

Use the cross-classification method, calculate the total non-work-based productions of each of the zones that are expected to contain the following mixtures of households.

Forecasted number of households
by household size and auto ownership

		TAZ 1			TAZ 2			TAZ 3		
		0	1	2+	0	1	2+	0	1	2+
Persons /HH	1	100	160	90	250	150	140	40	100	250
	2	30	450	200	150	100	160	55	250	240
	3	300	350	500	400	200	130	95	250	440
	4+	300	650	430	175	190	500	150	240	400

Vehicles/ HH

Home-based-non-work trip rates

Vehicles/ HH

		TAZ 1			TAZ 2			TAZ 3		
		0	1	2+	0	1	2+	0	1	2+
Persons /HH	1	0.37	1.25	1.82	1.97	2.02	1.99	1.94	2.32	2.09
	2	1.07	2.02	3.39	1.94	2.89	1.86	2.94	1.99	2.26
	3	3.27	4.22	5.89	3.94	5.05	5.96	3.34	3.99	4.56
	4+	4.55	6.7	8.27	6.32	7.87	7.74	4.82	5.99	6.99

Problem Practice 2: The trip distribution: Gravity Model

The trip generation characteristics of a four-zone city are shown below. The city has the following trip productions and attractions:

Trip production, attraction and travel time between zones

Zone	Trip production	Trip attraction	Travel time between zones			
			Zone 1	Zone 2	Zone 3	Zone 4
Zone 1	650	650	Zone 1 3	6	8	11
Zone 2	850	600	Zone 2 6	4	9	13
Zone 3	550	450	Zone 3 8	9	3	12
Zone 4	950	300	Zone 4 11	13	12	4

Travel time vs. friction factor

Travel Time (min)	F_{ij}
1	92
2	69
3	62
4	51
5	49
6	36
7	30
8	22
9	15
11	12
12	8
13	4

Distribute the trips for the city using the gravity model. Use the given data to develop a trip table for the city. For your analysis using the gravity model, assume the socioeconomic factor $K_{ij}=1.0$.

Practice Problem 3: Modal Split Model

Using the utility equation

$$U_i = \alpha_i - 0.005X_1 - 0.03X_2 - 0.02X_3$$

Where X_1 is the out-of-pocket travel costs in cents, X_2 is travel time in minutes and X_3 is waiting time in minutes.

1. Calculate the modal split of the following travel modes:

Table PP3.1

Mode i	A_i	X_1	X_2	X3
Automobile	-0.20	180	20	0
Train	-0.40	80	35	5
Bus	-0.60	50	45	20

2. Estimate the effect that a 50 percent increase in the out-of-pocket cost of an automobile will have on modal split. Based on the results, would you recommend an increase in fuel price to reduce the demand of automobile use and encourage public transit use?

Bibliography

Ben-Akiva, Moshe. 2008. "Travel Demand Modeling." *MIT Open Courseware, Civil and Environmental Engineering.* Massachusetts Institute of Technology (MIT)..

Edwards, John D. (Ed.). 1992. *Transportation Planning Handbook*, Prentice Hall

Fehrs and Peers Transportation Consultants. 2009. "Transportation Strategic Plan: Travel Demand Model Improvement Program." *Vision Los Angeles.*

ICPST. 2010. "CrimeStat." *Inter-university Consortium for Political and Social Reseach.* The National Institute of Justice.

Meyer, Michael, and Eric Miller. 2001. *Urban Transportation Planning: A Decision Oriented Approach.* 2nd ed. New York: McGraw-Hill.

NCHRP. 2012. *Travel Demand Forecasting: Parameters and Techniques.* National Cooperative Highway Research Program, National Academy of Sciences.

Sinha, Kumares, and Samuel Labi. 2007. *Transportation Decision Making: Principles of Project Evaluation.* New Jersey: John Wiley & Sons.

5

Impacts of Transportation
on the Environment and Society

Chapter Outline
- Introduction
- Auto Dependency and Its Impact
- Possible Solutions
- Travel Demand Management (TDM) as Environmental Solutions
  - o *Push Measures*
    - *Traffic Calming*
    - *Flexible Work Hours*
    - *Telecommuting*
    - *Congestion Pricing*
  - o *Pull Measures*
    - *Improving Public Transit*
    - *Improving Pedestrian and Bike Infrastructure*
    - *Land Use Alteration and Improved Accessibility*
- Other Sustainable Solutions
  - o *Hydrogen Fuel Cells*
  - o *Electric Cars*
  - o *Green Roads*
- Conclusion

Introduction

Some externalities associated with transportation such as local and global pollution, traffic congestion, accidents, noise, and oil dependency have undesirable and unintended impacts on society and the environment. Data demonstrate that about 40,000 people die on highways each year (NHTSA 2011); urban road congestion causes 3.7 billion hours of delay a year (Schrank and Lomax 2005); automobiles are a leading source of greenhouse gas emissions and local air pollutants; and gasoline accounts for nearly half of the nation's dependence on oil (Parry, Walls and Harrington 2007). Especially, the issue of transportation and the environment has historically been a much-debated subject for the last several decades. An international symposium on "Transportation and Environment Policies, Plans and Practices", held at the University of Southampton in 1973, is credited with creating awareness of the growing use of motorized transport, and also challenged the maintenance of many reasonable and acceptable standards in environmental planning. The major themes that emerged from this symposium included the idea of balance between transport and the environment, between control and freedom, between private and public transport and between long-term solutions and short-term resolution (Earp, McDonald and Thomas 1973).

Before the automobile, transport-related environmental problems involved horse manure and carcasses in the streets. By contrast, with automobiles, the problems range from slow moving traffic clogging streets to severe environmental damage. As society becomes increasingly reliant on automobiles, the rate at which we consume fossil fuels has become more and more of an environmental concern. As much as the automobile has enabled us to take care of our daily needs and has become a focal point and a symbol of socioeconomic status, it has also burdened society in terms of environmental and health cost. As the population increases at incredible rates, automobile needs, and its subsequent consequences also increase. With the problems of traffic congestion in urban areas, air pollution that comes from vehicle emissions become a growing concern for the general public, especially minorities and people of low-income living in areas where the freeways go through their neighborhoods. The high flow of traffic volumes through the low-income areas leaves the people exposed to higher volumes of air and noise pollution. Furthermore, the impacts of roads and automobile-related waste on the natural environment become a concern for society. Consequently, the jobs of planners today turn around mitigating the adverse effects of transportation on society and the environment.

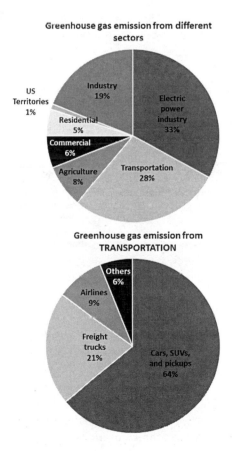

Figure 5.1 U.S. greenhouse gas emission (data: EPA, 2008).

Auto Dependency and Its Impact

AIR POLLUTION

The ecological impacts of excessive driving are significant and support persuasive arguments for decreasing car use. Air pollution is obviously one of the key concerns. Worldwide, approximately 68 percent of all carbon monoxide, 73 percent of sulfur oxides, 43 percent of nitrogen oxides and 42 percent of particulates come from the transportation sectors. The combustion of fossil fuels from the transport sector also accounts for 32 percent of total U.S. carbon dioxide emissions and 27 percent of U.S. greenhouse gas emissions (EPA 2014). The emissions of nitrogen oxides and volatile organic compounds from cars react with oxygen and sunlight to form ground-level ozone, also known as a photochemical smog, a brownish haze formed by chemical reactions. The formed ozone reacts with other air pollutants to form different secondary air pollutants that injure plant tissue, irritate eyes, and aggravate respiratory illnesses in humans and other mammals (Berg and Raven 1995).

Auto emissions also include carcinogenic compounds such as benzene, formaldehyde, toluene, acetaldehyde, xylene, and 1, 3-butadiene. Many of these particles are extremely fine, so fine that they find their way into our bloodstream via the lungs, bringing with them carbon, metals, and other harmful ingredients. Aside from the cancer-related impacts of these particulates and chemicals, studies have shown that many of the above mentioned toxic compounds emitted by automobiles also cause reproductive and neurological problems. As more vehicle miles are traveled, pollution from cars and trucks tend to increase, surpassing the air pollution improvements that have been made in the world over the last few decades (Gillham 2002).

Surface Runoff

The environmental impacts of driving are not just related to air pollution. Paved surfaces contribute to the pollution of water. The transportation system requires a vast system of *impervious surfaces* like roads and parking lots, which together take up about one-half of all urban space (Durning 1992). As of 2012, there exist approximately 8.6 million lane miles of road in the United States (ARTBA 2014). Not only do these synthetic surfaces keep rainwater from percolating into the water table, they allow rainwater to transport many transportation-related byproducts, such as oil, grit, and road salt, into streams, rivers and lakes during rain events. Parking lots and roadways also contribute heavy metals, hydrocarbons and volatile organic compounds (VOCs) to local storm drains.

The ubiquitous hardscape of urban regions also compromises the health of botanical life that keeps cities beautiful, shaded, and cool. Greyfield development and its accompanying road network is one of the key factors in what is called the urban heat-island effect. A surface's capacity to reflect light is known as albedo, and so the lower the albedo a surface has, the more solar heat it absorbs. A quick look at most of our urban centers via Google Earth not only reveals an overwhelming amount of hardscape, but a dark surface that helps make our cities much hotter places than the surrounding countryside.

Toxic Waste

The environmental impacts of driving can be found in expanding the system of landfills. With the development of the automobile in the early twentieth century, the nature of the waste stream slowly changed. As we shifted away from mostly organic materials to inorganic ones, the automobile became one of the main culprits in this change. Cars are manufactured from a host of materials, including iron, steel, and an increasing amount of plastic.

The United States disposes about one tire per resident which adds to landfills annually. Over three hundred million tires are disposed next to old washing machines, discarded food containers, and steamed medical waste. Over a billion cars are in use worldwide, translating to a little less than a trillion tires destined to be disposed (Weisman 2007).

Auto body shops typically generate several kinds of potentially hazardous waste, including waste solvent and coatings, contaminated rags, wipes, and absorbents, empty containers, used oil, waste antifreeze, sanding or grinding dusts, and contaminated wash waters. Off the road, junk cars pollute the environment because of lack of regulating the automobile recycling industry. In some cities, millions of tons of potentially toxic junk cars have been buried in municipal landfills, instead of being placed in the dumps for toxic materials. There are also cases where junk cars are transported to the developing world where environmental awareness and resources for treating toxic waste are scarce.

EXTINCTION OF WILDLIFE AND LOSS OF PRIME FARMLAND

One of the less recognized impacts of driving involves wildlife. Millions of animals die each year after being hit by automobiles and trucks. Moose, deer, snakes, toads, and raptors are just some of the creatures killed on roads. The real impact on wildlife, however, is much greater than the carnage on the roads. What we are seeing is a gradual process of large mammals "shifting their home ranges away from areas with high road densities" (Foreman 2004). Paved roads are barriers to movement; they fragment habitat and increase the chances for extirpation and extinction of various animal populations around the world. Conservation biologists, Trombulak and Frissel, claim that road construction in the United States has "destroyed 11,817,346 acres of land and water bodies that formerly supported plants, animals, and other organisms" (Foreman 2004). Gillham (2002) found that paving 30 percent of a given watershed with the impervious material will cause many species to disappear.

The U.S. Department of Agriculture's (USDA) National Resources Conservation Service reports, "we are losing land to development at an average rate of nearly two million acres per year" (Gillham 2002). From 1992 to 2007, about 11.5 million acres of new land developed was prime farmland, which is farmland that has the best combination of physical and chemical characteristics for agricultural production, and is considered to be of local economic importance (USDA 2013). Much of this lost land is developed into landscapes adapted to automobile use including large lots, separated strip development, and many other hardscape surfaces. As auto use increases, farmland disappears in the metropolitan fringe will likely only increase, along with its air and noise pollution and traffic problems (Gillham 2002).

URBAN SPRAWL AND SUBURBAN LIVING

There is a direct correlation between urban sprawl, land use patterns and automobile dependency. During the height of the railroad system in the United States, the location and placement of towns were determined by the transit routes and stops. After the age of trolley systems, the automobile became the preferred mode of commuting to the newly minted, sprawling suburban neighborhoods, with the white picket fence homes. While the distances between necessary stops of daily life expand, accessibility decreases, and automobile dependency increases.

An intricate system of regulations, codes, and standards exist that determine the shape of development across several cities. Oliver Gillham (2002) called this system the "genetic code of sprawl." It establishes the interrelated network of subdivision regulations, zoning codes and other rigid guidelines found in the "roadway manuals and standards issued by state and federal governments." Put simply, this code has been put into action to encourage the free movement of the private car. And while we cannot blame automobile technology itself for the present layout of arterial roads, freeways, and strip development, what has been established over the course of the twentieth century is a deep relationship between the automobile and the built landscape that is often hard to tease apart. The automobile and the expansive sprawled metropolitan area are one and the same. One does not exist independently of the other.

Kenneth T. Jackson, in his book, *Crabgrass Frontier: The Suburbanization of the United States*, defines the "drive-in culture of contemporary America" by pointing out the extreme post-war transformation of the American landscape. In his view, the garage shaped the single family home and fast became our portal to the outside world. As the garage moved from the back of the house to become attached to the dwelling, it grew bigger with each passing decade (Jackson 1987). The motel on the interchange replaced the hotel in the central business district as travelers began to bypass downtown. Drive-in theaters and fast food restaurants became the norm, both reliant on the highly mobile consumer. The gasoline service station gradually shed its role as a place of automotive maintenance and soon turned into another commercial stopover. One only fill up and buy snacks on the way to your destination; nobody checks oil anymore. Cities became centerless, sprawling areas of continuous growth, and the offices and other places of business spilled out into the former countryside. "Commercial, residential, and industrial structures have been redesigned to fit the needs of the motorist rather than the pedestrian." (Jackson 1987).

Possible Solutions

Providing efficient and practical alternatives to the automobile and redesigning our cities are the essential measures in reducing environmental and societal impacts of transportation. Societies have begun to acknowledge the prices they have already paid for excessive car use, whether in the form of lost productive time (or opportunity cost) due to highway congestion, personal medical costs due to accidents, or simply the polluted air due to car emission. The solution is pointed to reducing the absolute number of vehicles in use, curbing vehicle miles traveled, enhance the average vehicle fuel economy and invent new technologies. These solutions may reduce emissions, and air pollution while they decrease congestion and other impacts on the environment. The challenge to the automobile reduction strategies is that it will not be possible without efficient alternative and substitutes modes of travel. Some of these alternatives include improving public transportation and bicycle infrastructure, reducing urban sprawl, modifying the land use patterns, and making activity points more accessible. Today, many urban planners and geographers are promoting higher density, mixed-use housing and urban development as a solution to urban congestion and other environmental issues. "Smart growth" proponents point to highways and expressways as one of the leading causes of urban sprawl, low-density sub-cities, and scattered land use patterns. They believe the solution lies in developing higher density and more efficient land use patterns with transit-based accessibility.

The planning concepts that seek auto-dependency reduction are also known as travel demand management (TDM) strategies. Although TDM was originally intended as congestion relief mechanism, the strategies also have tremendous and sustainable effect on alleviating the environmental consequences of the automobile.

Travel Demand Management as Environmental Solutions

The original concepts of Travel Demand Management (TDM) took root in the 1970s and 1980s from legitimate desires to provide alternatives to single occupancy commuter travel for several reasons: to save energy, improve air quality and reduce peak period congestion. The Intermodal Surface Transportation Efficiency Act of 1991 gave metropolitan areas powers for regional transportation planning, followed by the Transportation Equity Act for the 21 Century (TEA 21) which mandated several factors to be included in transportation planning.

These factors include support for the economic vitality and productivity of the region; increased safety for all travelers, pedestrian, driver, and transit rider; increased accessibility and mobility for all people and goods; protection of the environment; conservation of energy; improved quality of life; increased connectivity of transportation across and between modes; promotion of efficient system management and operation; and effective maintenance and preservation of existing transportation systems.

This legislation reduced and restricted federal funding that forced regional planners to approach solutions by managing both the demand side for transportation as well as the supply side. The need of TDM comes with the recognition that with a growing economy and population (high demand), we are driving more than ever. Growth in demand has far exceeded growth in the supply of infrastructure, rendering a need for change in the planning ideology. TDM has emerged to contrast the traditional supply side practice that continued investment in road infrastructure.

TDM can be described as a set of tools to offer people better travel information and opportunities, and also to help them to reduce their need to travel especially by car. Travel Demand Management (TDM) is a general term, which includes strategies and programs that encourage more efficient use of transport resources (Litman 2003). It deals with developing and evaluating various strategies and policies to reduce traffic congestion, environmental pollution, and energy consumption, as well as to produce benefits such as improved traffic safety, consumer cost savings, etc. (Zaman and Habib 2011). Travel Demand Management is about providing travelers with choices, such as work location, route, time of travel and mode (FHWA 2006). Managing travel demand is geared toward optimizing transportation performance for work and recreational commutes. In doing so, Zaman and Habib (2011) argued that Travel Demand Management is considered to be the most effective means for achieving sustainability in the transportations sector.

At its most basic level, TDM attempts to reduce car use by influencing people's travel behavior (Meyer 1999). This is endeavored through numerous strategies categorized by Steg and Vlek (1997) as push and pull measures. Push measures refer to TDM strategies that attempt to discourage car use while pull measures group strategies that pull people into alternative modes of transportation (Steg and Vlek 1997). Congestion pricing, parking control, telecommuting and flexible work hours are pertinent examples of widely practiced push measures. Compared to pull measures, these strategies are often cheaper to implement and highly effective in reducing vehicle trips. The following sections address a few of the most popular TDM strategies. It is important to note that the potential successes of TDM strategies is dependent on residents' acceptance of these policies, the political feasibility of implementation and effectiveness of the program.

PUSH MEASURES

Traffic Calming

Traffic calming was based on the idea of residential areas being protected from through traffic and reducing vehicle speeds. Subsequently, it was mainly justified on the grounds of pedestrian safety and reduction of noise and local air pollution that are consequences of heavy traffic. Definitions of traffic calming vary, but they all share the goal of reducing vehicle speeds, improving safety and enhancing the quality of life. Traffic calming strategies include the so-called Three "Es," traffic education, enforcement, and engineering (Fehr and Peers 2014). Most definitions focus on engineering measures (infrastructural elements) to change driver behavior. Some focus on enforcement and education measures that compel drivers to slow down.

To improve the environment and livability of neighborhood streets, local planning agencies encourage citizens' involvement in the traffic calming process by incorporating the preferences and requirements of the residents. This promotes and improves real and perceived safe conditions for motorists, bicyclists, pedestrians, and residents. Designated bike lanes, raised islands located along the centerline of the roadway, rounded and raised pavement to slow vehicles (speed bumps), curb extension to narrow the road and crossings, road markings and the installation of traffic circles (roundabouts) are some techniques for calming traffic. According to Pharoah and Russel (1989), traffic calming schemes may reduce accident rates by up to 40 percent, as well as reduce the severity of accidents. While legal speed limits can be applied, these traffic measures create a physical restriction that is not limited to driver self-regulation and police enforcement.

These measures can be argued to provide a more socially equitable and efficient solution to accidents and noise pollution than increased regulation (Garrod, Scarpa and Willis 2002). However, a study by Anh & Ruhka, 2009 suggested that some speed bumps created congestion and increased fuel consumption. They also found that, in general, traffic circles allow smoother driving patterns with milder acceleration behavior when compared to speed humps and stop signs. Although some argue that calming traffic increases congestion, the introduction of traffic calming scheme is associated with improvements in health and health-related behaviors. A study by Morrison *et al.* (2004) found that there were increases in observed pedestrian activity after the introduction of traffic calming scheme. Another traffic calming study found that "success" in calming schemes depends, not only on objective empirical measures, but on the overwhelming support of the local community, which in turn depends upon the openness of policies and public outreach (Taylor and Tight 1997).

BOX 5.1 Road Diet case study: Stone Way North in Seattle

The road diet approach involves narrowing travel lanes or shoulders or eliminating some of them to provide more space for pedestrians and bicyclists. A typical road diet consists of converting a four-lane roadway (two in each direction) to a three-lane (one in each direction plus a center turn lane) and adding sidewalks and/or bicycle lanes. At times, this reconfiguration can be accomplished by simply restriping the lanes in conjunction with a resurfacing project. In theory, road diets have potential drawbacks, but, in fact, this approach offers a number of benefits in terms of traffic operations, safety, and livability when applied in the appropriate situations.

For almost three decades, Seattle, WA, has implemented road diets in an effort to improve the city's streets and encourage walking, bicycling, and transit use. Since 1972, the Seattle Department of Transportation (SDOT) has installed 29 road diets. In 2007, Seattle passed a Complete Street Ordinance that required SDOT to plan, design and construct new transportation improvements to accommodate pedestrians, bicycles, and transit while promoting safe operation for all users. Also, the ordinance required SDOT to incorporate complete streets principles into its transportation strategic plan, pedestrian and bicycle master plans, transit plan, and various other SDOT plans, manuals, rules, and regulations. A complete street is a nationwide movement to design and build road networks that are welcoming to everyone: young and old, motorist and bicyclist, walker and wheelchair user, bus rider and shopkeeper.

For a corridor to be considered as a candidate for a road diet, SDOT requires that it be identified in the city's list of complete streets capital projects or its pedestrian or bicyclist master plans. Another approach is for the candidate street's residents to request a road diet as part of the implementation of their neighborhood improvement plan. SDOT considers the following facets of transportation operations, mobility, and safety in the selection of a road diet corridor: Volume of traffic, number of collisions, vehicle speed, number of lanes, freight usage, bus stops and routing, travel time and accessibility.

In 2008, SDOT implemented a road diet on a 1.2-mile (1.9-kilometer) section of Stone Way North from N 34th Street to N 50th Street. Also to serving motor vehicles, this segment of Stone Way North helps connect a bicycle path with a park. Within five blocks are eight schools, two libraries, and five parks. The segment that was modified was originally a four-lane roadway carrying 13,000 vehicles per day. It had parking on both sides, a posted speed limit of 30 mi/h (48 km/h), and four uncontrolled, marked crosswalks that were noncompliant under SDOT's 2004 revised crosswalk guidelines. For this corridor, the city's 2007 Bicycle master plan recommended climbing lanes and shared lane markings (previously known as "sharrows"). The road diet cross section became two lanes plus a two-way left-turn lane, bicycle lanes, and parking on both sides.

Speeds decreased after the road diet installation. The 85th percentile speed was 37 mi/h (60 km/h) prior to the road diet. In the northbound direction, the 85thpercentile speed dropped to 36 mi/h (58 km/h) and, in the southbound direction, 34 mi/h (55 km/h). Three percent of vehicles traveled at 40 mi/h (64 km/h) and faster prior to the road diet. Less than 1 percent traveled at 40 mi/h and faster afterward. Average daily traffic (ADT) dropped 6 percent, which was consistent with a citywide trend between 2006 and 2008. Peak hour volume dropped approximately 5 percent. The off-peak volume increased south of 45th Street by 2 percent. Bicycle volume increased 35 percent, representing almost 15 percent of the peak hour traffic volume. Traffic did not divert after restriping, as indicated by the fact that volume did not increase on the four non-arterial streets commonly known as alternatives to Stone Way North. A comparison of 2 years of crash data before (2006–2007) and after (2008–2009) the installation showed an overall decline in incidents. Total crashes decreased 14 percent; injury crashes went down by 33 percent, and angle crashes dropped by 56 percent. Bicycle crashes showed no change, but the rate decreased because the number of cyclists increased. Pedestrian crashes declined 80 percent.

Adapted from "Going on a Road Diet" by Carol Tan, Federal Highway Administration, September 7, 2011.

Flexible Work Hours

Another TDM push measure is the implementation of a flexible work schedule. The general idea behind the flexible work schedule is altering the traditional 8:00 a.m. to 5:00 p.m. work day. Since this traditional work schedule correlates with peak hours of congestion, allowing for flexibility in home-work trip days and times can reduce commute times, vehicle trips at peak hours and local emissions. The compressed work week (CCW) is an example of a flexible work schedule that has been practiced by many employees. Sundo and Fujii (2005) define the compressed working week as, "a shortening of the traditional five-day working week, by extending daily work times to maintain the same number of weekly working hours as the five-day week." For example, workers may opt to work four 10-hour days per week, taking Monday or Friday off. Another flextime schedule is to work nine-hour a day Monday through Thursday, an eight-hour day on Friday, taking every other Friday off. Workers may arrange to coordinate their days off so that their responsibilities are adequately covered. Other workers may opt simply to come in early, such as 5 or 6 a.m., and leave in the mid-afternoon, or come in late and, therefore, leave late. Flextime may have been initially introduced to help employees with children who needed the flexibility to care for their children before and after school, but another benefit is the ability for some employees to schedule their departure time allowing them to evade rush hour traffic and congestion.

A case study conducted by Sundo and Fijii (2005) reveals the benefits of this scheme. Data collected from over 220 university employees noted a significant reduction in commute time. Although the reduced commute time stemmed from a change of schedule rather than a reduction in congestion, it is evident that the idea is a valuable strategy. Despite successes, the flexible hour scheme would render little impact on places with incessant traffic. Also, the prevalence of the private market creates a demand for employees to be present Monday through Friday from 8:00 a.m. to 5:00 p.m. Although these flex hour work schemes could provide personal congestion relief, the belief that they would have a substantial impact on congestion and environmental problems is difficult to comprehend.

There is a study conducted to determine the factors impacting the propensity to adopt a flexible work schedule, and establish how and to what extent the timing of work is influenced by information communication technologies and socio-demographic characteristics. The analysis by Alexander, Dijst and Dick (2010) suggests that work-related characteristics and information communication technology (ICT) seem to be more important for work-schedule flexibility than socio-demographic characteristics. Among the occupations that use ICT, are high-level professionals (scientific, technical, healthcare, information technology professionals, etc.) are more likely to make the shift and use flexible work schedule. This, however, might exclude low-level employees from the flexible time experience and keep them in the congested traffic.

A more comprehensive approach such as extended hours in childcare, banking, stores, and flextime working hours can have a significant impact on the space-time autonomy allowing communities of all social classes to have better accessibility to various opportunities (Hanson 2004). More studies have to be done to determine possible incentives to encourage businesses to offer flextime to their employees so that there is less time spent commuting.

Telecommuting

Telecommuting refers to any form of substitution of information technologies (such as telecommunications and Internet) for work-related travel. In other words, it is moving the work to the workers instead of moving the workers to work (Nilles 1998). Telecommuting is not limited to work, it has made strong headway in education as well with an increasing popularity of online classes, cutting down on traffic congestion and costs. Telecommuting is practiced by only a small fraction of the labor force, but it has become more common and will probably continue to increase. The idea of telecommuting is considered the most promising substitute for work trips and thus believed to be a good strategy for Transportation Demand Management (Yen 2000).

Ory & Mokhtarian (2006) conducted a study in which they explored the causal relationship between telecommuting and residential relocation to determine whether telecommuting prompts workers to move farther from work and increase their overall commute distance, or allows those who have already chosen to live in more distant locations to commute less frequently. Findings revealed that telecommuters are putting greater distance between their homes and workplaces than are non-telecommuters.

Choo & Sangho (2005), examined the propensity and frequency of workers to telecommute by using a rich set of individual demographic, work-related and industry characteristics, household demographics, and work location characteristics and found that women telecommuted less, yet the propensity to telecommute was equal to men. Similarly, the study showed that full-time employees telecommuted more than part-timers, yet again the propensity to telecommute was equal. These are encouraging findings that further strengthen telecommuting as a substitute (or a complement) for travel and imply that there is strong public support for policy makers to implement such change.

Besides, the existence of positive externalities suggests that the marginal social benefit of telecommuting is greater than its private marginal benefit. Even in the case where only the effect on congestion is taken into account, the size of telecommuting's positive external effects seems to be sufficient to justify a degree of policy support for this practice. As a form of substitution from physical commuting to virtual commuting, telecommuting is expected to have not only a direct impact on telecommuters but also an indirect impact on society as a whole (Mitmomo and Jitsuzumi 1999; Mokhtarian *et al.*, 1995). The drawback for telecommuting is that face-to-face contact remains a necessity for team development and is critically important in business.

Congestion Pricing

Congestion pricing is a system of surcharges for the use of a transportation system. Also known as road pricing, congestion pricing has two distinct objectives: revenue generation, usually for road infrastructure financing, and for demand management purposes (Small and Gomez-Ibancz 1998). It is usually intended for the private automobile users during peak hours. The fundamental premise behind congestion pricing is that the private vehicle users do not pay the full cost of vehicle use. Thus, congestion pricing is an efficiency pricing strategy that requires the users to pay more for the public good, thus increasing the welfare gain or net benefit for society. The economic theory of congestion pricing is that the use of the price mechanism is to make users more aware of the marginal costs they add when using the transportation system during the peak hour, and that they should pay for the additional congestion they create, thus encouraging the redistribution of the demand in space or in time (Button 1993). Congestion charging is increasingly being considered for implementation in some cities to reduce traffic congestion during peak periods.

If a congestion charging scheme is introduced with variable charges applied throughout the day, it is likely to achieve a shift in departure time from the peak period to less congested times. It is, therefore, imperative that the flexibility of departure time choice is addressed in the analysis of potential impacts of a charging scheme.

Congestion pricing is widely touted as the most effective TDM strategy employed today (Sweet 2011; Meyer 1999). The strategy also requires drivers to pay a highway toll that can vary according to the level of congestion to match the marginal social cost (Finch 1996). Four types of pricing schemes have emerged in recent years including variably priced lanes (variable tolls on separated lanes within the highway, variable tolls on entire roadways, cordon charges (charges to drive into a congested area within a city such as London's congestion charging), and area-wide charges (per mile charges on all roads within an area) (HOTM-FHWA 2006). Numerous congestion pricing schemes have been implemented worldwide, attesting to their success and applicability. These schemes have proven to reduce central city congestion (Transport for London 2007), improve traffic flows, and reduce daily vehicle trips (Meyer 1999).

In the United States, Highway Occupancy Toll Roads are the closest to congestion pricing. High occupancy toll lanes is a road pricing scheme that gives motorists in single occupant vehicles access to high occupancy vehicle lanes (or HOV lanes) by charging a toll. Tolls are collected either by manned booths, automatic number plate recognition or electronic toll collection systems. Some people argue that HOV lanes are often constructed within the existing road space which they criticized as being an environmental tax or perk for the rich ("Lexus lanes"). A study by The Brookings Institute also agrees that in practice, this idea would be unacceptable to most American drivers. They believe high tolls would force them off the best roads during the most convenient hours while wealthier commuters move rapidly on those roads (Downs, 2002).

Despite their success, congestion pricing is difficult to implement. With roads are seen as a public entity, owned by the taxpayers, the implementation of congestion pricing schemes is heavily contested. A case study conducted in Bangkok attests to the unpopularity of congestion pricing. Over 1000 daily commuters were surveyed and questioned about their preferences for numerous TDM strategies. Not surprisingly, congestion pricing was the least favorable among all available TDM measures (Debashish, *et al.*, 1997).

PULL MEASURES

Pull measures refer to strategies that reduce congestion through pulling people onto alternative modes of transportation. Park and ride schemes, improving pedestrian and bike infrastructure, altering land use and transit marketing campaigns are widely implemented pull measures that the TDM strategies use today.

Improving Public Transit

Although transit provides a relatively small portion of total travel, it tends to be concentrated in dense urban areas where automobile's external costs are high. As a result, it can provide significant benefits for congestion reductions, road and parking facility cost savings, users' cost savings and efficient land use and environmental protection. Where transit is a catalyst for smart growth land use, it can provide a variety of indirect benefits, including increased property values and improved community livability near transit stations, in addition to increased economic development. These benefits can be substantial, in some cases offsetting a significant portion of transit service public costs (Smith and Gihring 2003).

The low-level transit ridership in the U.S. challenges local governments' interest in providing quality public transportation service. With low ridership, governments are forced to increasingly subsidize mass transit systems, rendering a significant burden on taxpayers and municipal governments. Further compromising for transit ridership is the relative absence of efficient marketing campaigns. A survey of 85 randomly selected transit companies found that the average marketing budget rested just above $450,000 and rendered little to no influence on ridership. As customer-oriented businesses, transit companies are responsible for informing the public of their services and creating a rider-oriented culture (Smith, Razzouk and Richardson 1990). The success of public transit's marketing campaign illustrates the impact of marketing on ridership. For example, in Los Angeles, after LA Metro re-branding the entire service in 2008, using the media with creative advertisements and portraying the car as "cynical," ridership of discretionary riders (those who have a choice between transit and driving) grew from 24 percent to 36 percent (Arpi 2009). Often overlooked as a TDM measure, simple marketing is effective and efficient. With a well-financed and competently operated campaign, marketing can bring about the modal switch and increase ridership.

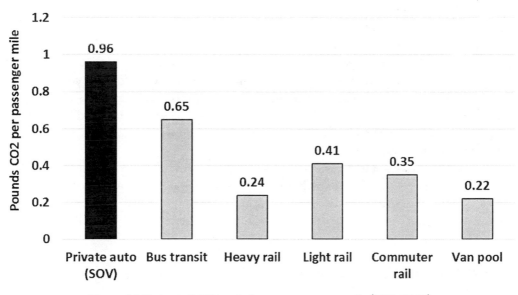

Figure 5.2 Estimated CO2 emissions per passenger mile (EPA, 2002).

Transit-oriented developments (TODs): Transit-oriented development is an integral land use development and is one of the efforts made toward reducing environmental impacts of transportation and creating easier access to public transportation. By definition, transit-oriented development (TOD) is a high-density, mixed-use residential and commercial area designed to maximize access to public transport and encourage transit ridership. Transportation hubs increase accessibility to provide better transit opportunities and, therefore, make transport more sustainable. TODs are a new-found solution, drawing the attention of new urbanists and architects. Such developments are planned to mix compact housing with commercial, public and open spaces and are designed to promote walking and the use of public transportation (Calthorpe 1993). Transit-oriented developments support personal, societal, environmental, and economic benefits. Some of the personal benefits from TODs include improving human health by promoting non-motorized modes of transportation such as walking and cycling. The societal benefits from TODs can include housing development and neighborhood revitalization, infrastructure efficiencies, decreased sprawl, and decreased automobile dependence and oil consumption (Brown and Werner 2011). Transit-oriented developments help to generate income for local businesses and increase public transportation ridership. A dissertation by Shah Imran (2012) titled "*Assessment of Transit Oriented Devel-*

opment Impacts" discusses the connection of TOD with smart growth, livable communities and sustainability that often creates new opportunities for the expansion and enhancement of transit services in communities while promoting alternative modes. TODs not only help the environment but promote health and a higher quality of life, thus planners are trying to help transit and health professionals better coordinate their efforts to create a more livable environment in various communities, and to offer people healthier and more sustainable transportation options.

Improving Pedestrian and Bike Infrastructure

Improving pedestrian and bike infrastructure is becoming a proven strategy that pulls people out of their cars and onto the streets as cyclists and pedestrians. Clearly, there is a link between the provision of quality walking and biking infrastructure and using active transportation. A study of over 2000 adults from neighborhoods across Stockholm, Sweden addresses this link and points to successes of walkable neighborhoods in encouraging active transport. Walkable neighborhoods (those with high residential density, street connectivity, and land use mix) had a higher level of people walking for transportation (as opposed to leisure) than those living in neighborhoods with low levels of walkability (Sundquist *et al.*, 2011). Integrating quality pedestrian and cyclist infrastructure with a compact city design, potentially deters people from driving.

In many places, the automobile is overused because of the absence of infrastructure for other travel modes. The provision of bicycle lanes and adequate walking facilities has high potential to increase walking and biking for transport. For example, New York City has made progressive efforts to improve bicycling safety and improve facilities. The city has extended the cycling network, provided favorable traffic conditions to bikes and has introduced bike sharing programs. Innovative bike policies and programs in the City of New York have led to a near doubling of bicycle trips since the year 2000 (Pucher, *et al.*, 2010).

Land Use Alteration and Improved Accessibility

Badoe and Miller (2000) discuss the relationship between transportation and land use but specifically, automobile ownership and land use. Their findings suggested that urban densities, traditional neighborhood designs, and land use mix have an impact on less auto ownership and land use. Over the last two decades, land development patterns that are favorable to the automobile were blamed for the decline in air quality, increased congestion, in both urban and suburban areas, and adverse impacts on the natural environment. As a result of cities consisting of specialized and spatially separated land uses, people are forced to travel long distances to access goods and services. Therefore, accessibility is considered to be one of the most important determinations of land use patterns. The relationship between land use and accessibility become dependent on the specific characteristics and locations of different land use types. However, accessibility cannot be measured only by distance. The quality of the transportation network and the cost of using a different mode of travel must be taken into account when measuring accessibility. The location of activities in space, together with the transportation resources connecting them, affects daily activity and travel patterns, which in turn affect land use and the transportation system. Consequently, the ability that people have to reach desired locations such as a market can influence both the extent and the location of land use alteration (Verburg, Overmars and Witte 2004).

BOX 5.2 Missoula, MT—Connecting transportation and land use to support livable communities

In rapidly growing Western Montana, Missoula County and the City of Missoula have entered into a cooperative agreement to enhance their ability to plan for future development so that a county-wide pattern of community-building, land use, and conservation that reflects the environmental, economic, aesthetic, and social values of city and county residents is achieved. The agreement created a City-County Office of Planning and Grants (OPG) responsible for land use permitting, long range planning, transportation planning, historic preservation, housing, the "Missoula in Motion" transportation demand management program, the Crime Victim Advocates Program and the Forum for Children and Youth. OPG works closely with city neighborhood councils and county community councils as it implements the city and county vision and mission as they related to existing and proposed land use and the built environment. Recent efforts conducted in support of livability include:

- The Urban Fringe Development Area Plan (UFDA), an innovative plan to allocate anticipated growth within the Missoula urban area through a cooperative effort of the county and the city. UFDA established development suitability criteria that seek to respond to an evolving market, provide housing choice, make efficient use of infrastructure, and protect sensitive lands. Progress is measured annually against a 2007 benchmark, allowing for course corrections and keeping the plan relevant.
- The Missoula Metropolitan Planning Organization (MPO) staffed by OPG created the "Envision Missoula" Transportation Plan, which won the Association of Metropolitan Planning Organization National Award for Outstanding Achievement in Metropolitan Transportation Planning for its linkage of land use and transportation planning and its inclusive process. Over 500 citizens participated in workshops and follow up "summit" meetings to confirm an inward focus to future regional growth. The workshops were followed by a telephone survey that confirmed the workshop findings and showed decision makers that the citizens actively participating in the project were representative of the community.
- The city's Brownfields Program is using the expertise of their Redevelopment Agency, Street Department, Parks Department, and the State Department of Environmental Quality to conduct environmental cleanup in support of redevelopment in the City.
- The city recently passed a complete streets policy. Also to slowing traffic, Missoula has developed over 400 miles of pedestrian facilities, including over 25 miles of separated bike paths and three bicycle/pedestrian crossings of the Clark Fork River. The City is moving forward to work to extend existing bicycle/pedestrian trails along the former Milwaukee Railroad corridor and the Bitterroot Branch rail line.

A new roundabout is also helping traffic flow smoothly, increasing safety and beautifying the area. "It's making travel along Higgins Avenue easier for drivers, bicyclists and pedestrians and making it safer for all to cross the east and west areas of the county," said the Mayor of Missoula. This $600,000 construction project was funded with American Recovery and Reinvestment Act funding.

Adapted from FHWA Livability Initiatives case Studies

Other Sustainable Solutions

There is a growing transition from vehicles powered by fossil fuels to energy-efficient vehicles. Commonly used energy efficient vehicles may include hybrids, hydrogen fuel cells, electric vehicles, liquefied petroleum gas and compressed natural gas. Using these types of vehicles lessens the environmental impact of transportation, but there are various obstacles that must be overcome to make the transition from fossil-fueled vehicles to a more sustainable and renewable fuel vehicle. In most situations, the biggest problem is cost. As long as governments continue to fund fossil fuel powered vehicles, it will continue to be extremely difficult for the average person to own one of these sustainable vehicles (Lovins 2012).

The fact that oil has been the only mass-produced fuel for transportation makes it hard for consumers to consider alternative fuel sources and switch over to more sustainable fuels. However, the benefits of switching to cleaner alternative fuels are measurable. For example, between 1999 and 2003, the Delhi, India municipal government made a substantial difference in air quality by converting the oil-based buses to CNG (Compressed Natural Gas) vehicles. Even as one of the most populated cities in the world in 1999, "Delhi bagged the Clean City International Award in May 2003 for successfully converting its 9,000 public buses to CNG" as only one of many instruments used (Kathuria 2005). Studies show that vehicle emissions can be reduced through the use of alternative fuels and new technologies. For example, "on a life-cycle basis, a blend of gasoline with 85% ethanol (E85) can reduce greenhouse gas (GHG) emissions by 15–20% compared to gasoline. Compressed natural gas (CNG) reduces CO_2 emissions up to 30%. Hybrid gasoline-electric vehicles (HEVs) reduce life-cycle GHG emissions by 30–50%." (Frey, Zhai and Rouphail 2009).

Hydrogen Fuel Cells

Hydrogen may become the solution or choice for future fuel of the combustion engine. Hydrogen is an environmentally clean source of energy to end-users, particularly in transportation applications because it does not release of pollutants at the point of end use (Yusibani, Kamil and Suud 2010). Hydrogen may be produced from water using the process of electrolysis. There is a slightly more inexpensive process called Steam Reforming, which consists of reacting methane and steam at high temperatures. "The holy grail of hydrogen production will be the efficient, direct conversion of sunlight through a photocatalytic process that uses solar energy to split water directly into its constituents, hydrogen and oxygen, without the use of electricity" (Edwards 2007). A U.S. Department of Energy (DoE) report suggests that the solar photodecomposition of water is probably the only major—but long-term—solution to a CO_2-free mass production of the immense volumes of hydrogen needed if the hydrogen economy is to emerge (U.S. Department of Energy, Office of Science 2003; Edwards, Kuznetsov and William 2007). Just like most forms of energy, hydrogen cannot be stored efficiently; there are various criteria that must be met in order to obtain hydrogen storage requirements for transportation. More research is required to understand the physical and chemical process needed to meet hydrogen storage requirements. To use hydrogen fuel cells as an energy carrier will depend solely on the availability of efficient, clean and economic techniques for its utilization.

There are also various safety concerns when it comes to implementation of hydrogen fuel cells, but some might insist that concerns are mostly perceived from psychological and sociological issues facing the adoption of the hydrogen economy. There is the unknown risk of environmental effects due to increased anthropogenic emissions of molecular hydrogen to the atmosphere. Hydrogen must first prove itself to the public eye as a safe means of energy production. An important factor in promoting public confidence will be the development and adoption of internationally accepted codes and standards. "Education projects, product exposure and marketing should be developed in order to facilitate a successful introduction and acceptance of hydrogen as an alternative fuel" (Edwards, Kuznetsov and William 2007). With these risk factors taken into consideration, hydrogen has a very high potential of becoming the next globally used form of energy because of its clean, renewable and sustainable nature.

Despite the concerns, the hydrogen fuel cars are slowly hitting the road. Although the relatively high cost of building the cars and extremely small number of hydrogen refueling stations would constrain the market for such vehicles for years to come, Hyundai, Honda, Toyota, Mercedes-Benz and other manufacturing companies are introducing hydrogen fuel cars to the market.

Electric Cars

Though the push to develop sustainable clean forms of energy has only recently become a widely discussed topic, the technology behind electric vehicles has existed for over a century. It began with the Electric Vehicle Company (EVC), a start-up company that took place in London in the early 20th century that had a vision for electrification of urban transit. Their goal was to "offer an integrated, all-electric urban transportation service that included road and rail based components" (Kirsch and Mom 2002).

The same principles developed by the EVC are being pursued today as more and more automakers are producing electric vehicles. Modern day electric vehicles are perceived as a more logical answer in purchasing a new sustainable vehicle. EVs are subsidized by government funds to help push the product into the market. "A fairly common view seems to be that although electric vehicles are not privately profitable, they are, or will be, socially profitable when the external costs are taken into account" (Carlsson and Johansson-Stenman 2003). The current upfront cost of an EV is relatively more expensive than that of a petrol fueled vehicle, but over time the EV will essentially pay itself off. One must also consider var-

Figure 5.3 Electric car charging station at CSUN (author's photograph).

ious other costs of EVs like that of a battery replacement although maintenance and repairs are hard to calculate upfront.

GREEN ROADS

Green automobiles seem to get most of the attention in the environmental protection field, but what about the roadways that these future "green" automobiles will travel on? Over the past few years, new technologies and new ideas have begun emerging to help transform traditional blacktop asphalt into more environmental friendly, cost-effective roadways that help not only the environment, but also the rising costs of infrastructure.

Green roads are made out of a permeable surface that allow rain and storm water to seep through them into the ground. The idea behind green roads is to capture the water that falls on them. The water then slowly percolates underground through the porous asphalt or concrete. The rationale for using permeable surfaces is to reduce stormwater runoff, which, in general, is damaging to the water environment. Future-thinking cities are looking to keep storm water out of their sewers in the first place.

Letting water percolate through the asphalt or concrete on the road is a very new concept in the industry. Some of the first instances of this idea being used are in the rainy areas such as Seattle, Washington and Portland, Oregon. Permeable roads could be ideal for low lying, flood prone communities. One such town on the East coast, Edmonston, Maryland, is incorporating permeable roadways. Construction workers replaced Edmonston's main road, Decatur Street, with environmentally friendly streets with rain gardens, porous brick and a drought-resistant tree canopy designed to shade the concrete and filter rainwater before it flows into the river. Decatur Street naturally treats more than 90 percent of the pollution from the 40 inches of rainwater that sweeps into the Anacostia each year. "We're a town that's been beaten up by floods," said Adam C. Ortiz, Edmonston's mayor and the key person behind the project. "We have to make things happen for us instead of making things happen to us" (Rein 2009). It seems only natural to allow water to seep through the asphalt or concrete. Permeable roads should be strongly considered for the new urbanism movement. Incorporating green roads with the rain gardens and such would be not only aesthetically pleasing, but also functional and sustainable.

Another aspect of green roads is in the construction process. The current construction process of just a single lane puts out more than 1,200 tons of CO_2. When we multiply that by the 32,300 miles of road paved every year; building roads emits 38,760,000 tons of CO_2 every year. That's the same as the annual energy use of 6 million homes (Singleton 2011). That is a lot of pollution that needs to be curtailed. Recycling the material of existing roadways, and finding more environmentally friendly materials are at the core of the green roads movement. The United States currently paves around 32,300 miles of road a year (ARTBA 2014). It has one of the most extensive paved road networks in the world. It is also very expensive: each year, we spend roughly 7 percent of our Gross Domestic Product (GDP) on transportation infrastructure. For the fiscal year of 2010, that amounted to nearly $1 trillion (Singleton 2011). An essential ingredient of these costs is the large amount of asphalt in current road construction. Some other substantial costs in the production of roads would be the aggregate materials. Aggregates are the small rocks that act as a binder for the road; they make up the base of the road. These small rocks are the most mined substance in the world and are also a non-renewable material.

One way to prevent the exorbitant amount of pollution would be to look into ways that renewable, unused, and untapped resources could be incorporated into the future building practices of roads. Switching traditional rock aggregates with renewable resources is a main idea in the practice of constructing green roads. Some popular fillers and aggregate replacements include rubber tires, roofing shingles, and even glass. Using recycled material for replacing aggregates in this way not only saves money, but it also makes use of a material that would otherwise remain unused. A mile of single-lane road using pulverized tires will use approximately 2,000 tires and save around $50,000 in expenses.

An example of a state in the country where this is practiced is California. The state of California leads the nation in the innovative waste reduction and recycling programs. A key component in the program is the recycling of tires for the re-pavement of roads. The state claims to use 75 percent of waste tires and considering that the state generates 40 million scrap tires every year, this is significant. California currently uses two different approaches to building green roads: RAC and TDA. RAC, or Rubberized Asphalt Concrete, is a road paving material made from ground scrap tires mixed with asphalt concrete. It is made by blending ground tire rubber with asphalt binder, which is then mixed with conventional aggregate materials. RAC is more durable, safer and quieter than traditional asphalt roads and uses thousands of scrap tires per paved mile. RAC is a proven paving material that has been used in California since the 1970s. It is a cost effective solution that requires little maintenance, is safer than older traditional roads being that it is skid-resistant and maintains a prolonged color contrast, and it also has the environmentally friendly feature of reducing noise pollution (Calrecycle 2011).

The other method being used is TDA or Tire Derived Aggregate. TDA is the second largest use of recycled tires in the United States and provides a cost effective alternative to conventional aggregate used in various civil engineering projects. Some uses of TDA include: retaining wall backfill, lightweight embankment fill, landslide stabilization, vibration mitigation, and various landfill applications. TDA is cost-effective, being less expensive than other lightweight fill materials. Also, its free-draining characteristics help solve engineering problems while also being environmentally friendly, and it reduces the need for mined resources such as pumice and gravel. These two methods of using recycled materials in road construction are great cost-savers by reducing the cost of aggregate by almost half (Calrecycle 2011).

Another way that green roads are being built is through Hot-In-Place asphalt recycling. The Asphalt Recycling and Reclaiming Association (ARRA) describes Hot-In-Place asphalt recycling as an on-site, in-place method that rehabilitates deteriorated asphalt pavements and thereby minimizes the use of new materials. The use of this technique has been proven to reduce material use by 80 percent and material transport by even more than 80 percent (Green Roads Recycling 2011). Hot-In-Place asphalt recycling is a three-part process. The first part of the process is to heat the asphalt on the roadway. This is done by a large machine built specifically for this purpose. Temperatures under the heater can reach 1,700 degrees Fahrenheit. After the old roadway is heated, the next process is to scarify or to cut up and scratch the roadway. This is done to help the new recycled material bind to the existing road. The final step in Hot-In-Place asphalt recycling is to pave with the new recycled material. Hot-In-Place recycling offers tremendous cost savings in material, labor, and a reduction in duration of the repair activities. Another great benefit from Hot-In-Place recycling is that it can turn a traditionally environmentally damaging process into a process with only minimal environmental effects. Energy savings primarily come from reduced aggregate haul and drying, and also asphalt transportation.

The practice of Hot-In-Place recycling has been used sparingly during the past fifty years, and only since the 1980s have acceptable processes and equipment been developed. Much of the technological development, experience, and Hot-In-Place technology has occurred in Canada, where highway agencies have embraced the concept and equipment manufacturers have provided the innovations. A factor that has held back more rapid acceptance of Hot-In-Place recycling is the poor quality often associated with the technique. Being that this technology is still in its infancy, it will only grow and become more accepted as the concept is understood and improved upon.

In conclusion, there is no single solution to fix all the environmental and societal problems that transportation has encountered. The solution to reducing or eliminating transportation impacts on the environment would be accomplished by promoting sustainable transportation developments such as reducing automobile dependency; improving public transit; encouraging non-motorized modes of transportation like walking and bicycling; planning high-density, mixed-use and transit-oriented developments; making effective land use patterns; and increasing accessibility. However, these solutions would happen over extended periods of time. Since there is no a "magic bullet", society have to take a comprehensive and integrated approach.

Travel demand management can provide cost effective ways to solve some transportation problems. Cost-effectiveness and public acceptance, coupled with necessary technical feasibility, are the key issues for managing travel demand. The major problem with all TDM solutions presented in this chapter is the ability to implement them on a large enough scale to make an impact on the environment. Solutions such as flexible work hours have been around since the 1980s and have not appreciably reduced pollution from congestion since the standard work schedule still dominates peak travel times. Improvements to public transportation, cycling and walking infrastructure, and land use alterations suffer from the same problem.

While planners continue to work with the public, environmental groups and political leaders on travel demand management strategies, scientists are making progress on technological options to reduce the impacts of travel. Hydrogen fuel cells and electric cars are technologies that will become increasingly relevant as the world's oil sources are depleted. There are still numerous technological and public acceptance challenges that must be overcome. Also, automakers will have to create a business model that makes these cars affordable for the majority of people, just as Henry Ford did for his Model T in the early 19th Century. For now, hybrid cars are available to serve as an intermediary between today's vehicles and the concept cars being developed. Other technologies such as green road infrastructure are also available today to reduce the impact of transport on the environment. While there is no single perfect solution, technologies coupled with smart city planning practices are a promising way to protect the society and the environment from transportation-related impacts.

Review Questions

1. How does society's dependence on the automobile affect the environment?
2. What is Travel Demand Management? Summarize the central tenants.

3. Summarize the push and pull measures of Travel Demand Management (TDM).
4. Define and elaborate on the 3E's of traffic calming.
5. What are the problems of congestion pricing strategies?
6. What are some of the concerns of the use of hydrogen fuel cells for powering transportation?
7. How does Transit Oriented Development enhance public transportation?
8. What is the "genetic code of sprawl"?
9. What are some ways the automobile can be improved to reduce environmental impacts?
10. What are "Green Roads" and how do they differ from most roads currently in place?

Project/Paper Idea

List the Transportation Demand Management (TDM) strategies being planned and implemented in your community by the local planning organization.

- Are they effective (add some statistics and personal experience)?
- Was there an issue in terms of public acceptance?

Also discuss the planning process by referring the planning documents or interviewing the planning officers.

Videos

Moving Beyond Auto America, *by Chip Taylor Communications, 1998 (30 min.)*: The information in this documentary confirms what most transportation professionals today agree on, that we cannot simply build our way out of urban congestion problems. Here we see highlights of innovative transportation systems, as well as interviews with national experts. Its goal is to raise awareness of the lack of public transportation and to encourage serious planning for the future. Viewers will learn that intelligent transportation systems provide the technology to enable people to make choices for travel, which will be better for our overall environment.

Internet Sources

- The Center for Transportation and the Environment, http://www.itre.ncsu.edu/CTE/About_CTE/index.asp

Bibliography

Alexander, Bayarma, Martin Dijst, and Ettema Dick. 2010. "Working from 9 to 6? An Analysis of In-Home and Out-Of-Home Working Schedules." *Transportation* 37 (3): 505–523.

Arpi, Ethan. 2009. "Transit Agencies Need to Invest in Marketing: A Lesson from Los Angeles." *The City Fix.* December 8. Accessed April 30, 2014. http://thecityfix.com/blog/transit-agencies-need-to-invest-in-marketing-a-lesson-from-los-angeles/.

ARTBA. 2014. *Transportation FAQs.* http://www.artba.org/about/transportation-faqs/#11.

Badoe, Daniel, and Eric Miller. 2000. "Transportation–Land Use Interaction: Empirical Findings in North America, and Their Implications for Modeling." *Transportation Research Part D* 5 (4): 235 263.

Berg, Linda, and Peter Raven. 1995. *Environment.* Fort Worth: Saunders College Publishing.

Brown, Barbara, and Carol Werner. 2011. "Before and After a New Light Rail Stop: Resident Attitudes, Travel Behavior, and Obesity." *American Planning Association* 75: 5–12.

Button, Kenneth. 1993. *Transport Economics.* 2. England: Edward Elgar Publishing Ltd.

Calrecycle. 2011. *Green Roads.* November 2. Accessed June 27, 2014. http://www.calrecycle.ca.gov/Tires/Green-Roads/rac.htm.

Calthorpe, Peter. 1993. *The Next American Metropolis: Ecology, Community, and the American Dream.* New York: Princeton Architectural Press.

Campbell, Scott. 2002. *Transit-oriented Development: An Overview*. Dissertation, Proquest UMI Dissertations Publishing.

Carlsson, Fredrik, and Olof Johansson-Stenman. 2003. "Costs and Benefits of Electric Vehicles: A 2010 Perspective." *Journal of Transport Economics and Policy* 37 (1): 1–28.

Cervero, Robert, and Kara Kockelman. 1997. "Travel Demand and the 3D's: Density, Diversity, and Design." *Transportation Research Part D: Transport and Environment* 2 (3): 199–219.

Choo, Sangho, Patricia Mokhtarian, and Ilan Salomon. 2005. "Does Telecommuting Reduce Vehicle-Miles Traveled? An Aggregate Time Series Analysis for the U.S." *Transportation* 32 (1): 37–64.

Debashish, Bhattacharjee, Haider Waqar, Tanaboriboon Yordphol, and Sinha Kumares. 1997. "Commuters' Attitudes towards Travel Demand Management in Bangkok." *Transport Policy* 4 (3): 161–170.

Downs, Anthony. 2002. Some Like It HOT: High-Occupancy Toll Lanes Work Best on High-Traffic Roads. Without Congestion, Drivers Have Little Incentive to Pay the Toll. Brookings Institute.

Durning, Alan. 1992. *How Much Is Enough? The Consumer Society and the Future of the Earth*. W.W. Norton.

Earp, John, McDonald, and Hopkin Thomas. 1973. "Transportation and Environment: Polices, Plans, and Practices." University of Southampton.

Edwards, Peter, Vladimir Kuznetsov, and David William. 2007. "Hydrogen Energy." *Philosophical Transactions: Mathematical, Physical and Engineering Sciences* 365 (1853): 1043–1056.

EPA. 2014. *Overview of Green House Gasses*. April 17. Accessed June 27, 2014. http://www.epa.gov/climatechange/ghgemissions/gases/co2.html.

Fehr and Peers. 2014. *Traffic Calming Definition*. Accessed June 27, 2014. http://trafficcalming.org/.

FHWA. 2006. "Managing Travel Demand: Applying European Perspectives to U.S. Practice." Federal Highway Administration, Department of Transportation.

Finch, Ginny. 1996. "Reducing Traffic Jams Through Economics." *Research and Innovative Technology Administration, National Transportation Library*.

Foreman, Dave. 2004. *Rewilding North America: A Vision for Conservation in the 21st Century*. Washington, D.C.: Island Press.

Frey, Christopher, Haibo Zhai, and Nagui Rouphail. 2009. "Regional On-Road Vehicle Running Emissions Modeling and Evaluation for Conventional and Alternative Vehicle Technologies." *Environmental Science & Technology* 43 (21): 8449–8455.

Garrod, Guy, Riccardo Scarpa, and Kenneth Willis. 2002. "Estimating The Benefits of Traffic Calming on Through Routes: A Choice Experiment Approach." *Transport Economics and Policy* 36 (2): 211–231.

Gillham, Oliver. 2002. *The Limitless City: A Primer on the Urban Sprawl Debate*. Washington, D.C.: Island Press.

Green Roads Recycling. 2011. *Green Roads Recycling*. October 26. Accessed December 2, 2011.

Hanson, Susan. 2004. "The Context of Urban Travel: Concepts and Recent trends" in the *Geography of Urban Transportation*, 3rd ed. By Susan Hanson and Genevieve Giuliano (eds.), Guilford Press.

HOTM-FHWA. 2006. *Congestion Pricing: A Primer*. Office of Transportation Management Federal Highway Administration, U.S. Department of Transportation, Washington, D.C.:

Imran, Shah. 2012. *Assessment of Transit Oriented Development Impacts*. Dissertation, ProQuest Dissertations & Theses.

Jackson, Kenneth. 1987. *Crabgrass Frontier: The Suburbanization of the United States*. New York: Oxford Press.

Kathuria, Vinish. 2005. "Vehicular Pollution Control in Delhi: Impact of Compressed Natural Gas." *Economic and Political Weekly* 40 (18).

Kirsch, David, and Gijs Mom. 2002. "Visions of Transportation: The EVC and the Transition from Service- to Product-Based Mobility." *The Business History Review* 76 (1): 75–110.

Litman, Todd. 2003. "Transportation Cost and Benefit Analysis Guidebook." Victoria Transport Policy Institute.

Lovins, Amory. 2012. "A Farewell to Fossil Fuels." *Foreign Affairs* 91 (2): 134–146.

Meyer, Michael. 1999. "Demand Management as an Element of Transportation Policy: Using Carrots and Sticks to Influence Travel Behavior." *Transportation Research Part A: Policy and Practice* 33 (7–8): 575–599.

Mitmomo, Hitoshi, and Toshiya Jitsuzumi. 1999. "Impact of Telecommuting on Mass Transit Congestion: The Tokyo Case." *Transportation Policy* 23 (10–11): 741–751.

Mokhtarian, Patricia, Susan Handy, and Ilan Salomon. 1995. "Methodological Issues in the Estimation of Travel, Energy, and Air Quality Impacts of Telecommuting." *Transportation Research A* 29: 283–302.

Morrison, David, Hilary Thomson, and Mark Petticrew. 2004. "Evaluation of the Health Effects of a Neighbourhood Traffic Calming Scheme." *Journal of Epidemiology and Community Health* 58 (10): 837–840.

NHTSA. 2011. *Fatality Analysis Reporting System*. Accessed June 27, 2014. http://www-fars.nhtsa.dot.gov/Main/index.aspx.

Nilles, Jack. 1998. *Managing Telework: Strategies for Managing the Virtual Workforce*. New York: Jon Wiley & Sons.

Ory, David, and Patricia Mokhtarian. 2006. "Which Came First, the Telecommuting or the Residential Relocation? an Empirical Analysis of Causality." *Urban Geography* 27 (7): 590–609.

Parry, Ian, Margaret Walls, and Winston Harrington. 2007. "Automobile Externalities and Policies." *Journal of Economic Literature* 45 (2): 373–399.

Pharoah, Timothy, and John Russel. 1989. *Traffic Calming: Policy and Evaluations in Three European Countries*. South Bank Polytechnic, London. London: South Bank Polytechnic.

Pucher, John, Lewis Thorwaldson, Ralph Buehler, and Nicholas Klein. 2010. "Cycling in New York: Innovative Policies at the Urban Frontier." *World Transport Policy & Practice*, 16 (1):7–50

Rein, Lisa. 2009. "Prince George's Town Aims to Pave a 'Greener' Path." *Washington Post*, July 23. Accessed December 1, 2011. <http://www.washingtonpost.com/wp-dyn/content/article/2009/07/22/AR2009072203470.html>.

Renne, John. 2009. "From Transit-Adjacent to Transit-Oriented Development." *Local Environment* 14 (1): 1–15.

Schrank, David, and Timothy Lomax. 2005. "The 2005 Urban Mobility Report." Texas Transportation Institute, The Texas A&M University.

Singleton, Derek. 2011. "Green Roads Construction: Are Contractors Our Roadblock?" *Software Advice Articles, News & Best Practices Guides.*

Small, Kenneth, and Jose Gomez-Ibanez. 1998. *Road Pricing for Congestion Management: the Transition from Theory To Policy.* U.C. Berkeley: University of California Transportation Center.

Smith, Jeffery, and Thomas Gihring. 2003. "Financing Transit Systems Through Value Capture: An Annotated Bibliography." *Victorian Transport Policy Institute.*

Smith, Laurence. 2011. *The World in 2050: Four Forces Shaping Civilization's Northern Future.* New York: Plume.

Smith, Marry, Nabil Razzouk, and Scott Richardson. 1990. "The Role of Marketing in Mass Transit: An Empirical Investigation." *Transportation Journal* 30 (1): 30–35.

Steg, Linga, and Charles Vlek. 1997. "The Role of Problem Awareness in Willingness to Change Car Use in Evaluating Relevant Policy Measures." In *Traffic and Transport Psychology: Theory and Application,* by Talib Rothengatter and Enrique Vaya, 465–475. Bingly: Emerald Group Publishing Limited.

Sundo, Marloe, and Satoshi Fujii. 2005. "The Effects of A Compressed Working Week on Commuters' Daily Activity Patterns." *Transportation Research Part A* 39 (10): 835–848.

Sundquist, Kristina, Ulf Eriksson, Naomi Kawakami, Lars Skog, Henrik Ohlsson, and Daniel Arvidsson. 2011. "Neighborhood Walkability, Physical Activity, and Walking Behavior: The Swedish Neighborhood and Physical Activity (SNAP) Study." *Social Science and Medicine* 78 (8): 1266–1273.

Sweet, Matthias. 2011. "Does Traffic Congestion Slow the Economy?" *Journal of Planning Literature* 391–404.

Tan, Carol. 2011. "Going on a Road Diet." *Federal Highway Administration.* September 7. Accessed June 26, 2014.

Taylor, David, and Miles Tight. 1997. "Public Attitudes and Consultation in Traffic Calming Schemes." *Transport Policy* 4 (3). 171–182.

Transport for London. 2007. "Central London Congestion Charging." Mayor of London.

USDA. 2013. *Farmland Protection Policy Act Annual Report FY 2012.* Natural Resources Conservation Service, U.S. Department of Agriculture.

Verburg, Peter, Koen Overmars, and Nol Witte. 2004. "Accessibility and Land Use Patterns at the Forest Fringe in the Northeastern Part of the Philippines." *The Geographical Journal* 170 (3): 238–255.

Weisman, Alan. 2007. *The World Without Us.* New York: St. Martin's Press.

Yen, Jin-Ru. 2000. "Interpreting Employee Telecommuting Adoption: An Economics Perspective." *Transportation* 27 (1): 149–164.

Yusibani, Elin, Insan Kamil, and Zaki Suud. 2010. "Hydrogen Gas Production from Nuclear Power Plant in Relation to Hydrogen Fuel Cell Technologies Nowadays." *AIP Conference Proceedings.* 70–82.

Zaman, Hamid, and Khandker Habib. 2011. "Commuting Mode Choice in the Context of Travel Demand Management." *Canadian Journal of Civil Engineering* 38 (4): 433–443.

Part II

*Planning for
Drive-Alternative
Means of Travel*

6

Driving Less: Changing Travel Behavior

Chapter Outline

- Introduction: Why Do We Need to Change Travel Behavior?
  - o *The Social Impacts of Excessive Driving*
  - o *The Economic Impacts of Excessive Driving*
  - o *The Health Impacts of Excessive Driving*
- Change Means Avoiding Unnecessary Car Trips
- Limiting Auto Use
  - o *Travel Feedback Programs of Japan*
  - o *InMotion of King County, Washington*
  - o *IndiMarket (Germany/Australia)*
  - o *Travel Smart of Australia*
- The Challenge: Convenience vs. Consciousness
- Conclusion

Introduction: Why Do We Need to Change Our Travel Behavior?

There are many benefits associated with automobile use; however, it is the "auto-dependency" that comes at a high cost to society and creates numerous challenges for providing sustainable transportation. Much of the recent research on the adverse impacts of auto-dependency focuses on impacts on the natural and built environments (as discussed in chapter 5). This chapter discusses the social, economic and health perspective of auto dependency to set the stage for a persuasive argument that changing individual travel behavior is one more step necessary to provide sustainable transportation and quality of life.

THE SOCIAL IMPACTS OF EXCESSIVE DRIVING

The social impacts of driving are either related to a general loss of the public realm or the trend of diminishing levels of civic engagement. The immediate concern is the gradual decline in the public realm. Since the World War I, the interest in the streetscape as a flexible and multi-purpose space has severely diminished. It is hard to find roads in the United States designed for slow speed. If we do find an active street life, it is either a self-contained space, a newly designed space, or unchanged historic space, all of which can serve a variety of users, including motorists, walkers, and cyclists. The cause of this decline in the public realm has to do with large-scale privatization and with consumer society's emphasis on the private realm. The city, according to Appleyard and Jacobs (2011), becomes "one of the closed defended islands with blank and windowless facades surrounded by wastelands of parking lots and fast-moving traffic." This placelessness, or urban blandness, can be found almost anywhere. The city street has become a place where one is not expected to linger or to interact with others.

Extreme control over urban space is now the norm. Both rich and poor communities wish to control access to their neighborhoods. This type of control increases physical and social fragmentation while upper-income lifestyle enclaves, like gated communities, emphasize only auto-based access via key cards and guard shacks. With the reliance on car-only access, residents are less likely to interact with the public unless they make a concerted effort. In such a space, you choose whom to interact with and to what degree.

Add this level of disconnect to the history of highway construction and the process of community destruction that came along with it. Freeways not only connected the nation, they also detached the city's people from their neighborhoods and places of meaning. Citizens were in the way of progress and were removed without much thought regarding just how their neighborhoods would be negatively impacted. The cities that fell prey to multiple highway projects often saw their street life erode soon after the new high-speed roads were built. And with highways came a general shift in attitudes towards urban design. This shift has been towards inwardness with the focus becoming exclusion, not inclusion. Even in rural America, when the interstates came through, small towns turned into hollowed-out shells, and many communities lost their face-to-face interactions.

The loss of public safety is another social impact of driving. In Managua, Nicaragua, socio-spatial segregation has been evolving over the last two decades. The city's fabric has been reconstructed to include new exclusive shopping areas and luxury housing for the elite. Unfortunately, all of this new construction is connected to a network of high-speed roads that allow the wealthy to move freely and safely (Rodgers 2004). The poor, on the other hand, risk their lives crossing roads that have no amenities for them or pedestrians generally. This extreme control over space, detailed above, manifests a kind of spatial segregation. Pedestrian conditions are not much better in the U.S. In 2012, 4,743 pedestrians were killed, and an estimated 76,000 were injured in traffic crashes. In 2006, 82-year-old Mayvis Coyle received a $114 jaywalking ticket for failing to cross an intersection in Los Angeles within the allotted thirty seconds. With a large percentage of the population behind the wheel, the mobility needs of other users get swept aside or forgotten (Gottlieb 2007).

The car and the commute can also be "demonstrably bad for community life" says Robert D. Putnam (2000), in his famous book *Bowling Alone: The Collapse and Revival of American Community*. He wrote that for every 10 minutes of commuting time, one's community involvement is cut by 10 percent. "Imagine what that means when it's not a matter of minutes but hours," was added by Michelle Conlin's article: *Extreme Commuting* in Bloomberg Business Week. As we spend more time behind the wheel, the spatial fragmentation between home and workplace is amplified by the general loss of citizen participation.

This leads us to the question: does driving enforce isolation and alienation or does it provide options for reaching out and engaging with others? Without looking too deeply, it would appear that driving from place to place, in a private-in-public situation, is a kind of "carcooning" (Durning 1992). The car insulates one from the outside world. "Dwelling at speed, car drivers lose the ability to perceive local detail, to talk to strangers, to learn of local ways of life, to stop and sense each different place" (Urry 2006). Strapped within the confines of the automobile, the driver shuts off from the physical environment with an array of temperature controls, digital music systems, seatbelts, and other safety features. This mobile form of privatization enables the driver to navigate the risks of high-speed transport and to protect himself from the streets inhabited by the homeless and any other undesirables. "The car is a room in which senses are necessarily impoverished" (Urry 2006). The driver is unable to move freely, restricted to only micro-movements of the hands and feet. The world is taken in through the windshield, much like a film, and the experience of moving through public space becomes a mostly passive activity.

Two of the more intriguing thinkers on the impact of the automobile on social life were Jane Jacobs and Lewis Mumford. Though Mumford was certain that the city streets of the post-war age must be turned over to the exclusive use of the automobile, with pedestrian activities to segregated walkways, the writer/activist Jane Jacobs saw the street as the very focus of urban culture. Her views differed slightly from Mumford's in her appreciation of the desirable congestion found in areas where multiple road users existed. Jacobs found herself interested in the mix of street ballet, mobile cart peddlers, and slow speed automobile movement. She found this diversity of road and sidewalk use to be the lifeblood of the city. While Mumford and Jacobs' view of the car and its impact on the city differed slightly, both had concerns that the car might destroy something unique that had evolved over time. Today we often hear the echoes of Jacobs and Mumford in the voices of many contemporary urban designers, planners, and activists who worry not only about the disruption brought on by increasing car traffic, but about the costs of isolation and detachment that have come with an unrestrained auto culture (Mumford 1950; Jacobs 1961).

THE ECONOMIC IMPACTS OF DRIVING

Auto dependency and excessive commuting can also have a diverse economic impact. As much as the automobile facilitates mobility and ease of access, the segregation of different urban functions and activities encourage excessive driving. At present, local and regional governments spend billions of dollars every year on road and other infrastructure development. Thus, auto-dependency is translated into excessive expenditures on roads, traffic services and parking facilities, often averaging hundreds of dollars annually per household. For example, transportation expenditures by federal, state and local governments totaled $167 billion in 2000, of which $104 billion was for roads, $15.9 billion for bus transit, $1.8 billion for demand response services and $16.7 billion for rail. The cost of parking at destinations is estimated to total more than $200 billion annually (Litman 2003).

Automobile dependency increases per capita vehicle and fuel expenditures, often increasing average annual household transportation expenditures by thousands of dollars and reducing expenditures on other consumer goods. This can have significant economic impacts, particularly because most vehicles and fuel are imported from other regions (Litman and Laube 2002).

Every year a large amount of time is wasted sitting in traffic. According to a survey of people living in 15 metro areas, 52 hours a year were spent in traffic in 2010 (" in traffic" is defined as wasted time that is above and beyond the natural length of the commute). In the Washington, D.C., Virginia and Maryland area alone, studies observed a 74-hour delay a year (TTI 2001). Wasted time means, in economic terms, reduced productivity and loss of capital.

Table 6.1 Congestion trends—wasted hours (yearly delay per auto commuter, 1982 to 2010)

Urban Area	Yearly Hours of Delay per Auto Commuter					Long-Term Change 1982 to 2010	
	2010	2009	2005	2000	1982	Hours	Rank
Very Large Average (15 Areas)	**52**	**52**	**60**	**50**	**19**	**33**	
Washington, D.C.-VA-MD	74	72	83	73	20	54	1
Chicago IL-IN	71	74	77	55	18	53	2
New York-Newark NY-NJ-CT	54	53	51	35	10	44	3
Dallas-Fort Worth-Arlington TX	45	46	51	40	7	38	6
Boston MA-NH-RI	47	48	57	44	13	34	8
Seattle WA	44	44	51	49	10	34	8
Houston TX	57	56	55	45	24	33	10
Atlanta GA	43	44	58	52	13	30	11
Philadelphia PA-NJ-DE-MD	42	43	42	32	12	30	11
San Diego CA	38	37	46	35	8	30	11
San Francisco-Oakland CA	50	50	74	60	20	30	11
Miami FL	38	39	45	38	10	28	16
Los Angeles-Long Beach-Santa Ana CA	64	63	82	76	39	25	23
Detroit MI	33	32	41	36	14	19	36
Phoenix AZ	35	36	44	34	24	11	79

- Very Large Urban Areas—over 3 million population.
- Large Urban Areas—over 1 million and less than 3 million population; Medium Urban Areas—over 500,000 and less than 1 million population; Small Urban Areas—less than 500,000 population.
- Yearly Delay per Auto Commuter—Extra travel time during the year divided by the number of people who commute in private vehicles in the urban area.

Source: 2011 Annual Urban Mobility Report, Texas A & M University

At the government level, the cost of air pollution (caused by cars) and health care costs are extremely high. Soaring health care costs can be partly attributed to health problems related to driving, such as asthma and obesity. In fact, Americans spend two times more on health care than those living in OECD (Organization for Economic Development and Cooperation) countries. According to the United Nations Human Development Report, based on 2004 World Health Organization (WHO) data, the U.S. spent $6,102 per person on medical care in 2004 –15.3 percent of the GDP. That's more than double the $2,552 median of the

30 OECD countries (UNHDR 2007). Although this is not entirely attributed to transportation, the health care cost related to transportation is evidently high. Moreover, increased automobile travel tends to increase traffic crashes that negatively impact people's lives. These costs are borne directly through increased insurance fees and lost worker productivity, and indirectly through taxes to cover injuries and disabilities (Litman and Laube 2002).

THE HEALTH IMPACTS OF EXCESSIVE COMMUTING

According to recent research on the relationship between commuting and health, walking, cycling and playing outside are the activities that burn the most calories. Instead of being able to engage in these activities in their locality, adults are driving, and children are increasingly being driven to organized activities. Researchers found that once at a given activity, children that had been driven were less active than those who walked or cycled. These combined effects lead to a substantial overall reduction in calories burned (Mackett and Paskins 2004).

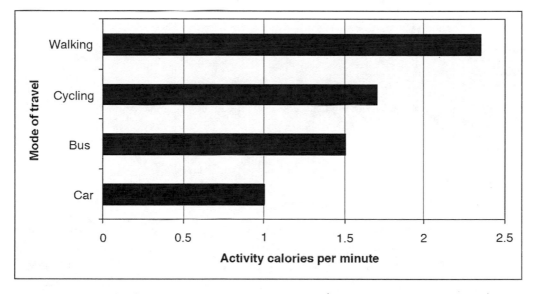

Figure 6.1 Mode of travel vs. activity calories per minute (data: Mackett and Paskins 2004).

Driving in congested situations is also associated with raised blood pressure, musculoskeletal disorders, increased hostility, lateness, absenteeism, and adverse effects on cognitive performance. Swedish researchers surveyed 21,000 workers ages 18 to 65 and found that those who commuted by car reported more everyday stress, exhaustion, missed work days and generally poorer health compared to the active commuters (Hansson, *et al.*, 2011). Thus, many improvements (i.e. encouraging driving-alternative modes of travel) would not only help ease congestion, but would increase public health.

Several other studies show that car dependency and obesity are positively correlated. This relationship is well stated in *New Urbanism on the News*:

Studies showed that the more a country depends on the car, the fatter its people are. It has also been shown through a variety of studies that people who live in walkable communities and use transit are more likely to reach physical activity targets and avoid obesity, along with its correlated problems. Such communities also allow people to spend their money on things other than cars, including healthier food and better health care. People living in these types of communities, who are not able to drive because of income or physical disability, could get better access to services, including medical care. The ability to exercise safely and casually mix with neighbors provides both physical and mental health benefits.

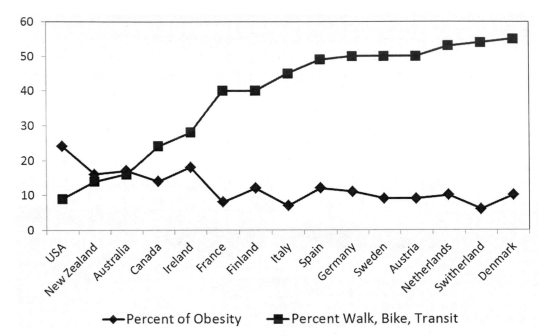

Figure 6.2 Alternative-to-driving vs. obesity (data: John Pucher, 2010).

Another study in the U.S., a National Analysis of Physical Activity, Obesity, and Chronic Disease, compared the counties' sprawl index to the health characteristics of more than 200,000 individuals living in the 448 counties. This study uses a large national health survey, the Behavioral Risk Factor Surveillance System (BRFSS), which is maintained by the Centers for Disease Control and Prevention (CDC). The results show that people in more sprawling counties are likely to have a higher body mass index (BMI), a standard measure of weight-to-height that is used to determine if people are overweight or obese. A 50-point increase in the degree of sprawl on the county sprawl index was associated with a weight gain of just over one pound for the average person. Looking at the extremes, the people living in the most sprawling areas are likely to weigh six pounds more than people in the most compact county. The study also found a direct relationship between sprawl and chronic disease. The odds of having hypertension or high blood pressure, are six percent higher for every 50- point increase in the degree of sprawl (McCann and Ewing 2003).

According to the *Cincinatti Post* (May 31, 2004), a "survey of 10,500 metro Atlanta residents found that for every extra 30 minutes commuters drove each day, they had a three percent greater chance of being obese than their peers who drove less. The survey also found out that people who lived within walking distance of shops, less than a half a mile, were 7 percent less likely to be obese than their counterparts who had to drive."

Another important health-related issue, traffic fatalities, also contribute to lower lifespan to the tune of 1.2 million potential years of life lost annually. If this number could be reduced, it would improve lifespan and reduce disabilities and health care costs.

Change Means Avoiding Unnecessary Car Trips

What type of car trip should be categorized as unnecessary? I might start by defining unnecessary car trips in this chapter's context. An unnecessary trip is any short trip we are making (say, less than a mile) using a car instead of walking, biking, or taking mass transit when adequate facilities are present. Driving to get coffee from a Starbucks two blocks away from home is probably an unnecessary car trip. If there was a good sidewalk system, a dedicated bike lane, or convenient mass transit, then it is clearly an unnecessary trip.

The unnecessary trip is the one we shouldn't be making by automobile or rather the one we should've bundled together with our other car-related errands. Perhaps it is the car itself that promotes the concept of the unnecessary trip (induced travel demand) since its ease of use prompts us to explore or to make additional trips that we wouldn't have made if we did not have access to a car. According to the Federal Highway Safety Administration, 40 percent of all daily trips made in the U.S. cover a distance of two miles or less, 90 percent of which are made by car. Most of those trips, even some with unfriendly pedestrian or cycling environments, could be made without the car. Biking and walking save money, reduces the risk of accidents, and relieves stress, but for many these alternative transport choices are not available. In North America, a high percentage of people live in places with certain infrastructure inadequacies, creating safety issues for pedestrians and cyclists. Taking this inadequate infrastructure into consideration makes defining an unnecessary trip more difficult.

According to Matilda Lee (2009) from *The Ecologist*, "questioning unnecessary travel really means choosing modes of travel available to reach your destination and choosing the one with the least carbon intensity." In this view, an unnecessary trip is one that is associated with unneeded pollution and greenhouse gas emissions. In deciding whether a trip is necessary, you must consider a trip's true cost: environmental, social, and economic. Labeling a trip unnecessary asks us to question our movements, how we move, and what the impacts may be on others (both human and non-human). The reasons below further elaborate on possible reasons why we make unnecessary car trips.

UNAWARENESS

Because cars are the default mode of travel for many, people may not think twice when it comes to mode choice. We go to our garage and put the key in the ignition. If we take a closer look, we are probably surrounded by options and opportunities (though it is understandable that not all areas are provided with options). Woldeamanuel and Welle (2012) conducted a survey of small town residents and one of the questions asked was: "is there a bus stop within a quarter of a mile of your residence?" About 80 percent of the respondents answered "yes." The follow-up question was "how often do you use buses?" 80 percent said "rarely" or "never." So it is not the lack of options but the lack of awareness of alternatives. That is why local governments and service providers ought to focus on campaigns and awareness programs to increase ridership and help people understand how the transit system works.

Car Culture

We love our cars. They not only take us to places we want but we sometimes eat in them, pray in them, and act like ourselves in them without breaking the codes of the public space. For many, it's great to be in a private space while being in public. The convenience of the automobile and the all-encompassing nature of car-culture has led us to believe that we can't live without them. We grow up driving them. We never forget that moment from our teenage years when our parents reluctantly handed over the keys to the family car. That was the day we were born into a new era of freedom and independence. And that perception becomes a learned behavior, a way of life, a culture. That is why it is difficult to get out of our comfort zone and give up our car, even for short trips.

Negative Perceptions of Alternative Travel Modes

Many think public transit is the "unsafe" means of travel; transit is associated with crime and poverty. Although public transit is mostly used by low-income and minority groups, studies show that the link between transit and crime is weak (Ihlandfeldt 2003). Over the past couple of decades, a culture of fear has fostered a suspicion of strangers. With the rise of surveillance cameras, as well as fences and walls shielding residents from one another, it is no wonder that a public bus or train is met with apprehension by those that are underexposed to public mass transit.

The car is undeniably necessary; however, unnecessary car trips are still a problem. Many trips are not "derived trips" (trips out of necessity and economic activity) but "induced trips" (created by the land use environment, government policies and most importantly by our own perception).

BOX 6.1 Induced traffic and VMT growth

"Induced traffic" is a term for traffic growth produced by the addition of highway capacity. The theory behind induced travel is that of supply and demand. Adding highway capacity (supply) reduces the cost of vehicle travel, particularly the costs associated with travel time. Demand is inversely related to cost. When cost goes down, demand goes up. As travel time and monetary costs fall, people travel more. Expansion in road capacity can have multiple effects on behavior. An increase in capacity may result in changes in travel route, timing, vehicle occupancy, or mode choice for any given trip. It may also result in changes in trip frequency and switches to alternative destinations. Of these effects, increases in trip making and mode switch clearly contribute to induced travel. Other effects, such as switching routes or changing travel times, may occur as well. Although these effects may reduce some of the expected improvement in traffic flow and savings in travel time associated with the road project, they do not constitute new vehicle travel. Different types of induced traffic are believed to occur in the short term and long term. In the short term, people may make more trips or switch from transit or carpools to driving alone because of improved traffic conditions. In the long term, reduced travel costs encourage more dispersed land use patterns that, in turn, can increase trip lengths and vehicle dependency.

Adapted from "Our Built and Natural Environments: A Technical Review of the Interactions Between Land Use, Transportation, and Environmental Quality (2nd Edition)" EPA, 2001.

Limiting Auto Use

Because of the reasons mentioned above (and with all the environmental problems discussed in chapter 5), societies face increasing pressure to mitigate the effects of car use. Where urban development and car infrastructure are two sides of the same coin, how can we retrofit the landscape, so it is suitable for other means of transport? Can our current ten-trips-per-day out of a typical single family house be changed?

While technological innovations discussed in chapter 5 may fix automobile problems, such solutions only solve the short-term problem but do not address the root of the problem. Many proposed solutions encourage more driving, more scattered living, more farmland conversion, and more congestion. The technological innovations need to be supplemented with a long-term solution to driving such as a change in travel behavior: either through education, urban-redevelopment, regulations or market-based strategies.

All successful travel-behavior-change programs, even those with a strong emphasis on improving infrastructure and services, involve education and information to promote changes. Most often, they target a broad population through traditional mass marketing techniques, such as advertising of the services and benefits available (Cooper and Meiklejohn 2003). The literature suggests that travel behavior is habitual, and, therefore, the success of travel behavior change strategies is dependent on being able to break the driving habit (Del Mistro, *et al.*, 2007). Travel behavior and the culture of habits are instilled while living in particular culture, along with various other factors such as socio-economic status and distance to work that determine the mode of travel taken.

The *indirect* way of facilitating behavioral change is through structural strategies such as changing the built environment (land use), the transit level of service and the walking/bicycling environments in order to regulate travel behavior (Giuliano and Joyce 2005). These measures are part of the Transportation Demand Management (TDM) (refer to chapter 5) that has attracted increasing attention by their success in curbing the excessive auto use and creating a modal shift from car to walking, biking and using public transit. As part of land use interventions, regulatory measures such as car-free zones and limiting parking are often considered as an indirect or passive method to create a steady and long-term travel behavior change. However, the focus of this chapter is the *direct* way of travel behavior change through education, campaigns and travel awareness programs.

As stated by the prominent travel behavior advocates, Satoshi Fujii and Ayako Taniguchi of Japan, the direct travel behavior change focuses on psychological and behavioral strategies of creating awareness to encourage voluntary travel behavior change. To influence travel behavior change, the most successful psychological and behavioral strategies are those that provide information on the environmental impacts of driving, existing public transport, travel campaign and travel education (Fujii, Garling and Ryuichi 2001; Taniguchi, *et al.*, 2003). Similar studies suggest that neighborhood residences, schools, universities and workplaces can be positive environments for the application of such direct behavior change programs.

According to Fuji and Taniguchi (2005), personalized communication is a more effective method for changing travel behavior than non-personalized mass communications. There are several awareness programs around the world being implemented to influence travel behavior to reduce the carbon footprint, use personal vehicles, and various other problems. Examples of personalized communication include individualized marketing: IndiMark® and

Travel Blending® of Australia, Personalized Travel Plans of the UK, InMotion in King County of Washington State, and the Travel Feedback program (TFP) of Japan (Fujii and Tanuaguchi 2005). In these active travel behavior change programs, residents usually receive information that is designed to encourage travel behavior change. Such feedback may be effective because it induces behavioral awareness, an essential element in change. This feedback may also prompt participants to increase their knowledge of specific methods for modifying their travel behavior. In such travel behavior change programs, people were given information on why an individual's travel behavior was necessary and how participants could change their travel behaviors. Thus, all the efforts mentioned above focused on psychological and behavioral strategies of creating awareness to encourage voluntary travel behavior change.

There is a variety of factors that influence human behavior and choices. Travel is derived from activity participation while travel behavior is a choice and influences the mode of travel, departure time and route selection and location decisions. The overall travel behavior changes over time along with the changes in social settings and the transportation system. The social settings and transportation system include transportation infrastructure and service as well as the social and institutional circumstances (Choi, *et al.*, 2014). It is important to understand changes in travel behavior in order to change necessary infrastructure and policy of transit and other drive-alternative travel modes; however, even with changes in transit, if the population at large is not aware of the modifications and improvements made to drive-alternative travel modes, then they are of limited value.

Though more countries recognize the importance of changing individual behavior, a few cities in Japan, Australia, the United States and Germany developed programs to change travel behavior of automobile use and encourage to use other modes of transportation such as a bus, train, bicycle, or just walking, to alleviate the negative consequences that comes with certain travel behaviors of using only an automobile as a means of transport.

Travel Feedback Programs of Japan

Travel feedback programs (TFPs) are interactive communication programs between target people and mobility management (MM) conductors. Mobility management focuses on making an effort to change travel behavior through communication. The communicative measures in the mobility management uses for travel behavior modification are called "soft measures"; they include the provisions of specific information on public transport, travel campaigns, and travel education (Fujii and Tanuaguchi 2006). Travel feedback programs can differ in many ways but they all share a common feature: the participants in each program receive information designed to modify behavior (Fujii and Tanuaguchi 2006). Such feedback may be effective because it induces behavioral awareness and may also prompt participants to increase their knowledge of specific methods modifying their travel behavior. The premise is that without some feedback, there cannot be change. Location, techniques for travel behavioral change, procedures, and communications media are useful parameters to the success of travel feedback programs.

The ten travel feedback programs implemented in Japan until 2003 resulted in a 19 percent reduction in CO_2 emissions, 18 percent reduction in car use, and a 50 percent increase in public transport use. There are too few travel feedback programs cases in Japan to allow a thorough investigation of all the factors that determine the effectiveness of travel feedback programs, however, travel feedback programs with behavioral plans yield the greatest reduction in CO_2, the most significant reduction in car use, and the greatest increase in public transit use (Fujii and Tanuaguchi 2006).

InMotion of King County, Washington

The program InMotion is a transportation demand management program (TDM) that encourages Kings County residents within targeted neighborhoods to use healthier and environmentally friendly travel options. Kings County Metro Transit, whose largest service cities include Seattle and Bellevue in Washington State, launched the InMotion programs in 2004 to encourage residents to walk, bike, take the bus, or carpool to reduce traffic congestion and reduce emissions while improving their own health (refer http://www.kingcounty.gov). When the program began, different neighborhoods were targeted based on certain criteria and encompassed a broad spectrum of the population for the pilot study. Based on surveys from the neighborhood, the program tailored its process to meet the needs of the neighborhood. A key element of the InMotion programs was that it utilized a community-based approach to craft messages that spoke to the particular motivations and barriers specific to a community, and delivered that message in a way that was acceptable to the community (Cooper 2007). Carol Cooper found that in all cases, the single biggest motivator was personal health benefits, and that became one of the biggest key components of the messaging.

Developing a community-based approach requires building partnerships with local organization and businesses. This allows the program message to be delivered by sources the recipients know, and, therefore, ensures that the InMotion program becomes part of the local community, rather than an abstract initiative that would be easy to ignore.

There were several unique projects that took place in Kings County. The first project in the Madison-Miller neighborhood that encouraged the personal health benefits and community connections of walking and biking for short trips to the stores, schools, and recreation, and was based on the initial survey that revealed residents were much more concerned about health rather than, for example, traffic congestion. Another project was in Renton and focused more on the potential time and financial savings of avoiding the construction impacts on the Interstate 405. In just a few years the results from 20 neighborhood projects collectively reduced their driving by 1.3 million miles, saved 66,040 gallons of fuel, and avoided 674 tons of CO_2 emissions. Participation levels average between 6 to 10 percent for each target neighborhood, and individual reports of approximate 20 percent decrease in solo car trips.

IndiMark (Germany/Australia)

IndiMark stands for "individualized marketing," and was developed as early as the late 1980s. The individualized market is a voluntary travel behavior-change program based on a personalized, customized, marketing approach. It is designed to shift travel behavior from the car to environmentally friendlier modes of transit that will be sustained in the long run. Germany and Australia recognized that there was a gap between an individual's perception of alternative modes of transport and the reality. Due to the lack of personal experience, or the lack of information about the readily available options, traveling by foot, by bicycle or by public transport can seem less attractive than it actually is. As a result, most people make their trips by car, although many could easily be replaced by other modes of transit.

The travel behavior change facilitation technique was based on four conceptual premises, but the main aim is to increase the amount of activities accessed by environmental friendly modes while decreasing the amount of car travel (Taylor & Ampt, 2003). The four premises are contact, motivation, information, and reinforcement. For example, in the South Perth, Australia, of the 400 households that were approached in the program, 36 percent expressed interests in switching from car to other modes, than those who participated provided with specific local information for the use of alternative modes. Initial results saw a 10 percent reduction in car driver trips; public transit trips increased 21 percent, cycling increased to 91 percent and walking increased to 16 percent. The follow-up evaluation conducted 12 months later saw that the initial changes were not only sustained, but there were further increases in walking trips and a corresponding decline in car driver trips (Taylor and Ampt 2003). From the groups that were interested, there was a significant impact on using alternative modes of transportation. The greatest increase and sustained travel behavior change was cycling. The program significantly increased the use of transit and improved personal health by having the community cycle more. Once an underutilized mode, the program made this mode of transit a viable option.

Just as South Perth was a trail for Australia, Germany conducted individualized marketing in the city of Viernheim. Viernheim was chosen because it has good infrastructure for bicycles and pedestrian traffic and made improvement for public transport (Taylor and Ampt 2003). It was the first city to apply individualized marketing to all environmentally friendly modes such as walking, cycling, and public transport on a large scale; therefore, the project is a pilot for the whole country. Germany had similar techniques to Australia, except instead of steps; they had different phases like the contact phase, segmentation phase, motivation phase, information phase, and persuasion phase. The difference is that the segmentation phase divided the groups of the population of the city into three subcategories: the households who have no interest in change and therefore no need for further contact, the households that are likely to change and receive the most attention, and the last group where one member of the households uses environmentally friendly modes regularly that would only need encouragement and support. The result was that walking increased seven percent, bicycling increased 10 percent, public transport increased 29 percent and journey by car was reduced by 12 percent. In the article *"Individualised Marketing Reducing Car Kilometres—A Global Approach,"* from the IndiMark program, they reported on average a relative reduction in car kilometers travelled by up to 19 percent in Germany and up to 17 percent in Australia (Socialdata 2004).

TravelSmart of Australia

The TravelSmart program of Australia began in response to the Metropolitan Transportation Strategy (1995) findings that recognized continuing trends in car use were not sustainable and that demand for car use would have to be managed to maintain a livable city (refer http://www.travelsmart.gov.au/). TravelSmart works directly with individuals to help them make informed travel choices about how to get to their destinations using their cars less and using environmentally friendly modes of transit more. There are a variety of TravelSmart programs in Australia that works with local communities, including local governments, schools, universities, hospitals, and workplaces, to help them make decisions about travel choices. A two-component-

Travel Blending is making one trip that covers several destinations rather than making several trips to multiple locations at different times.

model for behavior change was used: a community development approach and an individual conversation-based approach (Zhang, Stopherb and Hallingc 2013). A major project for travel behavior change was implemented in South Perth that included 15,300 household residents. Of those households, 45 percent took no interest in the programs, 40 percent actively participates in the program about how to change their travel habits, while 15 percent of the households were already regular users of walking, cycling or public transit users (Taylor and Ampt 2003).

The TravelSmart programs and the Indimark program work closely to change travel behavior in Australia. Both programs worked to identify households that could potentially change or want to change and continued to work with those who are already regular users of environmentally friendly modes of transit. The programs objective is to allow people to choose to change travel behavior rather than to expect or force reactions in response to external stimuli or pressures. This program was tailored to a group of individuals or worked at a local scale, but slightly larger than just neighborhoods. This program was also geared towards local organizations in the region such as schools and hospitals. The results were effective in changing travel behavior to include more walking and transit that were sustained in a long term rather than just immediate and short term results.

The Challenge: Convenience vs. Consciousness

When human beings started to harness animal power for mobility, they were exercising their freedom of movement beyond the means of their own feet. Over time, in the age of cities, this freedom of movement became even more apparent when humans started to live farther away from the inner core of the city. But in the age of automobiles, no other mode of transportation like the private car, has provided the actual (or perceived) comfort and convenience that works with one's own schedule like the private car. Despite the major developments in different modes of transportation, no other mode has received as much investment or transformed the natural landscape like the automobile. Throughout history, society has witnessed many changes in transportation. The twentieth century alone brought changes in energy sources, the development of high-speed trains, investment in air and surface travel and the invention of automobile's mass assembly. Of these developments, the automobile possesses the most notable grip on modern culture. Households and individuals were easily attracted to the automobile for its representation of prosperity and independence. This is coupled with the less emphasis local governments give for the development of drive-alternative travel modes such as public transit, walking and biking. And when government policies paved the way, the car went wherever and whenever it wanted. That is the challenge of travel behavior change.

As a society's consciousness towards environmental and social issues evolves, they are faced with the dilemma of whether or not to reduce car use. An individual leaving their comfort zone and choosing a different transportation method is a difficult decision. Adding to this dilemma, the unsettled political discourse on the question of whether human activities are responsible for environmental problems make the travel decisions more difficult. Michael Bronner (1997) suggested that society's ignorance of the malignant effects of automobile dependence allows the ill effects to grow beyond control. On the other hand, many believe that it is time to make a choice and adopt a more sustainable lifestyle. The real question is: how many of us are convinced of the far-reaching negative impacts of the automobile and are willing to take action? For the great majority, it is not about "not getting it" when it comes to human impacts on the environment, it is more about the dilemma of giving up our freedom.

For the most part, automobile use has determined the urban structure to the extent that cars are a necessity for most people. However, with depleting oil reserves, increased awareness of pollution and climate change, and growing city sprawl, the need to lessen automobile dependence has become more and more apparent (Amphlet 2008). It is argued that if car dependency is going to be significantly reduced, a large proportion of car drivers will need to shift to public transportation and other modes of transportation. The remaining critical question asks how we make the shift, in what time frame we can do it, and whether our communities are organized and dedicated enough to tackle such a project.

Keep in mind that the car is relatively fast, the cost of gas is relatively inelastic (though quickly changing), and the car works with most people's time budgets. Mass transit, on the other hand, is fragmented, requires more time, and is generally unfamiliar to most motorists. Cycling for many is inconceivable. It requires one to be relatively fit, be willing to sweat en route to one's destination, and it works best when one's destinations are within five miles or so. The alternatives to the car are enticing, but in many places, the convenience of the car is hard to beat.

For many, the car is perceived to be the safest way to get to one's destination, and for those who can afford the car, other options are less appealing. The automobile provides physical protection during accidents and is also very useful for safety as it provides safe passage when moving through problematic neighborhoods and poorly lit areas. One's personal safety is a very big issue and is hard to dismiss.

When motorists are confronted with decreasing their use of the car, a typical response is often something like, "what impact would it have if only I took my car off the road?" This type of response refers to the collective act of driving as a given and one that will not change until "they find some other way of transporting us around." To many, the choice is outside of our control; our mobile lives are shaped solely by the decision of others. So if one is aware of the numerous impacts of driving, how do we weigh the kind of consciousness we have against our need for convenience? Will we all be part of a wave of conscious consumers that will move us closer to a more sustainable economy, culture, and lifestyle or are we waiting for private industry (the design of less polluting or electric vehicles), or shall we wait for government policies to build a greater array of mass transit options along with the needed changes in land use policies favoring more compact development and decreased automobile use?

Another important factor in this discussion of consciousness vs. convenience is the fear of backsliding or sliding down the socio-economic ladder. People fear giving up a good thing, like the car and worry about not getting it back. In several cities, riding a bicycle for transportation and riding a bus is mostly an issue of class. Outside of a dense urban center like NYC, where mass transit is quite efficient, most of the transit riders are those that do not have an alternative transportation mode choice. They use mass transit, mostly buses or bicycles because these modes are less expensive than owning and maintaining an automobile. For many U.S. drivers, limiting or eliminating automobile use risks being perceived by others as part of a lower social class. The "humiliating" act of waiting at a bus stop is often used in car insurance commercials to remind us that one is not a fully functional member of society unless one drives.

In sum, it seems that the social and environmental consciousness vs. convenience dilemma is not easily solvable. In an age where more human beings are educated about the ecological, social, and economic impacts of driving, the convenience of the car is hard to give up. Bridging the gap from what we know to how we act has become increasingly difficult. A better way to approach this dilemma is to look at the issue of driving as connected to an entire list of other related issues like housing choices, urban design, safety and access issues, and the location of one's employment. *Driving less* is more than a decision of to drive or not to drive. It is one choice among a whole list of others, and all of these choices are connected. Until we see the relational nature of our individual choices, changing travel behavior will be difficult.

Review Questions

1. According to Robert Putnam, what is problematic about commuting by car?
2. Who are some individuals who are economically impacted by auto dependency?
3. What are some health problems associated with greater automobile use?
4. What are unnecessary car trips?
5. How do car culture and views of alternative transportation modes play a role in unnecessary car trips?
6. Why are technological improvements insufficient to solve all problems related auto dependency?
7. What are the direct and indirect ways of changing travel behavior? Elaborate.
8. Explain the Travel Feedback Program of Japan.
9. Explain the InMotion program in King County of the State of Washington.
10. What are the obstacles to changing driver behavior?

Project/Paper Idea

Do experimental research. Choose two groups of people, one experimental and the other a control group. At the beginning of the semester, conduct a pretest survey (that includes mode choice, trip characteristics, etc.) to both the experimental and control groups. Then, for the experimental group, provide detailed information about the adverse impacts of excessive driving, drive-alternative resources in the community, etc. Also, follow up with the experimental group with more information. At the end of the semester, conduct a posttest survey to both groups. Analyze the survey results to examine whether there is an impact of *information* on travel behavior.

Videos

Keep on Rolling: The Dream of the Automobile by *Films Media Group, 2012 (56 min.)*: Using archival footage, beautifully crafted contemporary animation, and interviews with astute cultural observers based outside the U.S., this program examines the implications of our love affair with the car. Viewers learn how, in just over a century, Henry Ford's innovations completely transformed human life, so much so that in some areas of the world, cars seem more important than human beings. In the West, for example, an estimated sixty-two percent of the urban space is now devoted to roads or car parks. The film also illustrates that devoting so much public and private space to an inefficient form of transportation has radically altered our relationship with the environment.

Internet Sources

- InMotion—King County, WA, http://www.kingcounty.gov/transportation/kcdot/MetroTransit/InMotion.aspx.
- Indimark—TravelSmart Australia, http://www.travelsmart.gov.au/training/packaging_comm_indi.html

Bibliography

Amphlet, Kieron. 2008. "Car Dependency in Australian Cities: A Discussion of Cause, Environmental Impacts and Possible Solution." *GEOview*. http://geoview.iag.org.au/.

Appleyard, Donald, and Allan Jacobs. 2011. *Toward an Urban Design Manifesto, Scottish Household Survey,* The City Reade, Routledge, New York, 518–529.

Bronner, Michael. 1997. "The Mother of Battles: Confronting the Implications of Automobile Dependence in the United States." *Population and Environment* 18 (5): 489–507.

Choi, Jinmu, Won-Do Lee, Woon-Ho Park, Chansung Kim, Keechoo Choi, and Chang-Hyeon Joh. 2014. "Analyzing Changes in Travel Behavior in Time and Space Using Household Travel Surveys in Seoul Metropolitan Area Over Eight Years." *Travel Behavior and Society* 1: 3–14.

Conlin, Michelle. 2005. "Extreme Commuting: More Workers Are Willing to Travel Three Hours a Day. But What Is the Long-Term Cost?" *Bloomberg business week*, February 12. Accessed May 2012, 2012. http://www.business-week.com/stories/2005-02-20/extreme-commuting.

Cooper, Bryony, and David Meiklejohn. 2003. *A New Approach for Travel Behavior Change In Universities.* Paper, Wellington, New Zealand: Paper presented at the 26th Australasian Transport Research Forum.

Cooper, Carol. 2003. "Showcase: In motion." *SMC*, 1–10.

_____. 2007. "Successfully Changing Individual Travel Behavior—Applying Community-Based Social Marketing to Travel Choice." *Transportation Research Record* (2021): 89–99.

Del Mistro, Romano, Roger Behrens, Lombard Mariana, and Ventor Christo. 2007. "The Triggers of Behavior Change and Implications for TDM Targeting: Findings of a Retrospective Commuter Travel Survey in Cape Town." *Proceedings of the 26th Southern African Transport Conference (SATC)* Pretoria, South Africa.

Durning, Alan. 1992. *How Much Is Enough? The Consumer Society and the Future of the Earth.* New York: W.W. Norton.

Fujii, Satoshi, Tommy Garling, and Kitamura Ryuichi. 2001. "Breaking Habitual Defecting by a Temporary Structural Change ." *Presented at the Ninth International Conference on Social Dilemma.* Chicago IL.

_____, and Ayako Taniguchi. 2006. "Determinants of the Effectiveness of Travel Feedback Programs—A Review of Communicative Mobility Management Measures for Changing Travel Behaviour in Japan." *Transport Policy* 13 (5): 339–348.

_____, and _____. 2005. "Travel Feedback Programs: Communicative Mobility Management Measures for Changing Travel Behavior." *Proceedings of the Eastern Asia Society for Transportation Studies.* 5.

Giuliano, Genevieve, and Dargay Joyce. 2005. "Car Ownership, Travel and Land Use: A Comparison of the U.S. and Great Britain." Working Paper, Transport Studies Unit, Oxford University Centre for the Environment, Oxford.

Gottlieb, Robert. 2007. *Reinventing Los Angeles: Nature and Community in the Global City,* MIT Press.

Hansson, Erik, Kristoffer Mattisson Mattisson, Jonas Björk, Per-Olof Östergren, and Kristina Jakobsson. 2011. "Relationship Between Commuting and Health Outcomes in a Cross-sectional Population Survey in Southern Sweden." *BMC Public Health* 11: 834.

Ihlandfeldt, Keith. 2003. "Rail Transit and Neighborhood Crime: The Case of Atlanta, Georgia." *Southern Economic Journal* 70 (2): 273–294.

Jacobs, Jane. 1961. *The Death and Life of Great American Cities.* New York: Random House.

Lee, Matilda. 2009. "Dilemma: How Do You Define Unnecessary Travel?" *The Ecologist.*

Litman, Todd. 2003. "Transportation Cost and Benefit Analysis Guidebook." *Victorian Policy Institute.*

_____, and Felix Laube. 2002. "Automobile Dependency and Economic Development." *Victoria Transport Policy Institute.*

Mackett, Roger, and James Paskins. 2004. "Increasing Children's Volume of Physical Activity Through Walk and Play." Paper presented at University College London, London.

McCann, Barbara, and Reid Ewing. 2003. "Measuring the Health Effects of SPRAWL: A National Analysis of Physical Activity, Obesity and Chronic Disease." *National Center for Smart Growth Research & Education.*

Mumford, Lewis. 1950. "The Sky Line: Civic Virtue." *The New Yorker*, 25 (509): 58–63.

Putnam, Robert. 2000. *Bowling Alone: The Collapse and Revival of American Community.* New York: Touchstone Books by Simon & Schuster.

Rodgers, Dennis. 2004. "'Disembedding' the City: Crime, Insecurity, and Spatial Organization in Managua, Nicaragua." *Environment and Urbanization*, 113–124.

Socialdata. 2004. "Individualised Marketing Reducing Car Kilometers—A Global Approach," Socialdata Australia PTY, LTD.

Taniguchi, Ayako, Fumihiro Hara, Shin-ei Takano, Sei'ichi Kagaya, and Satoshi Fujii. 2003. "Psychological and Behavioral Effects of Travel Feedback Programs for Travel Behavior Modification." *Transportation Research Record* 183: 182–190.

Taylor, Michael, and Elizabeth Ampt. 2003. "Travelling Smarter Down Under: Policies for Voluntary Travel Behavior Change in Australia." *Transport Policy* 10 (3): 165 177.

Travel Smart Australia. 2009. *Packaging the Travel Choices.* Accessed June 17, 2009. http://www.travelsmart.gov.au.

TTI. 2001. "Urban Mobility Report." *Texas Transportation Institute (TTI).*

UNHDR. 2007. "Human Development Report (UNHDR)." *United Nations (UN) Development Programme.*

Urry, John. 2006. "Inhabiting the Car Against Automobility." *The Sociological Review* (Blackwell) 54: 17–31.

Woldeamanuel, Mintesnot, and Erin Welle. 2012. "Analyzing Mode-Switching Behavior in Response to Transit-Oriented Developments ." *Studies in Regional Science* 42 (3): 607–620.

Zhang, Yun, Peter Stopherb, and Belinda Hallingc. 2013. "Evaluation of South-Australia's Travelsmart Project: Changes in Community's Attitudes to Travel." *Transport Policy* 26: 15–22.

7

Planning for Non-Motorized Transportation—Walking and Cycling

Chapter Outline
- Introduction
- The Benefit of Walking and Biking
  - o *Health Benefits*
  - o *Environmental and Economic Benefits*
  - o *Quality of Life Benefits*
- The Built Environment and Walking or Biking
  - o *Sidewalk Infrastructure*
  - o *Bicycling Infrastructure*
- Planning for Non-Motorized Transportation
- Successful Bicycling Practices

Introduction

As discussed in the previous two chapters, as we become more aware of the need to wean ourselves off of the automobile, we must look to and plan for alternative means of transportation. In addition to public transportation (which will be discussed in the next chapter), the means of travel that is suitable in almost all regards is walking and bicycling. This category is also referred as *non-motorized transportation* or *active transportation*. It is crucial that local planning agencies further develop non-motorized transportation infrastructure to encourage the use of alternative modes of travel. Planners and governments at all levels are starting to face some tough decisions as the demand for walking and cycling grows. When sprawl takes more and more land, pollution is on the rise, and the climate seems to be changing, so in the world of environmentalism, new urbanism, smart growth, sustainability and the buzz word "green," we see a push to active transportation. A question heard more often is how we get people choose a more sustainable mode of transportation. One important issue is how people view using a bicycle and walking for transportation. Especially in U.S., people look to the bicycle as a leisure, sport, enjoyment or something one uses during vacation whereas for the

Europeans and Asians, it is common to use a bicycle for commuting. In some places, there is a perspective that if you walk or are using a bike your standard of living is below that of someone driving a car. There is also the problem of drivers and bicyclists not being fully aware of the rules for each on the road. Not only the drivers, but also the law enforcement sometimes don't handle bicyclist the same as automobile drivers (Pucher, Komanoff and Shimek, 1999).

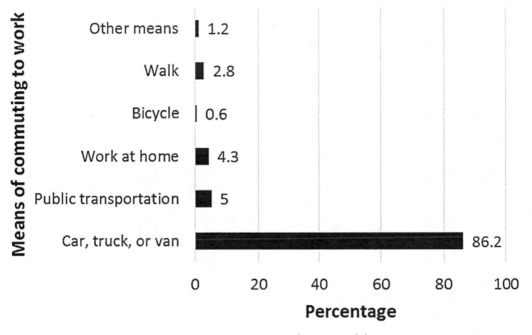

Figure 7.1 Means of commuting to work in U.S. in percent (2008–2012) (U.S. Census Bureau, American Community Survey, 2008–2012).

In the 1990s, The Federal Highway Administration described bicycling and walking as "the forgotten modes" of transportation (FHWA 2003). Many federal, state and local agencies had overlooked these non-motorized options for years, even as governments in other countries acknowledged their importance. Sources of funding were limited, with $6 million in federal funds spent on pedestrian and bicycle projects in 1990. Fewer than 4.4 percent of commuting trips in 1990 were made by bicycling and walking, down from 6.7 percent in 1980. Though these modes comprised only a small share of trips, bicycle and pedestrian crashes accounted for more than 15 percent of traffic fatalities. Recognizing the decline in walking and bicycling, and the rise in fatalities, the U.S. Department of Transportation (USDOT) adopted the first national transportation policy in 1994 to increase use of bicycling, and encourage planners and engineers to accommodate bicycle and pedestrian needs in designing transportation facilities for urban and suburban areas. The policy also aims to increase pedestrian safety through public information and improved design of crosswalks, signaling, school crossings and sidewalks (USDOT 2010). These priorities represented a significant shift in the attention given to bicycling and walking.

Despite the policy attention given to walking and cycling, fewer and fewer people are walking or bicycling for transportation. For example, according to a study by the U.S. Federal

Highway Administration, in 1969, about half of all U.S. students walked or biked to school (USDOT 1972). Similar studies showed that at the start of the 21st century, fewer than 15 percent of all school trips are made by walking or bicycling, and over half of all children arrive at school in private automobiles (NHTS 2001). This correlates to the various reasons why parents choose to drive their children to and from school. According to the U.S. Center for Disease Control (CDC), safety concerns influence parents' attitudes; parents consistently cite traffic danger as a reason why their children are unable to bicycle or walk to school (CDC 2005). Although there are objective measures of safety related to the physical environment, most parents decide based on *perceived* measures of the safety of the travel mode itself, or of the walking and bicycling environments. If other social and environmental factors support the behavior in question, then over time these perceived negative attitudes may lead to a lifestyle that doesn't include walking and biking (Johansson, *et al.*, 2011).

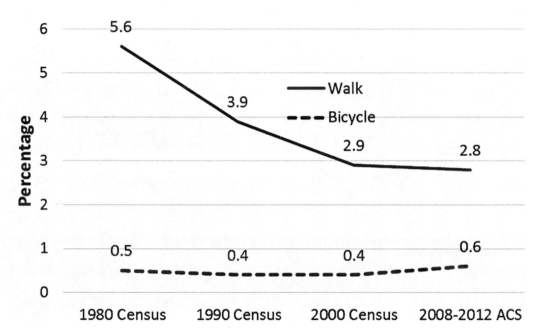

Figure 7.2 **Walking and bicycling to work: 1980 to 2008–2012. (U.S. Census Bureau, Decennial Census 1980, 1990, 2000 and American Community Survey, 2008–2012).**

The Benefit of Walking and Biking

Researchers have tried to determine the benefits of walking and bicycling on environmental and health measures and agreed that there are numerous benefits associated with those active transportation travel modes. Improved user convenience and comfort, accessibility for non-drivers, supporting equity objectives, reduced traffic congestion and road and parking facility cost savings are a few of the benefits. According to the Federal Highway Administration 2010, officials recognized the health, environmental, economic, and quality of life benefits and sought to encourage the use of bicycling and walking to reach environmental, health, and transportation goals (USDOT 2010).

HEALTH BENEFITS

Improved health is a crucial piece to examine when analyzing the benefits of active transportation. The theory goes, if we create a place (city, town, or community) that has design elements with opportunity for safe walking and bicycling, people will change their driving habits and adopt one or both of these alternative modes of transportation to their daily commute. Then in turn we will see an increase in health benefits in those that do. In fact, research found that the health benefits of regular physical activity related to walking and biking are far-reaching: reduced risk of coronary heart disease, stroke, diabetes, and other chronic diseases; lower health care costs; and improved quality of life for people of all ages. Even small increases in light to moderate activity, such as daily bike rides or 30-minute walks, can produce measurable benefits among those who are least active (USDOT 2010). This correlates with the recommendation of doing 30 minutes of physical activity a day, such as brisk walking. This does not have to be done in 30-minute intervals; it can be done 10 minutes at a time three times a day (Pucher, Komanoff and Shimek 1999). According to Hill (2003) if a person walked and extra 15 or 20 minutes a day they would burn and additional 100 calories that would eliminate the yearly weight gain if all other factors stayed the same. This would easily happen in communities that are designed to encourage walking and biking. In fact, a study has found that those who live in the most sprawl areas are six pounds heavier than those living in a pedestrian-oriented community (Pucher and Buehler 2010).

Research has also reported that 60 percent of Americans do not engage in physical activity on a consistent basis. Worse yet, 25 percent do not engage in any physical activity at all (Schmitz and Scully 2006). In a survey designed to determine why people do not exercise, the overwhelming answer was "not having enough time." With this information, researchers feel that to encourage people to engage in a daily activity, they need a destination close by such as work, drug store or doctor's offices that are reachable by walking or bicycling. A significant number of trips taken by car are one mile or less, and many of these could be walked or taken on a bike if the design of the community were walk or bicycle friendly (Schmitz and Scully 2006).

For any number of trips, people may not have a choice because the distance between their origin and destination and the safety to get there is a challenge. Urban planning that has been going on for decades has created a society that doesn't get out walking even for shorter trips. But research has found that people living in walkable communities walk a total of 70 minutes more each week which totals up to a loss of 4 pounds a year, and less air pollution because they use their cars less (Pucher and Buehler 2010).

Studies have found that moderate intensity physical activity numerous times a day is better than one extremely strenuous workout. This adds to the argument that people should increasingly use active transportation as a means to better health (Bors, *et al.,* 2009). Riding a bike or walking falls into the moderately intense workout category. There is an important distinction that must be made regarding active transportation, and that is the difference between regular physical activity and activity for the sake of transportation (Troped, *et al.,* 2003). Most believe that exercise must be for its own sake, but that is not the case. The truth is that biking or walking as a means of transport allows people to get from place to place while still participating in physical activity.

ENVIRONMENTAL AND ECONOMIC BENEFITS

The transportation sector accounted for nearly 30 percent of all energy consumed in the U.S., according to the Department of Energy. Transportation is also responsible for nearly one-third of greenhouse gas emissions, and 80 percent of U.S. carbon monoxide emissions. Replacing short trips with walking or bicycling can help reduce this level of energy consumption, while also decreasing emissions from cars. Economically speaking, the cost of owning and operating a car, currently estimated at $9,055 per year, can account for almost 18 percent of a typical household's income. Compare that with the $120 yearly operating cost of owning a bicycle, or essentially free travel by foot, and it is clear that walking and bicycling can provide options for those who would like to save money (USDOT 2010). Many communities are even using a bicycle and walking facilities to revitalize businesses and bring new economic life to downtown areas. It is hard to quantify the effects that less car use will have on the economy, but there is a study by Betts (2012) that has attempted to do just that, and the results are staggering. Eleven urban areas in the United States comprised the population that was examined in the study. The numbers show that if within a 5 month period all automobile trips of less than five miles were replaced with some form of active transportation or public transportation, the savings would amount to 8 billion dollars (Betts 2012). This is quite a significant number and shows the enormity of the money spent on trips just within 5 miles, which are easily accomplishable by walking and biking.

QUALITY OF LIFE BENEFITS

Providing more travel options can increase a sense of independence in seniors, young people, and others who cannot or choose not to drive. Increased levels of bicycling and walking can have a great impact on an area's sense of livability by creating safe and friendly places for people to live and work. As we have progressed into an automobile-centered culture, we have lost much of the basic interaction that used to bind communities. Gone are the days of sitting on the front porch and talking with neighbors. With a front door garage, it is possible to miss all opportunity for interaction with those in the community. This hinders the development of the strong community base that is essential to a healthy neighborhood. Increasing the community usage of active transportation increases the interaction among those in the community. More conversations and a stronger bond between individuals help not only to raise problems, but also solve them. The more time spent outside also strengthens ties to the physical environment that one lives in. It helps to identify problems and creates a more personal stock in the wellbeing of the area.

The Built Environment and Walking or Biking

Land use can either increase or reduce vehicle miles traveled and the use of walking and bicycling for transportation. Studies show that low density, single use land zoning produces longer travel journeys and greater reliance on the car as the principal means of transport. Conversely, higher density land use with mixed zoning and increased access to sustainable transport modes are more likely to promote sustainable travel behaviors. Cervero (2002) studied the impact of "new urbanist" areas on travel modes, specifically whether compact, mixed-use and pedestrian-friendly developments could have a significant influence. The author assessed three core dimensions of the built environment: density, diversity and design. The study found that density and mixture of land use were significant influences in determining travel mode, particularly in the decision to use public transport, walk, bike, share a car or drive alone. The study also showed that higher gross densities lowered the occurrence of driver-only car commuting. Also, workplace destinations with a higher density of mixed land use and a high sidewalk ratio produced a higher level of active transport use.

Goudie (2002) found that location played a large part in fuel consumption and distances traveled. People located in the outer urban/suburban areas used on average three times more fuel than more centrally placed participants. Outer urban dwellers had the least sustainable travel behaviors such as walking and biking, which the author felt posed a challenge for policymakers, developers and city planners. Guiliano & Narayan (2003) studied travel behaviors of U.S. and British populations and found that in the U.S., land use patterns reinforced vehicle dependence, particularly in the sprawling suburbs of the large metropolitan regions. The authors suggested that stronger urban planning and design controls in European countries contributed to a more compact and higher density urban form, and hence an increased use of walk, bike and public transport.

There are beliefs that the design of a community's built environment will have an effect on the physical and mental health of the residents (Dannenberg *et al.*, 2003), and that this is tied to mode choice. The design can also encourage more physical activity on a daily basis and have an indirect positive outcome on public health (Pucher and Buehler 2010). High density in neighborhoods with mixed land use that create closer destinations encourage more physical activity among youth, adults, and elderly over a sprawled development. Shops, restaurants, trails and parks should be within walking distance and no more than ½ mile apart. They need to be easily reached using well-planned connected streets that are designed to produce shorter routes (Dannenberg, Frumkin and Jackson 2011).

Research shows a significant correlation between travel mode choice and the built environment, with the built environment of neighborhoods in this case being measured by its physical characteristics and pedestrian perceptions. The attributes of the built environment include mixed land use, street connectivity, accessibility or proximity to services, aesthetics, sidewalks, safety, neighborhood type, availability and access to parks/open space, pedestrian infrastructure, pedestrian furniture and the upkeep of an area. So, the walkability of a neighborhood can determine how conducive the built environment is to the walking behavior of a community. The more an individual perceives the built environment as "walk-friendly," the more they will be inclined to walk or bike for pleasure or convenience (Forsyth and Krizek 2010). The pedestrian-friendly design encourages walking by providing a safer, more comfortable and enjoyable experience for non-motorist. The pedestrian-oriented design provides individuals with street furniture like benches, trees, shade, crossings and street lights. By implementing sidewalk features, such as protection from the weather and barriers from traffic, the pedestrian is more inclined to choose voluntarily to walk. These elements can make the pedestrian perceive the area as more inviting to walk or bike.

Design elements also bring up legitimate safety concerns. Elements such as street lights, islands, elevated curbs and crossings allow for refuge from danger. Such elements like trees and narrow streets can give the roadway a slimmer appearance that encourages the driver to be more aware of their surroundings. The pedestrian-oriented design also creates an environment for informal social interaction. Pedestrian design and streetscapes entice residents to walk around (Dannenberg, Frumkin and Jackson 2011), providing opportunities for relationships to build within a community.

Choosing alternatives to the private automobile is greatly dependent on the proximity between destinations. The biggest feature that determines one's choice is distance. Where we live, work, play, do our grocery shopping, where the nearest park is located, significantly determines our choice to walk or bike. According to the 2002 National Survey of Bicyclist and Pedestrian Attitudes and Behavior by the National Highway Traffic and Safety Administration and the Bureau of Transportation Statistics, the average distance people are willing to walk is 1.3 miles (based on responses from 10,000 respondents). Density, the proximity and street connectivity, which provides the ease of traveling between two points (Forsyth and Krizek 2010), has a great impact on whether one walks, drives or stays home. High density also offers other advantages like supports of local retail, social support, and perceived safety that encourages residents to enjoy their neighbors on a pedestrian level (Dannenberg, Frumkin and Jackson 2011). With increasing numbers on the sidewalks, the amount of people walking in the appearance of a larger crowd can represent a safer environment or social network. With street connectivity, the smaller blocks allow residents to choose their preferred routes that are convenient by avoiding dangerous routes or allowing for shortcuts. Also, a study by Owen, *et al.* (2007) also suggests that walkable neighborhoods encourage frequent walking trips if they promise a short journey to their destination. This trait of the built environment gives more choices and control to the pedestrian.

Not only density but also diversity encourages walking and biking. Diversity, one of the factors that encourage walking and biking, aims specifically at mixed land use. Mixed land use is having a variety of land uses in one area through zoning (Forsyth and Krizek 2010). Euclidean zoning, which is characterized by the segregation of land uses into specified districts and dimensional standards, can make it difficult for a diversity of amenities to be available to community members. Euclidean zoning is now the modern problem that can cause the isolation of amenities, especially for the less advantaged. Yet, diversity (mixed and use), is thought to provide pedestrians with more visual variety to capture the attention of pedestrians and have diverse land uses for physical space, including residential, office, retail/commercial, and public space within walking distance (Dannenberg, Frumkin and Jackson 2011). Pedestrians are more likely to walk if they believe they have access to a variety of

Euclidean Zoning is the common term that represents conventional zoning laws across the United States. Euclidean zoning is also referred to as **single-use zoning**. The basic component of Euclidean zoning is the classification, or segregation, of land use types, i.e. single-family residential; multifamily residential; commercial; industrial, etc. The term refers to a United States Supreme Court case from 1926, Village of Euclid, Ohio v. Ambler Realty Co. The Village of Euclid, as a means of preventing the invasion of Cleveland's industrial sprawl from their community, developed a zoning ordinance with six land use classifications. Ambler Realty Co. was a property owner in Euclid who sued the Village of Euclid for substantially reducing the value of their land by limiting its use. The Village of Euclid won the landmark case, creating a basis for the Supreme Court on zoning laws. Euclidean zoning spread across the United States shaping the first ring suburbs and exurban communities of our country. Even today, 85 years later, townships and municipalities use a variation of the original zoming laws to shape our automobile-centric environment. (Source: Urban Landscapes Blog).

activities (Forsyth and Krizek 2010). Walking is easier if an area has a diverse mixture of land uses and activities close enough together. Generating pedestrian traffic in a busy area can have a positive effect on the area and even generate informal policing, which creates a sense of place.

BOX 7.1 Safety and comfort for all street users: New Haven, Connecticut

In the city of New Haven, Connecticut, a variety of local factors mobilized members of the community to encourage the adoption of a complete streets policy in the fall of 2008. These factors included (1) a very high proportion of workers commuting on foot or by bike, carpool, or public transit; (2) two high-profile pedestrian fatalities; (3) data indicating a disproportionate rate of pediatric injury; and (4) the elevation of local streets as public places that define quality of life and the overall image of the city. Activists in the area made it a priority to rally public support for a comprehensive policy to make the streets of New Haven safer and more comfortable for all users. Activists and city officials worked together to draft and adopt a set of goals and develop an implementation program. The resulting policy explicitly outlines comprehensive steps to make sure that complete streets implementation will be a community effort. A steering committee has been tasked with developing a design manual, ensuring that engineers—key players in implementation—are not left out of the process. Further, the committee developed a process to involve the general public in the planning and design of complete streets in their neighborhoods. Although the city does not have the public funds available to support projects solely dedicated to completing the streets, a tremendous amount of private investment is available to the city despite the challenging economic times. Thus, the city has been using funds from private investors to develop its bikeway system and enhanced bicycle and pedestrian access to transit hubs.

Bureaucratic procedures have stood in the way of complete streets implementation in New Haven; however, the policy addresses this issue. According to Mike Piscitelli, city transportation director, "This policy was more about how to organize ourselves for the longer term. How do we create a lasting system?" City officials have found that the policy has created a more comprehensive and systematic approach as it coordinates the efforts of staff, who previously had worked in unrelated silos, to promote similar goals. The policy focuses on changing the way the administration does business so as to provide a sustainable, reliable transportation system for all roadway users well into the future. Finally, the policy emphasizes the importance of public education campaigns to promote complete streets principles. One campaign that stands out is the award-winning "Street Smarts," in which drivers take a pledge to be cognizant and respectful of other roadway users. In New Haven, citizens can receive training to become a "Smart Driver"; all city and school bus drivers go through this program. The city has emphasized the relation of the Street Smarts campaign to the complete streets legislation. According to Piscitelli, "Instead of focusing solely on regulations, we are addressing human behavior as the central focus of the safety campaign and then complementing education with physical improvements." This is one unique and, according to Piscitelli, successful aspect of the systematic change taking place in New Haven.

Source: The City of New Haven, www.cityofnewhaven.com/streetsmarts/index.asp. Accessed on August 14, 2014

Sidewalk Infrastructure

Sidewalks are an important city infrastructure that can create many possibilities for socialization, tie the community together, provide direct movement, and encourages people to walk freely and safely to move from place to place (Zelinka and Brennan 2001). Along with well-connected streets, it is important to include sidewalks to provide safety for pedestrians. When sidewalks have been included in city infrastructure, there has been an increase in children walking to school (Forsyth and Krizek 2010), and elderly adults can move more independently (if the sidewalk is a stable, smooth surface) (Dannenberg *et al.*, 2003; Zelinka and Brennan 2001).

Sidewalks are vital in promoting pedestrian mobility in urban and suburban areas; therefore their quality and connectivity must be included to assess the pedestrian accessibility of city spaces accurately. However, lack of sidewalks in most neighborhoods impede pedestrian access to desired destinations due to problems such as cracks and buckling, or the sidewalks being entirely absent (Evans-Cowley 2006). While the current trend of transportation favors automobile-oriented travel, planners and researchers are working to reduce motor vehicle dependency and encourage active transportation, which is facilitated through well-connected, high-quality pedestrian networks that allow foot travel to activity sites. Pedestrian mobility is significantly increased with improved accessibility to destinations, specifically well-connected street networks and availability of good quality sidewalk (Witten, *et al.*, 2012). A study by Ehrenfeucht and Loukaitou-Sideris (2010) expresses the importance of sidewalks to public and community health. The authors refer to them as "distinct public spaces" that act to facilitate transportation by creating a connectivity network in the city, as well as support stationary activities, while contributing to public access of activity hubs (Ehrenfeucht and Loukaitou-Sideris 2010). The authors further explain the importance of sufficient sidewalk presence and quality with respect to connecting various destinations. Research conducted by Suminski *et al.* (2007) supports the theory that sidewalk quality is important to physical activity, finding that there is indeed a relationship between sidewalk quality and pedestrian presence in spaces. Furthermore, a study by Saelens, Sallis and Frank (2003) evaluated the built environment's effect on the capacity of young adults to perform physical activity in an urban environments, and found that there was a direct connection between the environment in which physical activity occurred and the subject's ability to perform continuous moderate-intensity exercise. The study found that obstacles within the urban built environment, such as poor quality sidewalks, caused subjects to slow down or stop.

Recent research by McCormack *et al.* (2012) indicates that improvements to sidewalks may in fact increase pedestrian use, while Chin *et al.* (2008) found that the addition of pedestrian networks improved connectivity measures for conventional neighborhoods. McCormack *et al.* (2012) also analyzed characteristics of neighborhoods, including transportation-related walkability and sidewalk length and found that neighborhood sidewalk length and walkability were positively associated with a 2.97 and 2.16 percentage point increase in the probability of neighborhood-based walking for transportation, respectively. For each 10 km (6.2 miles) increase in sidewalk length, neighborhood-based walking for transportation increased by 5.38 minutes per week and overall neighborhood-based walks increased by 5.26 minutes per week (McCormack, *et al.*, 2012). Also, the pedestrian infrastructure was included in Cervero's analysis of TOD design factors to encourage walking to transit stations (Cervero and Kockelman 1997). The connectedness of the surrounding street network can significantly influence access to activity sites because high connectivity reduces walking distance and allows for ease of travel between two points (Aultman-Hall, Roorda and Baetz 1997; Saelens *et al.*, 2003; Witten *et al.*, 2012).

Table 7.1 Sidewalk infrastructure with varied quality

Grade	Description	Picture representation

Grade   Description   **Picture representation**

1   **EXTREMELY POOR QUALITY SIDEWALK:** Non-paved sidewalk, sloping, uneven dirt or grass. According to the grading scale, when grading a sidewalk with a grade of 1, a sidewalk would be non-existent. There would not be pavement nor would it be walkable due to holes, bumps, debris along the path or at an angle.

2   **POOR QUALITY SIDEWALK:** Paved sidewalk with intersections of the grass lawn, dirt or an even dirt path. A grade of 2 is represented by a sidewalk that is a paved sidewalk with possible intersections of grass lawns or dirt. This classification must be taken into account and separated from a grade 1 due to the commonality where some properties have a paved sidewalk in front and others have dirt or grass lawn. With public health being a concern, sidewalks of grades 2 are the most hazardous because they may seem walkable but can easily cause a person to fall, especially when the impediment is small and non-intrusive, which is often ignored.

3   **FAIR QUALITY SIDEWALK:** Paved sidewalk, which has obstacles such as large cracks or elevations that can cause a person to trip or fall. The importance of this grade is due to injuries that can arise from falls, especially in children and the elderly.

4   **VERY GOOD QUALITY SIDEWALK:** Paved leveled sidewalk no surface obstacles, *without* ADA-complaint ramps at the end of the block.

5   **EXTREMELY GOOD QUALITY SIDEWALK:** Paved and leveled sidewalk with no surface obstacles, *with* ADA compliant ramps at the end of the block.

WALK SCORE

In terms of analyzing and assessing the walkability of a particular neighborhood, a popular method is the use of a Walk Score. According to Cortright (2009), walkability is defined by the Walk Score algorithm, which works by calculating the closest amenities—restaurants, coffee shops, schools, parks, stores, libraries, etc.—to any U.S. address. The algorithm then assigns a "Walk Score" from 0–100, with 100 being the most walkable and 0 being totally car-dependent. Walk Scores of 70+ indicate neighborhoods where it's possible to get by without a car. By the Walk Score measure, walkability is a direct function of how many destinations are located within a short distance (between one-quarter mile and one mile of a home). A study found that in the typical metropolitan area, a one-point increase in Walk Score was associated with an increase in house value ranging from $700 to $3,000 depending on the market. The gains were larger in denser, urban areas like Chicago and San Francisco and smaller in less dense markets like Tucson and Fresno (Cortright 2009).

Walk Score®	Description
90–100	**Walker's Paradise** Daily errands do not require a car.
70–89	**Very Walkable** Most errands can be accomplished on foot.
50–69	**Somewhat Walkable** Some errands can be accomplished on foot.
25–49	**Car-Dependent** Most errands require a car.
0–24	**Car-Dependent** Almost all errands require a car.

Figure 7.3 Walk Score interpretation (www.walkscore.com).

Bicycling Infrastructure

European countries have made a long-term commitment to adopting policies to encourage bicycling. This has been done due to few socio-environmental reasons, such as reducing automobiles in the city and improving traffic flow in dense areas where there is little land for parking (Pucher, Komanoff and Shimek 1999). They have worked to make bicycling safe, convenient and efficient while at the same time making driving expensive and difficult. Educating the public was the big component and is very important to continue encouraging people to move from cars to a bicycle. The Netherlands and Germany are good examples of educating the public about bicycling. In these countries, their drivers training includes paying special attention to ways in which you can drive to avoid colliding with pedestrians and cyclists (Pucher and Buehler 2010). Additionally, laws in these countries are very strict on how automobile drivers react to pedestrians and cyclists, even if the pedestrians or cyclists are at fault. However, the pedestrians and cyclists are also more apt to receive a ticket for jay-walking, riding in the wrong direction, not stopping at a red light or walking when the pedestrian light is red. There are also other provisions made to provide safety for the cyclists. They have separate bike traffic signals with advance green lights, bicyclist-activated traffic signals at key intersections, and modification of street networks to create deliberate dead ends and slow, circuitous routing for cars but direct, fast connections for bikes (Pucher and Buehler 2010). This encourages users of all modes of transportation to take careful consideration as to how their actions on the street and sidewalk may affect those around them.

In the United States, we are starting to see more support for bicycling at the governmental level since the Intermodal Surface Transportation Efficiency Act in 1991. There has been a considerable increase in funding for bicycling facilities and new bike paths (Pucher, Komanoff and Shimek 1999). Each step is taken to make biking safer and easier sees increases in bicycle use. There are programs as simple as encouraging children to bike to school by having adults guide them to and from school each morning. More and more cities are including the bike share programs, where bikes can be found throughout the city.

Table 7.2 Classification of bicycle infrastructure in Los Angeles

Class	Description	Picture representation
Class 1-Bike path	A class one bicycle path is the one that is separated from automobile traffic with its own corridor. Class one paths are usually found along current transit systems, rivers, parks, and former train track corridors.	
Class 2-Bike lane	The more commonly seen in Los Angeles is a class 2 bicycle lane. A class 2 bicycle lane is in a street with painted markings along the length of the street next to the parked cars along the curb.	
Class 3- Bike Route	The bike lane is not a marked lane or a path. It is designated by a signpost informing cyclists and drivers to share the road.	

Class	Description	Picture representation
Class 4-Sharrow	A sharrow is not a lane or a path. However, there are markings with noticeable arrows pointing in the direction of traffic with a bicycle image beneath the arrows. A sharrow is a sign to automobile traffic, informing them to share the road with bicyclists.	

Cultural Infrastructure and Bicycling

Bicycling has two paradigms: transportation infrastructure studies and cultural studies. Transportation infrastructure studies focus on the physical geography of biking while cultural studies address the societal motivation to bike (Pelzer 2010). For example, the Update of Tennessee's State Bicycle Route Plan's transportation study showed that the quality of bike routes and the type of destinations are important, and the plan's cultural study showed that 80 percent of respondents have expressed formal and informal group rides as a motivation to bike (UTSBRP 2011). Bike movements, social networks, and cultural practices are "human infrastructures" that augment bicycling as a mode of transport. The human aspect and the built environment must be integrated for a truly functional cycling society (Lugo 2013).

More and more urban planning scholars are accepting that the effect of socio-cultural issues on cycling is a topic worthy of academic and political consideration. The range of this socio-cultural effect, for both commuters and recreational riders, includes physical infrastructure, socio-economic background, and cycling identity. There are many different cycling cultures, and the best way to promote cycling is to embrace the needs of the cyclists. These needs are both physical and social in form, ranging from improvements in physical infrastructure such as bike lanes, safety, and security, to efforts of instilling a positive attitude towards bicycling. Instituting these changes on a governmental level will boost the cycling culture so it may grow organically on its own. The widespread endorsement of festivals such as "critical mass" riding across socio-economic barriers, age groups, and cycling identities make it the optimum method for publicizing cycling. Accommodating the largest capacity of bicycle users, these events have quickly become one of the most advanced exhibits of cross-culturalism in transportation.

Research shows that in today's America, across cultures, there is already a desire to utilize alternative forms of transportation and live in walkable/bikeable cities. This fact, along with the new capacities of the Internet, supports the trend of Americans, especially young, driving far less than their predecessors.

In some other countries such as New Zealand, however, cycling was found to have decreased because it is perceived to be less safe and less convenient due to lack of supporting infrastructure. Research from 2008 to 2010 shows that only 2.5 percent of trips to work are by bicycle even though ⅔ of trips are less than 3.7 miles long, and only 1 percent of all trips are by bike (Smith, Wilson, & Armstrong 2011). This exemplifies the idea that when the policy provides new physical bicycle infrastructure, it also, inadvertently supports cultural infrastructure.

The relationship between physical and mental facets of bicycle use was analyzed by the

Department of Transit for Chicago to determine why users are provoked toward their mode of transportation. Mentally, exercise, health, fitness and pleasure were the main reported instigators of bike use. Over half of the time, a bicyclist's trip was for recreation, with fitness a mere 14 percent, and the total ride averaging 2–4 miles. Physically, paths and neighborhood streets were preferred over busy roads. In consideration of both factors, dedicated bike facilities and secure bike lockers were desired, but distance and too much to carry were also main reasons for nonuse (Wilbur Smith Associates 2005). San Luis Obispo's bicycle identity was also gathered in a survey, which revealed the major mental concerns such as personal safety and motorist behavior, followed by the physical concerns of bicycle facility availability and path connectivity. The main consensus was that cycling in San Luis Obispo would be more attractive if there were more bicycling lanes and paths (SLOCOG 2013).

BOX 7.2 Knoxville, TN, bicycle program-validating alternative modes of travel

Challenge-Effectively Promoting Alternative Modes of Travel

For the Knoxville region in Tennessee, an increase in bicycling represents a chance to alleviate poor air quality and roadway congestion while improving the overall quality of life for area residents. However, while most recognize the health and cost benefits associated with cycling, several concerns remain for those who wish to do so more than just recreationally. Many cyclists hesitate to ride due to safety concerns-the shoulder width, and road conditions may appear inadequate to maintain substantial distance between motorists and cyclists on the roadway, and the speed and volume of traffic can be intimidating. Weather conditions are sometimes prohibitive, and cyclists may feel limited in how far they can travel by bicycle. Cyclists may also worry about finding places to store their bicycles and whether motorists will make room for them on the roadways. Public support of the mode is the single-most important factor in its future development as a viable option for a larger constituency. The Knoxville Regional Transportation Planning Organization (TPO) seeks to enhance the public support while addressing these concerns.

Solutions—Making a Way for Bicyclists

The Knoxville Regional TPO has developed regional bicycle plans since 1975. The 2002 Plan established the Knoxville Regional Bicycle Program with the express purpose of implementing the Bicycle Plan. The Bicycle Advisory Committee (BAC), which administers the Bicycle Program, seeks to integrate bicycling into the transportation system. To date, the BAC has:

- Produced bicycle maps for Knox and Blount Counties
- Reviewed road plans to standardize the inclusion of bicycle accommodation for new and widened roads
- Administered bicycle/pedestrian counts at approximately 12 intersections in Knoxville and Blount County, biannually
- Installed bicycle signs, shared lane markings, and added over 500 bicycle racks
- Collaborated with law enforcement to ensure that bicyclists are appropriately accounted for on the roadways
- Educated citizens through bicycling classes, the "I Bike" awareness campaign, a Bicycling Ambassadors Program, and presentations to drivers' education classes on sharing the road with bicyclists.

Results—Visibility and Revitalization of Bicycle Culture

TPO and BAC initiatives have increased the visibility of bicycling as a practical form of transportation (in addition to recreation). They have effectively used social networks such as Facebook where they currently have several hundred fans. They have also provided links to other bicycle promotion initiatives such as Bike Knoxville, a blog that shows the most recent Bicycle Program news and provides an opportunity for members of the community to comment. There have also been in-person events that provide the community with a more tangible sense of the benefits and importance of bicycling. The Bicycle Program coordinates several classes, including Traffic Skills, Confident City Cycling, Bike Commuting, and Bicycling with Kids. Also, special functions such as Bike to Work Day and Neighborhood Bike Ride are held annually with increasing participation each year. Public health gains are clear. In 2010, according to the American Lung Association, the Knoxville region was still one of the "25 most polluted counties" in the United States in terms of ozone and year-round particulate matter, but in 2012 the county no longer appears on the list and air quality continues to improve. The region now meets all national ambient air quality standards. TPO and BAC's efforts have been rewarded by the public response and external recognition. Most recently, the League of American Bicyclists honored them with a bronze level designation in the "Bicycle Friendly Community" Award. Knoxville ranked equally with Santa Monica, Tulsa, and New York City, among others. This support points to a potentially promising future for alternative modes of travel throughout the Nation.

Adapted from FHWA, Livability Initiative Case Studies

When a person decides to make cycling their preferred form of transport, there is more to be considered than the tangible pros and cons such as money, health and efficiency. Other factors include the outside perception, social welfare, and self-perception on variant forms of transport. Social identities take the forefront in choosing bicycling as a mode of commute. For instance, biking in the UK is partially associated with negative youth crimes and poor parenting skills (Aldred, 2013). A completely different identity is found in Melbourne, where a new consumerist cycling culture has emerged, which excludes lower and working class citizens (Harland, 2010). Contrary to these negative stigmas, in Bryggebroen, Netherlands, the average age of cyclists is associated with a higher level of education. As far as use, "70% ride their bikes at Bryggebroen to go to/from work and 8% to go to/from school" (Andrade *et al.*, 2011). Another survey, held in the United States, also affirms that there are characteristics that correlate with bike use, namely: age, which has a negative effect, and education with a positive effect on choosing bicycling as a mode of transportation (Handy *et al.*, 2010).

An in-depth study of the proportionately cycle-based area of Cambridge in England revealed that the practice of bicycling creates a social identity that has "privileged views" from outside the car. This creates the "cycling citizen" persona, which affects how one perceives one's self about the social and natural environment specifically at a street level (Aldred 2010). The attitude of this particular identity has played a vital role in the success of many of Europe's bike friendly cities. For instance, feeling the weather, unrestricted sight, and using a modest form of transport makes cycling pleasant and cozy (Nelson & Scholar 2008).

Those mentioned above are intrinsic factors that affect the motivation of a person to choose cycling as their mode of transportation. Also, social support (family, peers, and community) plays a very important role, as well as having a friend to bike with, and or share the experience of biking to work with, and having amenities at the work site are all positive incentives to ride. For instance, a friend will continue the growth of cycling culture by inviting others to share in the enjoyment of riding to work by loaning bikes, showing routes and teaching bicycle maintenance (Rodriguez 2011). Some of the work force, in businesses and schools, was found to encourage cycling as a form of transport for social and physical health reasons, with one project even going so far as to provide electric and traditional bikes for employees to visit clients (Aldred 2012).

In addition to the well-known and effective concept of "If you build it they will come," the use of pro-bicycle programs in tandem with infrastructure provisions, supportive land use planning, and restrictions on car use are paramount to a successful cycling society (Pucher, Dill, & Handy 2010). Thus, in order to increase the use of bicycles for everyday commuting and to create a cycling culture, it stands to reason that a positive influence on bicycling culture needs to be evaluated with the same importance as a well-planned physical infrastructure. Hence, the distribution of funds for social/cultural infrastructure and physical infrastructure requires careful deliberation (Aldred & Jungnickel 2014). Even in Amsterdam, a well-revered bicycling community; there is a challenge for the allocation of funds for the information and promotion of bicycling (Ligtermoet 2010).

Due to this variance in perception, it is important to analyze all the prospective solutions that integrate the social/cultural and physical aspects of cycling. Although "Critical Mass" rides seek to create an alternative presence (that cycling is for professionals and exercise), they do not necessarily promote cycling as a form of commute (Nelson & Scholar, 2008). Rather, they could dangerously promote riding as a form of leisure. However, as with the aspiration of Ciclovia in Bogotá Colombia or CicLAvia in Los Angeles (refer BOX 7.2), they do challenge the utilization of road space in general as they challenge dominant views about the purpose of street space being mainly for cars (Aldred & Jungnickel 2012). In other words, the idea of using roads for something other than motorized vehicles is realized. Moreover, the critical mass of bicyclists gives support to the theory that having fewer cars, thus more cyclists, means more motorists are aware of bicycles and watch out for them (Nelson & Scholar, 2008).

BOX 7.3 CicLAvia, Los Angeles and bike culture

Los Angeles (LA) has been famous for many decades as a place designed around personal automobiles. What is less known, is that cycling has increased by as much as 165 percent in parts of central Los Angeles between 2009 and 2011. Historically cycling in Los Angeles is commonly considered a recreational activity instead of used for practical everyday travel needs. So then what can be the cause of the exponential growth in cycling in the past few years? One theory is that the current cohort of youth, the "Millennial Generation," has had declining interest in automobiles due to cultural changes caused by the Internet, urbanization, and the economic recession. The growth of cycling in Los Angeles is also believed to be part of the overall demographic change. In fact, one of the largest catalysts for increased cycling is believed to be the car-free streets festival known as CicLAvia. Inspired by massively successful reoccurring car-free street events in Bogotá,

Colombia known as Ciclovias, cyclists living in LA and associated with the Los Angeles County Bicycle Coalition began planning an L.A. event known as CicLAvia in conjunction with the Los Angeles Department of Transportation (LADOT)'s bicycle master plan update. The CicLAvia event closes down stretches of LA streets (usually between 6 and 10 miles) to cars and opens them up to cyclists, pedestrians, and other forms of non-automobile use. The first CicLAvia event occurred in October 2010 and was believed by event organizers to have had around 30,000 participants. Its route was mainly limited to smaller streets such as New Hampshire Avenue and 6th Street. By 2013, a single CicLAvia event attracted 100,000 participants according to estimates by planners, and the number of events per year had grown to three. Streets as large as Wilshire Boulevard and Venice Boulevard were being closed to cars for use as event routes.

Planning for Non-Motorized Transportation

Most of the urban transportation planning focuses on cars and public transportations (such as buses and subways). Planning agencies in most Metropolitan Planning Organizations and local agencies have little understanding how accessibility would improve through non-motorized transportation. Accessibility includes the ability people have to access different activity sites with non-auto modes. As explained in the article *"Measuring non-motorized accessibility: issues, alternatives, and execution,"* broadening the scope of accessibility to include a wide array of destinations and non-motorized modes, such as walking and cycling, has created a much-needed goal among planning initiatives (Iaconoa, Krizekb and El-Geneid 2010). The creation of these non-motorized transportation plans is to help give people the choice, as well as seemingly trying to encourage them to use non-motorized transit to access activity sites in their area. Not only does this reduce the amount of cars on the road, but it is linked to creating a healthier community. Studies show that there is a missing link between non-motorized transit behavior and planners. "Lack of reliable data, computational power, or knowledge of non-motorized travel behavior have hampered modeling non-motorized transit for metropolitan areas." (Jones 2012). After a non-motorized transportation plan is implemented, the planners should carry out surveys to understand how well the plan is implemented. These should be done before the plan is completed, as well after the project is completed. They should seek to learn the traffic patterns on the routes to understanding how effective the plan is. This should help direct planners to see what the next step to improvement in their plan could be.

Some issues faced when planning for non-motorized transportation may include different traffic patterns during different weather. "Ideally, travel survey data need to be collected year round and cover all seasons. More commonly, data are collected over a period of several months and reflect weather conditions prevailing at the time the survey data were collected. This is especially important in the case of non-motorized modes and in locations where significant seasonal climate variations exist." (Iaconoa, Krizekb and El-Geneid 2010). For example, there is probably much more non-motorized movement during summer in a place like Colorado, because it is very cold and snowy during the winter. By studying things such as the frequency of trips being made, the distance traveled, and the time traveled, planners can see what is working, and what is not. These studies are important because they constitute the theoretical and empirical foundation upon which policy makers and planners can anticipate the effectiveness of their interventions and base future policy decisions (Rodriguez and Joo 2004).

Safety is also another issue to be addressed with planning for non-motorized transportation. According to NHTSA Traffic Safety Facts, in 2012, 4,743 pedestrians, and 726 bicyclists were killed in crashes with motor vehicles. One may ask: is walking more dangerous than other modes of travel? Pedestrians are over-represented in the crash data, accounting for 14 percent of all traffic fatalities but only 12 percent of trips. But the fact is that as with every mode of travel, there is clearly some risk associated with walking. However, walking remains a healthy, inherently safe activity for tens of millions of people every year. The public health community recognizes that the lack of physical activity, and a decline in bicycling and walking, in particular, is a major contributor to the hundreds of thousands of deaths caused by heart attacks and strokes.

Encouraging walking and biking for transportation decreases the use of motorized transportation, which in turn can reduce the amount of traffic accidents on the road. Of course, deaths can still occur to pedestrians and bike riders from vehicles, but if more people are choosing to use non-motorized transportation because of better planning, this means less driving and more walking and biking. Consequently, non-motorized transportation plans need to be made effective and functional which results in creating a safe environment. Non-motorized transportation infrastructure and facilities required to meet the community's health and social objectives (Ramorobi, McGuigan and Mouws (2011) and planning agencies need to follow standard design guidelines.

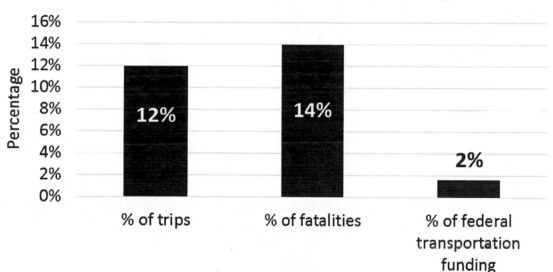

Figure 7.4 Level of bicycling and walking, bike/pedestrian fatalities and bike/pedestrian funding (data: Alliance for Biking and Walking 2010).

Successful Bicycling Practices

To increase bicycling and walking, it is crucial to learn from the successful policies and best practices implemented in other places, which have far higher levels of walking and bicy-

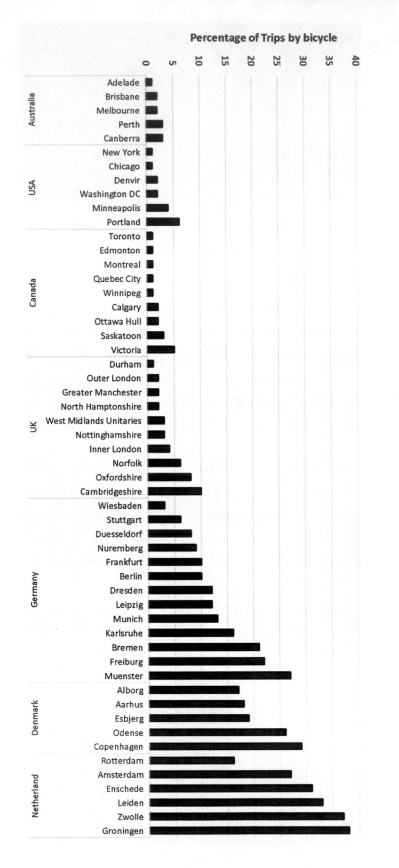

Figure 7.5 Bicycle share of trips in 55 cities in the U.S, U.K., Germany, Denmark and the Netherlands (data: Pucher and Buehler, 2008).

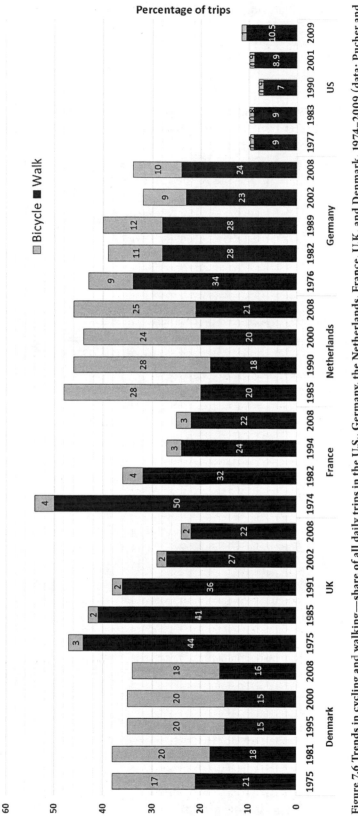

Figure 7.6 Trends in cycling and walking—share of all daily trips in the U.S., Germany, the Netherlands, France, U.K. and Denmark, 1974–2009 (data: Pucher and Buehler 2010).

cling as well as much better safety (Alliance for Bicycling and Walking 2012). There are many countries around the world that have taken to active and progressive transportation models, and it is important to take note and try to recreate these effective systems. Many European countries have been successful in limiting car usage through non-motorized transportation, and it shows in their lower transportation-related CO_2 emission levels.

A study by Pucher and Buehler (2010) found that walking and cycling accounted for only about 12 percent of all trips in the United States in 2009, which is similar to levels in Ireland and Canada, but only about a third as much walking and cycling as many European countries. Germany, Denmark, and the Netherlands set the standard for active travel with their bike mode shares up to 26 percent. These countries have roughly ten times as much cycling as the U.S. Similarly, the U.S. has only about half as much walking as most European countries. The variation among countries is confirmed by large differences among cities in active travel rates, with American cities lagging far behind European cities (Pucher and Buehler 2010).

In most large U.S. cities, the bicycle share of trips is less than 1 percent. Portland, Minneapolis, and Seattle have the highest bicycle to work share among cities: 5.5 percent, 4.1 percent, and 2.9 percent, respectively. By comparison, many cities in Germany, Denmark, and the Netherlands have bicycle trip shares over 10 percent. Examining bicycling and walking levels by trip distance shows that in the U.S., 38 percent of trips shorter than 1.6 miles (2.5km) were made by walking or cycling in 2009. For the same trip distance, the percent of short trips by walking or cycling was 63 percent in Germany, 70 percent in Denmark, and 54 percent in the Netherlands. The variation between the U.S. and other countries is greatest when looking at longer trip distances. Bicycling and walking account for only 3 percent of trips of 2.8 to 4 miles (4.5–6.5 km) in the U.S., compared to 16 percent in Germany, 21 percent in Denmark, and 27 percent in the Netherlands. Thus, at every trip distance, walking and cycling rates are much higher in Northern Europe than in the U.S. (Alliance for Bicycling and Walking 2012).

In fact, the geographic layout of these countries is more conducive to forms of active transportation. The transportation infrastructure in many European countries, as well as cities South America and Asia, is constructed around a bicycle culture. Bike lanes run along most streets to ensure safety and ease for the bike riders. It can be argued that the bike culture existed before the lanes were implemented.

In Austria, a study was done examining the reasons why individuals made the decision to either bike or take their car. This is very important in Europe, where 50 percent of all car trips are less than 5 kilometers (3.1 miles), making them very manageable bike rides (Titze, *et al.*, 2008). This study found that the safety and infrastructure of the active transportation systems had a large effect on the decision to bike or drive. A major issue hindering furthered active transportation is the danger and the difficulty that comes when trying to ride a bike simply instead of drive.

Another effective measure taken by many European countries is a bike sharing system. In the city of Paris, for instance, 10,000 bikes at 750 locations can be rented at a very low rate (Conlin 2007). Not everyone can afford a nice, comfortable bicycle and bike sharing systems give everyone the opportunity to travel free of cars and buses with the ease of bicycles while also avoiding costs such as parking. These systems are highly subsidized so that rates can remain extremely low, increasing accessibility. Bike sharing is starting to catch on in American cities, and yet the support isn't there to subsidize them at similar levels to Europe. Bike sharing as a business model is not profitable, and so it would need to cover by governmental subsidies, which is not easy to accomplish (DeMaio and Gifford 2004).

Europe is believed to be more progressive when it comes to drive-alternative modes, but it is not just the European countries that have attempted to cut down on their motorized transportation. The city of Bogotá in Colombia, for example, has implemented a wide-spread system of bike lanes. Unlike most other countries, the priority is given to the bikers as opposed to those driving on the streets. While such a system would be difficult to replicate in the U.S. due to the urban form and the culture, it shows the importance of building and planning for more effective active transportation.

In conclusion, as we understand from several studies, the safety and the basic infrastructure of an area can have a large impact on the decision to bike or walk. This proves the importance of effective planning for active transport. A strong correlation was found between the level of active transport and the effectiveness of the land use plan (Aytur, *et al.*, 2007). This essentially proves that when a better infrastructure for non-motorized transportation is provided people respond by being more active. In the United States, planning for active transportation can be effectively done. This is important because often when being compared to European nations, the differences in size and political environment allow people to dismiss the plausibility of such plans in the United States. As the experience of successful cities in the U.S. proves, through infrastructural improvement and community initiatives, active transportation can be effectively promoted.

Review Questions

1) Why are bicycling and walking the "forgotten modes" of transportation?
2) What are some of the benefits of bicycling and walking?
3) How do density, diversity, and design affect modal decisions?
4) What is the significance of the sidewalk in promoting walking for transport?
5) What legislative acts have marked a turning point for non-motorized transportation support?
6) What are some theories for recent increases in bicycling in Los Angeles?
7) What is the "Walk Score"? How does it function?
8) Why are European cities more conducive to non-motorized transportation?
9) What is the importance of the social/cultural infrastructure for creating or increasing motivations to bike?
10) Compare and contrast the walking/bicycling environments in the U.S. with that of Europe.

Project/Paper Ideas

Choose an activity site in your community (bus stops, parks, schools, etc.). Draw a buffer circle with a quarter of a mile radius, preferably using GIS software. Using a field observation or Google Earth, collect data on the availability and "quality" of all the sidewalks within the buffer. Quality can be defined as good, fair, bad based on the surface condition, width and availability of sidewalk amenities. What is the percentage of the good quality sidewalk out of the total street networks? Does it match with the Walk Score of the neighborhood? If not, why? Do this exercise for inner city neighborhood and suburban communities and compare the results

Videos

We Are Traffic! and **Return of the Scorcher** by Mill Valley, CA: Green Planet Films, 2005 (78 min.): These two classic bikeumentaries explore bicycle use and bicycle cultures in China, Europe, and the U.S. and show how bicycling is being taken up by many as a vital and powerful response to various environmental and social problems.

Internet Sources

- Alliance for Biking and Walking, http://www.bikewalkalliance.org/
- Rails-to-Trails Conservancy, http://www.railstotrails.org/
- Bikes Belong, http://www.peopleforbikes.org/
- Bicycle Dutch, https://bicycledutch.wordpress.com/

Bibliography

Aldred, Rachel. 2010. "'On the Outside': Constructing Cycling Citizenship." *Social & Cultural Geography*, 11(1), 35–52.

_____. 2012. *Cycling Cultures: Summary of Key Findings and Recommendations.* The University of East London: Economic & Social Research Council.

_____. 2013. "Incompetent, or Too Competent? Negotiating Everyday Cycling Identities in a Motor Dominated Society." *Mobilities*, 8(2), 252–271.

Aldred, Rachel, and Jungnickel, K. 2012. "Constructing Mobile Places Between 'Leisure' and 'Transport': A Case Study of Group Cycle Rides." *Sociology*, 46(3), 523–539.

_____, and _____. 2014. "Why Culture Matters for Transport Policy: The Case of Cycling in the UK." *Journal of Transport Geography*, 34 78–87.

Alliance for Bicycling and Walking. 2012. "Bicycling and Walking in the United States 2012 Benchmarking Report." ABW.

Andrade, V., Jensen, O. B., Harder, H., & Madsen, J. C. O. 2011. "Bike Infrastructures and Design Qualities: Enhancing Cycling." *Danish Journal of Geoinformatics and Land Management*, 46(0105–4570), 65–80.

Aultman-Hall, Lisa, Matthew Roorda, and Brian Baetz. 1997. "Using GIS for Evaluation of Neighborhood Pedestrian Accessibility." *Journal of Urban Planning & Development* 123 (1): 10–17.

Aytur, Semra, Daniel Rodriguiez, Kelly Evenson, Dianne Catellier, and Wayne Rosamond. 2007. "Promoting Active Community Environments Through Land Use and Transportation Planning." *The Science of Health Promotion* 21 (4): 397–407.

Baxandall, P., & Dutzik, T. 2013. *A New Direction: Our Changing Relationship with Driving and the Implications for America's Future.* U.S. PIRG Education Fund Frontier Group.

Betts, Kellyn. 2012. "Big Biking Payoff: Alternative Transportation Could Net Midwest Over $8 Billion." *Environmental Health Perspectives* 120 (1:a34).

Bors, Philip, Mark Dessauer, Rich Bell, Risa Wilkerson, Joanne Lee, and Sarah & Strunk. 2009. "The Active Living by Design National Program: Community Initiative and Lessons Learned." *American Journal of Preventive Medicine* 37 (6): 312–321.

CDC. 2005. *Barriers to Children Walking and Bicycling to School.* Morbidity and Mortality Weekly Report (MMWR). U.S. Centers for Disease Control & Prevention, 949–952.

Cervero, Robert. 2002. "Built Environments and Mode Choice: Toward a Normative Framework." *Transportation Research Part D: Transport and Environment* 7(4): 265–284.

_____, and Kara Kockelman. 1997. "Travel Demand and the 3Ds: Density, Diversity, and Design." *Transportation. Research Part D* 2 (3): 199–219.

Chin, Gary, Kimberly Van Niel, Billie Giles-Corti, and Mathew Knuiman. 2008. "Accessibility and Connectivity in Physical Activity Studies: The Impact of Missing Pedestrian Data." *Preventive Medicine* 45: 41–45.

Conlin, Jennifer. 2007. "Paris Joins 2-Wheel Trend in Europe." *New York Times*, July 8: 2.

Cortright, Joe. 2009. "Walking the Walk." CEOs for Cities. http://www.ceosforcities.org/.

Dannenberg, Andrew, Richard Jackson, Howard Frumkin, Richard Schieber, Michael Pratt, Chris Kochtitzky, and Hugh Tilson. 2003. "The Impact of Community Design and Land-Use Choices on Public Health." *American Journal of Public Health* 93 (9): 1500–1508.

_____, Howard Frumkin, and Richard Jackson. 2011. *Making Healthy Places, Designing and Building for Health, Well-Being and Sustainability*, Washington, D.C.: Island Press.

DeMaio, Pual, and Jonathan Gifford. 2004. "Will Smart Bikes Succeed as Public Transportation in the United States?" *Journal of Public Transportation* 7: 1–16.

Ehrenfeucht, Renia, and Anastasia Loukaitou-Sideris. 2010. "Planning Urban Sidewalks: Infrastructure, Daily Life and Destinations." *Journal of Urban Design* 15 (4): 459–471.

Evans-Cowley, Jennifer. 2006. "Sidewalk Planning and Policies in Small Cities." *Journal of Urban Planning and Development* 132 (2): 71–75.

FHWA. 2003. *Journey to Work Trends in the United States and Its Major Metropolitan Areas, 1960–2000.* FHWA-EP-03–058, FHWA.

Forsyth, Ann, and Kevin Krizek. 2010. "Promoting Walking and Bicycling: Assessing the Evidence to Assist Planners." *Built Environment* 36 (4): 429–446.

Giuliano, Genevieve, and Dhiraj Narayan. 2003. "Another Look at Travel Patterns and Urban Form: The U.S. and Great Britain." *Urban Studies* 11 (40): 2295—2312.

Goudie, Douglas. 2002. "Zonal Method for Urban Travel Surveys: Sustainability and Sample Distance from The CBD." *Journal of Transport Geography* 10 (4): 287–301.

Gray, Jennifer, Jennifer Zimmerman, and James Rimmer. 2012. "Built Environment Instruments for Walkability, Bike-ability, and Recreation: Disability and Universal Design Relevant?" *Disability and health* 5 (2): 87–101.

Handy, S. L., Yan Xing, & Buehler T. J. 2010. "Factors Associated with Bicycle Ownership and Use: a Study of Six Small U.S. Cities." *Transportation,* 37(6), 967–985.

Harland, J. 2010. Cycling Cultures and the Mismeasurement of Cycling. Melbourne.

Hill, James, Holly Wyatt, George Reed, and John Peters. 2003. "Obesity and the Environment: Where Do We Go from Here? " *Science* 299: 853–855.

Houston, Douglas, Victoria Basolo, and Dongwoo Yang. 2013. "Walkability, Transit Access, and Traffic Exposure for Low-Income Residents with Subsidized Housing." *American Journal of Public Health* 103 (4): 673–678.

Iaconoa, Michael, Kevin Krizekb, and Ahmed El-Geneid. 2010. "Measuring Non-Motorized Accessibility: Issues, Alternatives, and Execution." *Journal of Transport Geography* 18 (1): 133–140.

Johansson, Maria, Anders Raustorp, Fredrika Mårtensson, Cecilia Boldemann, Catarina Sternudd, and Maria Kyhlin. 2011. "Attitudinal Antecedents of Children´s Sustainable Every Day Mobility." *Transport and Health Issues* 3: 55–68.

Jones, Mark. 2012. *The Creation Of A Model to Estimate the Change in Non-Motorized Transportation Use After a Land Use Change.* Michigan State University, ProQuest Dissertations, and Theses.

Ligtermoet D. 2010. *The Bicycle Capitals of the World: Amsterdam and Copenhagen.* The Netherlands: Fietsberaad. Publication 7a.

Lugo, A. E. 2013. "CicLAvia and Human Infrastructure in Los Angeles: Ethnographic Experiments in Equitable Bike Planning." *Journal of Transport Geography,* 30, 202–207.

McCormack, Gavin, Alan Shiell, Billie Giles-Corti, Stephan Begg, Lennert Veerman, Elizabeth Geelhoed, Anura Amarasinghe, and J.C. Herb Emery. 2012. "The Association between Sidewalk Length and Walking for Different Purposes in Established Neighborhoods." *International Journal of Behavior Nutrition and Physical Activity* 9 (92).

Nelson, A., & Scholar, V. 2008. *Livable Copenhagen: The Design of a Bicycle City.* Copenhagen: Center for Public Space Research. University of Washington, Seattle.

NHTS. 2001. *Data from the 2001 National Household Travel Survey,* Federal Highway Administration, U.S. Department of Transportation.

Owen, Neville, Ester Cerin, Eva Leslie, Lorinne duToit, Neil Coffee, Lawrence Frank, Arian Bauman, Graeme Hugo, Brian Saelans, and James Sallis. 2007. "Neighborhood Walkability and the Walking Behavior of Australian Adults." *American Journal of Preventive Medicine* 33 (5): 387–395.

Pelzer, P. 2010. *Bicycling as a Way of Life: a Comparative Case Study of Bicycle Culture in Portland, OR, and Amsterdam.* Amsterdam: University of Amsterdam.

Pucher, John, Charles Komanoff, and Paul Shimek. 1999. "Bicycling Renaissance in North America?" *The Sustainable Urban Development Reader* 17 (2): 130–136.

_____, Dill, J., & Handy, S. 2010. "Infrastructure, Programs, and Policies to Increase Bicycling: An International Review." Elsevier: *Preventive Medicine,* 50, S106-S125.

_____, and Ralph Buehler. 2010. "Walking and Cycling for Healthy Cities." *Built Environment* 36 (4): 391–414.

Ramorobi, Tsepa, Derek McGuigan, and Jacqueline Mouws. 2011. "Prioritization of Non-Motorized Transport Projects." *Civil Engineering: Magazine of the South African Institution of Civil Engineering* 19 (8): 60–64.

Rodriguez, C. 2011. *A Case Study of American Bicycle Culture: How Cycling to Work Works in a Small Town in Kansas.* Kansas: University of Kansas.

Rodriguez, Daniel, and Joonwoon Joo. 2004. "The Relationship between Non-Motorized Mode Choice and The Local Physical Environment." *Transportation and Research part D* 9 (1): 151–173.

Saelens, Brian, James Sallis, and Lawrence Frank. 2003. "Environmental Correlates of Walking and Cycling: Findings from The Transportation, Urban Design, and Planning Literatures." *Annals of Behavioral Medicine* 25 (2): 80–91.

Schmitz, Adrienne, and Jason Scully. 2006. *Creating Walkable Places.* Washington, D.C.: ULI the Urban Land Institute.

SLOCOG. 2013. *2013 Bicycle Use Survey Results*. San Luis Obispo: San Luis Obispo Council of Governments.

Smith, P., Wilson, M., & Armstrong, T. 2011. *I'll Just Take the Car: Improving Bicycle Transportation to Encourage Its Use on Short Trips*. New Zealand: NZ Transport Agency.

Suminski, Richard, Katie Heinrich, Walker Poston, Melissa Hyder, and Sara Pyle. 2007. "Characteristics of Urban Sidewalks/Streets and Objectively Measured Physical Activity." *Urban Health* 85: 178–190.

Titze, Sylvia, Willibald Stronegger, Susanne Janschitz, and Pekka Oja. 2008. "Association of Built-Environment, Social-Environment and Personal Factors with Bicycling As a Mode of Transportation Among Austrian City Dwellers." *Preventive Medicine* 47 (3): 252–259.

Troped, Philip, Ruth Saunders, Russell Pate, Belinda Reininger, and Cheryl Addy. 2003. "Correlates of Recreational and Transportation Physical Activity Among Adults in New England Community." *Preventive Medicine* 37 (4): 304–310.

UTSBRP. 2011. *Update of Tennessee's State Bicycle Route Plan*. Tennessee: Tennessee Department of Transportation.

USDOT. 2010. "The National Bicycling and Walking Study: 15-Year Status Report." Federal Highway Administration, U.S. Department of Transportation.

USDOT. 1972. "Transportation Characteristics of School Children. Nationwide Personal Transportation Study." Federal Highway Administration, U.S. Department of Transportation, Washington, D.C.

Wilbur Smith Associates. 2005. *Chicago Bicycle Users Survey Report*. Chicago: Department of Transportation.

Witten, Karen, Tony Blakely, Nasser Bagheri, Hannah Badland, Vivienne Ivory, Jamie Pearce, Suzanne Mavoa, Erica Hinckson, and Grant Schofield. 2012. "Neighborhood Built Environment, Transport and Leisure Physical Activity: Findings Using Objective Exposure and Outcome Measure in New Zealand." *Environmental Health Perspectives* 120 (7): 971–977.

Zelinka, Al, and Dean Brennan. 2001. "SafeScape." *Planners Press*. Chicago.

8

Planning for Public Transportation

Chapter Outline

- Introduction
- Public Transportation in American Cities
- Health and Quality of Life Benefits
- Environmental Benefits
- Economic Benefit
- Transit-Oriented Developments
- Why Public Transit Is Not Popular in the United States
- Planning for Public Transportation
  - o *Assessing Quality Attributes of Bus Stops*

Introduction

Public transportation is defined as a shared passenger transport service that is available for use by the general public. Public transport has many variations, such as buses, trains, fairies, planes and gondolas. Buses are arguably the common form of public transportation, and they use different energy sources including diesel, electric, and natural gas, and come in many forms, shapes and sizes. Buses run in many cities throughout the world, are relatively frequent in service times and availability and are more easily incorporated into an area's planning. Another form of public transportation is known as the light rail, referring to the older types of tramways and the newer types of the subway system. Many times, one may only think of this kind of public transportation in big cities such as New York City, but this form is seemingly becoming more attainable in cities across the U.S. Light rail transit systems differ from the buses because they can usually hold a higher capacity, have much more frequent services, travel at faster speeds and often carry passengers who are traveling a relatively longer distance. As part of the public transportation system, there are a few types of demand responsive transit services such as dial-a-ride or care cab's that are meant for the assistance in transportation for the elderly and disabled population. Litman (2014) classified different modes of public transportation as follows:

- Heavy rail—relatively large, higher-speed trains, operating entirely on separate rights-of-way, with infrequent stops, providing service between communities.
- Light Rail Transit (LRT)—moderate size, medium-speed trains, operating mainly on separate rights-of-way, with variable distances between stations, providing service between urban neighborhoods and commercial centers.
- Streetcars (also called trams or trolleys)—relatively small, lower-speed trains, operating primarily on urban streets, with frequent stops that provide service along major urban corridors.
- Conventional bus transit—full-size buses on fixed routes and schedules.
- Bus Rapid Transit (BRT)—premium quality bus service with features that typically include grade separation, frequent service, attractive stations, quick-loading, and attractive vehicles.
- Express commuter bus—direct bus service from residential to employment areas.
- Ferry services—public transport that uses water bodies such as canals and rivers or oceans.
- Minibus—smaller buses or large vans used for public transit.
- Demand Response Paratransit—small buses or vans that provide direct (door-to-door) service, often intended primarily for people with disabilities.
- Personal Rapid Transit (PRT)—small, automated vehicles that provide transit service on demand.
- Shared Taxi—common in cities of the developing countries, shared taxis are smaller than buses and bigger that taxicabs, usually take passengers on a fixed or semi-fixed route without timetables, but instead commonly departing when all seats are filled.

Although public transit provides a relatively small portion of total travel, especially in the United States, it provides a much larger part of certain types of travel. It is considered a practical solution to transport problems such as congestion and pollution by supporting a variety of community development objectives. It is most suitable for medium-distance trips in urban areas or on any corridor with adequate demand, and as an alternative mode for travelers who for any reason cannot use a private automobile.

Public Transportation in American Cities

Until the turn of the 20th century, rail and horseback riding were the major forms of public transportation in American cities. According to an article "The Decline of the Urban Horse in American Cities" by McShane and Tarr (2003), horseback riding was the predominant form of local transportation in the late nineteenth century. Large nineteenth-century cities in the United States averaged roughly one horse for every nineteen people, although the ratio of humans to horses varied widely. Horses then decreased as streetcars and automobiles took over the streets. Many cities had trolleys and street cars including Los Angeles Pacific Electric System, San Diego Electric, Atlantic Avenue Railroad in Brooklyn, along with several other systems. According to the Muller (2004), in the 1950s, the automobile became popular, and the construction of the interstate highway system started. This caused a rapid decrease in ridership in the trolley systems, causing these systems to go out of business.

To fully understand the public transportation in American cities, we must analyze four aspects that shaped the evolution of the public transportation. First, electric streetcars, once the universal symbol of urban public transit, were replaced by motor buses in all but a few large cities. Second, urban public transit ridership experienced a harsh decline, interrupted by World War II. The decline was most noticeable earlier in smaller cities and eventually spread to larger cities, a pattern that matches the pattern of substitution of motor buses for electric streetcars. Third, private transit firms found it increasingly difficult to survive, especially after the mid–1950s. This steered the creation of subsidized, publicly owned transit districts which, in numerous cities and towns, could provide only minimal service. Fourth, the automobile replaced public transit as the dominant mode of urban transportation. Urban America took the approach of rural America by relying on the automobile for meeting most of its transportation needs (Clair 1981).

The development of the automobile is the most responsible for the public transit decline. The inability of urban public transit to compete with the automobile is most often mentioned as one of the crucial factors for the slow public transit development in the United States. The freedom and privacy the automobile offers to individuals explains the traditional argument that as automobile ownership grew, the public abandoned urban public transit. This caused the weakening in transit ridership, which resulted in the cut of revenues and profits of transit companies. Confronted with massive declining revenues and profits, urban transit companies pursued to reduce their costs and their investment by cutting service, and more importantly replacing electric streetcars with less expensive, more efficient, and more profitable motor buses.

Consequently, the shift from electric streetcars to motorized buses was credited to the superior operating economy of the motor bus and its supposed lower capital costs. Lower capital costs resulted because the motor buses did not require expensive electric overhead cables or tracks. Nonetheless, this shift to a superior technology was able only to delay temporarily the inevitable decline of urban public transit that ultimately was attributed to the increasing popularity of and preference for the automobile. By the 1950s, regardless of the massive replacement of streetcars by motor buses, urban public transit companies increasingly faced bankruptcy and most transit systems could survive only through the creation of public transit districts providing subsidized transit operations (Clair 1981). On top of that, many communities have automobile-oriented land use patterns that made access to public transportation difficult (Litman 2012).

In the second half of the 20th century, the U.S. Congress and several states have mandated a more systematic and comprehensive approach to public transportation planning and operations than in previous decades. Among such laws at the federal level are the Intermodal Surface Transportation Efficiency Act 1991 (ISTEA), the Clean Air Act Amendments of 1990 (CAAAs), the American with Disabilities Act of 1990 (ADA) and the Transportation Equity Act for the 21st Century of 1998 (TEA-21). In the State of Washington, for example, relevant laws include the Growth Management Act (GMA) of 1990 and revisions to that act passed in 1991, 1995 and 2001. These recent federal and state laws are the result of many experts and citizens that have advocated for diversifying the transport systems. To accomplish this, many cities have been investing in public transportation development and transit improvements, including rail transit system expansion. There is considerable debate over the merits of these investments. Critics argue that they are inappropriate and wasteful, but, on the other hand, the benefits are being noticed in several communities (Litman 2012). One example is the public transportation investment called Measure R of Los Angeles County. Measure R was a 30-year county-wide half-cent sales tax narrowly approved by LA voters in 2008. Measure R funding has been key to Metro's rail expansion, including the Gold Line Foothill Extension, Expo Line Phase 2, Crenshaw-LAX Light Rail, the Regional Connector, and the Purple Line Extension. Evidence are emerging showing that there is a significant increase in ridership in Los Angeles due to these expansions.

It is worth mentioning that public transportation is flourishing in cities such as New York, San Francisco, Boston and Washington, D.C., which are investing in the development of their public transit systems. These cities have developed their public transportation system to a level where they can accommodate the travel demands of their residents and alleviate problems such as congestion, pollution and social equity.

One interesting recent observation in public transit use in the United States is the positive perception and choice of the Millennial Generation, which contribute for the comeback of public transportation. The Millennial Generation is the largest and most diverse generation in American history. The key findings of a survey research by Sakaria and Stehfest (2013) for American Public Transport Association highlighted that:

- Millennials are multimodal, they choose the *best* transportation mode (driving, transit, bike, or walk) based on the trip they are planning to take.
- Communities that attract Millennials have a multitude of transportation choices, as proven by millennial hotspots, popular zip codes where residents have self-selected into a multimodal lifestyle.
- Public transportation options are considered the best for digital socializing and among the most likely to connect the user with their communities. Transit also allows Millennials to work as they travel; a trend noted by 40 percent of those surveyed in the study. These benefits of public transit need to be fully leveraged by the transit industry, as they provide a clear competitive advantage.
- Reasons and motivations for transportation choices are pragmatic, with 46 percent stating that a need to save money drives their choices; 46 percent note convenience, 44 percent want exercise, and 35 percent say they live in a community where it just makes more sense to use transit.
- Millennials would like to see in the next ten years: more reliable systems, real time updates, smartphone fare payment, Wi-Fi or 3G/4G wherever they go, a more user-friendly and intuitive travel experience. This will allow transit users to be more spontaneous, thus addressing the key competitive advantage of the car.

Health and Quality of Life Benefits

A well-developed transit system is a crucial element of creating healthier communities. Public transit motivates riders to walk and ride a bike as a portion of their daily routine. It helps reduce crash rates, improves air quality and at the same time improves accessibility for those who don't have cars. Using public transportation offers the opportunity to walk, which has immeasurable health benefits (as discussed in the previous chapters). If users of public transportation walk about 20 minutes to access the public transit, they build in extra activity into their daily activities. A study by Leyden, Goldberg and Michelbach (2011) found that there are aspects of the city that people do care about such as access to the arts and entertainment, and surprisingly, a *good public transportation* system and the aesthetics of the city are considered to be important elements of happiness.

The most significant benefit that public transportation can provide is the reduction of smog, noise, and stress in the congested streets of cities. Likewise, public transportation can reduce isolation for people that cannot afford to buy a car. Public transportation offers mobility and freedom for people from every socioeconomic background, especially for elders and persons with disability. A study done by Samimi and Mohammadian (2010), regarding health impacts of urban development and transportation, showed that increasing the transit use and decreasing the automobile use have a significant positive impact on almost all the health variables. It was found that every percent decrease in automobile use would reduce the chance of obesity by 0.4 percent, high blood pressure by 0.3 percent, high blood cholesterol by 1.3 percent, and heart attack by 1 percent. The study also notes that the difference is that people using transit still need to walk some distance while entering or exiting transit compared to those who drive vehicle and park as close as possible to their destination. Also, most food providing stores have a drive-through, so there is no need to leave the vehicle, which is believed to be one of the main reasons for obesity.

Another quality of life benefit of public transportation is safety. Todd Litman (2014), in his piece "Safer Than You Think" asserts public transportation is a safer mode of transportation than driving. Public transportation is overall a relatively safe (low crash risk) and secure (low crime risk) mode of transport, Litman argues. Transit travel has about a tenth the traffic casualty (death or injury) rate as automobile travel, and residents of transit-oriented communities have about a fifth the per capita crash casualty rate as in automobile-oriented communities. Transit also tends to have lower overall crime rates, and many transit service improvements can further increase security by improving surveillance and economic opportunities for at-risk populations.

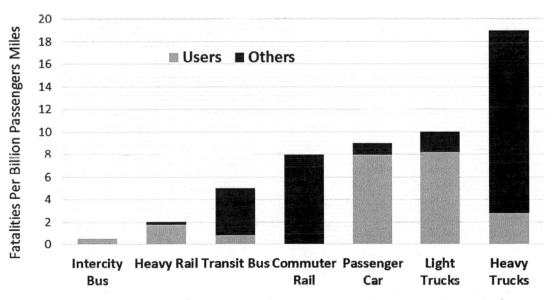

Figure 8.1 Transport fatalities (data: Litman and Fitzroy 2012, based on FHWA and APTA data).

Despite its relative safety and security, many people consider public transit dangerous, and so are reluctant to use it or support service expansions in their communities. Various factors contribute to this excessive fear, including the nature of public transit travel, heavy media coverage of transit-related crimes, and conventional traffic safety messages that emphasize danger rather than safety. Transit agencies can help create a new safety narrative by better measuring and communicating transit's overall safety and security impacts, and providing better guidance on how users and communities can enhance transit safety and security.

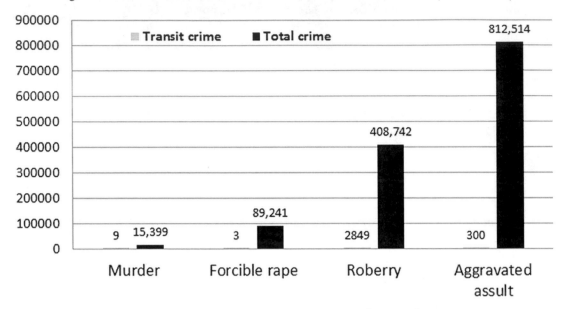

Figure 8.2 Transit vs national crime, 2009 (data: FBI).

Also, providing safe, suitable and convenient sidewalks, pedestrian crossings and transit stops is crucial to ensuring riders have a positive attitude towards public transportation, enhancing their experience and motivating them to continue using it. In communities where transit is intended to make the most out of the pedestrian experience, drivers move at slower traffic speeds, which reducing crash rates. Additionally, residents of transit-oriented communities often drive significantly less and rely more on walking, biking, and public transportation compare to residents of other neighborhoods that are mainly built to accommodate private vehicles.

Environmental Benefits

Public transportation produces 95 percent less carbon monoxide (CO), 90 percent less in volatile organic compounds (VOCs), and about half as much carbon dioxide (CO_2) and nitrogen oxide (NOx) per passenger mile, as private vehicles (APTA 2007). Air pollution is a severe problem in major urban areas due to increasing numbers of personal vehicles while few investments are made to improve public transportation. Given that the transportation sector is responsible for 28 percent of gross greenhouse gas emissions in the U.S., it will be important to identify cost-effective mitigation strategies, and encouraging the use of public transportation.

According to American Public Transportation Association (2012), one person switching to public transit can reduce daily carbon emissions by 20 pounds or more than 4,800 pounds in a year (APTA 2012). Furthermore, "a single commuter switching his or her commute to public transportation can reduce a household's carbon emissions by 10%, or up to 30% if he or she eliminates a second car. When compared to other household actions that limit CO_2, taking public transportation can be ten times greater in reducing this harmful greenhouse gas" (APTA 2012).

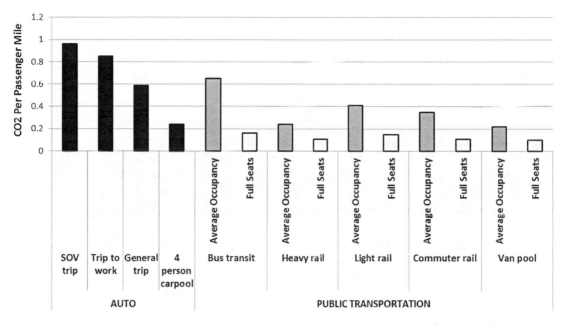

Figure 8.3 Estimated CO_2 emissions per passenger mile for different modes (EPA, 2002).

Economic Benefit

Public transportation saves money. The average household spends 18 cents of every dollar on transportation, and 94 percent of this goes to owning, preserving, and operating the vehicle, the second largest expenditure after housing. Households that are most likely to use public transportation daily may save about $10,000 every year (APTA 2012). These are just the benefits of saved money on fuel. Household transportation costs rise in areas with urban sprawl and few transportation options available. Communities living in areas served by public transportation save $18 billion annually in congestion costs. Also, transit availability can reduce the need for an additional car, a yearly expense of $6,251 in a household budget. Similar sources show that public transportation's overall effects save the United States 4.2 billion gallons of gasoline annually. That is more than three times the amount of gasoline imported from Kuwait. Similarly, households near public transit drive an average of 4,400 fewer miles than households with no access to public transit. This associates to an individual household gasoline reduction of 223 gallons per year.

It is estimated that every $10 million in capital investment in public transportation yields

$30 million in increased business sales, and that every $10 million in operating investment in public transportation yields additional $32 million in increased business sales. Businesses located near public transportation experience more employee reliability, and less absenteeism and turnover. Public transportation's role in reducing traffic congestion is significant. Without public transportation, travel delays in 2003 would have increased by 27 percent. Public transportation services in America's most congested cities saved travelers 1.1 billion hours of added travel time (APTA, 2007).

Transit-Oriented Developments

A Transit Oriented Development (TOD) is "a moderate to higher density development, located within an easy walk of a major transit stop, generally with a mix of residential, employment, and shopping opportunities designed for pedestrians without excluding the automobile. TOD can be new construction or redevelopment of one or more buildings whose design and orientation facilitate transit use." (Parker, et al., 2002). Although TODs have this basic definition, it is understood differently by scholars and planners that attempt to analyze them. Anastasia Loukaitou-Sideris (2010) defines a TOD as a project that runs adjacent to rail lines with an addition of mixed use projects. There is a checklist the author developed in order to rate how well a TOD functions. The article states that in order for a TOD to be rated successful, it must accommodate an increasing population without expanding its city limits. Den Belzer and Gerald Autler (2002) define TODs as a transit systems that are physically and functionally connected with its surrounding areas. They identify a TOD as a way to improve connectivity between homes and the workplace or other facilities. The article explains the importance of transitioning to transit-oriented developments as people move away from older sprawled developments. In order to rate the performance of a TOD, the authors take into account community members' income level, means of travel, and the characteristics of new developments along a selected corridor. They also found out that traffic levels, health and safety of the community and adequate connectivity are some of the ways used to rate a TOD.

Roberto Cervero and Jennifer Day (2008) identify TODs as cities served by rail systems in a sustainable manner. For the purpose of their research, the authors analyzed Shanghai, China, as it closely matched the description of what they consider a TOD. Twenty housing projects were selected as a sampling base in the area. Household members of the housing project twelve years of age and older were asked to complete a self-reported survey on travel behavior and household attributes. In addition, descriptive statistics was used to present the findings from the survey. Travel time, changes in the mode of transportation of choice, changes in job accessibility and what mode of transportation participants had opted for are identified as characteristics of TOD. John L. Renne (2009) identifies a TOD as an area within a ten-mile walk or a half-mile radius from a public transportation station. However, the distinction between transit-adjacent developments (TAD) and transit-oriented developments (TOD) is made by the author. The author analyzed the physical built environment to better understand the land use and design characteristics that lead to higher transit use, walking and bicycling and developed a checklist of what characteristic that would make an area be defined as a TAD instead of a TOD. A transit adjacent development is an area with a transit service but identified by the following characteristics: suburban street patterns; low densities; surface parking; limited pedestrian and bicycle accessibility; single family homes; industrial, segregated and auto-focused land use. On the other hand, TODs are comprised of housing, office, neighborhood retail, and civic uses, carefully designed to be pedestrian-friendly, human-scale communities where residents can live, work, and shop (Campbell 2002). Campbell (2002) and Lund *et al.* (2004) suggest that the most important aspects of a quality TOD site are transit ridership, quality of streetscape, density, quantity of mixed use structures, pedestrian safety and activity, increase in property value and tax revenue, parking, number of transit connections and positive public perception.

In whatever way it is understood, it is essential to recognize the vital components of a Transit Oriented Development (the four D's):

- Distance—shopping, medical services, recreational areas, and other services must all be within walking distance from the transit stations (no more than a mile) to promote walkability and biking.
- Density—this refers to reasonably high housing units or population per square miles.
- Diversity –this signifies a diversity of activities where people can have access to recreational areas, shopping, and other uses.
- Design –TOD connects transit, housing and retail centers with good walking and biking routes in a safe and pleasing environment.

Transit-oriented development was originally built with the idea of combating growing urban sprawl due to the rise of the automobile and "freeway suburbs." A TOD neighborhood typically has a center with a transit station or stop (train station, metro station, tram stop, or bus stop), surrounded by relatively high-density development with progressively lower-density development spreading outward from the center (Casey 2005).

Prior to the arrival of the automobile in the United States, most real estate development was arguably transit-oriented. "New Transit Town" characterizes transit-related development in the early twentieth century as "Transit Oriented Development." Electric streetcar systems evolved after the development of the electric traction motor in the 1890s. Unlike the horse-drawn streetcars, these new electric streetcars were faster and had extended lines. Real estate developers took advantage of this and built housing around these streetcar transit hubs. "Transit Oriented Development" occurred on the edges of most major U.S. cities of the time, which encouraged growth. Early examples of railroad and streetcar neighborhoods were characterized by small sized towns with small homes and distinctive street patterns with a focus on civic spaces for a sense of community. Transit oriented villages with these design principles include Backbay in Boston, Riverside in Chicago, and Roland Park in Baltimore. These neighborhoods also help preserve the natural environment. Not only were they walkable, but they appealed to many people due to their safety and aesthetic qualities.

CHALLENGES OF TODs

Sufficient funding, planning expertise and increasing success in all stages of TOD development serve to maximize the understanding necessary to create fully realized TODs (Center for State Innovation, 2008). The major barriers to implementing TODs include: transit system design, local community concerns, local zoning not being transit-friendly, higher developer risk and cost and finances difficult to obtain (Parker, *et al.*, 2002). The design of transit systems can be a major barrier to successful TODs. Stations often have poor pedestrian access, and broad expanses of surface-level parking lots often separate the stations for the surrounding community. Some stations and transit corridors are located in areas with little to no development potential, reducing transit's ability to link activity centers. Also, the proposals for TOD projects are met with concerns about changing the character of a community. Even with the quality design and appropriate density, and despite local government support for TODs, the community concerns about density and traffic can be huge hurdles to implementation. Besides, in many areas, local zoning has not been changed to reflect the presence of transit. Local development codes around stations tend to favor low-density, auto-oriented uses; creating and implementing transit-friendly zoning becomes an additional challenge. Another challenge is that mixed use, higher density projects with reduced amounts of parking can increase risks for developers and financiers with public financing available for implementing TODs is limited and difficult to obtain. TODs can be more costly, and subject to added regulations and more complex local approval processes when it compares to auto-oriented development. Lenders typically have concerns about financing mixed-use projects or those with lower parking ratios.

BOX 8.1 Measuring the benefits of TOD—the case of San Francisco Bay area

Using data gathered from over 15,000 households, the Metropolitan Transportation Commission conducted an in-depth analysis of the travel behaviors of Bay Area residents who live near rail and ferry stops in the region. The results, contained in Characteristics of Rail and Ferry Station Area Residents in the San Francisco Bay Area: Evidence from the 2000 Bay Area Travel Survey, published in September 2006, clearly indicate that those living (and working) close to rail and ferry transit stops use transit, walk and bike much more than people living farther from these facilities. The study does recognize that "self-selection," or the tendency for individuals with a high propensity for using transit to live in TODs, may also be a factor in these travel behaviors. Still, the study concludes that: "Whether being near rail/ferry transit simply allows people who prefer to drive less that personal choice, or whether it creates a greater interest in such travel options, this research demonstrates that policies to support transit-oriented development hold promise as one important tool, among others, in addressing congestion, transit usage, non-motorized travel, and air pollution in the Bay Area." Here are some spotlights of the study's key findings, which provide a kind of rough gauge to measure the potential benefits of individual TOD projects.

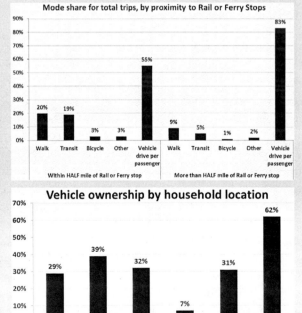

Proximity Matters

Bay Area residents who live within a half-mile of rail or ferry stops are four times as likely to use transit, three times as likely to bike, and twice as likely to walk as are those who live at greater distances.

Transit Favored for Commute

People who both live and work close to transit use it extensively to travel to their jobs. Individuals living and working within a half-mile of rail stations and ferry terminals use transit for 42 percent of their work commute trips, while people who neither live nor work within a half-mile of such facilities use transit for only 4 percent of their work commute trips.

Fewer Cars Owned

Almost 30 percent of households within a half-mile of rail or ferry stations do not have a car—they are "zero vehicle households." This means that fewer parking spaces are needed in these areas, allowing more land to be used for housing, parks, amenities and local-serving retail.

Less Driving

People living close to transit log fewer miles in the cars they do own—these households produce about half of the vehicle miles of travel of their suburban and rural counterparts. This dramatically reduces the level of air pollutants and congestion per household.

More Walking and Biking

People living close to transit also walk and bike for far more of their trips. Those who live within a half-mile of rail and ferry stops walk or bike for 16 percent of their work trips and 25 percent of their non-work trips, adding a vibrant presence on local streets and supporting a healthy lifestyle. This compares with 4 percent and 12 percent walk/bike rates for people farther from transit for work and non-work trips, respectively.

Adapted from New Places, New Choices: Transit-Oriented Development in the San Francisco Bay Area, Nov. 2006.

Why Public Transit Is Not Popular in the United States

Although there is an increase in recent years, American public transportation networks lag behind in terms of ridership. Is it because the notion that "public" is a collectivist ideology, as many conservatives argue, or the service is too bad in some cities so the public doesn't want to use it? The general explanation may go further than this. The cultural perception of public transport creates innate biases in transport decision making. This can be illustrated by what the Prime Minister of England Margaret Thatcher said in 1986: "A man who, beyond the age of 26, finds himself on a bus can count himself as a failure" (Milne 2012). Such cultural notions contribute to a reason for people using transit less (Lloyd 1981; Lee 2010).

Cultural attitude aside, there are several reasons for public transit's unpopularity in the U.S., and one of these could be the fact that U.S. has many low-density *suburban developments*. Many cities in Europe, Latin America and Asia have fewer suburbs, and the cities are more densely populated, so it is much easier for residents to use public transit rather than drive. Also, suburbanites think a public transportation system passing through their neighborhood disintegrates their sense of community by inviting strangers to the community. For example, the state of California passed a bill in 2008 that provided a bond to build a high-speed rail. As much as the plan's implementation was challenged with the reason that the state is facing a financial deficit and that the costs are higher than expected, the plan's popularity is also disputed by some suburban communities for passing through their neighborhood (Not in my Backyard-NIMBY).

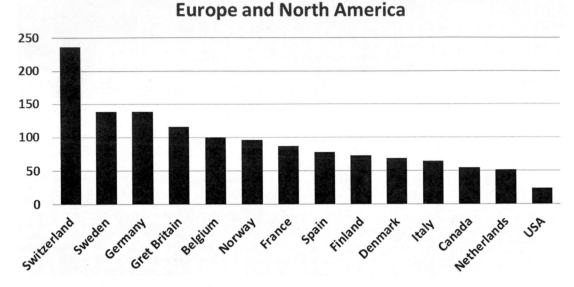

Figure 8.4 Annual public transportation trips per capita in Europe and North America (data: Ralph Buehler and John Pucher, 2012).

BOX 8.2 California High-Speed Rail (CHSR)

Argument: A TRAIN NOW AND HERE

A high-speed rail system will cost less to construct, take the pressure off the current infrastructure system, reduce the state's dependency on fossil fuels, and result in better air quality and community health in California. The high-speed rail system will take cars off the road and reduce daily flights, thus boosting California's economic productivity as more travelers and commuters take the train to get around the state. By 2040, the system will reduce vehicles miles of travel in the state by almost 10 million miles of travel every day. Over a 58 year period (from the start of operations in 2022 through 2080), the system will reduce auto travel on the state's highways and roads by over 400 billion miles of travel. Starting in 2030, the state will see a reduction of 93 to 171 flights daily. By 2040, the state will see a reduction of 97 to180 flights daily. The Authority has committed to using 100 percent renewable energy for powering the system. This will be achieved by procuring or producing enough renewable energy to offset the amount of energy it takes from the state's power grid to operate trains and facilities. This net-zero approach will increase the environmental benefits of the rail system and reinforce California's renewable energy economy while providing the Authority with a cost-stable source of electricity. Finally, the high-speed rail system will save 2.0 to 3.2 million barrels of oil annually starting in 2030.

In 2010 alone, U.S. GHG emissions totaled 6,821.8 million metrics tons of carbon dioxide (CO2). California leads the nation in working to reduce the level of GHG emissions. In 2006, the State Legislature passed Assembly Bill 32, also known as the Global Warming Solutions Act that directs the state to reduce statewide emissions to 1990 levels by 2020, a 17 percent reduction. In 2022, when the Initial Operating Section (Merced to the San Fernando Valley) is up and running, the resulting GHG reductions will be between 100,000 to 300,000 metric tons of carbon dioxide

(MtCO2) in the first year. That's the equivalent of from between 17,700 to 53,000 personal vehicles taken off the road. Between 2022 and 2040, the cumulative reduction of CO2 is estimated to be between 5 and 10 million metric tons.

Source: California High-Speed Rail Authority, 2013

Counter argument: A TRAIN TO NOWHERE

No matter how many times Governor Brown tout the mega-project as the job-creating wave of the future, he can't change the mountain of evidence that high-speed rail is, in fact, a boondoggle.

The latest authoritative warning came last week from the California High-Speed Rail Peer Review Group, which called the program "an immense financial risk" for the state and refused to recommend that the state legislature sell $2.7 billion in bonds to start a 130-mile initial stretch of the system. On the merits, high-speed rail would be a questionable investment even if California could afford to build it.

People marvel at bullet trains in Europe and Japan, insisting simplistically that we need them, too. But the sprawling, decentralized cities of the United States do not make convenient destinations for train travelers. International experience shows that high-speed rail entails expensive debt service and large operating subsidies. This would likely be the case here as well, since, for better or worse, rail must compete with well-established air and car options. Business travel is one ostensible purpose of bullet trains in California, but increasingly people meet via video conference. For these and other reasons, high-speed rail in the United States would lower carbon emissions and reduce traffic far less cost-effectively than would alternative solutions.

It's especially odd for a Democratic president and governor to saddle California with the cost of bullet trains when the state is facing chronic deficits, tax increases, and social spending cuts. Maybe this is why polls show that a majority of Californians have turned against the project. It's still not too late to hit the brakes.

Source: Charles Lane, January 9, 2012, The Washington Post

The second reason for resistance is the poor operation of the public transit services regarding punctuality, service frequency and spatial coverage. Public transportation in several cities is characterized by longer waiting times, missed departures, delays and lack of onboard information. In many cases, rail travel is slow and more costly than driving while in Europe it is faster and cheaper than driving.

The third reason is the hard-to-beat popularity of the automobile and the notion that public transportation is for the low income and the minority groups. The United States has more cars than any other country in the world and more miles of highways. In Europe, it is harder and expensive to get a driver's license, with many European countries having privatized driving schools that cost quite a lot. Most driver's start to drive in their early twenties, unlike in the U.S., where people drive at sixteen. Then, there is the cost of the tolls; the United States is one of the easiest countries to drive because most of the highways are free, and gas is cheaper compared to the other developed countries. Therefore, it has been easier just to buy a car and drive. Some are led to believe that public transportation is only for those who can't afford the privilege of driving, so many people who have cars may not even think of it as an alternative. This belief has been dated back in the 1950s when transit was predominately for working class inner city neighborhoods, where most minorities settled after the White flight (Sanchez, Stolz and Ma 2003). This vicious stereotype caused fear and has stopped many people from riding public transit.

Light rail, heavy rails and subways systems (the desired modes of public transit), have more upper-middle income riders than lower-class citizens on average. However, Pucher and Renee (2003) state different statistics. The majority of public transit riders of all systems end up being lower-class riders (those who have less than a twenty-thousand-dollar a year earning) who make up the largest percentage of over thirty-seven percent. However, according to an APTA report, "A Profile of Public Transportation Passenger," more than half of public transport passengers own automobiles. Many people only pay attention to the lower class numbers and don't realize that lower-class are not the only people who ride public transit, they just make up a large portion. People over the poverty-line including upper-middle and even some affluent, make up the rest, which is over half of transit users.

The fourth reason for low ridership is safety, which leads to an important question: is it more dangerous to ride public transit than drive? According to the Bureau of Transportation Statistics, the typical crimes that happen in public transit are theft, disorderly conduct, assault and battery, and sometimes homicide. These crimes have either remained steady for a very long time or decreased. Driving a car can be dangerous as well. According to the Center for Disease Control, for every one-hundred thousand people in the U.S., over ten percent will be a victim of a fatal car crash (CDC 2008). The chance of someone dying in a car accident is higher than getting stabbed or murdered on a train or city bus. Loukaitou-Sideris and her colleagues made extensive literature review from the various studies and summarized that transit crime have the following non-threatening characteristics:

- Transit crime is mostly a problem of the nation's larger cities.
- The majority of the incidents represent less serious crime and incivilities. A survey of 45 transit agencies showed that 22 percent (or 8,000 cases) of all reported incidents were of a serious nature. Of the serious crime, only 2,700 cases were violent. The vast majority of the less serious incidents involve vandalism, disorderly conduct, public drunkenness, theft, and harassment. These affect and intimidate other transit patrons, but tend to be underreported. Robberies, assaults, and batteries represent the majority of the reported serious crime.
- Crime levels vary for different parts of the transit system and are correlated with neighborhood crime.
- Most crime incidents occur in stations rather than on trains, and at bus stops rather than on buses, since the presence of the train crew or bus driver probably discourages potential offenders.
- Transit crime varies temporally and spatially. More serious crime tends to happen in late evening and night hours; while less serious incidents occur during rush hours.
- Different crimes occur in different types of environmental settings. Pickpockets and purse snatching typically happen in crowded situations, where the offender can easily hide in the anonymity of the crowd and rapidly escape the setting. Rape, homicide, and robbery usually occur in settings with low pedestrian traffic, low surveillance, and many concealed areas (dark corners, elevators, restrooms) (Loukaitou-Sideres, Liggett and Hiseki 2002).

Planning for Public Transportation

Public transportation planning needs to adapt to a changing environment such as air quality, technological advancement (such as intelligent transportation systems) and demographic change. Planning must also realize the current local and regional travel markets and needs. In terms of operation and management, transit planners need to consider new institutional arrangements, including public-private cooperative ventures, to provide, manage, and implement service and project initiatives. They must also implement expanded research and training programs that explore new approaches and incorporate them into current practice.

The urban planning field, in general, is changing, so transportation planning need to change with those realities. For example, neo-traditional development patterns (such as new urbanism and smart growth) are catching up in many localities, so transit planning needs also to be integrated with such developments. Changing demographics and the new interest of the Millenial generation in multimodality is an opportunity for transit planners.

According to Bickel (2000), the central role of public transit, particularly rail transit, in shaping transit-oriented development is gaining strength (even though the empirical evidence is still mixed). In encouraging Transit-Oriented Developments, efforts need to be made to foster multi-municipal planning and local–county cooperation in fragmented jurisdictions. There is the growing movement of state-level initiatives that offer a more consistent policy and coordinated infrastructure investment overlay of the county and local government planning activities. Also, public transportation planning needs to implement outreach techniques and public involvement programs to foster participatory planning (Bickel 2000).

According to Van As and Joubert (1990), when planning for public transportation, especially in choosing that transit mode is preferable for a given city or region, the following aspects can be taken into account.

- *Cost:* this includes the total cost per passenger mile, the capital cost (capital cost/passenger or capital cost/resident), capital cost/operating cost ratio, the sensitivity of the project to capital overruns and overestimates in passenger numbers and the percentage of cost recovery (to understand the subsidy required).
- *Demand:* the selected mode should be able to cope with the estimated volume of passengers expected to use the route. The travel demand forecast (as discussed in chapter 4) needs to include ways to estimate demand for public transportation.
- *Environmental Aspects*: This includes noise pollution and air pollution, and the project's visual intrusion as well as the consumption of energy.
- *Time Savings:* the magnitude of these savings will depend on the number of passengers and the value placed on the time saved by each passenger. Most passengers on transit are commuters making non-business trips. Some authorities consider that no value should be placed on time saved in making non-business trips while others suggest that it is equivalent to 25- 35 percent of the income earning rate.
- *Safety*: usually expressed as the expected number of fatalities, injuries or collisions. These parameters would need to be defined on a per passenger or per passenger-mile basis.
- *Less Quantifiable Aspects*: comfort and convenience of the passenger, number of transfers, predictability, flexibility, reliability and overall image.

Once the service is operational, transit agencies need to make a periodic evaluation of the service based on defined transit Level of Services (LOS). Transit Level of Service (LOS) refers to the convenience, comfort and security of transit travel as experienced by users. The level of Service (LOS) ratings, typically from A (best) to F (worst), are widely used in transport planning to evaluate problems and potential solutions. Such rating systems can be used identify problems, establish performance indicators and targets, evaluate potential solutions, compare locations, and track trends. They can also be used for travel demand modeling, to identify the types of improvements that could increase transit ridership (Litman 2014).

Table 8.1 Public transportation Level-of-Service rating factors

Feature	Description	Indicators
Availability	Where and when transit service is available.	• Annual service-kilometers per capita. • Daily hours of service. • Portion of destinations located within 500 meters of transit service. • Hours of service.
Frequency	Frequency of service and average wait time.	• Trips per hour or day. • Headways (time between trips). • Average waiting times.
Travel Speed	Transit travel speed.	• Average vehicle speeds. • Transit travel speed relative to driving the same trip. • Door-to-door travel time.
Reliability	How well service actually follows published schedules.	• On-time operation. • Portion of transfer connections made. • Mechanical failure frequency.
Boarding speed	Vehicle loading and unloading speed.	• Dwell time. • Boarding and alighting speeds.
Safety and security	Users perceived safety and security.	• Perceived transit passenger security. • Accidents and injuries. • Reported security incidents. • Visibility and lighting. • The official response to perceived risks. • Absence of vandalism.
Price and affordability	Fare prices, structure, payment options, ease of purchase.	• Fares relative to average incomes. • Fares relative to other travel mode costs. • Targeted discounts or exemptions as appropriate. • Payment options (cash, credit cards, etc.) • Ticket availability (stations, stores, Internet, etc.)
Network and system integration	Ease of transferring between transit and other travel modes (bus, train, ferry, airport, etc.).	• The quality of transit service to transport terminals. • Ease of accessing transit service information from transport terminals.
Comfort	Passenger comfort	• Seating availability and quality. • Space (lack of crowding). • Quiet (lack of excessive noise). • Fresh air (lack of unpleasant smells). • Temperature (neither too hot or cold) • Cleanliness. • Washrooms and refreshments (for longer trips).

Feature	Description	Indicators
Accessibility	Ease of reaching transit stations and stops.	• Transit Oriented Development. • Distance from transit stations and stops to destinations. • Walkability (quality of walking conditions) in areas serviced by transit.
Baggage capacity	Accommodation of baggage.	• Ability, ease and cost of carrying baggage, including special items such as pets.
Universal design	Accommodation of diverse users including people with special needs.	• Accessible design for transit vehicles, stations and nearby areas. • Ability to carry baggage. • Ability to accommodate people who cannot read or understand the local language.
User information	Ease of obtaining user information.	• Availability, accuracy and understandability of route, schedule and fare information, at stops, stations, destinations; by Internet and mobile telephone; and by transit agency staff and other information providers. • Real-time transit vehicle arrival information. • Information available to service people with special needs (audio or visual disabilities, inability to read or understand the local language, etc.)
Courtesy and responsiveness	Courtesy with which passengers are treated.	• How passengers are treated by transit staff. • Ease of filing a complaint. • Speed and responsiveness with which complaints are treated.
Attractiveness	The attractiveness of public transit facilities.	• Attractiveness of vehicles and facilities. • Attractiveness of documents and websites. • Quality of nearby buildings and landscaping. • Area Livability (environmental and social quality of an area) and community cohesion (quantity and quality of positive interactions among people in an area). • Number of parks and recreational areas accessible by non-motorized facilities.
Marketing	Effectiveness of efforts to encourage public transportation.	• Popularity of promotion programs. • Effectiveness at raising the social status of transit travel. • Increases in public transit ridership in response to marketing efforts.

Source Litman 2014; adapted from The Florida Department of Transportation (FDOT 2007)

ASSESSING QUALITY ATTRIBUTES OF BUS STOPS

Correct planning and management of a public transportation system are ultimately the keys to offering potential users a mode of transport which can be competitive with the private car (Ibeas *et al.*, 2010). Underneath this planning and management are the proper locations as well as physical designs in and around bus stops, to which there are indeed ways to improve user-friendliness and overall appeal.

According to Hamby and Thompson (2006), bus stops are a vital link in the journey of a bus rider. If a passenger cannot get to the stop and thereby use it, an otherwise accessible bus remains a distant goal. That being the case, most bus stops are located at a walking distance greater than what is recommended by numerous research examples. According to Bert (2003), urban planners typically assume that people will comfortably walk approximately one-quarter mile (1,320 ft or 400 m) to reach transit stops or stations. Given a potential user's origin point, a distance set beyond such numbers can act as a barrier in terms of desire to use the system; something only exacerbated if surroundings are not pleasant or safe (Hess 2012).

So as not to develop the notion that convenience is all that matters, there is also an element of safety to be involved in location. Loukaitou-Sideris (1999) has assessed in her study that conditions in and around bus stops can have an impact, noting that elements such as surrounding litter, graffiti, exterior dilapidation, or social behaviors inclusive of rowdiness, drunkenness, and panhandling lead to increased crime. Yet another aspect about safety is proper lighting. According to Gil-de-Castro *et al.* (2013), public lighting systems in cities are a basic and vital service for all users of public space; the light they provide allows for persons such as public transit users to have a sense of safety and comfort as they walk towards a bus stop or any other destination.

Apart from location and safety, there is the design of the stop itself. The most prominent feature of a bus stop is the stop sign that designates it. Gonzalez-Diaz and Montoro-Sanchez (2011) studied 29 news reports in economic journals regarding road passengers' complaints, with one of the major ones being about badly located, designed or maintained sign posts. These signs, if not located properly (out of view, missing, etc.) mean that not only are passengers at a loss when it comes to locating the bus stop, but inexperienced bus drivers who are new to the route may simply bypass it even when riders ring the bell (Kay 2010). And not completely forgetting about safety, improperly placed signs at a bus stop could also lead to pedestrian fatality. According to National Highway Traffic Safety Administration, Traffic Safety Facts 2004, 2 percent of pedestrian fatalities in the United States are associated with buses due to lack of proper infrastructures, including signs. Of additional note is also the ability of the signs themselves to be understood, which suggests that present bus stop signs must be capable of being understood by the diverse body of individuals to which they serve.

Amenities also constitute as parts of the design, and are considered as elements that enhance comfort and convenience. One basic amenity that is many times overlooked by transit authorities is the availability of a seating area at bus stops. Quite often buses do not reach their stops on time due to traffic, mechanical breakdown or closure of roads. These unfortunate happenings lead to increased passenger waiting time at stops, and a lack of seating area only serves to make the wait time seem even longer. According to Ben-Akiva and Morikawa (2002), travel comfort includes seat availability. Hence, a lack of seating leads to a decrease in ridership that in turn increases dependency on private automobiles.

Another such amenity that should be provided is a form of shelter/shade. Bus shelters provide protection from extreme weather conditions especially during hot summer months and rainy seasons. The barrier to installation though is as stated by Hess *et al.* (2010): "municipalities determine the location of bus shelters usually using rider volume as criteria." However, if the overall issue being discussed is attracting more riders, how can such be done if agencies are not willing to provide shelters that could attract more riders to begin with? Such criterion for determination does not seem to be very fitting. If shelter is provided though, it is also worth noting that not only is elemental protection offered, but that protection also has a socio-cultural function imbued within it, as the enclosed physical environments can facilitate interaction amongst their users; something that helps to build community (Ely *et al.*, 2012).

Also to be considered in bus stops is sanitation. The absence of a clean area in and around a bus stop would deter an individual from using public transit. In a confined and crowded space such as a bus stop, maintenance of public health should be of significant concern to transit authorities. In regards to this, an often detached but important sanitary item comes into play: the trash bin. Research conducted by Rodríguez *et al.* (2009) suggests that there is an increase in pedestrians' usage of public space if the space is provided with trash bin. However, if trash bins are provided by transit authorities, they must be emptied and cleaned periodically to maintain hygienic conditions. According to Parizeau (2006), failure to find local solutions to the city's waste-related problems has led to a different set of unsustainable practices inclusive of declines in public transit usage rates. Without sufficient care and cleanup, a bus stop could potentially create a blighted condition in a neighborhood, which would invite anti-social elements into the community. Citing James Q. Wilson and George Kelling's "Broken Windows" theory, Adams (2006) remarks that areas which show lack of care invite unsavory individuals and activities such as drug dealing, petty theft, and prostitution. When such elements are inserted into an area, remarks Adams: "residents become yet more fearful and withdraw further from community involvement and upkeep." Succinctly speaking, an unkempt bus stop has negative implications for not only the transit service, but also the area being served.

Since bus stops are located on sidewalks, it is imperative that sidewalks must also be given proper attention. This is to say that sidewalks must be designed and maintained in a manner that keeps in mind many users with different needs; specifically speaking, those with disability or mobility functional needs. Regarding bus stops, an absence of well-maintained sidewalks can lead to decreased ridership in the groups mentioned above. In a word, accessibility is the primary concern here. With the passage of the Americans with Disabilities Act in 1990, access to public transportation is a civil right for people with disabilities (Hamby and Thompson 2006). It is the duty and responsibility of the government to remove all architectural barriers on public spaces that render them inaccessible to certain groups of individuals. There are numerous qualitative characteristics of sidewalks that should be taken care of leading to a bus stop. For one, sidewalks should have a smooth, crack-free and continuous surface. For those individuals propelling a wheelchair, bumps, curb descents, and uneven driving surfaces become obstacles that carry with them consequences. These obstacles cause vibrations on the wheelchair and in turn, the wheelchair user, which through extended exposure can cause low-back pain, disc degeneration, and other harmful effects to the body (Wolf *et al.*, 2005). Additionally, sidewalks leading to a bus stop should be constructed using all-weather materials. Usage of unfinished gravel, stone, or dirt for sidewalks would be unsafe for many users traveling during rainy seasons, or at the very least prove to be difficult to traverse. Walkability is also of some note here, bearing in mind that in order to promote walking in a city and perhaps increase transit patronage to a desirable level, engineers and policy makers must make pedestrians feel more comfortable walking than driving. The suggestion here being that sidewalk width should be increased to engender such feelings (Kim *et al.*, 2010).

Review Questions

1) What is the most common type of public transportation? What are some of the sub-categories of this mode?
2) What are the key factors that induced a shift away from public transportation in the 20th Century?
3) How might Millennials change the transportation paradigm in the U.S.?
4) What quality of life augments do researchers make to improve public transportation?
5) How is public transportation potentially good for business?
6) What is TOD? Explain.
7) What are the four D's? How do they apply to public transportation?
8) What are the potential benefits of TOD?
9) Why is public transportation less popular in the U.S. versus other parts of the world?
10) Discuss the relationship between the bus stop quality and ridership.

Project/Paper Idea

Some people may be frequent riders of public transportation, and some may not. This assignment challenges each student to ride a local Metro system (if you are a regular user choose a route that is new to you). Students should then evaluate the system based on their experience. Instead of choosing a particular direct route, choose an origin A and a destination B. That way, you can involve in planning the trip, transferring and first and last mile experience. Based on your experience write a 2–3 pages summary of what worked well and what could be changed or improved. Use the following attributes for your evaluation. At the end of your evaluation, offer your recommendations to improve the public transits system.

1. Frequency of service/waiting time at bus stop
2. Punctuality
3. Directness of route (from origin A to destination B)
4. Cleanliness of the bus
5. Design (barrier free? Usable by all regardless of disability, gender?)
6. Convenience
7. Bus stop quality and convenience (shelter, bus stop information (panels))
8. Driver behavior
9. Behavior of other passengers
10. Coverage of important locations (urban activities)
11. Pre-journey an on-board information system
12. Availability of seats in the bus
13. Temperature on the bus (is it air conditioned?)
14. Ease of boarding
15. Ease of transfer

Videos

Tango 73: A Bus Rider's Diary by New Day Films*, 1998 (28 mins.)*: This documentary is about riders and drivers on AC Transit line 73 in the East Bay Area, showing the vital importance of public transportation in urban areas.

Internet Sources

- American Public Transportation Association, http://www.apta.com/Pages/default.aspx
- Transportation Alternative, http://www.transalt.org/
- Online TDM Encyclopedia, http://www.vtpi.org/tdm/

Bibliography

Adams, Joan. 2006. "The 'Broken Windows' Theory: Stopping the Little Things Will Deter Bigger Infractions." *Supply House Times*, 49: 395.

APTA. 2007. "Public Transportation: Benefits for the 21st Century." American Public Transportation Association Resource Library, U.S. DOT.

_____. 2012. "Ridership Report." American Public Transportation Association Resource Library, U.S. DOT.

Belzer, Den, and Gerald Autler. 2002. "Countering Sprawl with Transit-Oriented Development." *Issues in Science And Technology* 51–58.

Ben-Akiva, Moshe, and Takayuki Morikawa. 2002. "Comparing Ridership Attraction of Rail and Bus." *Transport Policy*, 9: 107–116.

Bert, Ray. 2003. "Streets and the Shaping of Towns and Cities." *Civil Engineering-ASCE*, 73: 79.

Bickel, Richard. 2000. *Key Issues Confronting Public Transportation Planning and Development*. Washington, D.C.: Transportation Research Board.

Campbell, Scott. 2002. *Transit-Oriented Development: An Overview*. Dissertations Publishing, Proquest, UMI.

Casey, Mark. 2005. *Transit-Oriented Development Smart Answer to High Oil Prices*. Boulder County Business Report.

CDC. 2008. *Accidents and Unintentional Injuries*. National Center for Health Statistics, United States Department of Health and Human Services, Atlanta, GA: Center For Disease Control And Prevention.

Cervero, Robert, and Jennifer Day. 2008. "Suburbanization and Transit-Oriented Development in China." *Transport Policy* 315–323.

Clair, David. 1981. "The Motorization and Decline of Urban Public Transit, 1935–1950." *Journal of Economic History* 41 (3): 579–600.

CSI. 2008. "Transit Oriented Development." *Center for State Innovation*. Accessed September 16, 2013. http://www.stateinnovation.org/publications/all-publications/TOD.aspx.

Ely, Vera Helena Moro Bins, Jonara Machado De Oliveira, and Louise Logsdon. 2012. "A Bus Stop Shelter Evaluated from the User's Perspective." *Work* (Reading, Mass.), 41: 1226–1233.

Gil-De-Castro, A., A. Moreno-Munoz, A. Larsson, J.J.G. De La Rosa, and M.H.J. Bollen. 2013. "LED Street Lighting: A Power Quality Comparison Among Street Light Technologies." *Lighting Research & Technology*, 45: 710–728.

González-Díaz, Manuel, and Ángeles Montoro-Sánchez. 2011. "Some Lessons from Incentive Theory: Promoting Quality in Bus Transport." *Transport Policy*, 18: 299–306

Hamby, Beth, And Ken Thompson. 2006. "New Toolkit Provides Practical Tools to Build Better Bus Stops." *Journal-Institute of Transportation Engineers*, 76: 22–26.

Hess, Daniel Baldwin. 2012. "Walking to the Bus: Perceived Versus Actual Walking Distance to Bus Stops for Older Adults." *Transportation*, 39: 247–266.

_____, Paul David Rayc, Anne E. Stinsonb, and Jiyoung Parka. 2010. "Determinants of Exposure to Fine Particulate Matter (Pm 2.5) For Waiting Passengers at Bus Stops." *Atmospheric Environment*, 44: 5174–5182.

Ibeas, Ángel, Luigi Dell'olio, Borja Alonso, and Olivia Sainz. 2010. "Optimizing Bus Stop Spacing in Urban Areas." *Transportation Research Part E*, 46: 446–458.

Kay, Liz F. 2010. "Missing Bus Stop Sign Diverts Passengers." *Baltimore Sun*.

Kim, Sangyoup, Jaisung Choi, and Yongseok Kim. 2010. "Determining the Sidewalk Pavement Width by Using Pedestrian Discomfort Levels and Movement Characteristics." *KSCE Journal of Civil Engineering*, 15: 883–889.

Lee, Shin. 2010. "Transport and the Recession: an Opportunity to Promote Sustainable Transport." *International Planning Studies* 15 (3): 213–226.

Leyden, Kevin, Abraham Goldberg, and Philip Michelbach. 2011. "Understanding the Pursuit of Happiness in Ten Major Cities." *Urban Affairs Review* 47 (6): 861–888.

Litman, Todd. 2012. "Evaluating Public Transportation Benefits and Cost." *Victoria Transport Policy Institute*.

_____. 2014. "Public Transit Improvements." *Victoria Transport Policy Institute*.

_____. 2014. "Safer Than You Think! Revising the Transit Safety Narrative." *Victoria Transportation Policy Institute*.

Lloyd, William. 1981. "Understanding Late Nineteenth-Century American Cities." *Geographical Review* 71 (4): 460–471.

Loukaitou-Sideris, Anastasia. 1999. "Hot Spots of Bus Stop Crime—The Importance of Environmental Attributes." *Journal of The American Planning Association*, 65: 395–411.

_____, Anastasia. 2010. "A New Found Popularity for Transit-Oriented Developments? Lessons from Southern California." *Journal of Urban Design* 15 (1): 49–68.

_____, Anastasia, Robin Liggett, and Hiroyuki Hiseki. 2002. "The Geography of Transit Crime. Documentation and Evaluation of Crime Incidence On and Around the Green Line Stations in Los Angeles." *Journal of Planning Education And Research* 22: 135–161.

Lund, Hollie, Robert Cervero, and Richard Willson. 2004. *Travel Characteristics of Transit-Oriented Development in California.* Caltrans Transportation Grant—Statewide Planning Studies.

Mcshane, Clay, and Joel Tarr. 2003. "The Decline of the Urban Horse in American Cities." *Journal of Transportation History* (24) 2: 177–198.

Milne, Eugene. 2012. "A Public Health Perspective on Transport Policy Priorities." *Journal Of Transport Geography* 21: 62–69.

Muller, Peter. 2004. "Transportation and Urban Form ." In *The Geography of Urban Transportation*, by Susan Hanson and Genevieve Giuliano, 59–85. New York: The Guilford Press.

National Highway Traffic Safety Administration. 2004. *Traffic Safety Facts 2002.* U.S. Department of Transportation.

Parizeau, Kate. 2006. "A World of Trash." *Alternatives Journal*, 32: 16.

Parker, Terry, Mike Mckeever, GB Arrington, and Janet Smith-Heimer. 2002. *Statewide Transit-Oriented Development Study: Factors for Success in California, Final Report.* Division of Mass Transportation, Transportation and Housing Agency, California Department of Transportation.

Pucher, John, and John Renne. 2003. "Socioeconomics of Urban Travel: Evidence from the 2001 NHTS." *Transportation Quarterly* 57 (3): 49–78.

Renne, John. 2009. "From Transit-Adjacent to Transit-Oriented Development." *Local Environment* 14 (1): 1–15.

Rodríguez, Daniel A, Elizabeth M. Brisson, and Nicolás Estupiñánc. 2009. "The Relationship Between Segment-Level Built Environment Attributes and Pedestrian Activity Around Bogotá's BRT Stations." *Transportation Research Part D*, 14: 470–478.

Sakaria, Neela, and Natalie Stehfest. 2013. *Millennials & Mobility: Understanding Themillennial Mindset and New Opportunities for Transit Providers.* Transit Cooperative Research Program, Transportation Research Board.

Samimi, Amir, and Abolfazl Mohammadian. 2010. "Health Impacts of Urban Development and Transportation Systems." *Journal of Urban Planning and Development* 136 (3): 208–213.

Sanchez, Thomas, Rich Stolz, and Jacinta Ma. 2003. *Moving to Equity: Addressing Inequitable Effects of Transportation Policies on Minorities.* Cambridge, MA: The Civil Rights Project at Harvard University and Center for Community Change.

Van As, S.C, and H.S. Joubert. 1990. *Traffic Flow Theory.* SARB Chair in Transportation Engineering, Department of Civil Engineering, University of Pretoria.

Wolf, Erik, J. Pearlman, R.A. Cooper, S.G. Fitzgerald, A. Kelleher, D.M. Collins, M.L. Boninger, and R.Cooper. 2005. "Vibration Exposure of Individuals Using Wheelchairs Over Sidewalk Surfaces." *Disability and Rehabilitation*, 27: 1443.

Part III

*Planning for Safety
and Social Equity*

9

Traffic Accidents and Safety Issues

Chapter Outline

- Introduction
- History of Automobile Safety in the United States
- Causes of Traffic Accidents
  - o *Driver Behavior—The Human Factor*
    - *Driving Under the Influence of Drugs and Alcohol*
    - *Distraction and Inattentiveness*
    - *Reckless Driving*
    - *Driver Fatigue*
  - o *Mechanical Failure—The Vehicle Factor*
  - o *Road Design—The Environmental Factor*
- To Stop or Not to Stop: Safety at Intersections
- Measures to Reduce Traffic Accidents
  - o *Drunk Driving Prevention*
  - o *Safety Improvements on Vehicles*
  - o *Safety for Youth Driver and Children*

Introduction

Fatalities and injuries caused by traffic accidents are considered to be global public health problems. According to the U.S. National Highway Traffic Safety Administration (NHTSA) and the National Safety Council (NSC), motor vehicle traffic fatalities are the leading cause of death among people from the ages of 5–34 each year, claiming the lives of about 40,000 men, women and children annually. These account for nearly 5 percent of the total death rate in the United States. As a result, of all the systems that people have to deal with on a daily basis, road transport is considered as the most complex and the most dangerous one. In 2012, there were 34,080 fatalities on U.S. highways and roads, including drivers, motorcyclists, cyclists, and pedestrians. The figure represents a 5.3 percent increase over the 2011's total of 32,367, reversing a long-running trend of declining deaths from motor vehicle crashes. In 2011, there were 1,987 traffic deaths of drivers between 15 and 20 years old while 5,401 people 65 and older were killed in crashes (Seckan 2013). Also, the estimated annual cost of traffic fatalities and injuries in the U.S. exceeds $99 billion. Worldwide, the number of people killed in road traffic crashes each year is estimated at almost 1.2 million while the number injured could be as high as 50 million. This makes road traffic injuries the third top cause of death globally (Peden, *et al.*, 2004). Globally, estimates of annual road fatalities vary as a result of the limitations of injury data collection and analysis, problems of underreporting and differences in interpretation. The figure ranges from around 750,000 to 1,183,492 annually, representing over 3000 lives lost daily. Around 85 percent of all global road deaths and 90 percent of the disability-adjusted life years lost are due to crashes. 96 percent of all children killed worldwide as a result of road traffic injuries occur in low-income and middle-income countries. Over 50 percent of deaths are among adults in the age range of 15–44 years. Among both children aged 5–14 years, and young people aged 15–29 years, road traffic injuries are the second-leading cause of death worldwide (Peden, *et al.*, 2004).

Table 9.1 The changing order of 10 leading causes of global deaths

	2000		2012		2020
Rank	**Cause of death**	**Rank**	**Cause of death**	**Rank**	**Cause of death**
1	Lower respiratory infections	1	Ischaemic heart disease	1	Ischaemic heart disease
2	Diarrhoeal diseases	2	Lower respiratory infections	2	Unipolar depressive disorders
3	Ischaemic heart disease	3	Stroke	3	**Road injury**
4	Stroke	4	Preterm birth complications	4	Cerebrovascular disease
5	Preterm birth complications	5	Diarrhoeal diseases	5	Chronic obstructive pulmonary disease
6	Birth asphyxia and birth trauma	6	Chronic obstructive pulmonary disease	6	Lower respiratory infections
7	HIV/AIDS	7	HIV/AIDS	7	Tuberculosis
8	Chronic obstructive pulmonary disease	8	**Road injury**	8	War
9	Malaria	9	Unipolar depressive disorders	9	Diarrhoeal diseases
10	**Road injury**	10	Birth asphyxia and birth trauma	10	HIV/AIDS

Source: WHO

In response to a general concern for citizens' well-being on the road, governments at various levels have had to implement policies to help regulate driving on streets. Policymaking enabled governments to set specific standards for motor vehicle users and manufacturers to promote a safe driving environment. Through this process, society has made significant advances to decrease injuries and deaths resulting from traffic accidents. Policy mandates have forced car engineers to produce safer cars that limit the human damage from collisions. Still, there has been controversy over the actual positive effects these policies have shaped, and whether more should be done to minimize the automobile death rate. Furthermore,

more than 90 percent of traffic accidents are caused due to human error, so some public safety scholars argue that the policy debate must continue to focus on how to educate people and change driving behavior.

History of Automobile Safety in the United States

In the beginning of the 20th century, government concern over driving practices inspired the creation of the first national conference in 1924 addressing driving as a health issue, resulting in the development of the first research on physical principles in automobile driving. This study, conducted in 1927 by the National Academy of Sciences, National Research Council at Ohio State University was the first publication on transportation safety. This innovative transportation safety study was a catalyst for further automobile safety research by private companies, universities and government organizations.

The early traffic research reports conducted showed that the greatest risk factor was speed, along with the steady increase in automobile ownership on poor capacity roadways. Baker (1971a) elaborates: "During a 35- year period (1935- 1969), the number of vehicles had increased from 25 to 104 million, the number of vehicles miles of travel had increased from 280 billion to 1 trillion, and the number of drivers 38 million to 108 million. The trend for higher speeds led to an increase in the average speed from 47 in 1942 to 59 mph in 1968." Increased speeds continued to after World War II, and once more an increase in vehicular registration and vehicle miles traveled. To add to the growing concern about traffic safety, Ralph Nadler (1965) published *Unsafe at Any Speed* on November 1965, which stated that driving at any speed, was unsafe, blaming the automobile companies for focusing on style and sales, rather than personal safety. It was clear that something had to be done to limit the deaths, and some reports suggested that if no government action were taken, the total fatality rate would reach 150,000 by the end of 1966. Examining another report, over a 27 year period from 1934 to 1961 showed a rise in the number of deaths from 36,101 to 38, 091, while the next seven-year cycle exhibited a larger increase in vehicle fatalities to 55, 200 (Baker 1971b).

After the publication of such statistics, it became clear to the public that automobile companies were not doing much to minimize deaths and instead looked to elected officials to promote and regulate vehicular fatalities. Safety research, along with citizen protest, ultimately led to the creation and implementation of the National Highway Safety Act of 1966, originally under the National Highway Safety Bureau, which later became the National Highway Traffic Safety Administration (Forbes, 1972). The National Highway Safety Act of 1966 and Motor Vehicle Safety Act of 1966 were responsible for developing safety standards and programs to help decrease the number of collisions, and more importantly, the fatality rate. The implementation of these two laws was the greatest leap forward and was the first body of legislation that had any power to create and recommend adequate vehicular safety policies. The Acts mandated automobile manufacturers to improve overall safety and made twenty standard requirements, including: rules requiring installation of seat belts for all occupants, impact-absorbing steering columns, padded dashboards, safety glass, dual braking systems, vehicle identification numbers, rearview mirrors, anchorage of seats and windshield wiping with defrosters (Olmstead 2004). In time, federal motor vehicle safety standards have expanded to cover many other aspects of motor vehicle safety, including everything from windshield wipers, lights, and rearview mirrors to door locks, head restraints and fuel tanks (Blomquist 1988). These laws finally made the automobile manufacturers responsible for complying with safety standards. Standards were maintained by fining auto companies a $1,000 civil penalty for each offense, up to a maximum of $400,000 for a related series of violations (the maximum penalty was increased to $800,000 in 1974) (Olmstead 2004). By having the listed automobile safety standards, consumers now were more protected and aware of safety requirements on the market. Another positive outcome was competition among automobile manufacturers to implement new ideas in safety and enticing customers with the safety of the vehicle rather than just the style and performance that once dominated the car market. Furthermore, there was a standard set on overall safety, which made it easier to reduce the overall number of fatalities and created a way to analyze important variables that could be linked to vehicle accidents.

The legislation also helped reduce deaths by encouraging, enforcing and funding highway safety programs. Initially, thirteen plans were adopted, mainly focusing on highway design, traffic control and driving behavior. Examples of the plans range from driver education, traffic records, motor vehicle registration, traffic courts, traffic control devices and most importantly, driver licensing. The establishment of such programs was made mandatory for states, as the refusal of implementation resulted in a cut of 10 percent in federal highway funding. However, states benefited from the implementation of programs as they were subsidized by the federal government in a 75 percent/25 percent federal/state fund matching system. The programs helped decrease the car mortality rate by making drivers aware of the responsibility they have on the road. Programs like public service announcements and required driver training courses significantly improved driver's ability to perform better on the road.

In addition to these positive changes, the programs also created better automobile regulation at the local level. This was done by improving vehicle information, such as proper licensing and registration, along with keeping current records for drivers that had been suspended. The total number of deaths prevented because of policy implementation in 1969 was estimated to be 150,000, but it is hard to estimate accurately because the collection of data had only begun in 1963 (Baker 1971a). Overall, the National Highway Safety Act of 1966 and Motor Vehicle Safety Act of 1966 greatly contributed to the reduction of deaths by holding automobile driver and manufacturer accountable for traffic safety.

In the 1970s, the National Highway Safety Administration (NHTSA) was founded in order to meet safe driving demands for future generations. The NHTSA incorporated new boards within the department, from research to recalls. The research board's objective is to evaluate the performance of experimental vehicles, concerning crash protection, fuel economy, crash avoidance, pedestrian hazard, susceptibility to damage, and marketability (Blomquist 1988). The NHTSA has conducted an array of safety studies ranging from the crashworthiness of cars, safety belts, the impairing effect of alcohol or other drugs on driving, and public attitude regarding speed limit mandates. Some of the research has proven to be influential in creating political change in favor of the automobile consumer, as noted in the Motor Vehicle Information and Cost Savings Act of 1972. This new act made the NHTSA responsible for testing new commercial automobile models on the market by giving them a rating on how good they performed in a collision. The safety rating is published for the public in an effort to discourage automobile consumers from buying poorly designed vehicles.

The other power the NHTSA has earned is the ability to announce automobile recalls, whether it is a safety unit of the car or the whole car. The recall board is in charge of recalling vehicles, by making phone calls, and sending letters to those drivers affected, and more recently alerting the press and major television news networks. Policy outcome does not always improve the quality of life, but traffic safety laws from 1966 to 1979 helped reduce the rate of fatalities by 39 percent. This number mainly credits the safety program campaigns that were run as it did most successful in declining the death toll.

Perhaps the most important safety technology in automobiles is a seat or safety belt. However, a study conducted by researcher Peltzman (1975) calculated that these devices would only yield a seven to sixteen percent reduction in the fatality rate. Also, energy absorbing steering columns were shown to have a four to seven percent reduction. Overall Peltzman concluded, "for all five major design changes, the expected reduction in the 1972 occupant fatality rate was in the 10 to 25 percent." Because of the large fleet of automobiles already in use, it is hard to save lives in vehicles that are not equipped with the new mandated safety features. It is important to note that as more people purchase automobiles after 1966, the rate would increase more, as Peltzman projected that reduction would reach be in the 35 percent range. The differentiation of opinion caused many studies to be conducted to examine the total human lives saved due to those safety measures.

One regression report conducted by Robertson (1984) and Orr (1984), took into consideration model years (base year) along with estimated total miles driven, and unlike the Peltzman study, excludes trucks, as they were not mandated to have the same vehicle safety standards as regular automobiles. Robertson and Orr's data was gathered by calculating 120 fatal crashes and involved fifteen model years. Robertson and Orr also conducted studies on non-occupants to include motorcyclists, cyclists and pedestrians. Non-occupant studies were calculated by dividing the number of pedestrians killed in an accident with a vehicle of a specified model year of vehicle. Similarly, multiple regression analysis was applied to fatalities of motorcyclists and cyclists, which were independent of pedestrians. Finally, a total fatality crash involvement rate was calculated and analyzed with the same specification for regression analysis. Robertson and Orr's more in-depth study summarized the reduction of deaths during the 1975 to 1978 period due to improvements in vehicle standards to over 37,000 people: 26,500 occupant, 7,600 pedestrians, 1,000 cyclists and 2,000 motorcyclists. Such results, if combined during the three years analyzed, exhibit a substantial improvement; automobile fatalities were 16 percent lower, pedestrians 20 percent, motorcyclists 12 percent, and cyclists' fatalities were 21 percent lower. The data shows impressive reductions in car occupant fatalities. Thus, it is surprising to have data that shows a positive outcome for non-occupants as well. The reduction of fatalities for non-automobile travelers can be linked to the mandated technological innovation for newer automobiles. Such innovative safety features, such as windshield defrosters, headlights, turning signals, rear-view mirrors and horns were contributing factors in making non-occupants more visible. For example, the reduction of pedestrian fatality by 20 percent can be attributed to the incorporation of better driver visibility from the automobile by using rear-view mirrors, and during cold weather, by the application of windshield defrosters. Motorcyclists and cyclists benefited from vehicle safety standards, by automobiles being equipped with headlights making for better awareness of all drivers, and also by the much needed turning signals making motorists more aware of upcoming vehicular moves on the road. Robertson and Orr's study suggested a positive outcome, yet it is important to note that their study only included three years and as such, does not include automobiles made before mandates were applied, and also omits vehicles that were manufactured after the mandates were enacted.

Oscar Cantu (1980) conducted a study analyzing traffic fatality rates from 1947 to 1977, adding 28 previous years to yield a better total. Cantu used the same regression analysis as Robertson and Orr, but included alcohol as a variable with an alcoholic content of beverage consumption per capita of the drinking population. Additionally, he included a measure of the extent of regulation, the percentage of the car stock of 1964, and a qualitative (0–1) variable for the energy crunch, which occurred in 1974. Cauntu's findings correlated with that of Peltzman except for a small, but significant effect of regulation on total fatality rate. Cantu estimated that in 1977, there was a reduction of only 0.2 percent of possible fatality, which ended up causing a national fluctuation of overall car death reduction. More interestingly, he concluded that non-occupants did not benefit from the Motor Vehicle Safety Act. This information contradicts what Robertson and Orr's study about the non-occupant increase survival outcome. However, his study lacked quantitative numbers to yield such a finding and does not take into consideration motorcyclists and bicyclists.

Although several studies conducted through the 1990s and 2000s, there have not been many recent changes in traffic policies, yet there is a continuing pressure to implement more laws to create a safer driving environment.

Causes of Traffic Accidents

Traffic accidents are related to three factors, namely driver's personal behavior (human factor), geometrical design of the road (environmental factor) and factors related to the mechanical failure of the vehicle itself (vehicle factor). It is well established in literature and law enforcement documents that, of the three factors, drivers' personal behavior contribute to most of the accidents on the road.

Some injury epidemiologists use a schematic approach to the identification of risk factors called the Haddon Matrix. The Haddon Matrix organizes risk factors, according to a three-phase conceptualization of the event sequence (pre-crash, crash, post-crash) as it relates to the three factors: human, vehicles, and environments. This approach is believed to be advantageous because it promotes consideration of a wide array of factors that can influence the likelihood of a harmful outcome in a format that is easy to interpret. The Haddon Matrix has been credited with broadening the focus of highway safety efforts from a preoccupation with accident preven-

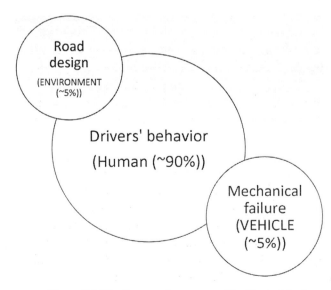

Figure 9.1 The three major causes of traffic accidents.

tion to an increased emphasis on the crashworthiness of vehicles and the quality of emergency medical care (NTSB, National Transportation Safety Board: Safety Study 2002).

Table 9.2 The Haddon matrix with example risk factors from the highway mode

Phase	Human/Host	Vehicle/Agent	Physical environment
Pre-crash	Driver intoxication	Poor visibility from inside vehicle	Narrow road, poor lighting, and sharp curves
Crash	Lack of restraint use	Reaction of vehicle structures to impact forces	Hard structures adjacent to the roadway
Post-crash	Hemorrhaging	High difficulty and cost to repair vehicle	Remote area

Adapted from W. Haddon, Jr. "Approaching the Reduction of Road Losses—Replacing the Guesswork with Logic, Specificity and Scientifically Determined Fact," a paper presented at the National Road Safety Symposium, 1972.

The Human Factor: Driver Behavior

Driver behavior is a significant contributor to road deaths. In 2011, 31 percent of total traffic fatalities involved alcohol. Texting and cell phone usage are also on the rise, contributing to 3,300 traffic deaths, according to the U.S. Department of Transportation. Research has shown that drivers who use a cell phone while driving can exhibit greater impairment than intoxicated drivers (Seckan 2013). Of motorcyclists or their passengers who died, 40 percent were not wearing helmets at the time of the crash. According to the Center for Disease Control (CDC), 16 percent of traffic crash fatalities were vulnerable road users: pedestrians, bicyclists, and others.

DRIVING UNDER THE INFLUENCE OF DRUGS AND ALCOHOL

The National Highway Traffic Safety Administration (NHTSA) Fatality Analysis Reporting System (FARS) estimates that in 2011, there were 9,878 alcohol-impaired driving fatalities, which represented 31 percent of all highway fatalities. Although the FARS database has limitations, such as variability in how well states report their driver Blood Alcohol Content (BAC) levels, it is generally considered the most comprehensive source for national data on fatal traffic crashes. A study by Miller *et al.* (2012) compared police and hospital records for nonfatal crashes in seven states and found that both sets of records substantially underreported alcohol involvement. Based on comparisons of the two datasets, the authors estimated that 12.9 percent of all nonfatal crashes involved alcohol. For the subset of nonfatal crashes that caused severe injury, the authors estimated that 22.6 percent of them involved alcohol. These estimates are considerably higher than, for instance, estimates based on police-reported data alone, which indicate that 4.4 percent of all nonfatal crashes and 11.4 percent of the serious injury crash subset, respectively, involved alcohol. The National Transportation Safety Board (NTSB) conducted an analysis of injury data for the years 2000–2011 using the NHTSA General Estimates System database, which is a nationally representative sample of police-reported motor vehicle crashes. Although there was a 43 percent reduction in injuries from alcohol-involved crashes during this period, in 2011 alone, more than 173,000 people received nonfatal injuries in alcohol-involved crashes, including more than 27,000 who received incapacitating injuries. The NTSB analysis also found that nearly twice as many people in alcohol-involved crashes are killed or injured (32 percent) compared, to those in non-alcohol-involved crashes (17 percent) (NTSB 2013).

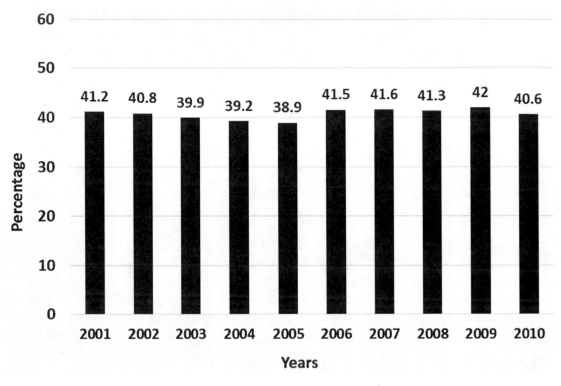

Figure 9.2 Fatalities involving alcohol as percentage of total fatalities (data: USDOT, National Highway Traffic Safety Administration, Fatality Analysis Reporting System Database as of April 2012).

According to NTSB's analysis of FARS data, between 1982 and 2011, annual impaired driving fatalities went from 21,113 to 9,878, a 53 percent reduction. During that same period, there was a 74 percent decline in the fatality rate. This shows a period of rapid decline in alcohol-impaired fatalities relative to non-alcohol-impaired fatalities between 1982 and 1994; however, since 1995, the proportion of fatalities associated with alcohol-impaired drivers has remained between 30 and 32 percent.

Although the NTSB data shows a very promising trend, every year thousands of adults make a deadly decision to climb into their vehicles while under the effects of alcohol and other illegal substances such as marijuana, cocaine, heroin, etc. Not only are they significantly increasing their chances of being involved in a serious accident on the streets or highways due to their reduced reaction time and impaired judgment, putting their own lives at risk, but also they endanger the lives of unsuspecting, innocent motorists, pedestrians or cyclists and their families, who ultimately end up paying the price for another person's fault. In the article *Drugs and Alcohol Involvement in Four Types of Fatal Crashes*, Romano and Voas (2011) break down the accidents caused by intoxicated drivers into four separate categories: speeding, inattention, failure to obey/yield and seat belt non-use. In California alone, drugged and drunk fatalities from 2000–2009 have reached an astonishing 12,389, accounting for 30 percent of all intoxicated accidents in the United States (40,507 total) (Romano and Voas 2011). According to the study, among all drivers fatally injured in speed-related crashes, 25.5 percent were found to be under the influence of drugs while 47 percent were over the legal limit for alcohol. For drivers that failed to obey traffic signs/yield, 20 percent tested positive for drugs and 18 percent for alcohol. Those who did not utilize their seat belts properly tested 21.4 percent for drugs and 25 percent for alcohol. And finally, drivers who were inattentive to the road and their surroundings tested 24.6 percent positive for drugs and 34 percent for alcohol (Romano and Voas 2011). The reason these statistics are immensely important is because they add significant evidence and truth to the fact that drugs and alcohol distort a person's judgment and reasoning, especially when it comes to the speed and high risk of driving an automobile.

DISTRACTION AND INATTENTIVENESS

Distraction and inattentiveness of drivers are demonstrated on streets and highways every day, with a cellular phone or mobile device used for texting, making phone calls, sending emails or social networking. In *The Six Most Common Causes of Automobile Crashes* at sixwise.com, Mark Edwards, Director of Traffic Safety at the American Automobile Association (AAA) stated, "The research tells us that somewhere between 25–50 percent of all motor vehicle crashes in this country really have driver distraction as their cause." The distractions are many, but according to a study conducted by Atkins (2003), texting and rubbernecking, or slowing down to gawk at another accident, caused the most accidents, accounting for 16 percent of all distraction-related crashes. After rubbernecking, other common driver distractions included: driver fatigue (12 percent), looking at scenery (10 percent), other passengers or children (9 percent), adjusting the radio, cassette or CD player (7 percent), reading the newspaper, books, maps or other documents (less than 2 percent) (Atkins 2003).

It seems that with the expansion of technology, people are more interested in socializing rather than their own safety as well as that of passengers and pedestrians. Driving and talking on a cell phone at the same time quadruples the risk of crashing, which is why many cities have recently begun banning the use of cell phone while driving, unless a hands-free device is used. The article "Risk Perceptions of Mobile Phone Use While Driving" by White, Eiser and Harris (2004) states that at any given moment, 2–3 percent of all motorists on the road will be using their mobile phones, increasing a driver's risk of having or causing an accident due to speed maintenance, following distances, poor reaction time and situational awareness (White, Eiser and Harris 2004). Since cell phone use involves visual, manual and cognitive distractions, an insignificant phone call or text message may remove a person's hands from the steering wheel, eyes from the road, and attention from their surroundings, leaving them at risk for potential disaster that they may never see coming. According to the National Safety Council (NSC), in 2010, an estimated 28 percent of all accidents and fatalities on U.S. Highways were caused by distracted drivers on their cellular phones, a startling 10 percent increase from 2009 (Professional Safety 2011).

The lure to look at and answer the cell phone "ping" signaling an incoming text message or phone call is incredibly strong. This has caused a dramatic increase in distracted driving, causing more accidents to occur. Since the arrival of cell phones, and in particular the past decade, as cell phone usage has dramatically increased, they have been a focus of public safety, raising awareness of the dangers of using the cell phone while driving. Texting and driving can be as impairing as driving while intoxicated, slowing reaction times by 35 percent when typing a text message. To combat this problem, over 19 states and the District of Columbia have banned texting while driving. However, four of these states have a law in place in which the officer has to have a reason to pull over the car, instead of just seeing the driver on their phone (Halsey 2010).

Reckless Driving

Reckless driving is voluntarily speeding, street racing, and failing to obey traffic signs and laws. The term "reckless" describes driving habits of new as well as experienced motorists who, despite having knowledge of the dangers, regulations and etiquette of the roads, decide to deliberately disobey the law and risk their lives and those of others in an unnecessary and preventable manner. With flashier, faster and more powerful cars being produced annually, and the image of street racing being glorified in movies, music and video games, speeding and street racing has become an immensely dangerous issue. In films such as *The Fast and the Furious* series and *XXX*, as well as video games like *Need for Speed* and *Grand Theft Auto*, underground law breakers are seen as heroes to young teenagers and some adults for the actions and adventures they embark on once they hit the streets. In a study conducted by Sheila Sarkar and Marie Andreas (2004) entitled *Acceptance of and Engagement in Risky Driving Behaviors by Teenagers*, 2,230 new and student drivers in Southern California, ages 16–19, were asked about their experiences with risky and dangerous driving practices. 44.2 percent of these teenagers admitted to having been in a vehicle with a person that was involved in a drag race while 20.9 percent of them had participated in an illegal street race themselves. 53.6 percent had ridden in a car with a reckless driver, and 27.2 percent of them confessed to being the reckless driver themselves. Although most kids may find this amusing and simple fun to be had with their friends, they are not realizing the potentially catastrophic results that their decisions may entail. Reaching speeds of 100 to 150 miles per hour in a matter of seconds greatly reduces a person's reaction time if another vehicle, pedestrian or even an object may cross their path. With drivers attempting to do whatever they can to win and show off to their friends, they are not taking into consideration their inexperience and inability to control a massive object such as a car, traveling at such a high velocity with very little to absolutely no room for error. According to Michael Berenis of the Examiner, there are an average 135 fatalities every year caused by street racing, accounting for 0.3 percent of the total automobile deaths in the United States. On the other hand, and just as dangerous, there are quite a lot of drivers that have been deciding that they will not obey traffic signs (stop signs, signal lights, etc.), causing an estimated 1,922 deaths in the United States in 2009 alone. This stands as the 3rd leading cause of fatal accidents in the United States.

Speeding is a multi-tiered threat because not only does it reduce the amount of time necessary to avoid a crash, it also increases the risk of crashing and makes the crash more severe if it does occur. In fact, according to the Insurance Institute for Highway Safety (IIHS), when speed increases from 40 mph to 60 mph, the energy released in a crash more than doubles.

DRIVER FATIGUE

Drowsy drivers account for about 100,000 accidents every year in the United States, according to the U.S. National Traffic Safety Administration (NHTSA, Traffic Safety Facts 2001). The risk is greatest from 11 p.m. to 8 a.m., the time when most people are used to sleeping. However, some people also become drowsy from noon to 2 p.m. Symptoms of driver fatigue include heavy eyelids, frequent yawning, a drifting vehicle that wanders over road lines, varying vehicle speed for no reason, misjudging traffic situations, seeing things "jump out" in the road, feeling fidgety or irritable and daydreaming. For most people, having four hours or less of sleep and then getting behind the wheel is like having two drinks prior to driving.

Vehicle's Mechanical Failure

In most cases, the mechanical failures can be attributed to normal wear or a lack of proper vehicle maintenance, not necessarily poor design or manufacturing defects. Manufacturers are required by law to design and engineer cars that meet a minimum safety standard. Computers, combined with companies' extensive research and development, have produced relatively safe vehicles that are easy and safe to drive. The most cited types of equipment failure are loss of brakes, tire blowouts or tread separation, and steering/suspension failure. Except the rash of Firestone light-truck tire failures, combined totals for all reported equipment failure accounts for less than 5 percent of all motor vehicle accidents.

Since the first automobile in history, manufacturers are continuously improving the performance of cars to avoid accidents caused by mechanical failure. Brake failure is almost an unlikely event with modern dual-circuit brake systems. If one side of the circuit fails, the other side is usually sufficient to stop a vehicle. Disc brakes, found on the front wheels of virtually every modern vehicle, are significantly more effective than the older drum braking systems, which can fade when hot. ABS (Anti Blockier System) or anti-lock brakes prevent the wheels from locking up during emergency braking maneuvers, allowing modern vehicles to avoid many accidents that would have previously occurred. Uneven or worn-out tires are the next most serious problem and can also lead to tire failure. Uneven wear is caused by improperly balanced tires or misaligned or broken suspensions. Car suspension keeps tires in contact with the roadway in a stable and predictable manner. Steering enables drivers to go around road obstacles and avoid potential accidents. Even a safe, well-trained driver is helpless in the event of a steering or suspension system failure. Such failures are catastrophic, especially at high speeds. With regular component inspections by trained individuals, equipment failures can be virtually eliminated (smartmotorist.com).

Road Design and Environmental Factors

Permanent roadway hazards consist of intersections, merging lanes, bends, crests, school zones, and animal or pedestrian crossings. Temporary hazards include road construction, parked or disabled vehicles, accidents, traffic jams, and wild animals. Roadway design may be blamed for accidents, but it's rarely the cause. Civil engineers, local governments, and law enforcement agencies all contribute to the design of safe road layouts and traffic management systems. State and federal governments provide guidelines to their construction, with design flexibility to suit local conditions.

Engineers can use different surfaces depending on the environment, traffic speed, traffic volume and location of the roadway. Roadway markings let drivers know about their ability to pass safely, the location of the roadway in inclement weather and where road surface ends and the shoulder begins. Traffic light signals, speed limit signs, yield and stop signs, school & pedestrian crossings, turning lanes, traffic circles or roundabouts, built-in obstacles that limit the ability of a vehicle to speed (including crash barrels, speed bumps, pedestrian islands, raised medians, high curbing, guardrails, and concrete barriers) are some engineering solutions to reduce traffic accidents. Rural two-lane roadways are statistically the most dangerous because of a high incidence of deadly head-on collisions and the difficulty impatient drivers' face while overtaking slower vehicles.

Related to environmental factors, inclement weather, including heavy rain, hail, snowstorms, ice, high winds and fog can make driving more difficult. Drivers need more time to stop and may have trouble seeing the road clearly. Of the 5,870,000 vehicle crashes each year, twenty-three percent (23 percent) of these crashes—nearly 1,312,000—are weather-related. Weather-related crashes are defined as those crashes that occur in adverse weather (i.e., rain, sleet, snow, fog, severe crosswinds, or blowing snow/sand/debris) or on slick pavement (i.e., wet pavement, snowy/slushy pavement, or icy pavement). On average, 6,250 people are killed and over 480,000 people are injured in weather-related crashes each year (Murphy, *et al.*, 2012). The vast majority of weather-related crashes happen on wet pavement and during rainfall: Seventy-four percent (74 percent) on wet pavement and forty-six percent (46 percent) during rainfall. A much smaller percentage of weather-related crashes occur during winter conditions: Seventeen percent (17 percent) of during snow or sleet, twelve percent (12 percent) occur on icy pavement and fourteen percent (14 percent) of weather-related crashes take place on snowy or slushy pavement. Only three percent (3 percent) happen in the presence of fog (Murphy, *et al.*, 2012).

Table 9.3 Weather-related crash statistics (annual averages)

Road Weather Conditions	Weather-Related Crash Statistics		
	10-year Average (2002–2012)	10-year Percentages	
Wet Pavement	959,760 crashes	17% of vehicle crashes	74% of weather-related crashes
	384,032 persons injured	16% of crash injuries	80% of weather-related injuries
	4,789 persons killed	13% of crash fatalities	77% of weather-related fatalities
Rain	595,900 crashes	11% of vehicle crashes	46% of weather-related crashes
	245,446 persons injured	10% of crash injuries	52% of weather-related injuries
	2.876 persons killed	8% of crash fatalities	46% of weather-related fatalities
Snow/Sleet	211,188 crashes	4% of vehicle crashes	17% of weather-related crashes
	58,011 persons injured	3% of crash injuries	13% of weather-related injuries
	769 persons killed	2% of crash fatalities	13% of weather-related fatalities
Icy Pavement	154,580 crashes	3% of vehicle crashes	12% of weather-related crashes
	45,133 persons injured	2% of crash injuries	10% of weather-related injuries
	580 persons killed	2% of crash fatalities	10% of weather-related fatalities
Snow/Slushy	175,233 crashes	3% of vehicle crashes	14% of weather-related crashes

Road Weather Conditions	Weather-Related Crash Statistics		
	10-year Average (2002–2012)	10-year Percentages	
Pavement	43,503 persons injured	2% of crash injuries	10% of weather-related injuries
	572 persons killed	2% of crash fatalities	10% of weather-related fatalities
Fog	31,385 crashes	1% of vehicle crashes	3% of weather-related crashes
	11,812 persons injured	1% of crash injuries	3% of weather-related injuries
	511 persons killed	2% of crash fatalities	9% of weather-related fatalities
Weather-Related *	**1,311,970 crashes**	**23% of vehicle crashes**	
	480,338 persons injured	**20% of crash injuries**	
	6,253 persons killed	**17% of crash fatalities**	

Source: *Ten-year averages from 2002 to 2012 analyzed by Booz Allen Hamilton, based on NHTSA data*

To Stop or Not to Stop: Safety at Intersections

Stop signs at intersections, predominantly used in the U.S. and Canadian cities, play a crucial role in regulating the movements of traffic and pedestrians and, thus, avoiding traffic accidents. The Fatality Analysis and Reporting System of the U.S. National Highway Traffic Safety Administration (NHTSA) shows that there were 34,017 fatal crashes related to junction and traffic control devices in 2008 (NHTSA, Traffic Safety Facts, 2010). According to the 2009 NHTSA Annual Report on Traffic Safety Facts, 36 percent of fatal crashes at intersections are at stop signs, whereas 33 percent are at traffic signals, 25 percent at no traffic control devices, and the remaining at traffic control devices labeled as "other/unknown." The same data source reports that injury crashes at intersections are also higher at stop signs than other traffic control devices (NHTSA 2011). A similar report revealed that there was an increase in urban accidents, although a 7.1 percent decline in intersection crashes were observed between 2009 and 2010 (NHTSA 2012). However, statistical projection of traffic fatalities for the first half of 2012 shows that there was a 9.0 percent increase in traffic fatalities from the first half of 2011 (NHTSA 2012b).

Several other studies have reported that many injuries and fatalities occurred at intersections (with signals or stop signs) (USDOT 2004; Retting, Weinstein and Solomon 2003; NHTSA 2001; Van Houten and Retting 2001). As 50 percent of all urban accidents occur at intersections, studying drivers and pedestrians' behavior is of vital importance for public safety (Neuman, *et al.*, 2003).

At unsignalized stop-controlled intersections, drivers who fail to stop, or after stopping proceed without looking for traffic on the major road, create a substantial crash risk (Van Houten and Retting 2001). According to a survey by the National Safe Kids Campaign (2003), nearly half of the 25,660 vehicles surveyed at intersections marked with stop signs violated the stop signs by not coming to a complete stop at intersections. The same study shows that more than a third of motorists rolled through the stop signs, whereas nearly a tenth of motorists did not even slow down for the stop signs. There are various explanations as to why drivers are not complying with the stop signs as required by law. Although ecological issues such as the built environments, stop sign visibility and road design played a significant role, the compositional variables, such as drivers' behavior, explained in terms of carelessness, lack of attention, or unnecessary overconfidence in controlling their surroundings, and the driver's socio-demographic background, cause a failure to comply with the law of making a complete stop. The compositional variable may also include age, gender and hand-held cell phone use while approaching a stop sign. There are also studies that attempted to create relationships between the socio-economic backgrounds of the travelers, their trip making circumstances and their stopping behavior. For example, Kishore *et al.* (2009) conducted an observational study to determine the percentage of vehicles completely stopping at stop sign intersections. According to the results of the study, the greatest contributing factors that caused most drivers to completely stop were the presence of conflicting vehicle movement, followed by movement of vehicles, vehicle arrival sequences and the driver's age group. The study also found that drivers, during off-peak periods, have a higher probability of not completely stopping than those during peak periods because of less conflicting movement (either pedestrians or vehicles from other directions).

Other studies identified speeding as an influencing factor. For example, according to a study by NHTSA (2004), speeding was the dominant factor in the fatal vehicle crashes in which the driver violated the traffic signal/stop sign while inattention ranked second. Van Houten and Retting (2001) assessed several studies on the subject and documented that poor compliance at stop signs, characterized by failure to stop or to look adequately for oncoming traffic, improper lookout, and stop-sign visibility to be the leading cause of crashes. Age also played a significant role in influencing the behavior of drivers at stop signs. A study by Preusser *et al.* (1998) shows that drivers aged 65 and above are 2.3 times more at risk of being involved in accidents at all-way stop sign intersections when compared with being 1.3 times more at risk in other situations. Drivers aged 85 years and older are 10.6 times more at risk at stop-sign intersections. Braitman *et al.* (2007), in their comparative analysis between groups of drivers ages 35–54 and drivers ages 70 and older, found that crashes where drivers failed to yield the right of way increases with age and occurred mostly at stop sign controlled intersections.

The stopping behavior of the drivers can also be influenced by pedestrian movements at intersections. According to the National Safe Kids Campaign (2003), motorists were more likely to stop when pedestrians were present. However, the same study shows that nearly a third of motorists violated the stop signs when child pedestrians were present. Nearly half of motorists violated the stop signs when no pedestrians were present. Drivers were more likely to stop for pedestrians who were crossing than for those waiting to cross, although a significant percentage of drivers did not come to a complete stop at intersections where pedestrians were crossing. Traffic volumes, urban settings, and the behavior of other drivers can also have an influence on the way drivers behave at stop signs (Keay, *et al.*, 2009; Kishore, Kronprasert and Veknkateshwar 2009).

Measures to Reduce Traffic Accidents

Traffic accidents involve multiple contributing factors. Generally, the 4E's of safety measures are used by law enforcement to avoid or minimize the occurrence of traffic accidents.

- Engineering (road design, maintenance, operations and planning);
- Enforcement (state and local law enforcement, legislative mandates);
- Education (driver education, citizen advocacy); and
- Emergency response (medical, fire emergency, etc.).

Engineers approach a safety problem from the roadway and vehicle perspectives, law enforcement focuses on road user behavior, education concentrates on prevention, and emergency response personnel concentrate on post-collision care. Each approach is required for integrated, comprehensive, data-driven planning. Public agencies, private companies, elected and appointed officials, and the public all have a role in transportation safety.

Prevention strategies vary considerably from one travel mode to another mode because many of the factors affecting accident likelihood are mode-specific. In general, prevention strategies seek either to minimize the likelihood of a particular kind of harmful event (for example, a crash), or to minimize its impact (in terms of property damage, injury or environmental pollution). Over the years, government and other groups have implemented laws, programs and strategies for reducing traffic injuries and fatalities. They have succeeded in reducing the number of injuries and fatalities and overall car accidents. Various campaign groups such as Mothers Against Drunk Driving (MADD) and American Academy of Pediatrics (AAP) have helped with getting the word out about safe driving practices. Also, car manufacturers continue to improve and add safety mechanisms to the vehicles they manufacture and laws regarding youth drivers continue to be evaluated and changed.

Drunk Driving Prevention System

Car manufacturers are trying to include a drunk driving prevention system. While drunk driving kills thousands of people yearly, only two percent of people who drive while intoxicated get caught. In other terms, 98 percent of the people who drive drunk on a giving night will not be taken into account. That is why the drunk driving prevention system is a very important addition to car manufacturing. For example, Nissan is introducing a hi-sensitivity alcohol sensor built into the transmission shift knob, which is able to detect the presence of alcohol in the perspiration of the driver's palm as he or she attempts to start driving. When the alcohol level detected is above the pre-determined threshold, the system automatically locks the transmission, immobilizing the car. A "drunk-driving" voice alert is also issued via the car navigation system.

Additional alcohol odor sensors are also incorporated into the driver's and passengers' seats to detect the presence of alcohol in the air inside the vehicle cabin. When alcohol is detected, the system issues both a voice alert and a message alert on the navigation system monitor. The device is feared to be easily manipulated so that the intoxicated driver is still able to get behind the wheel and put others in danger.

Safety Improvements on Vehicles

According to a study by the U.S. Department of Transportation's National Highway Traffic Safety Administration NHTSA (2012), better-designed, safer vehicles have contributed to an overall decline in crashes, deaths and injuries on U.S. roadways. The agency's analysis of police-reported crash data estimates that design improvements between Model Year 2000 and Model Year 2008 cars helped save 2,000 lives and prevented one million occupant injuries in the 2008 calendar year alone. The NHTSA report also shows the likelihood of escaping a crash uninjured improved from 79 to 82 percent as a result of improvements between the 2000 and 2008 cars. The report used statistical models to isolate vehicle improvements from human and environmental factors. NHTSA data shows traffic fatalities have been on a steady decline in the past decade, falling to 32,885 in 2010—the lowest level in six decades—despite

Americans driving more miles than previous years (Glassbrenner 2012). The agency expects this trend to continue as automakers add advanced safety features to their fleets and continue to improve vehicle designs to earn top safety ratings under the newly updated 5-Star crash-test program. The United States Department of Transportation suggests the new system gives vehicles one overall safety rating, as well as many sub-ratings, with one star being the worst and five stars being the best (Mitchell 2010). To achieve more gains in safety, the government is making it harder for cars to receive five-star safety ratings, which can make the manufacturers more willing and motivated to produce safer cars. Recent car models have anti-lock brakes, electronic stability control, tire pressure sensor monitors, and multiple air bags.

SAFETY FOR YOUTH DRIVER AND CHILDREN

Youth drivers, simply because of their age, are involved in more crashes than almost any other age group. For people under the age of 21, more than 5,000 deaths occur annually as a result of car accidents. Drivers aged 16 to 19 are involved in 20 crashes per million miles driven versus five crashes per million miles for all drivers other than those over 80 years of age. The primary reason in this sad statistic is a lack of maturity and lack of experience (Porter 2009). Most states require classroom time, a certain amount of behind-the-wheel hours, and having adults present in the vehicle for a pre-determined number of months after the license is obtained. Also, in some places, night curfews, and zero tolerance alcohol laws have been enacted (Porter 2009).

Regarding children, strategies recommended by the American Academy of Pediatrics (AAP) include having rear-facing car seats for children under the age of two or until they reach the height and weight restrictions for the car seat. A rear facing child seat distributes the force of the collision over the entire body. There have been some studies in the last few years that showed it's safer to be rear-facing because the child get better support for the head and neck in car crashes (Suwanski 2011). Another recommendation by the AAP is that children should always ride in the back seat of a car until at least the age of 13 (Suwanski 2011). Also, it has been recommended having children in booster seats until they are 4 feet 9 inches tall, usually between the ages of 8 and 12. The AAP stated that the rate of deaths in motor vehicles for people under the age of 16 had decreased by 45 percent from the years 1997 to 2009. One shocking statistic is that these crashes are still the leading cause of death for children aged four and older, so much more is still needed to be done to lower that number.

BOX 9.1 Arlington's Safe Routes to School (SR2S) program

Arlington's Safe Routes To School program (SR2S) program was started in 2000 by the National Park Service's Rivers and Trails Program in coordination with Walk Boston. Arlington (population 42,389) is an older suburb of Boston (population 589,141) that was developed before World War II. The project started with three schools in Arlington. During the first year, two schools in Boston were added. Arlington city and its suburb are both densely populated, and neighborhoods are considered walkable. However, many lifestyles do not lend themselves to walking to school, and schools in both cities actively discourage cycling. This SR2S project concentrated on community education, as well as parent and student encouragement efforts, believing these to be the greatest needs. Numerous strategies and activities encouraged thousands of parents and children to get involved, resulting in substantial gains in the number of Arlington children walking to school.

Description of Efforts

- Sponsored Walk to School Days, a six-week Step into Spring walking contest, led neighborhood walks with classes, developed walking games and activities, conducted a "walking school bus" week, and gave children pedometers so they could measure how far they walked.
- Produced six SR2S newsletters that showcased crossing guards, students, and parents who regularly walked; newsletters included photographs and walking activities.
- Hired parents of students at participating schools as SR2S coordinators to work 10–15 hours per week.
- Emphasized the fun aspects of walking, avoiding messages that focused on negative concerns such as overweight children.
- Recruited parents at PTA meetings and through informal networks such as SR2S coordinators "talking up" the program daily with parents as they arrived at school with their children.
- Worked with town councils on ways to make routes to school safer.
- Promoted the use of public transit, in conjunction with walking, for middle school age children.

Effects

- In the two elementary schools in Arlington that participated in SR2S, the percentage of students walking to school increased from a baseline of 42 percent to a current rate of 56 percent. At the participating middle school in Arlington, walking to school increased from 19 percent to 24 percent.
- At these Arlington schools, more than 150 students walk to school regularly, who did not walk before.

Lessons Learned

The project focused on the fun aspect of families walking together. Elementary children were very enthusiastic, and parents who remembered walking to school when they were students were willing to try walking; though, developing a culture of walking in a community requires a sustained effort. Teachers are more willing to participate and integrate activities into their curriculum when given ready-made lesson plans.

Adapted from, "Safe Routes to School Practice and Premise," National Highway Traffic Safety Administration.

Review Questions

1) Who published the report "Unsafe at Any Speed," and what did the report accuse automobile companies of doing?
2) What significant legislative acts were responsible for developing safety standards and programs for the United States?
3) Discuss the significance of the Haddon Matrix in understanding traffic risk factors.
4) Discuss the effect of weather on traffic safety.
5) Discuss driving behavior at stop sign controlled intersections.
6) Discuss the three factors that relate to driving accidents.
7) Explain the roles of campaign groups such as MADD and AAP in reducing accidents to youth drivers and children.
8) What are the 4Es of traffic safety? Explain.
9) What are some methods for improving vehicle safety?

Project/Paper Idea

Design a field research. The task is observing driver's behavior at stop-sign controlled intersection. Prepare a field checklist with stopping type (complete stop, rolling stop, no stop). Also include in your checklist variables such as gender of the driver, intersection type, the dominant building types (business, residential, etc.), passenger volume, availability of law enforcement officials, numbers of passengers, etc. Make observations at different times of the day. What variable has a significant impact on the stopping behavior of motorists?

Video

Missing Persons: Drunk Driving Holocaust by *Films Media Group, 2005 (26 min.)*: This video brings the real-life consequences of mixing alcohol with driving into the classroom. Hard-hitting footage helps young adults realize the consequences of drunk driving, for the victim and the driver. Bereaved parents and friends, permanently disabled victims, and young inmates convicted of vehicular homicide explore the relationship between alcohol, death, and prison. Members of MADD (Mothers Against Drunk Driving), SADD (Students Against Drunk Driving), and CAR (Convicts After Recovery) discuss how the thoughtless act of driving drunk impacts people's lives.

Internet Sources

- American Academy of Pediatrics (AAP), http://www.aap.org/en-us/Pages/Default.aspx
- Mothers Against Drunk Driving (MADD), http://www.madd.org/
- National Highway Traffic Safety Administration, http://www.nhtsa.gov/

Bibliography

Atkins, Anne: 2003. "VCU Study Finds Cell Phones Are Not the Leading Cause of Distracted Driving," *Virgina Commonwealth University News.*

Baker, Robert. 1971a. *Attacking the Problem: The Highway Risk Problem: Policy Issues in Highway Safety.* New YorK: Wiley-Interscience, 53–67.

_____. 1971b. *Setting Goals for Highway Safety & Developing Highway Safety Programs: The Highway Risk Problem, Policy Issues in Highway Safety.* New York: Wiley-Interscience, 117–154.

Berenis, Michael. 2008. "Districts Metro Station Entrances to Get Crime Cameras." *The Examiner.* ProQuest Newsstand.

Blomquist, Glenn. 1988. *The Regulation of Motor Vehicle and Traffic Safety.* Boston. Boston: Kluwer Academic.

Braitman, Keli, Bevan Kirley, and Neil Chaudhary. 2007. "Factors Leading to Older Drivers' Intersection Crashes." *Traffic Injuries and Prevention* 8: 267–274.

Cantu, Oscar. 1980. *An Updated Regression Analysis on the Effects of the Regulation of Auto Safety.* Working Paper No. 15, Yale School of Managment.

Forbes, T. W. 1972. *Introduction: Human Factors in Highway Safety Research.* Canada: John Wiley & Sons.

Glassbrenner, Donna. 2012. *An Analysis of Recent Improvements to Vehicle Safety.* Department of Transportation, National Highway Traffic Safety Administration.

Halsey, Ashley. 2010. "Cellphone Use, Texting in 28 Percent of Crashes; Traffic Study Results Inspire Group to Fight Distracted Driving." *The Washington Post.*

Keay, Lisa, Srichand Jasti, Beatriz Munoz, Kathleen Turano, Cynthia Munro, Donald Duncan, Kevin Baldwin, Karen Bandeen-Roche, Emily Gower, and Sheila West. 2009. "Urban and Rural Differences in Older Drivers' Failure to Stop at Stop Signs." *Accident Analysis and Prevention* 41: 995–1000.

Kishore, Raj, Nopadon Kronprasert, and Reddy Dhomadugu Veknkateshwar. 2009. *Observational Study for Determining the Percentage of Vehicles Completely Stopping at a Stop-Sign Intersection: Transportation Safety Final Report.* National Capital Region: Virginia Tech.

Miller, Ted, Rekaya Gibson, Eduard Zaloshnja, Lawrence Blincoe, John Kindelberger, Alexander Strashny, and Andrea Thomas. "Underreporting of Driver Alcohol Involvement in United States Police and Hospital Records: Capture-Recapture Estimates." *Annals of Advances in Automotive Medicine* 87–96.

Mitchell, Josh. 2010. "Crash Tests Dent Car-Safety Scores." *Wall Street Journal*, October 6.

Murphy, Ray, Ryan Swick, Booz Hamilton, and Guevara Gabe. 2012. "Best Practices for Road Weather Management." Office of Transportation Operations, Federal Highway Administration, Washington, D.C.

Nadler, Ralph. 1965. *Unsafe at Any Speed: The Designed-In Dangers of the American Automobile.* Grossman Publishers, New York.

Neuman, Timothy, Ronald Pfefer, Kevin Slack, Kelley Hardy, Douglas Harwood, Ingrid Potts, Derren Torbic, and Emilia Rabbani. 2003. *A Guide for Addressing Unsignalized Intersection Collisions: NCHRP Report 500.* National Cooperative Highway Research Program, Washington, D.C.: Transportation Research Board.

NHTSA. 2001. *Traffic Safety Facts.* Washington, D.C.: National Highway Traffic Safety Administration.

_____. 2004. *Analysis of Fatal Crashes Due to Signal and Stop Sign Violations.* Department of Transportation, Washington, D.C.: National Highway Traffic Safety Administration.

_____. 2009. "Traffic Safety Facts: A Compilation of Motor Vehicle Crash Data from the Fatality Analysis Reporting System and General Estimation System." National Highway Traffic Safety Administration, Department of Transportation, Washington, D.C.

_____. 2010. "Fatality Analysis and Reporting System (FARS)." National Highway Traffic Safety Administration, U.S. Department of Transportation.

_____. 2012. "Fatality Analysis Reporting System (FARS) Encyclopedia." *National Household Traffic Safety Administration.*

NSKC. 2003. *Stop Sign Violations Put Child Pedestrians at Risk: A National Survey of Motorist Behavior at Stop Signs in School Zones and Residential Areas.* Washington, D.C.: National Safe Kids Campaign.

NTSB. 2002. *National Transportation Safety Board: Safety Study.* Washington, D.C.: Transportation Safety Databases.

_____. 2013. *Reaching Zero: Actions to Eliminate Alcohol-Impaired Driving: Safety Report.* Washington, D.C.: National Transportation Safety Board.

Olmstead, Todd. 2004. "Seat Belts in Numbers: National Traffic and Motor Vehicle Safety Act of 1966." Vol. 3. New York: Macmillan Reference.

Orr, Lloyd. 1984. "The Effectiveness of Automobile Safety Regulation: Evidence from the FARS Data." *American Journal of Public Health* 74 (12): 1384–1389.

Peden, Margie, Richard Scurfield, David Sleet, Dinesh Mohan, Hyder Adnan, Eva Jarawan, and Matners Colin. 2004. *World Report on Road Traffic Injury Prevention.* World Health Organization.

Peltzman, Sam. 1975. "The Effects of Automobile Safety Regulation." *The Journal of Political Economy* 83 (4): 677–726.

Porter, Richard. 2009. *Economics at the Wheel.* San Diego: Academic Press.

Preusser, David, Allan Williams, Susan Ferguson, Robert Ulmer, and Helen Weinstein. 1989. "Fatal Crash Risk for Older Drivers at Intersections." *Accident Analysis and Prevention* 30 (2): 151–159.

PS. 2011. "Cell Phone Use While Driving & Employer Liability Professional Safety." *Professional Safety* 56 (12): 18–19.

Retting, Richard, Helen Weinstein, and Mark Solomon. 2003. "Analysis of Motor Vehicle Crashes at Stop Signs in Four U.S. Cities." *Journal of Safety Research* 34: 485–489.

Robertson, Leon. 1984. "Automobile Safety Regulation: Rebuttal and New Data." *American Journal of Public Health* 74 (12): 1390–1394.

Romano, Eduardo, and Robert Voas. 2011. "Drug and Alcohol Involvement in Four Types of Fatal Crashes." *Journal of Studies on Alcohol & Drugs* 72 (4): 567–576.

Sarkar, Sheila, and Marie Andreas. 2004. "Acceptance of and Engagement in Risky Driving Behaviors by Teenagers." *Adolescence* 39 (156): 687–700.

Seckan, Bakary. 2013. "Road Safety and Motor Vehicle Accidents: Surveying Global and U.S. Data." *Journal Resource.* Harvard Kennedy School, Shorenstein Center on Media, Politics, and Public Policy.

Suwanski, Rich. 2011. "Rear-Facing Car Seats Urged for Kids Until Age 2 More Protection in Case of Wreck, Study Says." *Messenger-Inquirer.*

USDOT. 2004. *Analysis of Fatal Crashes Due to Signal and Stop Sign Violations.* Washington, D.C.: U.S. Department of Transportation.

Van Houten, Ron, and Richard Retting. 2001. "Increasing Motorist Compliance and Caution at Stop-Signs." *Journal of Applied Behavior Analysis* 34: 185–193.

White, Mathew, Richard Eiser, and Peter Harris. 2004. "Risk Perceptions of Mobile Phone Use While Driving." *Risk Annals* 24 (2): 323–334.

10

Social Equity and the Transportation-Disadvantaged

Chapter Outline

- Introduction
- Challenges of the Low-Income
  - o *Spatial Mismatch Theory*
  - o *Low-Income Women—A Unique Challenge*
- Challenges of the Elderly
- Challenges of the Disabled
- Challenges of New Immigrants
- Planning for the Disadvantage
  - o *Smart Growth*
  - o *Universal Design and Complete Street*
  - o *Demand Responsive Transit—Planning and Policy*

Introduction

Most of the time, plans are designed and implemented with little consideration of certain groups of people who, as Falcocchio and Cantilli (1984) have been categorized as "disadvantaged," such as the poor, the aging, the youth, those with physical or cognitive limitations, ethnic minorities and new immigrants. Cities are planned with automobile dependency in mind, giving little or no attention to the portion of the society which relies on various alternative modes of transportation for commuting. But in fact, a great portion of members in low-income, elderly and minority households disproportionately depend on public transit (Garrett and Brian 1999; Ross and Prchal-Svajlenka 2012). A detailed analysis of commuting behavior in the Northeast corridor of the United States found that approximately ten percent of commuter households do not own a car and overall, 23 percent are low-income. Generally, low-income households are unduly dependent on transit more than affluent households. Yet, the higher demand for public transit by low-income communities, in particular, may not be associated with adequate levels of public transit services overall. This is the same for the elderly and people with disability. In fact, neighborhoods often have a variety of transportation needs along with differing levels and availability of public transit services that are not necessarily in alignment with the observed demand for transit options. Neighborhood differences in available public transit services could result in commute inequities that create critical disparities in commute time and monetary costs of travel (Wells and Thil 2012). For example, in the Washington, D.C., metropolitan area, although transit coverage is most robust in low-income neighborhoods, service frequency is less favorable for those low-income neighborhoods in the outer suburbs (Ross and Prchal-Svajlenka 2012).

Limited transportation options for low-income and minority families influence critical access to potential job opportunities in the local and regional labor market. Irregular and uncertain transportation options may result in higher job search costs, and when jobs are secured, longer commute times may be more costly as well (Clark and Huang 2003). In fact, evidence about public transit commute times in the largest metropolitan areas indicates that only about 25 percent of low-skilled jobs are accessible within 90-minute commute, while nearly 34 percent of high-skilled jobs are accessible in 90 minutes via public transit. Much fewer low-skilled jobs are accessible within a 60 or 45 minute public transit commute time (Tomer, *et al.,* 2011).

Mobility goes hand in hand with equity. In a society where not everyone can afford the luxuries of owning a personal car and going wherever they want, whenever they want to, transportation problems for the disadvantaged is a critical social issue to be addressed. This is mostly because spatial distribution of private and public goods and services have been changing through the last several decades. Under the impetus of economic scale and, ironically, increased mobility for the majority of the population, many local private and public services have failed or have moved to suburban areas (Briggs and McKelvey 2006). Moreover, the poorer urban residents live in depressed urban areas because of the high costs of transportation with the more affluent urban residents living on the fringes. Because of their physical location as well as their economic challenges, the poor usually need more time, greater effort, and higher marginal capital to reach the same destinations as the people owning cars living in the inner areas (Soltani and Ivaki 2011). For the elderly, youth and the disabled who live in the suburbs, the far proximity of urban activities and health facilities creates a major challenge in their mobility.

Challenges of the Low-Income

Low-income groups reside in areas that do not facilitate proper access to services. Besides, they lack sufficient money, have limited access to jobs/opportunities, as well as limited access to health and education facilities (Gomide 2008). The vast majority of the lower income groups are faced with such constraints because they lack the ability to access affordable personal transportation that in turn limits their mobility, and this lack of mobility constrains access to employment and education opportunities (Faiz 2011). Gomide further adds that

> Urban poverty manifests itself through the spatial segregation of the poorest areas characterized by inadequate public services and deficient infrastructure, where the provision of mass transit is inappropriate in terms of price as well as availability. These limitations constrain income and employment opportunities for the urban poor because of lack of mobility and access. The

urban poor are forced to restrict their travel to essential trips related to work, education, and shopping.

Income often determines one's mode of transportation. For instance, it has been found that owning and using a personal car increases with income; if income is limited, then an alternate mode of travel must be used. The lower income population often relies on walking, biking or public transit, assuming that the weather and topography allow for such movement. It has also been found that in autocentric society there is less ridership on public transit, which hurts the funding for public transit that is heavily used by lower socioeconomic demographics (Faiz 2011).

The travel demand of lower income groups is often neglected when making transportation plans/policy. This results in social and environmental justice issues that can be manifested in the following areas:

- While some communities have better accessibility and relief, others face fewer benefits from transportation spending programs.
- Low-income neighborhoods are negatively impacted by certain transportation projects, being exposed to pollutants and community disruption.
- Low-income communities pay higher transportation taxes and fares compared to others.
- Low-income residents receive a small share of the jobs that were created by the construction and operation of transportation facilities.
- Low-income and minority communities are less represented when it comes to policy decisions in terms of transportation resources. (Forenbrock and Schweitzer 1999; Cairns, Greig and Wachs 2003).

With regards to the built environment, the design of the poor communities often have highly walkable streets compared to affluent neighborhoods; however, these areas are often blighted, aesthetically unpleasant, high in crime, heavy in traffic and often lack social cohesion (Cutts, *et al.*, 2009). Also, when compared to affluent neighborhoods, the poorer neighborhoods lacked trees, landmark buildings, clean streets and access to street cafés (Neckareman *et al.*, 2009). Other environmental disparities that are found within the community design of ethnic and less affluent areas are lack of proper pedestrian infrastructure, poor physical amenities, visual qualities and maintenance, which leaves the population not feeling particularly safe (Zhu and Lee 2008). Often the sight of such characteristics could deter individuals from partaking in active transportation (such as walking and biking) in these well-connected and highly walkable communities, limiting overall physical activity. This shows that the perception of the physical and social environment influences how the community moves and conducts themselves.

Affordability is also a major factor for those in lower income neighborhoods in determining what mode of travel to utilize. Garrett and Taylor (1999), explained how the choice of mode of public transportation can be differentiated by income. In the article, they mention how urban bus riders made less than those who either rode a commuter rail or drove by themselves. According to U.S. Department of Transportation, the median household income of an urban bus passenger was below $20,000 compared to over $40,000 for commuter rail patrons and over $45,000 for drivers of private vehicles.

Blumenberg and Ong (2001) discussed the struggle between spatial separation from jobs and employment for welfare participants. The article reveals that "welfare recipients" do not usually own personal vehicles. Supporting this, data from the U.S. Department of Health and Human Services, automobile ownership among welfare recipients is 6.7 percent nationally. Thus, accessibility is a major challenge for low-income groups. Research on accessibility has found that spatial patterns affect the ability to obtain jobs. Roberto's article for the Metropolitan Policy Program at Brookings found that households make trade-offs in housing and transportation expenses, spending more for housing located near jobs or choosing more affordable housing farther away from jobs with higher transportation costs, including long and expensive commutes (Roberto 2008).

Spatial Mismatch Theory

To understand the gap between neighborhood need and transportation supply, it is worthwhile to understand the concept of spatial mismatch, which is an old problem that still impacts workers in metropolitan areas. The concept originated with John Kain (1968) and was used to help explain persistent inferior job attachment and wages of black men who lived in central cities in the mid to late 1900s. Over four decades of supporting research on spatial mismatch has provided an extensive body of evidence that manufacturing job decentralization and residential sprawl have contributed to higher unemployment rates for African American and to a lesser extent, Latino workers (Kain 1968; Kain 1992; Kasarda 1983; Gobillon, Selod and Zenou 2007; Covington 2009). Despite the wide acceptance of the spatial mismatch hypothesis, a few have challenged the classic view that spatial separation from skill matched jobs and residential location drive higher unemployment rates for blacks and Latinos. These works have asserted that factors such as employment discrimination are likely more important in explaining persistent black and Latino unemployment (Ellwood 1986; Hellerstein, Neumark and McInerney 2008). Scholars have noted an increasing geographic separation between job opportunities and downtown centralized locations. Today, there are more jobs in suburban locations than in cities (Kneebone and Berube 2013). Surprisingly, only 23 percent of metropolitan jobs are located within three miles of downtown; more than 43 percent are more than ten miles from downtown (Kneebone and Berube 2013). Between 1990 and 2000 a significant number of minority (Michael and Raphael 2002) and poor households (Hellerstein, Neumark and McInerney 2008) were moving toward job-rich metropolitan areas to overcome problems of job accessibility. In a metropolitan region, where employment is dispersed all over the metropolitan area, physical distance then needs to be recognized as an impediment to access to jobs. Certainly, car ownership seems to minimize spatial mismatch impacts. Ong and Miller (2005) examined the impact of spatial mismatch, car ownership and employment outcomes in the Los Angeles primary metropolitan area, focusing on the relationship of transportation to employment-to-population ratio and the unemployment rate. Study results indicate that a 10 percent increase in the carless rate results in a 3 percent drop in employment (Ong and Miller 2005). These results are promising for car owners or for people able to afford a car, but there are millions of households unable to afford cars in suburban neighborhoods in the U.S. and these households are dependent on other transportation options. Thus, transit accessibility can be a mediator to poor job access neighborhoods. Available and quality transit services may provide residents access to jobs in the surrounding area.

Though studies on spatial separation of jobs and car ownership exist, only few studies have considered the relative impacts of the spatial distribution of public transit services (Sanchez 1998; Zumaeta 2003) in relationship to the job attachment of residents. Take, for example, a study by Sanchez (1998) where he uses a Geographic Information System (GIS) to analyze the location and employment characteristics of workers with varying levels of accessibility to transit. Utilizing a variety of spatial measures, a two-stage least squares regression is used to estimate the relationship of transit accessibility with labor force participation levels for the cities of Portland, Oregon and Atlanta, Georgia. The results suggest that transit access is a significant factor in determining average rates of labor participation within these two cities (Sanchez 1998). In the Sanchez (1998) article, the stated direction of the relationship is that transit accessibility is associated with greater labor force outcomes. It is also possible that as a symbol of transit demand, it may be the case that labor force participation rates can influence public transit administrative decisions. Furthermore, there seems to be a correlation between transporting the disadvantaged and social exclusion. For example, New South Wales, Australia, "public transport services are very limited and often non-existent, impacting the opportunities for social inclusion. Access to employment, particularly for youth and low-income households, often of culturally and linguistically diverse (CALD) or Aboriginal background, are common problems" (Battellino 2009). By using strong words like "common problems," the author captures the harsh conditions in which those who are disadvantaged must live. Social exclusion plays a big role in the life of the disadvantaged as they have limited mobility and access to employment opportunities, therefore, are more likely have a low income. Also, they may not have adequate housing, health care, or possibly even education.

Low-Income Women—A Unique Challenge

One of the particular disadvantaged groups that continue to be marginalized in the transportation sector is low-income, minority women. Race and gender play a part in low-income transportation behaviors and deficiencies. In Scholl's article, research is conducted on transportation affordability for low-income groups of the San Francisco Bay Area. In the article, Scholl discusses how women are the largest group who are the most transit dependent: "Women continue to shoulder much more of the household responsibility than men, resulting in their increased likelihood to chain trips together, with this difference being greatest among whites who have higher incomes than among people of color" (Scholl 2002). When it came to the topic of race, the article discussed that blacks, Asians, and Latinos had lower rates of automobile ownership than whites. Thus, gender and race are important factors in the overall discussion of transportation for the low income. Women who are considered low income have been analyzed by Evelyn Blumenberg (2004) as she discusses the way women are prone to work in areas far from their homes and how their destinations lack the supporting transportation. In her article, *Engendering Effective Planning; Spatial Mismatch, Low-income Women, and Transportation Policy*, Blumenberg highlights the effect that transportation has on women's employment decisions. For example, the article points out the problem that the transportation system presents to mothers that are low income and are part of a welfare program and are then sent to working locations nearly impossible to reach. Therefore, obtaining employment is just one more disadvantage that these women face due to the lack of accessibility they encounter. Many of these women are forced then to travel longer distances for employment and take three times as long to get to their destination due to an inconsistent transportation system that goes from the city out to the suburbs.

The other groups of women that are at a disadvantage in terms of transportation are low-income single mothers. In Lisa Bostock's *Walking as a Mode of Transport Among Low-*

Income Mothers, the disadvantage that single mothers face in terms of transportation is well documented. For single mothers, the fact that they are low income demands a high number of chained trips. This then is seen as a problem because it brings about high levels of physical fatigue and psychological stress. Their challenges are presented as both physical and physiological due to the transportation they are forced to depend on.

Challenges of the Elderly

As one reaches the later stages of life, he/she may discover declines in their physical and cognitive abilities. As a result, many older adults find themselves asking for assistance with accomplishing some of the basic tasks in their day-to-day lives. Due to the fact that this is a universal inevitability, it seems logical that cities and communities can and should be considering designs to help older adults to increase their mobility and provide access to medical care and other neighborhood amenities. As Kochera and Bright (2005) state, "Poorly designed housing, inadequate sidewalks, limited mobility options, and few supportive services can make it difficult for people to remain active and engaged with friends, family, and neighbors." To accomplish this goal, planners would be prudent to incorporate Stafford's Four Domains of an Elder-Friendly Community: address basic needs, promote social and civic

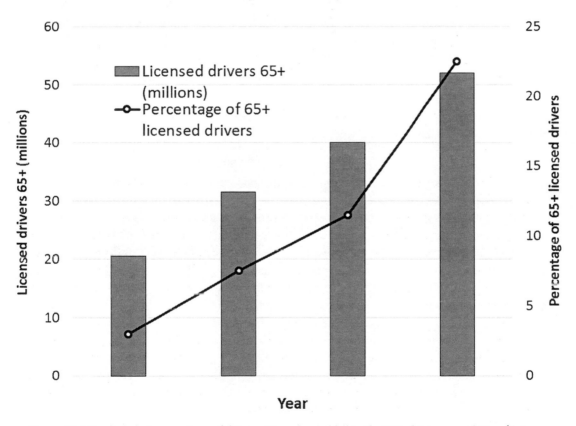

Figure 10.1 Number and percentage of drivers 65 years or older in the U.S. driving population (data: Federal Highway Administration statistics and predictions).

engagement, optimize physical and mental health and well-being, and maximize independence for frail and disabled (Stafford 2009).

Public transit should accommodate the elderly so that they are not driving on the road where they can potentially harm themselves or others around them. Elderly drivers are more likely than other drivers to be involved in collisions because of a traffic violation, such as failure to yield right-of-way or to disregard the traffic signal. These types of crashes tend to increase with age, especially after the age of 80 (Robertson and Vanlaar 2008).

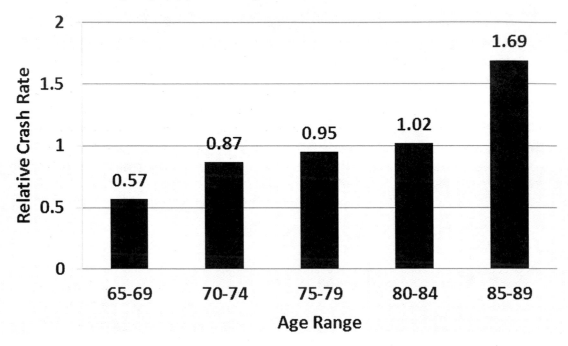

Figure 10.2 Relative crash rates in the 65 and over population (data: Fitten LJ, 2005).

But obviously, cars are private modes of transportation that provide more independence to the elderly than public transportation. About 90 percent of all trips made by individuals between the ages of 65 and 84 are in private vehicles, either as a passenger or driver. Only 3 percent of trips made by older people use public transportation (Pepper Institute on Aging and Public Policy 2006). The elderly strongly prefer driving over transit, as driving associates with freedom, convenience, and independence (Chase 2011). The number of drivers who are 65 and up has been steadily increasing throughout the years. More and more elderly people are getting licenses and more and more are renewing their licenses. Consequently, accommodating transportation for the elderly is beginning to be an issue in the current transportation planning process. Planning agencies are developing projections of how these needs will change, and exploring strategies to satisfy the anticipated demands (Wachs 1979).

The elderly, as well as the disabled, start struggling with mobility when their ability to drive a car is restricted. A common reason elderly are no longer able to drive their car is due to poor eyesight. With age, vision becomes impaired, which means inability to read road signs. Also, they might have slower reaction times and reduced mobility. Cars and roadways are built for the average driver's reflexes, ability, and vision. The size of sign wordage, distance from warnings to hazards, size and brightness of lighted signals and many other features make roads less accommodating to elderly drivers (Pickut 2013).

The freedom of leaving their homes anytime they desire is no longer an option. They can either ask a friend or family member, which is very common or change their modes of transportation and start riding the bus. There are millions of senior citizens who depend on others for their transportation. Constantly asking their friends and siblings for favors causes the elderly to be discouraged. This issue also applies to the disabled that range in age. To resist becoming a burden to family and friends, they decide to isolate themselves and discontinue daily routines that would let them socialize with others (Pickut 2013). A mode of transportation that does not require asking friends or family for rides would be public transportation. However, public transportation is not a common preference amongst both elderly and disabled. Holly Chase (2011) in her research paper "Transportation Planning Options for Elderly Mobility," discusses how the main reason the elderly avoid public transportation is due to their perception. She claims "public transportation does poorly on a measure of acceptability. The elderly often associate public transportation with long waits, uncertainty, and hard-to-read schedules. The same features that increase effectiveness for providers make transit less attractive for elderly users." When using public transportation, the elderly are most likely to encounter being pushed amongst crowded spaces in buses or trains. Another issue that creates an inconvenience for the elderly to use public transportation is the location of transit stops. Currently, there is a high amount of elderly people living in the suburbs, and it is hard for them to access bus stops because public transportation doesn't reach most suburbs. Public transportation tends to centralize its services in the city where more people use buses and trains. An example of this problem is discussed in a study done in Minneapolis, Minnesota by Marlys Harris (2012). In her article *What's Better for Old People: City or Suburb?* She claims that "access to transit varies widely"; when the study examined the 13-county Twin Cities metro, it found that only 10 percent of in-town seniors aged 65 to 79 had poor access to public transit; by 2015 that would increase slightly to 11 percent. In suburban areas, however, boomers will live in a public transit desert. Some 69 percent in the suburbs of Twin Cities metro won't have any access, up from 64 percent the previous year. This study does not only apply to Minnesota. The lack of public transportation in suburbs is an issue that affects most users in the U.S. while at the same time the number of elderly in suburbs continues to grow.

Walking accessibility plays a crucial role in the life of an elderly and disabled person. It allows them to interact with the community by either walking around the neighborhood or walking to the nearest bus stop. Sometimes, streets are not physically built to accommodate the needs of the elderly and disabled. A very common problem that both the elderly and the disabled face is having enough time to cross the street. Without having a safe right of way, the elderly and disabled are in danger even going from one street block to another. A study was done where the British Geriatrics Society tested 355 people over 60 to find out how fast they walked and found that half of those over 80 were not able to get over pedestrian crossings before the "red man" light appeared. Many could walk at speeds of less than one meter per second, far below the average 1.2 meters per second used to calculate pedestrian crossing timings. The British Geriatrics Society concluded that "not being able to cross roads in time could leave many older (and disabled) people frightened to leave their homes and reluctant to walk long distances."

Challenges of the Disabled

Disabled persons account for 15 percent of the world population and face several social, accessibility, communication and legislative challenges that somehow limit them from being active in life. Many of the problems that plague the aging community and limit their transportation options are also faced by the non-elderly disabled population. Blindness or other physical limitations prevent such individuals from being able to utilize personal vehicles. The physically disabled can be marginalized by not having their needs accommodated in the planning process. Also, the psychological effects poor transportation planning causes is not usually taken into account. As with the elderly, transportation challenges force the disabled to become dependent on someone else which often leads to isolation due to the lack of independence. In the past several years, adjustments have been made to the transportation systems to meet their needs, but the physical plan has yet to meet their needs.

Personal cars are not purpose-built (although can be custom made) for the disabled, which leaves disabled people without a range of choices like many other people when buying a car. These cars also cost more depending on what features would be needed to provide the most comfort for the user. The cost associated with modifying a vehicle is very expensive.

As elderly people, the disabled have their issues with public transportation. Some people require wheelchairs due to their disability, and sometimes wheelchair spaces are not available if they are trying to ride the bus. Buses have space for only two wheelchairs. After this capacity is reached, a disabled person using a wheelchair would most likely be left behind to wait for another bus. Another problem that wheelchair users may encounter is a crowded bus. If a bus is full, then the bus driver may be able to squeeze one more person in, but it is most likely that the bus driver will not even stop for the wheelchair user, knowing they require more space than most people. These issues make it difficult for wheelchair users to get to their destination on time.

Despite all of the challenges the disabled (and the elderly) face with mobility, there have been actions that have had a positive impact on transportation planning. There are legal actions, such as federal laws that specifically target the rights of an elderly or disabled person. The Rehabilitation Act of 1973, as amended, provides discrimination protection to persons with disabilities. People with disabilities are no longer to be excluded from, denied the benefits of, or be subjected to discrimination under any program or activity that receives Federal financial assistance. The Americans with Disabilities Act (ADA) of 1990, as amended, requires accessibility in public transportation by intercity and commuter transit services.

Some State Department of Transportation agencies provides grants so that organizations can offer transportation services for the disabled. An example of this is New York State, where they have funded a program that provides capital-only funding for the transportation needs of elderly individuals and individuals with disabilities. Through the NYSDOT Section 5310 Grant Program, funds are used to purchase accessible buses for not-for-profit organizations throughout the State of New York. The program funds 80 percent of the vehicle purchase cost, with the remaining 20 percent provided by the applicant organization as the local match. There are no operating funds provided under this program, and recipients are responsible for 100 percent of their ongoing operating expenses.

Challenges of New Immigrants

In addition to cultural, language, and economic barriers that immigrants face when taking up residence in a new country, they also face many transportation challenges. A key issue that they face is the challenge of acquiring a sufficient mode of transportation that makes everyday life easier. For new immigrants, commuting to different places such as work, the grocery store, school, and leisure activities are all dependent on a reliable and, more importantly, accessible mode of transportation. The notion of transportation challenges and securing a job are interrelated since accessibility to a job is dependent on the access to a car or another form of transportation. Researchers have also found strong positive effects of car ownership on the likelihood of being employed, with particularly large effects for minority workers (Holzer, Quigley and Raphael 2003).

Naturally, one is going to need a job to survive in a new country when a strong kinship and resources are initially limited. One of the biggest challenges immigrants face in their process to assimilate into society is finding a job (Kim 2009). Ong and Houston (2002) found 40 percent of low-income residents (including immigrants) in the U.S. have no access to a car; this is key finding in that such a large portion must rely on some other means other than a car. Since so much emphasis is related to owning a car or having one accessible to use to make an impact on employment, the 40 percent without a car have an employment disadvantage. The aspects that contribute to the issue of accessibility to employment are correlated to the fact that it takes long time for immigrants to assimilate to the norms of owning a car and the lack of accessible transportation in their neighborhoods.

Table 10.1 Work trip characteristics by immigrant history

		Immigrants 1 Year	Immigrants 1<Years<5	Immigrants 5 Years	Non-Immigrants
Number of	None	26.7%	16.1%	6.7%	2.8%
vehicles in	One	37.2%	33.3%	21.1%	17.7%
household	Two or more	36.1%	50.5%	72.2%	79.5%
Commuting	Drive alone	30.5%	45.0%	69.3%	82.5%
mode	Carpool	31.4%	28.7%	15.4%	10.5%
	Public Transit	17.2%	14.0%	10.1%	3.2%
	Walk/bike	16.5%	8.4%	3.9%	2.7%
	Other	4.3%	3.9%	1.4%	1.1%
Commuting	1–15 min.	41.7%	38.0%	35.3%	43.8%
time	16–30 min.	36.5%	37.0%	36.7%	32.6%
	31–60 min.	10.2%	13.2%	14.3%	13.4%
	More than 60 min.	11.7%	11.8%	13.7%	10.2%

Source: Sungyop Kim, Cityscape: A Journal of Policy Development and Research, Volume 11, Number 3, 2009.

The information in the above table shows a descriptive analysis of commuting travel characteristics of individuals by their immigration history. Immigrants are increasingly likely to have two or more vehicles in their households the longer they have been in the country, and non-immigrants have the highest percentage of two or more vehicles. Non-immigrants also have shorter average commuting times than immigrants. This gives a better gauge to the argument of assimilation because the immigrants over time get adjusted to the lifestyle of the American citizen and the "American Dream" of buying a house, getting a car, starting a family and living comfortably. Going from mainly public transportation to owning a car is also shown in the table, as the longer the immigrant is in the country, the public transportation mode of commuting steadily decreases while driving alone to wherever they have to go increases. Commuting modes change amongst immigrants, making planning for new immigrants easier to forecast because of the trends in how they travel but there is more work needed to be done with the steady flow of immigrants and the resources they require to travel.

Vehicle availability is often considered one of the most significant factors in work-trip mode choice for immigrants (Titheridge and Hall 2006). This transportation challenge is interrelated with the challenge of attaining employment since much is dependent on access to a mode of transportation, ideally a private automobile. Access to reliable private automobile transport has been recognized as an effective way to overcome employment barriers and achieve economic objectives among low-income immigrant workers (Taylor and Paul 1995). A study done by Liu and Painter (2012) have showed that new immigrants are less likely to drive alone, with much higher likelihoods of taking public transit and carpooling than immigrants who have been in the United States for more than ten years. Part of the explanation lies in the fact that on first arrival, many immigrants lack the institutional knowledge of owning a cars, although driving alone is characterized in its instant availability, convenience, flexibility, and high speed which are not comparable to other alternative transportation modes (Anable and Gatersleben 2005). Another reason as to why some immigrants do not have a car is due to lack of sufficient income. Low-incomes may prevent poor immigrant families from purchasing or maintaining automobiles and some immigrants may be less likely than others to have had drivers' licenses, driven cars, or owned automobiles in their countries of origin (Blumenberg 2008). Though it may seem subtle, the facts that drive-alone behaviors among immigrants occur gradually is an indication of assimilation.

While some may argue that immigrants may be moving to places that already have transit, the fact that researchers do not find such strong results in the newer immigrant gateway metropolitan areas and among other minority populations suggests this is not the case (Liu and Painter 2012). Besides, transit services of most metropolitan areas do not provide viable connections between inner-city and suburban areas with abundant employment opportunities (Chang 1986).

Language Barrier and Cultural Considerations

A language barrier is one of the challenges faced by new immigrants. Many immigrants coming to a new country are not fluent in the primary language of the country. This makes it hard to understand the signs, read bus schedules, airplanes times or even ask questions to help get them to their destination and back safely. As long as the population of immigrants continues to grow, which it has, planners will need to better understand how immigrants use transportation. Continued growth in immigrant populations could impact changes in demand in the types of transportation services and systems needed—including the demand for mass transportation services, sidewalks, and bike lanes. Improving knowledge of how immigrants use transportation and assimilate to the new country's norms can help planners identify those needs. Only recently have demographers and transportation researchers begun to explore the transportation behavior of immigrants. This is something that is often overlooked when thinking about immigrants in general because of the assumption that they know the nuances of the transportation system and even etiquette in certain situations. Language is something that can be an intimidating thing for a new immigrant. It takes a good amount of dedication to learn a new language and its signs in a new country. American major metropolitan cities are some of the best at accommodating to this. That is why new immigrants are more likely to move to one of the 25 metropolitan areas because they have family or a job lined up for them there. Los Angeles, for example, has one of the most diverse populations. From areas of the city such as Chinatown, Koreatown and a large Latino population, amongst others, it makes it easier for an immigrant to be more comfortable in those ethnic enclaves initially because they'll be able to read some of the signs and be more likely be able to get to and from those areas with relative ease.

Culture also influences travel behavior amongst immigrants in different ways. Francis Douma, from the University of Minnesota, held focus groups with homogeneous groups of Latino, Somali, and Hmong immigrants in both urban and rural areas of Minnesota to identify ways of better meeting their travel needs. The focus groups showed that Latino immigrants are open to transit and more "social" types of travel while privacy was an important consideration for the Hmong. All groups were found to prefer to drive themselves rather than use public transit (Douma 2004). Similarly, Evelyn Blumenberg (2008), found in her paper *"Immigrants and Transport Barriers to Employment,"* that Southeast Asian welfare recipients in California tend to use private vehicles more than other racial and ethnic groups. On the other hand, Lovejoy and Handy (2008), who conducted focus groups with recent Mexican immigrants in California, found high dependency on private vehicles among this group, including use of vehicles other than those owned by the household. Similarly, carpools provide an important alternative to either owning one's car for immigrants or to using public transit.

It is important for planners to understand that it is a process of many cultural aspects from others countries that factor into how immigrants decide to take and use transportation. There need to be comprehensive plans and studies done of cultural norms of travel, and a consensus arrived at on how to better understand the needs of immigrants in the transportation system.

BOX 10.1 Including people who are underserved by transportation

Public involvement needs to encompass the full range of community interests, yet people underserved by transportation often do not participate. Not only are they frequently unaware of transportation proposals that could affect their daily lives, but they also may have no means to get to a public meeting or have long work hours that preclude them from attending.

Many people in low-income communities, as well as those with low literacy and/or limited English proficiency, have traditionally been underserved by conventional outreach methods. Written notices in English language newspapers may not be read by everyone an agency wishes to reach. People may not feel safe or welcome at a meeting held in government offices. People may be unable to attend public events if they do not own a car, if they cannot afford child care, or if they work late shifts or more than one job. Failing to account for the variety in cultural expectations, language, literacy, or income and affordability can create barriers to full participation. In order to have the participation that can ultimately inform decision-making, agencies must identify the project area demographic(s) and develop an effective approach for outreach and communication. Recent efforts to include many different cultural or disadvantaged groups in transportation decision-making have been designed to assure basic, equitable access rather than to favor one group over another.

So we need a tailored outreach. Tailored outreach simply means selecting and adjusting public involvement techniques in order to effectively connect with the people affected by a project, whoever and wherever they are. Tailored outreach recognizes that "traditional" techniques are not always the most effective. Creating effective outreach requires knowing the constituency and taking steps to ensure that the public involvement process is accessible to everyone in the community. Agencies must also be sensitive to the limitations experienced by some individuals due to any number of reasons. Typical meeting announcements in newspapers and on the radio, for example, may not reach underserved populations. Agencies need to understand how these populations get information. This could be via bulletins from religious centers, on grocery store or laundromat bulletin boards, or at community meeting places. Understanding the full range of a community's needs enables an agency to create more responsive and even innovative plans. Interacting with community members yields insight into the reasons why they agree or disagree with proposed plans or projects. The perspective of traditionally underserved people can inform the goals and outcomes of planning and project development. Such individuals can suggest fresh approaches to transportation issues that otherwise would not be raised. However, input from underserved people is not "separate" from other input or given more weight; rather, to be most useful, it is integrated with and balanced by the needs and concerns of all interests. Examples of how tailored outreach has benefitted the process include:

- **Participation establishes trust and openness in the decision-making process.** The St. Louis, Missouri, MPO works in close collaboration with minority, ethnic, and low-income groups from the beginning of planning and throughout the transportation decision-making process, fostering a sense of ownership of the outcome.
- **Local leadership may become more active.** For the past 15 years, the Metropolitan Transit Authority of Harris County in Houston, Texas, has had a good working relationship with all segments of the community, especially underserved populations. As a result, their leaders have been very active in the decision-making process.
- **Agencies can address issues specific to a particular demographic.** At the inception of its long-range plan, the Georgia Department of Transportation (GDOT) had special forums for minorities so the planning process could address their concerns from the outset.
- **Agencies may discern new or improved transportation options.** Input from predominantly Mexican-American communities led to a hybrid option for transit in the Los Angeles Metro Red Line Eastside Corridor. In a mid-range of cost, the new option has the highest potential ridership and offers significant service advantages. The region's leadership and project planners agree that the new alternative is the best solution and readily admit it would not have been identified without the help of ethnic constituents.

Adapted from USDOT Federal Highway Administration/Federal Transit Administration

Planning for the Disadvantaged

A significant obstacle for the disadvantaged of all types to overcome, especially from the planning perspective, is the suburbs. Many cities practice a method of segregated zoning, whereby large tracts of land are zoned to be used exclusively for either industrial production facilities, commercial and retail establishments or residential housing (Scharlach 2009). Consequently, residents are required to travel greater distances from their homes to acquire goods and services than may be necessary. This often leads these residents to become reliant on personal automobiles as communities discover mass transit becomes too expensive to install and maintain in suburban areas. Furthermore, the great distances between suburban neighborhoods and local commerce prevent residents from being able to walk from one destination to another with relative ease. Another consequence of the suburban development scheme is the lack of easily accessible local meeting areas, such as community or senior centers, coffee shops, or parks. This can lead to a feeling of isolation for older adults and the physically impaired who are unable to drive and lack access to transportation alternatives (Kochera and Bright 2005). The following are some suggested solutions to close the transportation demand-supply gap for disadvantaged communities.

SMART GROWTH

Within the planning profession, a frequently discussed alternative to "traditional" zoning practices is to incorporate elements of "smart growth" into the planning process, specifically embracing the concept of higher-density, mixed-use developments. This process, which is frequently found in many European cities that were established long before the creation of the automobile, is believed to offer solutions to the problems created by the suburban culture. The mixed-use development offers a number of benefits for the disadvantaged with regards to transportation options. The traditional view of mixed-use development involves commercial establishments on the ground level with housing units located on the floors above. Such a design allows for older adults and the handicapped and those with no car to live in a neighborhood with a number of amenities located within walking distance of their homes. Instead of requiring a twenty-minute drive to the nearest big-box supermarket or retail chain, one can simply take an elevator to the ground level or travel to a corner store or a nearby coffee shop.

Another advantage of mixed-use development is that it allows for the ability of public transit to be established and operate at a more efficient cost. This allows residents of all ages and abilities in the community to travel to many distant destinations without the reliance of personal transportation. For the economically disadvantaged, this provides opportunities to seek employment over a wider are of the city, hopefully allowing them the chance to pull themselves out of poverty. For older adults and others with physical limitations, this can provide opportunities for socialization, as well as the ability to maintain their mental sharpness by easing their ability to reach recreation facilities such as libraries, theaters, museums, city parks and senior or community centers.

UNIVERSAL DESIGN AND COMPLETE STREET

According to Litman (2014), Universal Design (also called Inclusive Design, Accessible Design or Just Accessibility) refers to transport facilities and service designs that accommodate the widest range of potential users, including people with mobility and visual impairments (disabilities), and other special needs. Although Universal Design standards address the needs of people with disabilities, it is a comprehensive concept that can benefit all users. Increased walkway widths, low-floor buses, and smooth walking surfaces improve convenience for all travelers, not just those with mobility impairments. Curb ramps are necessary for people using handcarts, scooters, baby strollers and bicycles, as well as wheelchair users. Automatic door openers are another example of Universal Design features that can benefit many types of users. Universal design should be comprehensive, meaning that it results in seamless mobility options from origin to destination for the greatest possible range of potential users. It should consider all possible obstacles that may exist in buildings, transportation terminals, sidewalks, paths, roads and vehicles. There are communities in which neighborhood sidewalks stretch the length of a block but end at a six-inch curb when meeting a crossing street. For an individual in a wheelchair or motorized mobility unit, or even a parent pushing a child in a stroller, this type of situation is not only difficult to maneuver, but is likely to be hazardous. As a result, the walkability of the neighborhood declines, once again leaving residents to resort to either rely on other modes of transportation such as driving, or to remain isolated where they are, unable to access the greater community around them. Fortunately, many communities have discovered this issue and now design their sidewalks to incorporate ramps to ease the transition from the elevated sidewalk to the lower, paved street. Additionally, cities can install devices at frequently used intersections that audibly inform vision impaired pedestrians when it is safe to cross the street.

A complete street is also a similar concept that encourages the use of streets by all users. Everyone knows of the infamous phrase, "it's not the destination that matters, but the journey." Looking at it with a more literal perspective, it is evident that the roads and sidewalks that provide access to transportation should accommodate everyone, elderly, bicyclists, drivers, etc. Streets need to be complete, and a complete street is a road that is designed to be safe for drivers, bicyclists, transit vehicles, and users, and pedestrians of all ages and abilities. The complete street concept focuses not just on individual roads but on changing the decision-making and design process so that all users are routinely considered during the planning, designing, building, and operating of all roadways" (LaPlante and McCann 2008).

Demand Responsive Transit—Planning and Policy

A demand responsive transit (DRT) system is a means of transportation for the public that is known by its flexible routing and scheduling. Having the availability of this type of transportation system has been especially beneficial for that segment of society with limited access to conventional public transportation. According to the TCRP (Transit Cooperative Research Program) (Ellis and McCollom 2009), there are about 1,500 rural and 400 urban DRT systems in the United States.

The definition of "demand responsive transit (DRT)" has been continuously developed throughout the years. It is generally characterized by its flexible routing and shared rides, and the Federal Transit Administration defines it as a "transit mode comprised of passenger cars, vans or small buses operating in response to calls from passengers." (KFH Group Inc. 2008). DRT has been identified with other terms such as dial-a-ride, flexible transport service and demand responsive service (Dessouky, Rahimi and Weidner 2003; Gupta, Chen and Surya 2012; Crainic, *et al.*, 2010). With DRT having a large range of definitions, it confirms that not all providers of DRT systems are identical. DRT serves a variety of riders and is not focused on any particular type of rider.

Fixed-route transit (FRT) and demand responsive transit (DRT) systems are the two broad categories in transit systems. The most cost-effective are the FRT systems, having a large loading capacity and a predetermined schedule (Li 2010). In comparison with fixed-route services, the DRT still has low productivity and high per-trip costs (KFH Group Inc. 2008). The flexibility of the DRT system is what makes it more appealing than FRT. The movement of individuals from inner cities to the suburbs has created less demand for the fixed-route transit options and also increased the price per rider. Therefore, in the less dense areas, the DRT system can be more cost-efficient by having dispersed trip destinations.

Since the 1960s, demand responsive transit systems have been proposed, although it was not until the 1970s that the simple DRT systems were implemented in the United States (Teal 1993). During this time, the manual dispatching system in use was expensive and excessive. Since then, there has been an incredible increase in the use of DRT systems. A significant increase in 1990 was due to the Americans with Disabilities Act (ADA), which required the availability of "paratransit" services for individuals unable to use the fixed-route services (Khattak 2004). Many of the riders who currently use DRT are in rural areas with limited access to a privately owned vehicle (POV). Based on Government Accountability Office's survey, the demand for ADA paratransit trips in the United States increased since 2007 for some transit agencies, and costs for providing the trips remain high. The average number of annual ADA paratransit trips provided by a transit agency increased 7 percent from 2007 to 2010, from 172,481 trips in 2007 to 184,856 trips in 2010. Increases in demand for ADA paratransit services were driven by the ten largest transit agencies, measured according to the population size of their service areas. Also, ADA paratransit trips are much more costly to provide than fixed-route trips. Similarly, the average cost of providing an ADA paratransit trip in 2010 was $29.30, an estimated three and a half times more expensive than the average cost of $8.15 to provide a fixed-route trip. The average cost of providing an ADA paratransit trip increased 10 percent from 2007 to 2010.

Flexibility and the Role of Technology: Within the DRT system, scheduling and routing are flexible. Having the ability to create different schedules and routes is what makes DRT different from an FRT service. Some DRT services allow scheduling up to two weeks in advance (Crainic, *et al.*, 2010), and some even allow same-day scheduling if the room is available (Ellis and McCollom 2009). Those DRT services that provide ADA paratransit are required to accept a trip on a next-day basis. Among the added benefits of the DRT system, the flexible scheduling remains essential.

Research conducted by Monast and Worthy (2012) indicated that by applying a "well-planned scheduling structure," the performance of DRT can be further improved. Similar studies show that implementation of more advanced technologies could improve the DRT system. Palmer, Dessuky and Zhou (2008) discuss in their research how the advanced technologies have improved the DRT systems' efficiency. The benefits of these advanced technologies include the response to changed client schedules and improvements to the reliability of trip schedules.

Significance and Performance: Many perceive a DRT system is working in only dense areas with a greater number of destinations. However, the TRCP Report mentions that there are a greater number of DRT systems in rural areas than there are in urban settings. The DRT system in rural areas proves useful by helping to improve the mobility of many individuals who do not have access to privately owned vehicles.

DRT services in urban areas tend to experience high demand with simultaneously high costs. For example, the urban region of King County, Washington proved to have low ridership and high operating cost. The DRT performance within urban areas is not as efficient compared to suburban and rural areas because of the traffic congestion and complicated street networks. There also tends to be greater competition in urban areas with multiple services, including buses and taxis. Because there is such a high demand for DRT systems in dense urban areas, studies have been done to improve their efficiency. In Europe, Jenny Mageean (2003) argued that by implementing telematics-based DRT, limitations in urban areas could be addressed.

The DRT systems have created better options for rural areas since most lack any form of public transportation. With greater flexibility, the DRT gives rural populations greater access to medical facilities that are usually located around urban centers, as access to medical facilities becomes less difficult when the distance is served by the DRT system. Thus, mobility between rural and urban areas is served incredibly well by the DRT system. These rural areas now have a greater amount of accessibility and can do so in a shorter time period. With the greater availability of rural to urban transport, communities are provided better accessibility not only to medical facilities, but also to other critical services.

Performance is an important factor to evaluate in DRT because the system can understand what does work and fix what could work better. The performance of DRT systems has been widely researched for the last decade. When it comes to the performance of the DRT systems in the world, many studies have shown that they desperately need improvement. Kai Monast and Joshua Worthy (2012) researched the rural DRT system, concluding that it is inefficient to deliver, time-consuming to schedule and requires a large vehicle fleet. Although there are positive and negative aspects of rural DRT service, helping these communities have the greater mobility to "activity sites" outweighs the hardships within the service. Each study looks at different variables when assessing the performance of the DRT systems. Luca Quadrifoglio's performance measures include total trip miles, deadhead miles, and fleet size, while Kurt Palmer includes passenger miles and trips per vehicle as well as operating expense per passenger trip and mile in his performance measurement. Although both look at different variables and conclude separate results, both established that there still needs to be further research done to assess the performance of the DRT system. The TRCP report indicates that because of the growing demand for service, many DRT systems are under pressure to improve their performance. This TRCP report used similar performance measures as Kurt Palmer.

Another factor studied regarding performance of DRT is traffic conditions in urban areas compared to rural areas. In urban areas, there tends to be a great deal of congestions, which impacts the DRT systems' overall performance. Urban and rural areas should have different variables reviewed when assessing performance because they have different factors influencing them. In rural DRT, according to the Ellis and MeCollom (2009), the performance variables should also include deadhead time and miles, which were also included in Quadrifoglio's study on DRT performance. By researching the factors influencing DRT performance, both urban and rural areas can improve their systems.

Demand-Adaptive System: The newer transit system known as the demand-adaptive system (DAS) displays features of both fixed-line bus service and DRT (Crainic, *et al.*, 2010). The DAS bus line has mandatory stops in its schedule, which follows the fixed-line bus service pattern. On the other hand, it also follows the DRT service by giving individuals the option to issue requests for minor detour stops. This DAS service creates strategic plans in the scheduling phase, compared to DRT service, in which schedules are created a short period before issuing service. Although DAS provides some flexibility in its service, the DRT still offers the maximum flexibility for users.

Review Questions

1) What modes of transportation does the low-income population rely on, and why?
2) What is spatial mismatch theory and how does it apply to transportation? Explain.
3) How are women disadvantaged when it comes to transportation? Explain.
4) What is the relevance of the Americans with Disabilities Act in relation to transportation?
5) Discuss the transportation challenges of new immigrants
6) What are some transportation challenges for the disabled?
7) What considerations should be made for immigrants and transportation?
8) How can smart growth and mixed-use development benefit the disadvantaged?
9) Discuss the significance of tailored public participation approach that includes people who are underserved by transportation.
10) What is "demand responsive transit"?

Project/Paper Idea

Using the National Household Travel Survey (NHTS) from http://nhts.ornl.gov/, analyze your state's immigration history versus the work/school related travel characteristics. There is information in the survey about "foreign-born/born in US." Sort the ones who were not born in the United States to do your analysis. The task is to create a table similar to Table 10.1 for your state.

Video

Race: The Power of an Illusion: The House We Live In (Episode 3): by California Newsreel, 2003: Episode three focuses on how our institutions shape and create a race.

Internet Sources

America in the first decade of the new century, http://www.s4.brown.edu/us2010/index.htm
National center on Senior Transportation, http://www.seniortransportation.net
The Stanford Center on Poverty and Inequality, http://web.stanford.edu/group/scspi/issue_transportation.html

Bibliography

Anable, Jillian, and Birgitta Gatersleben. 2005. "All Work and No Play? The Role of Instrumental and Affective Factors in Work and Leisure Journeys by Different Travel Modes." *Transportation Research Part A: Policy and Practice* 39 (2–3): 163–181.

Battellino, Helen. 2009. "Transport for the Transport Disadvantaged: A Review of Service Delivery Models in New South Wales." *Transport Policy* 16 (3): 123–129.

Blumenberg, Evelyn. 2004. "En-Gendering Effective Planning: Spatial Mismatch, Low-Income Women, and Transportation Policy." *Journal of the American Planning Association* 73 (3): 269–281.

_____. 2008. "Immigrants and Transport Barriers to Employment: The Case of Southeast Asian Welfare Recipients in California." *Transport Policy* 15 (1): 33–42.

_____, and Paul Ong. 2001. "Cars, Buses, and Jobs: Welfare Participants and Employment Access in Los Angeles." *Transportation Research Record* 1756: 22–31.

Bostock, Lisa. 2001. "Pathways of Disadvantage? Walking as a Mode of Transport Among Low-Income Mothers." *Health Social Care Community* 9 (1): 8–11.

Briggs, Ronald, and Douglas McKelvey. 2006. "Rural Public Transportation and the Disadvantaged." *A Radical Journal of Geography* (Antipode) 7 (3): 31–36.

Cairns, Shannon, Jessica Greig, and Martin Wachs. 2003. "Environmental Justice and Transportation: A Citizen's Handbook." *Institute of Transportation Studies.*

Chang, Yi. 1986. "Transportation Research Record: Impact of Public Transit on Employment Status: Disaggregate Analysis of Houston, Texas." *Journal of the Transportation Research Board* 137–144.

Chase, Holly. 2011. *Transportation Planning Options for Elderly Mobility.* Thesis, Massachusetts Institute of Technology. Accessed March 4, 2014. Dspace.mit.edu.

Clark, Williams, and Yuqin Huang. 2003. *Black and White Commuting Behavior in a Large Segregated City: Evidence from Atlanta.* University of California Transportation Center, Los Angeles and State University of New York, Albany.

Covington, Kenya. 2009. "Spatial Mismatch of the Poor: An Explanation of Recent Declines in Job Isolation." *Journal of Urban Affairs* 31 (5): 559–587.

Crainic, Teodor, Fausto Errico, Federico Malucelli, and Maddalena Nonato. 2010. "Designing the Master Schedule for Demand-Adaptive Transit Systems." *Annals of Operations Research* 194 (1): 151–166.

Cutts, Bethany, Kate Darby, Christopher Boone, and Alexandra Brewis. 2009. "City Structure, Obesity, and Environmental Justice: An Integrated Analysis of Physical and Social Barriers to Walkable Streets and Park Access." *Social Science & Medicine* 69: 1314–1322.

_____. 2010. "Green Man Traffic Light Is 'Too Quick,' Say the Elderly." *Associated Newspapers.*

Dessouky, Maged, Mansour Rahimi, and Merrill Weidner. 2003. "Jointly Optimizing Cost, Service, and Environmental Performance in Demand-Responsive Transit Scheduling." *Transportation Research Part D: Transport and Environment* 8 (6): 433–465.

Douma, Francis. 2004. *Using ITS to Better Serve Diverse Populations.* State and Local Policy Program, Hubert H. Humphrey Institute of Public Affairs, University of Minnesota.

Ellis, Elizabeth, and Brian McCollom. 2009. *Guidebook for Rural Demand-Response Transportation: Measuring, Assessing, and Improving Performance.* Washington, D.C.: Transit Cooperative Research Program.

Ellwood, David. 1986. "The Spatial Mismatch Hypothesis: are There Jobs Missing in the Ghetto?" in *The Black Youth Employment Crisis,* edited by Richard Freeman and Harry Holzer. University of Chicago Press.

Faiz, Aysha. 2011. "Transportation and the Urban Poor." *Institute of Transportation Engineers* 81: 40–43.

Falcocchio, John, and Edmund Cantilli. 1984. *Transportation for the Disadvantaged: The Poor, the Young, the Elderly, and the Handicapped.* Lexington, Massachusetts: D.C, Heath, and Company.

Forenbrock, David, and Lisa Schweitzer. 1999. "Environmental Justice in Transportation Planning." *Journal of the American Planning Association* 65: 96–111.

Garrett, Mark, and Brian Taylor. 1999. "Reconsidering Social Equity in Public Transit." *Berkeley Planning Journal* 13: 2–27.

Giuliano, Genevieve. 2004. "The Context of Urban Travel." In *The Geography of Urban Transportation,* by Susan Hanson, 3–29. New York: Guilford.

Gobillon, Laurent, Harris Selod, and Yves Zenou. 2007. "The Mechanisms of Spatial Mismatch." *Urban Studies* 44 (12): 2401–2427.

Gomide, Alexandre. 2008. *Mobility and the Urban Poor.* London School of Economics, London, United Kingdom: Urban Age.

Government Accountability Office. 2012. "ADA Paratransit Services: Demand has Increased, But Little Is Known About Compliance."

Gupta, Diwakar, Hao-Wei, Miller, Lisa Chen, and Fajarrani Surya. 2012. "Improving the Efficiency of Demand-Responsive Paratransit Services." *Transportation Research Part A: Policy and Practice* 44 (4): 201–217.

Harris, Marlys. 2012. "What's Better for Old People: City or Suburbs?" *MinnPost,* June 11. Accessed March 4, 2014.

Hellerstein, Judith, David Neumark, and Melissa McInerney. 2008. "Spatial Mismatch or Racial Mismatch?" *Journal of Urban Economics* 64 (2): 464–479.

Holzer, Harry, John Quigley, and Steven Raphael. 2003. "Public Transit and the Spatial Distribution of Minority Employment: Evidence from A Natural Experiment." *Journal of Policy Analysis and Management* 22: 415–441.

Kain, John. 1968. "Housing Segregation, Negro Employment, and Metropolitan Decentralization." *The Quarterly Journal of Economics* 82: 175–197.

_____. 1992. "The Spatial Mismatch Hypothesis: Three Decades Later." *Housing Policy Debate* 3: 371–460.

Kasarda, J. 1983. "Entry-Level Jobs, Mobility, and Urban Minority Unemployment." *Urban Affairs Quarterly* 19: 21- 40.

KFH Group Inc. 2008. *Guidebook for Measuring, Assessing, and Improving Performance of Demand-Response Transportation .* Washington, D.C.: Transit Cooperative Research Program.

Khattak, Asad and Youngbin Yim. 2004. "Traveler Response to Innovative Personalized Demand-Responsive Transit in the San Francisco Bay Area." *Journal of Urban Planning and Development* 130 (1): 42–55.

Kim, Sungyop. 2009. "Immigrants and Transportation: An Analysis of Immigrant Workers' Work Trips." *Cityscape* 155–169.

Kneebone, Elizabeth, and Alan Berube. 2013. *Confronting Suburban Poverty in America.* Washington, D.C.: The Brookings Institution.

Kochera, Andrew, and Kim Bright. 2005. "Livable Communities for Older People—Generations." *Journal of the American Society on Aging* 32–36.

LaPlante, John, and Barbara McCann. 2008. "Complete Streets: We Can Get There from Here." *Institute of Transportation Engineers* 24–28.

Li, Xiugang and Luca Quadrifoglio. 2010. "Feeder Transit Services: Choosing Between Fixed and Demand Responsive Policy." *Transportation Research Part C: Emerging Technologies* 18 (5).

Litman, Todd. 2014. "Community Cohesion as a Transport Planning Objective." Victoria Transport Policy Institute.

Liu, Cathy, and Gary Painter. 2012. "Travel Behavior Among Latino Immigrants The Role of Ethnic Concentration and Ethnic Employment." *Journal of Planning Education and Research* 32 (1): 62–80.

Lovejoy, Kristin, and Susan Handy. 2008. "A Case for Measuring Individuals' Access to Private-Vehicle Travel as a Matter of Degrees: Lessons from Focus Groups with Mexican Immigrants in California." *Transportation* 35 (5): 601–607.

Mageean, Jenny, and John Nelson. 2003. "The Evaluation of Demand Responsive Transport Services in Europe." *Journal of Transport Geography* 11 (4): 255–270.

Michael, Stoll, and Steven Raphael. 2002. *Modest Progress: The Narrowing Spatial Mismatch Between Blacks and Jobs in the 1990s*. Washington, D.C.: Brookings Institution.

Monast, Kai, and Joshua Worthy. 2012. "Applying Structure Scheduling to Increase Performance in Rural Demand-Response Transportation." *Journal of Public Transportation* 15 (3): 61–76.

_____, and Douglas Houston. 2002. "Transit, Employment and Women on Welfare." *Urban Geography* 23 (4): 344–364.

Ong, Paul, and Douglas Miller. 2005. "Spatial and Transportation Mismatch in Los Angeles." *Journal of Planning Education and Research* 25 (1): 43–56.

Palmer, Kurt, Maged Dessuky, and Zhigiang Zhou. 2008. "Factors Influencing Productivity and Operating Cost of Demand Responsive Transit." *Transportation Research Part A: Policy and Practice* 42 (3): 503–523.

Pickut, Walt. 2013. "Top Ten Problems the Elderly Face with Transportation." *Livestrong*. Augest 16. Accessed March 4, 2014. www.Livestrong.com.

Quadrifoglio, Luca, Maged Dessouky, and Fernando Ordaez. 2008. "A Simulation Study of Demand Responsive Transit System Design." *Transportation Research Part A: Policy and Practice* 42 (4): 718–737.

Roberto, Elizabeth. 2008. *Commuting to Opportunity: The Working Poor and Commuting in the United States*. Metropolitan Policy Program at Brookings, 1–20. Accessed March 2014, 4.

Robertson, Robyn, and Ward Vanlaar. 2008. "Elderly Drivers: Future Challenges?" *Accident and Analysis Prevention* 40 (6): 1982–1986.

Ross, Martha, and Nicole Prchal-Svajlenka. 2012. *Connecting to Opportunity: Access to Jobs via Transit in the Washington. D.C. Region.*: The Brookings Institution.

Sanchez, Thomas. 1998. "The Connection Between Public Transit and Employment." *Presented at the Association of Collegiate Schools of Planning Annual Conference*. Pasadena, CA.

Scharlach, Andrew. 2009. "Creating Aging-Friendly Communities." *Journal of the American Society on Aging* 33 (2): 5–11.

Scholl, Lynn. 2002. *Transportation Affordability for Low-Income Populations*. Public Policy Institute of California, 1–96.

Soltani, Ali, and Yousef Ivaki. 2011. "Inequity in the Provision of Public Bus Service for Socially Disadvantaged Groups." *Journal of Sustainable Development* 4 (5): 229.

Stafford, Philip. 2009. *Elderburbia: Aging with a Sense of Place in America*. Santa Barbara, CA: Praeger.

Taylor, Brian, and Ong. Paul. 1995. "Spatial Mismatch or Automobile Mismatch? an Examination of Race, Residence, and Commuting Time in U.S. Metropolitan Areas." *Urban Studies* 32 (9): 1453–73.

Teal, R.F. 1993. "Implications of Technological Developments for Demand Responsive Transit," *Transportation Research Record*, 1390:33–42.

Titheridge, Helena, and Peter Hall. 2006. "Changing Travel to Work Patterns in South East England." *Journal of Transport Geography* 14 (1): 60–75.

Tomer, Adie, Elizabeth Kneebone, Robert Puentes, and Alan Berube. 2011. *Missed Opportunity: Transit and Jobs in Metropolitan America*. Brookings Institution.

Wachs, Martin. 1979. *Transportation for The Elderly: Changing Lifestyles, Changing Needs*. University of California Press.

Wells, Kirstin, and Jean-Claude Thil. 2012. "Do Transit-Dependent Neighborhoods Receive Inferior Access? A Neighborhood Analysis in Four U.S. Cities." *Journal of Urban Affairs* 43 (1). 43–63.

Zhu, Xuemei, and Chanam Lee. 2008. "Walkable and Safety Around Elementary Schools: Economic and Ethnic Disparities." *Amercian Journal of Preventive Medicine* 34: 282–290.

Zumaeta, Jorge. 2003. *Spatial Mismatch and Transportation Accessibility of Community Resources Urban Welfare to Work Transitions*. Florida Institute for Applied Research and Evaluation Florida Atlantic University.

Part IV

Urban Transportation Outside the United States

11

Urban Transportation in Europe

Chapter Outline

- Introduction
- Transportation and the European Union
- A Paradigm Shift in Car Ownership and Use: Germany
- Sustainable Transportation in Europe
  - o *Public Transportation*
  - o *Walking and Biking*
- Special Features of European Transportation
  - o *Congestion Pricing in London*
  - o *The German Autobahn*
- Lessons Learned from European Transportation
  - o *Multimodality and Drive-alternative Options*
  - o *Public Participation*
  - o *Integrated Land Use and Transportation Planning*
  - o *Financing and Taxing Systems That Encourage Sustainable Transportation*

Introduction

Most European nations are part of the ancient civilizations that created the first long-distance roads to connect their major cities. They also created the early shipping routes that connected most of the Europe's coastal cities and cities of other continents. The early land and marine based modes of transportation remained through the twenty centuries although, throughout the industrial revolution, transportation went through a vast transformation. During the industrial revolution, Europe was the center of innovations, which shaped the modern transportation system. Now, transportation in Europe has a comprehensive and complex design, which has created the greatest concepts of transportation and brought diverse systems of travel to the region.

Looking back to history, in the mid-nineteenth century, based on the same ideas such as a horse-drawn carriage and the first roads, came the creation of the steam engines and electric motors, which provided the desired speed, power, and comfort- a great achievement for European society. The steam-engine gave way for economically inexpensive transportation of both people and goods. Meanwhile, the first automobiles came to be a part of this great transportation evolution. During the late nineteenth century, and with the discovery of oil for combustion engines, many automobiles were produced to accommodate the travel demand. Since most of the cities and capitals of Europe were made for the pedestrian and horse-driven carriages, the roads were narrow and without sidewalks and most were paved with stone bricks. Most of these old cities were designed in a radial system making it hard for automobiles to move fast and freely. On top of that, the industrial revolution created over-populated cities due to migration from rural areas to inner city neighborhoods, generating

Key

A Bus priority fault detection and performance monitoring reports		**H** Bus door sensor
B System databases		**J** GPS receiver
C O Bus priority radio link		**K** Central system server (located remotely)
D Bus processor (contained within traffic signal controller)		**L** iBIS plus unit
E Traffic signal controller		**M** GPS satellites
F O Bus detection points		**N** Bus garage (when bus is in garage, it is linked to the central system server to send and receive bus priority data)

Figure 11.1 iBus system in London (Bus Priority Team).

more transportation accidents and fatalities. The industrial pollutants that came with the industries also created disease-prone areas in the metropolitan regions.

So, since then most European countries had to work with wide-ranging and complex transportation designs and models to accommodate better, cleaner, and efficient types of transportations, relevant to their geographical and geological positions. The growth of the urban population favored the construction of efficient public urban transport systems. The denser land use patterns found in European cities and suburbs and infrastructure investments that create safe, comfortable facilities for pedestrian and cyclists make short trips conducive to biking and walking. According to a report by USDOT FHWA (2001), what makes sustainable transportation planning practice that focuses on walking cycling and public transit different in Europe is that social, economic, and environmental objectives are integral part of transportation planning, rather than constraints or the focus of mitigation efforts. This change in perspective has led Europeans to develop new procedures and methods for developing sustainable transportation system.

Technology also plays a role. Take bus travel as example, several technological breakthroughs have made to make it a more attractive alternative to personal vehicles in Europe. In 2008, five hydrogen fuel-cell and five hydrogen internal combustion engine buses were ordered for implementation in London for 2010. These are believed to be one of the first commercial contracts for hydrogen-powered buses (Fuel Cells Bulletin, 2008). To further bus effectiveness, Automatic Vehicle Location (AVL) systems are being introduced. London's iBus is an example of one of the largest of GPS tracking systems being used today (Hounsell, Shrestha and Wong 2012). The iBus offers real-time tracking that monitors buses' location on their routes. The bus locations and expected arrival times can then be followed using a smartphone, or watching LED displays at transportation centers, bus stops, and on the buses themselves. Knowing when a bus is supposed to arrive helps passengers to utilize their time more efficiently, which can lower stress. An added benefit is the ability to give buses priority at traffic signals which speeds up travel and improves rider comfort; however, these applications have been deemed too expensive for continued use in London. Importantly, these systems supply invaluable data for later analysis by transportation authorities around Europe (Hounsell, Shrestha and Wong 2012).

Transportation and the European Union

Transport is an essential component of the European economy. According to European Commission (2009), the transport industry at large accounts for about 7 percent of GDP and over 5 percent of total employment in the European Union (EU). The European Transportation Policy (ETP) has contributed to a mobility system that brings efficiency and effectiveness to the economy of advanced regions of Europe. The ETP has assisted social and economic cohesion and promoted the competitiveness of the European industry (European Commission 2009).

With the emergence of the European Union (EU) in 1993, the need for a more cohesive transportation network was apparent, to help solidify the economic and social bond of the union. Transportation policy challenges in Europe arise from the existence of separate sovereign nations now being united under one governmental system, and transportation is one of the connecting principles of the European integration policy (Martin 2011). Recognizing the importance of transportation, an EU commission report stated,

> An efficient European transport network cannot be developed without a fully European perspective. Up until recently, this perspective did not really exist, with transport infrastructure being planned from purely national priorities. To make matters worse, the different transport modes were developed separately, rather than as the different elements of an integrated system. The result is a patchwork of road networks, railway systems, waterways, ports and airports that neither interface well nor, in many cases, even use the same technical standards. This poorly built jigsaw puzzle simply cannot satisfy the needs of a continental-sized economy and society. (European Commission Innovation Program, 1996)

At the beginning of the unity, there were difficulties in implementing the Central Transport Policy (CTP) developed by the Treaty of Rome. Therefore, it was necessary to initiate the Treaty of Maastricht's Trans-European Network (TEN) with the purpose of reinforcing the political, institutional and budgetary foundations for transport policy. Trans-European Transport Networks (TEN-T) policy has much increased the coordination in the planning of infrastructure projects by the Member States. Progress in implementation has also been substantial, and about one-third of the necessary investments (EUR 400 billion) in the TEN-T has been made. Much remains to be done, but the TENs have already gone a long way in linking EU markets and people. Progress has been achieved in reducing air pollution and road accidents. As a result, air quality in European cities has significantly improved through the application of ever-stricter Euro emission standards. Regarding road accidents, with more than 39,000 deaths in the EU in 2008, transport by road remains far too costly in terms of human lives. In the maritime sector, marine pollution and maritime accidents were considerably reduced, and the EU has established one of the most advanced regulatory frameworks for safety and pollution prevention. In aviation, it has adopted a comprehensive set of common, uniform and mandatory legislation covering all the key elements affecting safety (aircraft, maintenance, airports, air traffic management systems, etc.). Safety agencies have been set up for aviation, maritime affairs, and rail transport (European Commission 2009).

The Trans-European Transport Networks (TEN-T) upgraded infrastructure (highways, inland waterways and ports, seaports, airports), creating a more fluid multimodal high-speed, and long-distance travel network. The idea was to improve accessibility and unity while upholding environmental protection requirements and promoting sustainable development (Martin 2011). In 2001, the European Commission proposed more than 50 measures to develop a transport system that balanced modes of transportation, revitalizing the railways, promoting transport by sea and inland waterways and controlling the growth of air transport. Several technical standardizing measures with the aim of speeding construction of an integrated network were proposed for the revitalization of European railways (Martin 2011). The original TEN plan outlined in 1994 allotted 70,000 kilometers of rail consisting of high-speed and regular corridors dedicated to combined transport, increasing access to ports and regions (Gordon 2005).

According to the European rail industry association, the European market for trains is forecasted at more than 13 billion euros per year between 2015 and 2017. This greatly exceeds expected orders of 4 billion euros for North America for the same years (Comtex 2012). Bombardier is one of the leading innovative train manufactures answering the call for environmentally friendly, sustainable, multi-track and high-speed trains. The newest revolution in light rail technology is witnessed in the BOMBARDIER PRIMOVE e-mobility solution that operates using an overhead catenary (overhead electric wire system) or a wireless catenary-free system. A pickup coil underneath the vehicle creates electricity out of a magnetic field produced by cables in the ground (Glickenstein 2010). This allows the light train to operate without the clutter of overhead wires or with any existing infrastructure. For safety reasons, the cables only energize the area underneath a PRIMOVE vehicle. Moreover, the PRIMOVE system can be incorporated with buses, cars and trucks. These vehicles are also equipped with a BOMBARDIER MITRAC Energy Saver, batteries located on the roof that store energy released as a vehicle brakes. MITRAC saves 30 percent of energy, consequently reducing costs of electricity and greenhouse gases. Furthermore, light rail trains have lower flooring for a better center of gravity and ease of access (Glickenstein 2010). In the realm of high-speed trains, Bombardier has the highly praised BOMBARDIER ZEFIRO family. These trains are capable of adapting to other EU nations' rail networks, which will result in fewer train transfers (Comtex 2012). Advanced aerodynamics and design ensure passenger comfort because noise pollution formed from rushing air and cabin pressure changes experienced while entering and exiting tunnels at high speeds are reduced. This makes high-speed rail competitive with air travel for distances up to 700km (435mile)(Comtex 2012). Complementing air travel by rail, rather than the two competing, is a priority for the EU. For example, linking rail lines to airports is a tool Heathrow airport utilized to provide an alternative form of transport during peak times (Behrens and Pels 2012). Speaking of air travel, deregulation of the industry produce a more cooperative network among the member nations allowing EU citizens to travel freely and smoothly throughout the union. The packages called for a trans-European network of 267 airports using modern IT air traffic management systems to coordinate a smooth flow (Gordon 2005). Also included was the standardization of air traffic controller qualifications, adjusted airport charges, environmental rules reducing problems such as noise pollution, the establishment of the European Aviation Safety Authority, which upholds safety measures, and supporting passenger rights (Martin 2011).

A Paradigm Shift in Car Ownership and Use: Germany

With an average of 231 people per square kilometer (598 people per square mile), Germany is one of the most densely populated countries in Europe, surpassed only by Belgium and The Netherlands. Not only is Germany as a whole densely populated, but German cities are quite compact, with four times the average population density of the largest American cities. In Germany, as in the rest of the world, the private car is a popular mode of transport, providing levels of comfort, convenience, speed, and flexibility. Thus, as incomes in Germany have risen over the past decades, car ownership, and use has increased as well (Pucher 1998).

In 1950, West Germany had one of the western world's lowest rates of car ownership: only 12 cars per 1,000 inhabitants. Between 1950 and 1992, however, car ownership skyrocketed to 492 cars per 1,000 inhabitants, a 41-fold increase, giving West Germany the second highest rate of car ownership in the world. The motorization rate of the unified Germany in 1992 was somewhat lower than the rate for West Germany alone (470 vs. 492 cars per 1,000 inhabitants). Although car ownership in East Germany had doubled in the 3 years after the reunification, it was still about 10 percent lower than the West German rate in 1992, thus bringing down the average for Germany as a whole. Between 1992 and 1995, car ownership in both Eastern and Western Germany continued to grow, and by 1995, the unified Germany again had the second highest rate of car ownership in the world (at 494 cars per 1,000 inhabitants). In 2011, the car ownership of Germany was 588 cars per 1,000 inhabitants.

As car ownership has increased, so have vehicle kilometers traveled by car. The data series for car mileage in West Germany starts in 1952. In the 40 years from then until 1992, car use rose from 18.2 billion km to 409.8 billion km, a 23-fold increase. Of course, the extremely rapid growth in car ownership and use far exceeded population growth rate, which was only 36 percent for the entire 42-year period from 1950 to 1992 (excluding the increase due to the reunification of East and West Germany). The first consolidated statistics for the unified Germany were collected in 1992, and it is shown that vehicle kilometers of car use have continued to increase by 44 billion vehicle km or about 3 percent per year; (Pucher 1998).

However, recent studies on German travel demand forecast showed that after heavy travel demand increase rates in the eighties and the first half of the nineties, a paradigm of stagnation in car use have been observed in the last years, in spite of increases in the total number of cars in individual households (Zumkeller and Chlond 1997). There is a sluggish change in the number of passenger cars starting from the year 1999 (the year from which annual vehicle stock data is available). For many years, metropolitan-wide public transport systems have provided high quality, well-integrated services, and large subsidies have enabled them to offer regular riders inexpensive monthly tickets. Virtually every German city has extensive car-free pedestrian zones, traffic-calmed residential areas and a network of bikeways that encourage walking and bicycling, generally complementing public transport use. Having improved these transport alternatives, German policies have also greatly restricted car use in cities. Lower speed limits, shared rights of way, lane restrictions, limited parking supply, car-free districts and preferential traffic signals for public transport have made car use more difficult in inner city areas. Additionally, high motor vehicle fees, license fees, fuel taxes and parking fees make car ownership and use quite expensive in Germany. It is believed that only such a two-fold strategy can really change travel behavior: restricting car use and increasing its cost, while facilitating walking, bicycling and public transport use. These transport policies in Germany show that it is possible to reduce the private car by limiting its use in central cities and providing travelers with an attractive choice of alternative transport modes (Pucher 1998; Zumkeller and Chlond 1997).

Sustainable Transportation in Europe

In Europe, sustainability is seen as a much broader concept having economic and social as well as environmental dimensions. Sustainable development is viewed as development that improves service quality, the standard of living and quality of life, while at the same time protecting and enhancing the natural environment and honoring local culture and history (USDOT FHWA, 2001). The USDOT FHWA report, after assessing sustainable transportation practices of four European countries namely Germany, Sweden, The Netherlands and United Kingdom, discussed what is unique about the sustainable transportation in European context:

Sustainable transportation is safe, high quality, and accessible to all; ecologically sound; economical; and a positive contributor to regional development. Specific goals for sustainable transportation include improved service quality and quality of access to goods and services, safety, improved air quality, noise reduction, improved water quality, protection of habitat and open space, historic preservation, reduced carbon emissions, increased social equity, economic development, and a satisfying quality of life, plus local goals consistent with the overall objective. It is observed that there is a high degree of agreement on the goals and objectives of sustainable development and sustainable transportation among the four countries and at various levels of government (national, state, regional, and local). This common understanding and approach is the result of long-term and ongoing efforts to build consensus through international negotiations and EU policy development, bolstered by the emphasis on leadership, education, and use of incentives to win support and develop a sense of common cause among all levels of government (pp. 14–15).

The coordination of land use and transportation is a fundamental element in European efforts to improve sustainability. Local and regional land use strategies are viewed as important ways to manage demand and transportation impacts. In each country, policies governing the location of land uses are designed to reduce trip lengths and facilitate the use of transit, biking and walking—an approach referred to many European nations as the "short trip" land development strategy.

Berveling and van de Riet (2012) argued that in Europe, the amount of CO_2 produced is regarded as a major policy problem, so the problem is dealt within a European context. Europe's goal is to decrease total CO_2 emissions by 80—95 percent in 2050 compared to CO_2 emissions levels in 1990. In March 2011, the European Commission proposed in a *"Road Map to a Competitive Low Carbon dioxide Economy in 2050,"* to spread the 80 to 95 percent objective across various sectors (European Commission 2011a). For the transport sector, this amounts to a 60 percent decrease in CO_2 in 2050, as compared to 1990 levels (European Commission 2011b). For example, according to Berveling and van de Riet (2012), the Netherlands has committed to a total CO_2 emissions reduction of 80 to 95 percent in the EU context. This is a major policy objective that is only possible if the transport sector is a major contributor.

According to the report by European Commission (2011b), future development that ensures sustainability must rely on some sustainability strategies:

- improving the energy efficiency of vehicles across all modes and developing and deploying sustainable fuels and propulsion systems
- optimizing the performance of multimodal logistic chains, including greater use of inherently more resource-efficient modes, where other technological innovations may be insufficient
- using transport and infrastructure more efficiently through use of improved traffic management and information systems, advanced logistic and market measures such as full development of an integrated European railway market, removal of restrictions on cabotage, abolition of barriers to short sea shipping, undistorted pricing, etc.

BOX 11.1 European low car(bon) communities

The report, Europe's Vibrant New Low Car(bon) Communities describes eight European communities that apply smart urban and transport planning to significantly reduce car ownership and vehicle travel rates. As a result, these communities have less pollution, greenhouse gas emissions, public health issues and other negative externalities associated with driving. These new developments use a combination of "push" measures to discourage private car use and "pull" measures to improve the attractiveness of walking, cycling, transit and various forms of shared vehicle use. Each case study includes background information on the origins of the development and how these best practices were incorporated at early stages of the developments' planning processes. The top lessons learned from these case studies include:

- Develop neighborhoods for walking and prioritize bicycling networks: The majority of developments in the case studies provide direct, safe and comfortable walking and cycling routes and plentifully covered cycle parking. They also use a technique called "filtered permeability" to make travel by bicycle or foot more direct than by car, and locate bicycle parking closer to homes than car parking. This gives walking and cycling a competitive advantage over the car. Some are beginning to use bike sharing to encourage occasional bike use by visitors and residents alike.
- Provide high-quality transit: The transport in all of the case study areas is responsive to resident needs, and, therefore, has a high mode share. Stops are within half a kilometer of every home, and service frequencies are at least every 15 minutes. Integration into the regional transit network and long service hours all make riding convenient while low-cost period passes keep it affordable. By optimizing conditions for walking, cycling and transit, living car-free becomes more realistic. Many developments also provide nearby car sharing locations to help residents feel more comfortable giving up their private cars.
- Create compact regions with short commutes and zone new developments for mixed use: These case studies also suggest that new developments should be planned as closely as possible to existing job centers and other destinations. This makes investments in transit and cycling networks more efficient and effective. Mixed uses (housing, jobs, leisure facilities, shops, grocery stores, etc.) should be incorporated into new developments at site selection and master planning stage, to minimize travel distances, enabling residents to make routine trips on foot or by bicycle, with convenient public transportation offering a realistic alternative to the car.
- Reduce driving by regulating parking and road use: In addition to the nudges the urban design of these communities provide, many also use regulations to incentivize and in some cases mandate reduced car use. In many of the cases, parking supply has been reduced and the parking that does exist is separated spatially and fiscally from housing units.
- Market sustainable transportation: Many of these developments make ongoing efforts to reinforce their founding vision and to empower residents and visitors to make sustainable travel decisions by offering tailored mobility advice, running marketing and awareness campaigns and through promotions such as free or discounted transit passes or car-sharing membership for new residents. Ongoing measures to encourage low-emission travel behavior are important to ensure the long-term transport sustainability of residents.
- Don't forget the larger policy context: Transportation policies at the city, regional and national levels play a key role in shaping daily travel behavior and residential locations in the longer-term. Congestion charges, citywide parking management policies, high fuel prices, and high quality transit all influence mode choice, reinforcing site-specific measures such as car access restrictions, provision of high quality walking and cycling facilities and filtered permeability. All of the case study cities are served by national railroad systems, providing an alternative to the car for longer-distance journeys, thereby complementing measures to discourage car ownership and use in the local area.

Adapted from TDM Encyclopedia, Victoria Transport Policy Institute, 2014. More information on the case studies http://www.gwl-terrein.nl/files/artikelen/low%20carbon%20communities.pdf.

PUBLIC TRANSPORTATION

There are several public transportation systems installed in most of the technologically advanced nations of Europe. In Europe, there are sixteen long-distance high-speed rail companies, including French Train a Grande Vitesse (TGV), which connects France with Switzerland, Germany, Italy, Luxembourg, Belgium, and Spain. Similarly, Thalys (THA) of France connecting it with Belgium, Netherlands, and Germany. Likewise, the Intercity-Express (ICE) connecting Germany to Austria, Netherlands, Switzerland, France, Denmark, and Belgium. The X 2000 (X2) of Sweden & Denmark making it the shortest high-speed rail system of Scandinavia Peninsula.

It has become a primary focus of the European Union to create fast and efficient public transportation system, and High-Speed Rail appears to be the solution. The first big proposal for a network of the High-Speed Rail came in 1990. Special action was taken in December of 1994 at the Essen European Council to develop a policy for the implementation of this new rail system. The three main justifications for this new network were to improve capacity on heavily used rail corridors, to increase travel speeds and to allow better access to underserved regions (Vickerman 1997). A recent manifestation of Europe's commitment to High-Speed Rail came in 2010 when Spain opened a new high-speed rail line from Valencia to Madrid. Before the line opened, the journey took over 4 hours to complete. After the line had been completed, the journey took just 90 minutes, a significant improvement. Train speeds on the line run up to 205 miles per hour. Up to 30 trains are planned to operate on the route at the same time once capacity is reached with 294 passengers on each train (Minder 2010).

The monorail is another type of the rail-based transportation system, which is suitable for EU nations due to the dense population in major cities. The monorail operates on an elevated platform where the train is suspended on a single track of rail. Monorails are usually

Figure 11.2 Public transportation in Berlin, Germany (author's photograph).

placed in crowded areas where regular trains would be hazardous, and underground tunnels are not permitted.

Subway or "the tube" is an underground high-speed railway used by most capitals of modern European nations. These railways transport people in the intercity region and connecting them to their origins hubs on the outskirts of the suburban areas. This is an example of the interurban transportation system. They are oriented in a way that would stop only on the major hubs of the city and departs quickly, with no delays. The subway system also is using electricity to move the trains, and due to the cheap price and clean and safe environment, it attracts the majority of the urban population.

The oldest urban rail transportations of Europe are streetcars and cable cars. The single and sometimes double streetcars use electricity and electrical motors to move the passengers. The streetcars use overhead cables for power while cable cars use a cable system that runs underneath the vehicle.

The freight trains are also one of the oldest transportation systems that transfer larger numbers of goods and some percentage of passengers. They are not as fast as passenger trains, however, can be operated during heavy snowstorms and the winter. They use diesel fuel to be able to haul the heavy cargo cars, thus creating smoke and emitting CO_2. As Rotenberg *et al.* (2011) stated in their article, these vehicles all fall under the CO_2 emission limit set by the Kyoto Protocol, making them a liability for the nations operating them. Most of the European freight railways start and end their trip in a coastal city, a place that transportation of passenger and goods end or start a new journey.

According to Gori, Nigro and Petrelli (2010) different elements, criteria and policy have been underlined as important components to building a competitive public transport system as part of sustainable urban development. The approaches include improving the transit system performance and modifying the land use characteristics. The USDOT FHWA (2001) reports also observed that transit improvements are the key element of the European strategy for sustainability. Specific strategies to improve transit service include the development of extensive systems of priority lanes for buses, high-quality architecture and landscaping at transit stations and stops, planning for door-to-door service (including walk and bike access planning as part of transit planning), improved intermodal transfers, and high-quality customer information services.

BOX 11.2 Multimodal transportation in Cologne, Germany

With a population of 1.1 million in the city of Cologne and more than 3 million in the region, more than 400,000 workers commute into Cologne each day from seven principal origin areas. Only four bridges cross the Rhine, and these carry 120,000 cars per day. Some 180,000 vehicles a day uses the Autobahn east of Cologne, which is part of a 52-km ring road system. As such, the roads into and around Cologne are heavily congested. Of the 12,000 km of federal roads in the Cologne area, 2,000 or one-sixth are congested during much of the day. Today, there are significant pressures to expand the road system in an already very dense urban area and, indeed, lanes are being added to the ring highways to the west and east. But traffic management is a key part of the solution as well. Congestion costs billions of euros each year and the benefits of managing traffic not only include addressing congestion, but also reducing accidents and emissions. Traffic control systems have been developed by the Federal Ministry of Transport, but traffic in and around Cologne is managed by both the city of Cologne and the State of North Rhine-Westphalia. The state controls the highway system, and the city controls arterials and the public transport system. In fact, 84 percent of the transportation budget in Cologne is spent on public transit, 15 percent on roads, and 1 percent on traffic management. The city estimates that it receives six times the benefits for each euro spent on its overall transport program.

In addition to widening of the Cologne ring highways, the public transport system is being improved and expanded. The Kolnerverkehrsbetriebe (KVB) system, including trams, buses, and an underground system, carries 230 million riders per year. The KVB is in the middle of a U.S. $1.25 billion (€1 billion) improvement program over 12 years to upgrade right-of-way, rolling stock and stations and expand the system, notably the tram network. Improvements include the introduction of low-floor vehicles, prioritization schemes to increase speeds, an advanced schedule information system, dynamic information displays at platforms, and fare system integration. A park-and-ride system has been established along key arterials feeding into the city center where travelers can park and transfer to streetcars. There are five integrated park-and-ride facilities at tram stations, including 2,300 spaces. One innovative aspect of these facilities is the information system that provides drivers with real-time travel time comparisons. When approaching a park-and-ride lot and tram station, drivers can read a dynamic display panel, which shows the current travel time into the city center, the equivalent travel time by public transport, and how soon the next tram will arrive. This enables drivers to make informed choices about staying on the road or transferring to public transport. This travel time comparison initiative was integrated into the park-and-ride system as part of the Stadtinfoköln project.

Adapted from "Managing Travel Demand: Applying European Perspectives to U.S. Practice," FHWA, Office of International Programs

WALKING AND BIKING

Even though winters can be harsh in these countries, bicycling is recognized as an important transport mode, particularly for short trips. Extensive systems of bikeways, bike parking and facilities for bikes on transit have been established. Traffic controls, including signalization and signage, are designed to accommodate the slower speeds and accelerations of bicycles and to improve bike visibility and safety (USDOT FHWA, 2001).

More endeavors in Europe that promote alternative travel modes to cars can be witnessed in the bicycle culture displayed in several countries. Multiple provisions for safety, convenience, encouraging healthy lifestyles and an overall positive cultural perception towards bicycling are observed in those countries. Key policies for encouraging cycling include separate cycling facilities that include separate bicycle paths, color-coded signs and pathways, and short-cuts for pedestrians and bicycles only. Intersection designs from advanced waiting positions, to separate lanes that turn green early for bikes, to flashing bollards that signal the right speed needed to catch green lights that are synchronized to cyclists speeds are just some of the items found at intersections. Traffic calming strategies using physical deterrents, bicycle rights of way, and very low-speed limits of 30km/hr in residential and 7km/hr in "Home Zones" have also been implemented. Adequate, well lit, video-surveillance bike parking and bike rental facilities are integrated with public transportation to encourage multimodal travel (Pucher and Buehler 2008). These policies promote a positive perception of bicycle travel, strict traffic enforcement by police and courts in favor of cyclists regarding cyclist's rights and accidents. Health campaigns, bicycle festivals and competitions, and public participation in bike planning are some more practices that boost bicycle culture in bike-successful European countries. Despite these efforts, there has been a dramatic increase in the use of cars in all Eastern Block European countries that experienced a governmental transition after the end of the Cold War. This is due to the increased economic prosperity, better jobs, easier access to cars and new-found freedoms enjoyed by citizens of these nations (Pucher 1994).

Table 11.1 Main mode of transport for daily activities

Country	Bike (%)	Car (%)	Public transport (%)
Netherlands	31.2	48.5	11.0
Hungary	19.1	28.2	35.3
Denmark	19.0	63.4	11.8
Germany	13.1	60.9	14.8
Slovakia	9.5	32.3	30.9
Italy	4.7	54.4	18.2
Ireland	3.2	67.7	14.2
France	2.6	63.7	20.1
UK	2.2	57.6	22.1
Spain	1.6	47.4	30.2
EU27 average	7.4	52.9	21.8

Source: European Commission Future of Transport report 2011. 1,000 people in each country were asked; what is your main mode of transport for daily activities?

Smart Bikes: one component of the European cycling infrastructure is smart bikes. Bike sharing programs (or smart bikes) are one of the advances in transportation in Europe. The idea originally started in Amsterdam in 1968 with what were known as the "white bikes." Unfortunately, the system only lasted a matter of days due to a lack of proper use and theft. The idea disappeared for several years until 1995 when Copenhagen introduced a coin-operated system. This system worked much better than the system in Amsterdam although the theft was still an issue. In the late 1990s, a new system was created that gave each patron a magnetic card that would track their bike and have their information in case the bike was not returned. Additionally, there were boundaries instituted for where the bikes could be taken. If the bicycle left the zone, the patron would be charged. These zone maps were posted at each bicycle station. This system has proved quite successful all across Europe. As of 2003, ten different types of smart bike systems have been established. Some benefits of the system include access to an inexpensive transportation system in areas where transit is not feasible, increased exercise and reduction in air pollution (DeMaio 2003). In the years since, cities in the United States like New York and San Francisco are experimenting with systems like these as a means of inexpensive transportation option (Lippelt 2013).

Special Features of European Transportation

CONGESTION PRICING IN LONDON

Over the last 50 or so years, roads in London have become increasingly congested with travel as slow as pre-auto days within the central city. Much thought and effort has been given to alleviating the congestion. The solution that eventually was thought up was congestion pricing, which began in 2003. As stated in previous chapters, congestion pricing is a daily fee that is imposed on driving a car into the central city and parking within it. This all began with a report in the early 1990s that claimed that congestion pricing would significantly reduce the amounts of traffic within the city while promoting transit use. The report, which was published in 1995, called for a $7.50 daily charge for cars wishing to enter the city. This charge has subsequently increased to $15 recently. This fee increase was brought into effect to reduce the congestion by an additional 30 percent. For those who live within the city and want to leave and re-enter the city, there is a 90 percent discount as long as they have off-street parking. Additionally, motorcycles, bicycles, buses and taxis are not subject to the charge. Rather than having toll booths, the payment is collected through a variety of means including kiosks, telephone, text messages, retail outlets and on the internet. Payment is enforced by cameras that capture the vehicle's license plate when passing into the zone (De Palma and Lindsey 2011). The license plate is then recorded into a database. When paying, the customer enters their license plate number along with their payment and the license plate number is removed from the database. The system has overall proven itself to work with a 27 percent reduction in vehicles coming into the zone. Additionally, there has been a 28 percent increase in the number of bicycles coming into the city. This modal shift has reduced traffic and air pollution and promoted the physical exercise that is associated with bike riding. The average vehicle speed within the zone has increased from an average of 8.9 miles per hour to 10.4 miles per hour. This is an increase of about 17 percent. While there is much good news, the positive results may have come at a cost. A study done by several retailers within the city found a statistically significant negative effect on sales. Although in a survey, the majority of retailers were found to agree that the charge has increased both the quality of life and reputation of Central London while having a neutral impact on the economy. Overall, the congestion pricing has proven itself to be effective in London (Leape 2006).

THE GERMAN AUTOBAHN

How about driving at any speed on a highway? It has been thought that you can drive at any speed on the German Autobahn. To some, this may sound unsafe, but when closely examined it can be seen that in many respects, the Autobahn can be seen as a safer alternative to the conventional speed-regulated freeway. The Autobahn has a variable speed limit. Unlike the speed limits in the United States that are fixed speeds with the highly subjective caveat of whatever is safe for the conditions, the German Autobahn has speed limits posted that adapt to conditions (Moulson 2007). For the variable system to work, a combination of weather conditions and traffic, data processing, and a speed limit display is needed. The weather data collected is from the weather forecasting service, and the traffic data collected from something called an inductive loop detector. Loop detectors are integrated into the pavement and can provide such information as number of vehicles, vehicle speed and number of passengers in the vehicles. Pavement condition is also something that is taken into account. These are components that must be considered in the formulation of the posted speed. So far, Germany is not alone in its

Figure 11.3 A "no speed limit" sign for Germany's Autobahn

use of this variable speed limit system. Australia, Finland, the Netherlands, and the United Kingdom have all employed such systems with great success. In the United Kingdom, speed limits are adjusted based on the number of vehicles on the road; the greater the number, the lower the speed limit. For instance, when there is an excess of 1,650 vehicles per hour per lane, the speed is reduced from 70 miles per hour to 60 miles per hour. The number of display signs varies depending on region, but there are no less than 2 per kilometer. This keeps the drivers informed of the ever-changing limit. Additionally, the sign is posted directly over each lane to ensure that the driver can easily see the sign in plain sight. The signs usually use fiber optic technology along with LED light bulbs. The speed limit number is posted in white numbers inside a red circle. This strategy has been found to do the best job of capturing driver's attention (Sisiopiku 2001).

Lessons Learned from European Transportation

MULTIMODALITY AND DRIVE-ALTERNATIVE OPTIONS

According to an analysis by Charles Knutson (2013), multimodality is the European solution to reduce car use and encourage the use of alternative modes of travel. Multimodality is understood to be the use of different modes of transportation for a single trip that is fully accessible to anyone. For example, in Brussels, city leaders are taking a systematic and multimodal approach to traffic problems. Brussels anticipates that its population will increase by another 200,000 people by 2020, adding significant pressure to an already strained transportation grid. To plan for the future, leaders are working to reduce car traffic in the city by 20 percent in the next five years by promoting bicycle and transit use. Automobile speed limits on key routes have been reduced to make bike riding safer. On other streets, cars are prohibited from passing bikes, and some lanes are dedicated entirely to bike use. The city has also implemented a major public bike-sharing system called "Villo!" Bikes are placed in strategic places around the city about a quarter of a mile apart to ensure that one is always within walking distance. Bike and public transportation riding is also taught to adults through a public outreach program and to kids through holiday camps.

PUBLIC PARTICIPATION

In most cases, citizens are involved in the planning process. For example, the Fehrman Belt tunnel in Denmark initially met resistance from neighbors concerned about increased traffic, and from environmental groups concerned about perceived impacts on marine life. Project supporters worked to engage citizens early on, listened to their input, and made several changes to the design to address their concerns. Likewise, the Brussels Bike program initially faced opposition from conservative political parties. Through data gathered and public input, leaders gradually saw the transportation and monetary benefits of increasing multimodal choices (Knutson 2013). Another example cited by Buehler and Picher (2011a) is the city of Freiburg in Germany. Since the 1970s, citizen participation has been a key aspect of transport and land use planning in Freiburg. For example, citizen groups worked with the city administration to redevelop Vauban community into an environmentally friendly car-free neighborhood. Moreover, Freiburg's latest land use plan has been developed with the sustained input of 900 citizens. Citizen involvement and public discourse kept the environmental sustainability of the transport system in the news in Freiburg for decades. Over time, public opinion in Freiburg has become more and more supportive of sustainable policies. Even politicians from the conservative party have accepted restrictions on car use and have promoted public transport, bicycling, and walking as alternatives (Buehler and Pucher 2011a).

INTEGRATED LAND USE AND TRANSPORTATION PLANNING

Coordinating transport and land use planning involves policies promoting public transport, cycling, and walking that rely on a settlement structure that keeps trip distances short and residences and workplaces within reach of public transport. There are already some successful examples in the United States such as Washington, D.C., and Portland, Oregon. In Europe, integrated policy-making is gaining more attention. A report of the European Conference of Ministers of Transport states that more sustainable policy-making for urban travel requires a more holistic approach in which transport, land use and the environmental decisions are made together, not in isolation from each other. Current policies call for new forms of co-operation and government involvement, based on new ideas in public administration such as network management. This trend has developed over the last decade and is partly in reaction to previous policies that were characterized by central steering, autonomous policy developments for specific domains and a hierarchical set of relations (ECMT 2001; Geerlings and Stead 2002). European cities such as Freiberg, Germany has development of light rail systems, the planning of desirable land uses around rail stops, the restrictions on suburban sprawl and the focus on strengthening the central city and neighborhood-based commercial centers (Buehler and Pucher 2011a).

FINANCING AND TAXING SYSTEMS THAT ENCOURAGE SUSTAINABLE TRANSPORTATION

In the United States, the federal gas tax, generating nearly 90 percent of the federal transportation revenue, has not been raised in nearly 20 years, not even to keep pace with inflation. So, as the rate effectively declines, so does the purchasing power of the fund. The current 18.4 cent per gallon tax in the U.S. is far less than in European competitor nations. Unlike the U.S. gas tax, a VMT fee that is being practiced in some European countries, would be unaffected by the greater use of more efficient vehicles. Also, it provides a price signal that encourages drivers to minimize roadway congestion. A VMT fee is also very flexible—it allows pricing to vary depending on the actual cost of capacity, allowing for higher fees during congested periods and lower fees when traffic is free-flowing. Germany currently uses a similar system (Robert and Tomer 2009). Over the past two decades, Germany has also improved its public transport services, increased productivity, reduced costs, cut subsidy requirements and at the same time increased ridership. During the same period, transit ridership has increased in the United States but at a far higher cost, requiring much larger government subsidies and attracting fewer additional riders (Buehler and Pucher 2011b).

Overall, Europe has been at the forefront of transportation innovation. With programs such as the Smart Bike bicycle-sharing program in Copenhagen, people are getting out of their vehicles and onto bicycles that are both good for the environment and the individual's health. Innovations such as the Autobahn's adjustable speed limit system both assist in decreasing traffic bottlenecks and increasing highway safety. An investment in High Speed

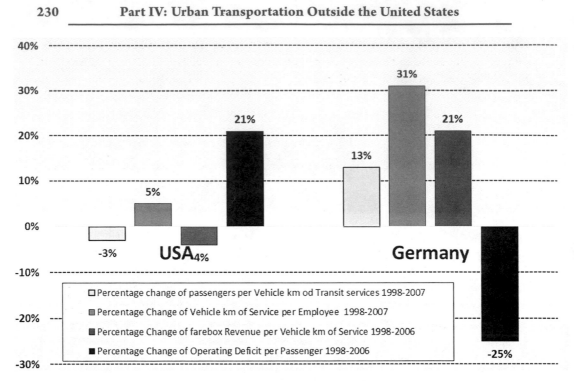

Figure 11.4 Percentage change of public transport productivity and financial efficiency indicators in Germany and the U.S. (data: Buehler and Pucher, 2011).

Rail has allowed drivers to forget the airport, leave their car at home and jump onto a quick, clean, and efficient modern day train that is both good for the environment and the economy. While there is still room for much improvement, Europe seems to be making the right steps in developing a transportation system for the future. It seems that what Europe has to go for it is the political will for such innovative transportation projects. Also, on an important note, the density and land use within European cities has been more supportive of modes of transportation other than the car than in the United States, although this is changing.

Review Questions

1) How were early European cities designed in relation to transportation?
2) What technological breakthroughs have made bus travel an attractive alternative to personal vehicles?
3) What is the "Trans-European Network" and how did it change Europe?
4) What are the major justifications for High-Speed Rail in Europe?
5) According to the European Commission report what standards must future developments rely on to achieve sustainability?
6) Discuss the paradigm shift in the use of the car in Germany.
7) What are "Smart Bikes"? How has technology made this a more practical alternative mode?
8) Why is cycling so popular in the Netherlands?

9) Why could the German Autobahn be safer than the conventional highways?
10) What are some of the components of smart urban and transportation planning in Europe low carbon communities?

Project/Paper Idea

Compare and contrast the transportation planning practices in the Northern America and Europe in terms of:

- Planning, policy, enforcement, etc.
- Land use
- Mode choice
- Pricing and regulatory measures

Is the comparison fair? What are the social, cultural and demographic factors for the different travel characteristics of the two regions? Is it feasible for the U.S. to adopt some of the European Transportation policies (or the vice versa)? What are some of the possible challenges?

Video

A Toute Vitesse: Commuting and Traveling by Public Transport by Films Media Group, 2011 (14 min.): Too many cars and never enough parking spaces: that's Paris! In this program, everyday people talk about what they think of traffic, how they commute to work, and how to buy a train ticket. In addition, a police officer explains the daily challenges of directing traffic in Paris—compounded by a state visit from the president of Egypt—and residents of Strasbourg debate the benefits and drawbacks of a controversial tramway system intended as a primary means of getting around in their city.

Internet Sources

- European Commission: Mobility and Transport, http://ec.europa.eu/transport/index_en.htm
- Transportation and the Environment, http://www.transportenvironment.org/
- Trans-European Network, http://ec.europa.eu/transport/infrastructure/tentec/tentec-portal/site/index_en.htm

Bibliography

Amann, Markus, Imrich Bertok, Jens Borken-Kleefeld, Janusz Cofala, and Chris Heyes. 2011. "Cost Effective Control of Air Quality and Green House Gases in Europe: Modeling and Policy Applications." *Environmental Modeling and Software* 26 (1): 489- 1501.

Behrens, Christiann, and Eric Pels. 2012. "Intermodal Competition in the London–Paris Passenger Market: High-Speed Rail and Air Transport." *Journal of Urban Economics* 71 (3): 278–288.

Berveling, Jaco, and Odette Riet. 2012. *Towards a Sustainable Car Fleet.* KiM Netherlands Institute for Transport Policy Analysis, Association for European Transport and Contributors.

Buehler, Ralph, and John Pucher. 2011. "Making Public Transport Financially Sustainable." *Transport Policy* 18 (1): 128–136.

_____, and _____. 2011a. "Promoting Sustainable Urban Transport: Lessons from Germany." *Presentation at: "Lessons from Europe"—Jean Monnet Research Workshop, Rutgers Center for European Studies, September 29–30, 2011*

Comtex. 2012. "Bombardier Highlights Innovative Transport Solutions at the World's Largest Rail Show." *Comtex news network.* http://www.comtex.com/.

DeMaio, Paul. 2003. "Smart Bikes: Public Transportation for the 21st Century." *Transportation Quarterly* 57: 9–12.

De Palma, Andre, and Robin Lindsey. 2011. "Traffic Congestion Pricing Methodologies and Technologies." *Transportation Research Part C: Emerging Technologies* 19 (6): 1377–1399.

European Commission. 2009. *A Sustainable Future for Transport—Towards an Integrated, Technology-Led and User-Friendly System.* Luxembourg: Publications Office of the European Union.

_____. 2011a. *A Roadmap for Moving to a Competitive Low Carbon Economy in 2050,* Brussels: European Commission.

_____. 2011b. *Roadmap to a Single European Transport Area—Towards a Competitive and Resource Efficient Transport System, Final.* Brussels: European Commission.

European Conference of Ministers of Transport (ECMT). 2001. *Implementing Sustainable Urban Travel Policies.* Report CEMT/CM(2001)13, ECMT, Paris.

Frémont, Antoine, and Pierre Franc. 2010. "Hinterland Transportation in Europe: Combined Transport Versus Road Transport." *Journal of Transport Geography* 18 (4): 548–556.

Geerlings, Harry and Dominic Stead. 2002. " Integrating Transport, Land Use Planning and Environment Policy in European Countries," *European Journal of Transportation and Infrastructure Research,* 2 (3/4): 215–231.

Glickenstein, Harvey. 2010. "Metro Rails Transportation Systems." *IEEE Vehicular Technology Magazine,* 14–90.

Gordon, Cameron. 2005. "Transportation Policy in the European and American Unions Compared: Lessons in Transportation Federalism." *Public Works Management & Policy* 9 (4): 292–304.

Gori, Stefano, Marialisa Nigro, and Marco Petrelli. 2010. *Land Use Characteristics for Sustainable Urban Mobility.* Association for European Transport and Contriibutors.

Hounsell, N, B Shrestha, and Alan Wong. 2012. "Data Management and Applications in a World-Leading Bus Fleet." *Transportation Research Part C: Emerging Technologies* 22: 76–87.

Knutson, Charles. 2013. *Europe on the Move: Public Transportation Lessons for the U.S.* http://blog.gmfus.org/.

Leape, Johnathan. 2006. "The London Congestion Charge." *Journal of Economic Perspectives* 20: 157- 176.

Lippelt, Jana. 2013. *Worldwide Bike Sharing Programs.* DICE Report, 50–52.

Martin, Juan. 2011. "Transportation Changes in Europe." *Transportation Journal* 50 (1): 109–124.

Minder, R. 2010. "Spain Pushes on in High-Speed Rail." *International Herald Tribune,* 18–24.

Moulson. 2007. "Speed Limits on the Autobahn? Never! Germans Declare." *Transport Topics,* A5.

Pucher, John. 1994. "Modal Shift in Eastern Germany Transportation Impacts of Political Change." *Transportation* 21 (1): 1–22.

_____. 1998. "Urban Transport in Germany: Providing Feasible Alternatives to the Car." *Transportation Review* 18: 285–310.

_____, and Ralph Buehler. 2008. "Making Cycling Irresistible: Lessons from the Netherlands, Denmark and Germany." *Transport Reviews* 28 (4): 495–528.

Robert, Puentes, and Adie Tomer. 2009. *Untangling Transportation Funding.* The Brookings Institution.

Rotenberg, Caroline, Peter Nijkamp, Henri De Grout, and Erik Verhoef. 2011. "Residents' Benefits of Multi-functional Land Use Projects: A Stated Preference Approach to a Case Study in Amsterdam." *International Planning Studies* 16: 397–417.

Sisiopiku, Virginia. 2001. "Variable Speed Control: Technologies and Practice." *Proceeding of the 11th Annual Meeting of ITS America.* 1–11.

USDOT, Federal Highway Administration. 2001. "Sustainable Transportation Practices in Europe." November, FHWA-PL-02–006

Vickerman, Roger. 1997. "High-Speed Rail in Europe: Experience and Issues for Future Development." *Regional Science* 31: 21–38.

Zumkeller, Dirk, and Bashtian Chlond. 1997. "The German Mobility Panel: Options, Limitations and the Complimentary Use of Secondary Data." *International Conference on Transport Survey Quality and Innovation.* Grainau, Germany.

12

Urban Transportation in the Developing World

Chapter Outline

Introduction: Cities and Transportation in the Developed World

Following the conclusion of World War II in 1945 and the onset of the Cold War, the term "Third World" was first applied to countries that were not directly aligned with the United States or Soviet Union. Now, the term Third World is outdated. However, people use it out of habit or just for the sake of simplifying the category of poor or developing countries, although the original concept has never been economic or developmental. The definition of "the developing world" in this chapter coincides with terms used in several official documents from UN and World Bank that includes "developing countries," "Less developed countries (LDCs)" or in general, "the Global South." For a long time, countries in the developing world were recognized as places of inequality and conflict, with rapid urbanization. Cities in the developing countries have struggled with constraints that arise from having center-periphery relations with the world economy (Mumme, Bath and Assetto 1988). At the same time, the developing countries has recently been seen to be instruments of development, wealth and social dynamism (Gottman 1983).

One of the characteristics of the developing world is accelerated urbanization and fast growing cities, faster than anywhere else in the world. According to data from the United Nations on world urbanization, 36 of the top 50 most populated city regions in the world are in the developing countries, representing 72 percent of the total top fifty places (measured as urban agglomerations or metropolitan statistical units depending on the country). In fact, only two cities in the top ten are in the developed countries: New York and Tokyo, with the rest being cities in less developed countries.

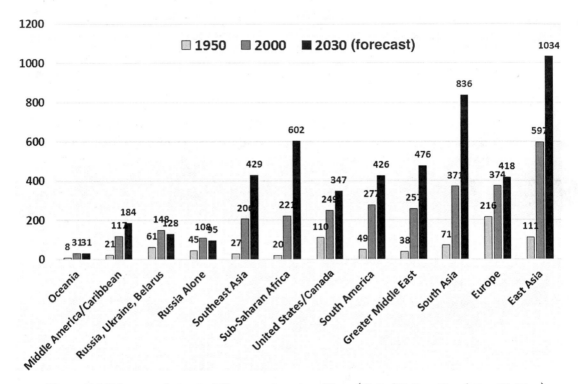

Figure 12.1 Urban population in different regions, in millions (United Nations Population Division).

Cities in the developing world have varied histories of transportation development. Some have a long history of transportation infrastructure development while some are recently emergent metropolises such as in South Asia and Africa. With accelerated urbanization, there is an increased demand for travel, which creates an immense challenge for cities. Transportation is a very critical sector for the social and economic function of cities. Consequently, mobility in the developing world is characterized by a travel demand that far exceeds supply (Darido 2003).

Public transportation is an important means of travel, especially in cities where there is a low level of car ownership. Travel needs in developing countries are mostly served by public transportation systems, especially bus transportation. Low-cost mass transit, jitneys/shared taxis, bus rapid transit (BRT) and massive state-run transportation are some of the various methods of urban mass transit in developing countries. In cities with a strong state mass transit system, the microbuses serve as feeders to the system, improving access for rural migrants and squatters from the fringe of the city (Cervero 1998). Informal transit service has been a preferred method of transportation in the developing world, but many cities have found success in BRT. Even developed cities have looked to cities of the developing countries for inspiration in urban planning and transportation (for example, BRT of Curitiba, Brazil).

In cities of the developed world, the urban poor are often a minority. Although equity considerations are important in all cities, in cities of the developed countries, these concerns are often focused on politically justifying urban transport subsidies of public transport systems used by only a minority of the population. In many cities of the developing world, on the other hand, the urban poor represent the majority of the population. This creates a significant burden on the existing public transportation system as car ownership rate is very low. In developing countries, car ownership rates are typically less than 100 cars per 1000 people, and even in higher income developing cities car ownership is less than 200 per 1000 people. This compares to car ownership rates of around 400 per 1000 people in Europe, and more than 500 per 1000 people in many cities in North America and Australia (GTZ SUTP 2010).

Today, developing countries are facing challenges in their journey towards economic development, be it socio-economic changes, education, health or the environment. However, urban transport remains largely unaddressed (Phanikumar and Bhargab 2006; UITP 2003). At the same time, public transportation use is receiving considerable attention as a means of reducing greenhouse gas emission, accidents and congestion as well as tackling existing high travel demand cities of the developing countries face. In an endeavor of creating a Transit-Oriented Society through compacted city development, many developing countries are encouraging the use of public transportation. Public transportation is playing an important role in those cities because (a) it is a relatively affordable means of transportation, (b) it reduces congestion as the road infrastructure is not sufficient enough to promote private vehicle ownership and (c) it reduces environmental pollution and traffic accidents. Even though the role of public transportation is more than noteworthy, in many cities the service provision is not enough to tackle the demand as well as to satisfy regular users. Moreover, in some cities of developing countries, public transportation is perceived to be a service for the "poor" so that many try to avoid it once their socio-economic status is improved. There is still a notion that public transportation, especially bus, is for a certain part of the society. Therefore, increasing public transportation users' level of satisfaction with the service and creating positive perception is important for the use of the service to the fullest extent possible. As the population in general and the number of public transportation passengers in particular increase, the quality of the service need to increase to persuade the city's residents who perceive that public transportation is something to avoid when one is up to the economic ladder. To change people's perception and satisfaction level, local governments and service providers have to improve the overall service and develop specific public transportation quality attributes.

Bogotá's TransMilenio

Bogotá is the capital and most important city in Colombia, and the majority of its resident's daily trips are made by public transportation. A report on "TransMilenio Busway-based Mass Transit, Bogotá, Colombia" which was prepared by John Cracknell in 2003 for the World

Bank, summarizes Bogotá's TransMilenio as a transportation service that provides a successful, high quality bus-based mass transit system with many positive attributes. The report stressed that TransMilenio is not just a busway; it is a bus-based mass transit system with the following elements of mass transit:

- high capacity vehicles
- frequent services provided by trunk line buses; services, both express and stopping, geared to meet passenger demand
- rapid and reliable services obtained through the use of exclusive and segregated lanes (busways)
- integrated fares and efficient fare collection
- high-level image and the appearance of a "quality mode" with well-designed bus stations with appropriate signage, bus livery, publicity, passenger assistance, etc.
- rapid passenger entry, facilitated by high-level platforms, prepayment and multiple doors
- efficient and equitable use of road space. Over 70 percent of travelers in Bogotá use public transport while it is estimated that prior to TransMilenio, public transport was allocated only 5 percent of road space. Therefore, the re-allocation of road space to TransMilenio busways and bus stations is both efficient and equitable
- high cost effectiveness and the provision of a service quality which is at least equivalent to any tram or LRT at a fraction of the cost—about U.S.$5 million/km for civil works and U.S.$8 million/km, including vehicles and infrastructure

Figure 12.2 TransMilenio BRT bus and bus station. Bogotá, Colombia (© 2011 Mariodo59).

- attractiveness to the traveling public, resulting in greater passenger demand than originally predicted. The original forecast for TransMilenio was 600,000 passenger trips/day while it carried more than 800,000 passengers/day.

Before TransMilenio was started in 2000, the Bogotá bus system was a de facto unregulated system with bus license/franchise conditions barely enforced and with services delivered by a large number of small, poor-quality, polluting buses. The creation of a single agency with powers to plan, design, implement and regulate the new bus system was a large reason for its success. However, the resolution of technical issues was only part of the answer; the city government actively sought the participation and collaboration of the existing transport companies and operators in the new system. TransMilenio has demonstrated that it is possible to develop a bus-based, high-capacity, and high-quality mass transit system in a very short time. The Cracknell (2003) report added that TransMilenio has integrated all the features system-wide which include:

- median bus stations, which are used by buses in both directions; this is made possible by providing doors on the "wrong" side of buses. The advantage is that road space requirements for bus stop platforms are less than for conventional layouts, where bus stop platforms are provided for each direction of travel. The disadvantage is that these buses cannot be used on other routes where bus stops/stations are located on the "conventional" side that, in the TransMilenio system, is of little importance since the trunk buses are never intended for use outside the busways
- the use of 2 bus lanes in each direction to permit a mix of stopping and express services; this has been possible in Bogotá because of the very wide road rights of way (rights of way of 25–40 meter are not available in many cities) and by the willingness of the city to widen roads, where it was/is necessary
- the use of ramped stops to allow level passenger boarding/alighting to/from high floor buses
- the use of stored value tickets as part of the system, which do not only make the trunk and feeder system more convenient to users, but speeds passenger boarding/alighting.

Curitiba's BRT: A Model for the World

Fast and efficient transit system, green city, open space- the Brazilian city of Curitiba has it all. Curitiba has gone through a historical evolution to obtain the progress that the city has reached today. Many factors helped the city address the transportation issues it had faced in the past. One primary solution was an integrated land use and transportation system that creates a unique BRT system that currently is being used as guidelines for many cities in the world (Pedreira and Goodstein 1992). Curitiba had almost 200,000 residents in 1950, grew to twice that in 1960, and had about 2 million residents in the urban region by 2000 (Macedo 2004). City master plans in the 1960s and 1970s were initiated due to the travel demand created by exponential population growth. The plan called for transportation development along linear transit corridors. Ultimately, constrained by funds, the decision was made to build busways rather than Metro. Public transit started as a system of high capacity bus corridors that have express service and feed-in service by regular bus lines and neighborhood circulators

(Macedo 2004). Initial routes into the downtown opened in 1974 and attracted ridership of 54,000 passengers a day. This had grown to 1.6 million per day with a fully realized network by 2000. The most far-reaching innovation was a bus rapid transit line known as the "Direct Line" that was opened in 1991 and deliberately designed to mimic rail-based transit operations, including now famous tube station boarding areas, of which there are now over 350 across the city (Macedo 2004).

Now the famous BRT is the special feature that the city of Curitiba is known for. The transit system of the city is achieving the goal of reversing automobile dependence by implementing measures in favor of public transport, non-motorized modes, integrated urban land use and transport planning, coordination of institutions and allocation of funds (Khayesi and Amekudzi 2011). "The transportation system became famous because of the successful association of land use and streets hierarchy aiming at a consistent public transport demand" (Miranda and da Silva 2012). Accessing the bus became easier by having waiting hubs, "with the boarding floor at the same level of the bus floor; and the fare was paid off the bus before embankment" (Fábio, Firmino and Prestes 2011). Having the boarding floor at level of the bus floor gave access to people on wheelchairs, elderly with reduce mobility and parents with strollers.

Figure 12.3 Bas Rapid Transit in Curitiba, Brazil (copyright © 2013 Mariodo59).

The BRT system in Curitiba on average makes more than 21,000 trips a day and travels more than 275,000 miles (Carvalho, Mingardo and Van Haaren 2012). Since the buses are always running, one would think that the buses would be creating air pollution. In Curitiba, the buses use biodiesel as a clean-tech innovation to help minimize this problem. The bus system is organized in a way where each bus line is color-coded by six different colors: orange, red, yellow, gray, blue and white (Miranda and da Silva 2012). The orange buses serve as a regional bus, the red buses serve as above ground transit and can carry up to 270 passengers, the yellow buses are city street buses, grey buses are the express service, the blue buses are the health care transit that allow direct access to health facilities and the white buses are used for tourism to allow for sightseeing of the city of Curitiba (Carvalho, Mingardo and Van Haaren 2012).

Curitiba's network has also made accommodations to better serve passengers by allowing free transfers on a single fare so as to help residents who might otherwise have low system mobility with low wages. Despite its success, the system does not provide opportunities for multi-modal travel (Macedo 2004), as cycling is not accommodated. While Curitiba is hailed as a model for the ecologically planned city, has had its transit and land use patterns grow incrementally over several decades, often lagging behind the rapid growth in population.

BOX 12.1 Curitiba's bus system is model for rapid transit

The bus system of Curitiba, Brazil, exemplifies a model Bus Rapid Transit (BRT) system, and plays a large part in making this a livable city. The buses run frequently—some as often as every 90 seconds—and reliably, and the stations are convenient, well-designed, comfortable, and attractive. Consequently, Curitiba has one of the most heavily used, yet low-cost, transit systems in the world. It offers many of the features of a subway system—vehicle movements unimpeded by traffic signals and congestion, fare collection prior to boarding, quick passenger loading, and unloading—but it is above ground and visible. Around 70 percent of Curitiba's commuters use the BRT to travel to work, resulting in congestion-free streets and pollution-free air for the 2 million inhabitants of greater Curitiba.

Thirty years ago, Curitiba's forward-thinking and cost-conscious planners integrated public transportation into all the other elements of the urban planning system. They initiated a system that focused on meeting the transportation needs of all people—rather than those using private automobiles—and consistently followed through with a staged implementation of their plan.

A previous comprehensive plan for Curitiba, developed in 1943, had envisioned exponential growth in automobile traffic with wide boulevards radiating from the core of the city to accommodate it. Rights of way for the boulevards were acquired, but many other parts of the plan never materialized. Then in 1965, prompted by fears among city officials that Curitiba's rapid growth would lead to unchecked development and congested streets, they adopted a new Master Plan. Curitiba would no longer grow in all directions from the core, but would grow along designated corridors in a linear form, spurred by zoning and land use policies promoting high density industrial and residential development along the corridors. Downtown Curitiba would no longer be the primary destination of travel, but a hub and terminus. Mass transit would replace the car as the primary means of transport within the city, and the development along the corridors would produce a high volume of transit ridership. The wide boulevards established in the earlier plan would provide the cross section required for exclusive bus lanes in which an express bus service would operate.

Curitiba's Master Plan integrated transportation with land use planning, calling for a cultural, social, and economic transformation of the city. It limited central area growth while encouraging commercial growth along the transport arteries radiating out from the city center. The city center was partly closed to vehicular traffic, and pedestrian streets were created. Linear development along the arteries reduced the traditional importance of the downtown area as the primary focus of day-to-day transport activity, thereby minimizing congestion and the typical morning and afternoon flows of traffic. Instead, rush hour in Curitiba has heavy commuter movements in both directions along the public transportation arteries. Other policies have also contributed to the success of the transit system. Land within two blocks of the transit arteries is zoned for high density since it generates more transit ridership per square foot. Beyond the two blocks, zoned residential densities taper in proportion to distance from transitways. Planners discourage auto-oriented centers and channel new retail growth to transit corridors. Very limited public parking is available in the downtown area, and most employers offer transportation subsidies, especially to low-skilled and low-paid employees.

The popularity of Curitiba's BRT has effected a modal shift from automobile travel to bus travel. It was estimated that the introduction of the BRT had caused a reduction of about 27 million auto trips per year, saving about 27 million liters of fuel annually. In particular, 28 percent of BRT riders previously traveled by car. Compared to eight other Brazilian cities of its size, Curitiba uses about 30 percent less fuel per capita, resulting in one of the lowest rates of ambient air pollution in the country. Today about 1,100 buses make 12,500 trips every day, serving more than 1.3 million passengers—50 times the number from 20 years ago. Eighty percent of travelers use the express or direct bus services. Best of all, Curitibanos spend only about 10 percent of their income on travel—much below the national average.

Adapted from "Issues in Bus Rapid Transit" by Joseph Goodman, Melissa Laube, and Judith Schenk, United States Federal Transit Administration (FTA) Office of Research, Demonstration and Innovation.

Transportation in Chinese Cities

China has grappled with an increasingly motorized population while having a large population on bicycles, which at one point in the late 1980s comprised almost half of worldwide bicycles. Despite this, China symbolizes the up-and-coming motor-hungry developing world that eyes the United States' personal automobile infrastructure while planning large-scale mass transit projects (Karp 1997). China (and India) characterizes the concerns over the global consequences of mass motorization. At present, vehicle ownership level in China is still less than 100 vehicles per 1000 inhabitants, according to the World Bank data for 2009–2013. In comparison, the United States has 769 vehicles per 1000 inhabitants while the average for Western European countries is approximately 430 vehicles per 1000 inhabitants (Whitelegg and Haq 2003). However, according to Wang *et al.*, 2012, in 2010, China surpassed the U.S. and all other countries in vehicle sales, and will no doubt retain its number one ranking for decades. Rapid Chinese motorization has alarming implications for both the environment and global energy resources. China is already the world's largest CO_2 emitter and second-largest oil importer. Most forecasts anticipate Chinese growth leveling off at an ownership rate of about 200–300 vehicles per 1,000 persons in 2030 or soon after that. Several major studies also forecasted 6 to 11 percent annual growth rates in car ownership levels in the Chinese vehicle market (Yunsh, Teter and Sperling 2012). In the meantime, Chinese cities have seen rapid restructuring of their public transportation systems. In 2005, the Chinese government issued a policy formally giving transit a priority in development (Zhang and Wang 2013), leading to over 25 new rail and BRT systems in the country and national high-speed-rail service by 2010. This kind of massive state-sponsored mass transit construction has rarely been seen and even more rarely has been constructed in such a short time frame.

The GTZ SUTP, 2010 report analyzes that while countries such as China and India are starting from relatively low car ownership levels, both are entering the income zone of heightened vehicle purchasing. If China were to reach an ownership level equal to that of the U.S., the global vehicle fleet would grow by approximately 1 billion. If India were included in this scenario, then another 740 million vehicles would be added to the global fleet. Even at European ownership levels, China is still adding nearly 550 million vehicles. Apparently, the automobile is officially touted as a symbol of progress and modernity for both China and India. Ultimately, Chinese government surveys indicate that families are likely to be prepared to spend two years of income for a car.

The trends in car ownership are spurring a spending spree on road-based infrastructure as well. At the end of 2004, China had 34,000 kilometers of highways, more than double the 2000 figure. Just 21 years ago, the nation had no highways. By the end of 2009, China has almost doubled the length of its highway again. China is effectively attempting to replicate U.S.-styled motorization in the span of just a few decades. The impact on air quality has been profound.

Shanghai officials, though, have become alarmed at the extreme growth rate of cars in the city and have implemented a system to ration vehicle registration. A monthly auction system has been in place for several years. Nevertheless, the permitted number of registrations is being increased on a regular basis, which has no effect on tackling motorization. Even as the auction price becomes quite costly, even by developed-nation standards, demand shows no slowing (GTZ SUTP 2010). Chandler (2003) observed that cars have launched a new cultural revolution, transforming Chinese life and society in ways that bear a surprising resemblance to what happened in America 50 years ago. Many major Chinese cities have been also actively discouraging bicycle use through priority measures for automobiles and the neglect of non-motorized infrastructure. A few Chinese cities have even banned bicycles from large sections of the urban area (GTZ SUTP 2010).

Figure 12.4 Transportation in Dalian, China (author's photograph).

BOX 12.2 Chinese cities vehicle restrictions

Large Chinese cities, Shanghai, Beijing and Guangzhou, have implemented various policies to control car ownership growth. Since 2005, a national public-transit-priority strategy has been established. Many cities invested heavily in building public transit infrastructure and upgraded policies to encourage people to take buses and subways. The first and most famous city in China that regulates car ownership is Shanghai. In 1986, Shanghai instituted a bidding mechanism (with a reservation price) in allocating licenses to automobile owners. The bidding mechanism has undergone several major changes since then. The policy was also modified when national and local economic planning and policy changed. For example, the automobile industry was promoted in 1994 as the pillar industry by the national government to boost economic growth. As one of the manufacturing centers for automobiles, Shanghai adopted temporary policies to stimulate car sales of local manufacturers by issuing low-cost licenses at that time. In 2003, the bidding mechanism was homogenized between imported vehicles and domestic vehicles.

As vehicle registration fees in other provinces are much lower, many people choose to register their vehicles elsewhere to avoid the auction process. To discourage local residents from doing so, the Shanghai government stipulates that during peak hours (7:30–9:30 a.m. and 4:30–6:30 p.m.), vehicles with non-local license plates cannot enter the elevated roads or the intra-city expressway system. With this restriction in place, the auction can effectively control the annual growth of private cars. Meanwhile, revenues from the auction have been spent on the improvement of ring roads and the development of the public transit system. These two measures are combined to buy time to develop the public transit system so that it can keep pace with rapid urban expansion.

The 2008 Olympic Games provided a valuable testing ground for implementing innovative transport management measures. During the Olympics, the right to drive alternated according to whether the plate number was an odd or even number. After the Olympics, the policy was modified to factor in the last digit of the plate number, and each car had to be off the road at least one day per week.

Starting January 2011, to further reduce road traffic, the Beijing government started a lottery system. This policy has three key elements:

1. The quota for annual vehicle growth and its structure are set according to an analysis of road capacity, environmental sustainability and projected demand;
2. Currently, monthly quota is set at 20,000, with 88 percent to individuals, 10 percent to companies and other organizations, and the remaining 2 percent to operators of transportation services;
3. Companies and individuals go through separate lottery processes to get their rights to own. This right is non-transferable and effective for six months. It lapses if the individual or company fails to register a car before the deadline. Companies and individuals who already own a car license can renew their license on a new car if the old car is sold or scrapped. This right also lapses within six months.

Meanwhile, Beijing's generous subsidy to transit fares and construction of BRT pulled many people away from their cars. These measures all facilitated the smooth implementation of Beijing's integrated transport management plan.

Starting July 2012 Guangzhou began a mixed-quota system that combines a lottery and an auction to allocate vehicle registrations. The annual quota is set at 120,000 or 10,000 per month. There are three categories: a lottery for alternative energy vehicles, a lottery for regular vehicles and an auction for regular vehicles. In the auction, the reserve price is ¥10,000. Each month the allotted quotas for these categories are approximately 1,000, 5,000, and 4,000 respectively. From the quota of each category, 88 percent goes to individuals, and the remaining 12 percent is assigned to companies, organizations, and government agencies. The new regulation also restricts the road rights of those vehicles registered elsewhere. This aims to prevent residents of Guangzhou from registering their vehicles elsewhere.

Adapted from "Vehicle Restrictions Limiting Automobile Travel at Certain Times and Places," TDM Encyclopedia, Victoria Transport Policy Institute, Updated 22 May 2014

Transportation in Africa

Transportation is considered as a backbone of development, especially for the African continent. However, from a transportation perspective, the region is perceived as not having enough road networks as well as lacking transportation policies. The lack of roads, especially rural roads, is viewed as a major physical constraint propagating poverty in the continent. Africa is a continent with diverse culture composed of several countries. As diverse the population is, the transport systems of Africa also exhibit a significant contrast in coverage and efficiency. For example, in 2011, while Chad has only 206 km (128 miles) of urban roads that are paved, Tunisia, South Africa, Namibia and Botswana boast over 5000 km (3107 miles) paved urban roads.

Sub-Saharan Africa has a much lower density of paved roads than any other region in the world. It has only 204 km (127 miles) of roads per 1000 square kilometer (386 square miles) of land area, with only one quarter being paved. This compares with a world average of 944 km (587 miles) of roads per 1000 square kilometer of land area, with over half paved. Its spatial density of roads is less than 30 percent of the next worst provided region, South Asia, with half being paved, and only 6 percent of North Africa, with two third paved. Apart from the problem of inadequate and ill-maintained transport infrastructure, the continent is burdened with institutional hurdles, including cumbersome administrative and custom procedures, corrupt officials and staff, lack of transportation policy and a list of other deficiencies (Njoh 2007).

However, there are recent improvements in the transportation sector in African countries. Cities of some countries in Africa are exhibiting a remarkable overall economic growth, and it is reflected in the transportation sector. For example, in Addis Ababa (the capital of Ethiopia), the city's performance in the transportation sector had been so remarkable that the total road length grew from 1360 km (845 miles) in 1998 to 3192 km (1983 miles) in 2010, i.e., 135 percent growth in a period of 12 years. Also, according to Tsitsi Mutamambara (2008), in the southern part of Africa, each country has been taking initiatives to rehabilitate, upgrade and maintain existing road networks as well as construct new roads. For example, in Lesotho, the road network is constantly being expanded and upgraded, especially with the Lesotho Highlands Water Project, as the development of road network seeks to access the most remote areas. In Madagascar, reforms and rehabilitation are taking place through the Transport Sector Program. In Mozambique, the Roads and Coastal Shipping Program led by the World Bank has made developing the internal transport system a priority.

Despite the progress, there are still several challenges for Africa's transportation industry. Although the major problem is a lack of transportation policy that guides development, there are also poor institutional frameworks and lack of technical and financial resources. Regarding the physical condition of roads, severe problems of early cracking in bituminous pavements are frequent in especially Sub-Saharan countries, as well as rutting of paved surfaces not long after their construction. The explanation of these phenomena may sometimes be found in the choice of a weak road structure, and sometimes in poor workmanship. Related to this, corruption of some African officials and technicians plays a significant role as well (Martinez 2001). Also, civil unrest and border wars have caused disruption in the progress of road network improvement.

Conflicts and wars in many countries have ruined the efforts carried out in the transportation sector. Since their independence, almost all 43 Sub-Saharan countries have been involved in civil wars or wars with other countries and they have suffered from serious problems of internal disorder. The prolonged civil wars in some countries resulted in significant damage to road and rail networks, and the effects continue to be felt despite current initiatives to rebuild the networks (Niekerk and Moreira 2002).

COLONIAL INFLUENCE

Africa's transportation evolved through the colonial influence that focused on the development of transport infrastructure facilitating links with Europe. This was to support the economic interest of the colonial power, which meant providing raw materials to their "homeland." As a result, Africa is characterized by limited internal linkages, with only major cities being linked to international gateways (seaports) that serve foreign markets. Colonial authorities paid little or no attention to road building. For instance, as documented by Jeffrey Herbst, in the case of French West Africa, there were hardly any roads outside a few urban areas in the region in 1914 (Herbst 2000). The colonial powers invested almost exclusively in transportation infrastructure such as railways, which brought them economic benefits. Their need to minimize cost led them to build only those roads and streets that were necessary for colonial governance. At the same time, colonial powers recognized the importance of their physical presence throughout the colonies as a critical element of control. Accordingly, they proceeded to build a few roads linking some hinterland areas to the colonial government centers. In the area of air transportation, only very few airports were developed in Africa during the colonial era. These airports were designed to link the colonies to the colonial master nations. Thus, little if any efforts were made to link African cities by air.

Even several decades after independence, the transportation infrastructure of African countries didn't show signs of remarkable growth, and there was no single transportation policy that is guiding the development of transportation infrastructure. There are a number of reasons for sluggish growth, including poor economic and political performance, topographic condition and administrative incompetence. However, in recent years, with the help of the global financial institutions and the involvement of China, many African countries are exhibiting a remarkable growth in the transportation industry.

The Sub-Saharan Africa Transport Policy Program (SSATP)

If there is one program that defines Africa's (especially the Sub-Saharan Africa) transportation policy, it is the Sub-Saharan Africa Transport Policy Program (SSATP). As summarized by John Thompson (2011) from the World Bank, the conception of the SSATP started with a small group of African and international engineers and policy makers who were deeply concerned with the poor condition of the regions' road network. Despite some nations investing billions in road network funds, these nations were running out of treasury funds and by the early 1980s, only 20 percent of the classified road networks were in excellent condition. Another conundrum was that poor nations in the region couldn't afford the refurbishment of their existing networks let alone help fund the construction of the extensive road network of the entire region. So, funding was a problem. Countries with deteriorating road networks would decline economically, and poverty would increase. With these challenges present, the founders devised policies such as institutional arrangements and capacity building. The policies were intended to stop the unproductive cycle of road building, collapsing and rebuilding for African countries. In 1986, the founding group members met at the United Nations Economic Commission for Africa (UNECA) to develop a program that would address the neglect of the regions road networks. The 1987 inaugural meeting in Oslo led to the creation of the International Advisory Committee (IAC), which was a joint committee of the World Bank and UNECA. Offices were located in Addis Ababa, Ethiopia. However, program operations stalled due to funding limitations until 1988, when it relocated to the World Bank's offices in Washington, D.C., and renamed itself as the Sub-Saharan Africa Transport Program.

In its early days, the SSATP addressed a wide spectrum of issues such as road maintenance, railway managements, low volume roads, rural travel and transport, development of agriculture and transport, taxations in transport and many other issues. The program attracted several agencies from African countries and some international agencies. In a short time, these stakeholders limited the range of the program to focus on policy issues renaming the program to its current name. By 1992, the program was implemented through seven components: Road Maintenance Initiative (RMI), Rural Travel and Transport Program (RTTP), Urban Mobility (UM), Trade and Transport (T&T), Railway Restructuring (RR), Human Resources and Institutional Development (HRID) and Transport Data (TD). RMI is meant to facilitate policy reforms, resulting in sustainable maintenance and financing of public roads. RTTP is designed to better the livelihood of rural people by improving access to basic goods and services. UM's goal is to support and facilitate the provision of safe, efficient and less polluting transport in cities of Sub-Saharan Africa. T&T is to reinforce the international competitiveness of Sub-Saharan African economies. RR is to help countries establish efficient and financially sustainable railway enterprises. HRID focuses on the capacity building for policy reforms. Lastly, TD is designed to provide information systems to support policy preparation (Thompson 2011).

The nine founding member countries, supported by small groups of donors, requested the UNECA and the World Bank to continue serving as executing agencies through the seven components. Membership grew from nine to seventeen member countries in the 1990s. The RMI component was the main attraction to the SSATP because it sought to bring roads to the marketplace. Towards the end of the 1990s, African countries felt the SSATP was too donor-oriented because they were able to earmark funds towards specific projects that were geared towards donor's interest. With fluctuating finance and weakening leadership in SSATP, African countries felt increasingly marginalized. Donors were also frustrated with the lack of management reporting, and they did not sufficiently recognize the program's policy principles aimed at poverty reduction. The concerns of African countries and donors were confirmed in the 1999 management review and concluded that there needed to be an improvement in the management framework of the program.

UNECA and donors gathered in 2000 to conduct a detailed analysis of the program. Conclusions of the seminal meeting changed the program, resulting in a new mission statement, a new governance framework, the setting up of an Executive Board, the formation of a Ministerial Advisory Group and the recruitment of a full-time program manager. In 2001, further review was conducted in five African countries that the program impacted, and recommendations were made for the need to be more African-focused in program management. The recommendations led to the implementation of national and African regional coordinators based in Africa. Hence, SSATP became a stronger partnership with a sound governance structure. By 2003, Thirty African countries were engaged in different components of the program, and an increase in donor confidence was restored. The RMI and RTTP were popular of all the components. By 2006, the number of members increased to thirty-five.

Since the program's implementation, especially the last decade, SSATP reports that countries have economically improved. Ten of the 48 Sub-Saharan African countries have had economic growth in excess of five percent each year since 2005. There is no doubt that improved transport has contributed significantly to Africa's growth. The social landscape has improved with many more people having access to health centers and more children able to attend schools. The SSATP has a distinguished history of supporting information gathering, analysis and dissemination. This has led to the development of principles, themes and areas of focus that have a substantial impact on some countries' transport policy formulation and implementation. Some of the impact is being seen with the recent program resurgence and widening influence on the policies and operations of countries, regional economic organizations, aid agencies and international organizations such as the World Bank, UNECA and the European Commission. On an overall program level, the SSATP is focusing efforts on national transport policies and programs that support poverty reduction strategies specifically in clarifying the key role of transport in achieving the goals of other sectors such as health, education, and agriculture.

The influence of principles and themes championed by SSATP components on transport sector development has been strong and consistent. For instance, the influence can be clearly seen in Ethiopia, where an agriculture-led development plan triggered a comprehensive road sector development program (RSDP), which enjoys the support of many donors. The RMI principles; ownership, stable financing, responsibility, and good management; all support the theme of commercialization and have been central to the Ethiopian RSDP. Similar principles championed by the RTTP such as ownership, good management and adequate funding have been applied not just to policy but to actual or pending improvements in many country programs that enjoy widespread support.

Transportation in Addis Ababa

Addis Ababa, Ethiopia is one of the rapidly urbanizing African cities. Addis Ababa is set on a 50-year trajectory to become an African megacity with a population of more than 10 million people (AACPPO 2012). At an average altitude of 2400 meters, Addis Ababa is the administrative, economic and social capital of Ethiopia. The city serves as an important political hub for the African continent as headquarters of the African Union, the UN Economic Commission for Africa and regional offices of several international organizations. Like many African cities, Addis Ababa's economy is undergoing a rapid expansionary period as the Ethiopian government estimates national economic growth at 11 percent annually (USDS 2012). While GDP, foreign investment and incomes are rising, the city has substantial unmet demand for public services, such as access to quality transportation. Additionally, the city has undergone substantial urban to rural land conversion in the previous decades, which will continue to be perpetuated by population and economic growth. Between 2002 and 2012, Addis Ababa's municipal revenue grew by $1 Billion USD, granting the city government one of the largest local budgets in Africa for its relative size (AACPPO 2012). There is, however, a deficit of public services to low-income earners who make up a large portion of the city. Economic and population growth has created a shortage of affordable housing near the urban core, significantly reducing accessibility to employment and service centers for low-income earners. In the midst of interminable real estate development, there exist large areas of informal housing that pose health, safety and environmental concerns (Wubneh 2012). There is also a lack of adequate road infrastructure and poor street conditions, which have resulted in traffic safety and circulation problems (Berhanu 2004). The local government has a daunting task of correcting these issues and providing adequate services in the wake of massive population growth.

Addis Ababa, like many African cities, is culturally primed for sustainable development principles and mass transportation. Under the current transportation paradigm, walking, mini buses and taxis dominate the modal split. Pedestrian activity and public transit account for 45 percent and 46 percent of transport, respectively. The Anbassa City Bus Service transports about 400,000 passengers daily (AACPPO 2012). Although car ownership is still low in Addis Ababa, it is rapidly increasing mainly due to economic growth and the introduction of low-cost private vehicles into the local market. The key determinant of rising automobile use in Addis Ababa is growing per capita income (Kutzbach 2009). Income inequality may also increase automobile use over time. As the wealth of the population grows, and low-cost cars are introduced, it is expected that the demand for private transport will substantially grow, as well as infrastructure to support automobiles.

Even with low automobile ownership, auto-related congestion is already a problem in Addis Ababa's dense urban center. Congestion resulting from automobiles use significantly impacts bus efficiency. The result is negative feedback that further stimulates demand for cars (Kutzbach 2009). Thus, when automobiles begin to dominate local roadways, they create a self-reinforcing effect thus, by reducing the utility of public transit. The rising use of cars presents an apparent threat where they share the road with buses, which comprise a major transport share in Addis Ababa's and much of Africa. Approximately 38,000 vehicles are being added every year to the local transportation market. By 2020, Addis Ababa will have in the vicinity of 486,000 vehicles, 82 percent of which will be for private transport and only 12 percent projected to account for taxi cabs, buses and trucks (Haregewoin 2010). This growth in automobile travel will greatly overextend the limited street infrastructure currently in place. Additionally, many streets are dilapidated, and only about 35 percent of the current road network is pedestrian-accessible (Demdime 2012). For centuries, there exists no rail system to transport passengers from the periphery to the urban center (although construction of a light rail system is underway) (Wubneh 2012). This is problematic, as a larger portion of the city's workforce live away from job centers and must cover a significant commute distance (Tafesse 1989).

As a response to increasing automobile use, lack of infrastructure and a need for mass transportation, the city government of Addis Ababa has adopted a city-wide transportation

Figure 12.5 Minibus taxis in Addis Ababa (author's photograph).

master plan designed to modernize public transport, improve pedestrian environments and tackle the congestion that is generated from the increasing use of private vehicles (Voukas and Palmer 2012). Addis Ababa's transportation plan is rather ambitious, though, necessary to meet the immense population and development-driven demand in the city. The plan calls for the organization of a strong mass transit system to serve millions of people. The transportation master plan includes the construction of seven BRT (Bus Rapid Transit) and two LRT (Light Rail Transport) corridors, as well as improvements in pedestrian facilities, non-motorized transport and parking management (Voukas and Palmer 2012). The plan also calls for an integration of land use planning and transportation planning, which is essential for maximizing returns on transit investment. Under the framework of sustainability principles, the city plans to develop new transit corridors and terminals into an integrated multi-modal transportation system. The construction and upgrading of primary roads are planned with pedestrian infrastructure and designated transit lanes (AACPPO 2012). The separation of buses from vehicle traffic, through designated lanes, will help to maintain transit as a drive alternative as the city accrues wealth by maximizing consumer surplus for transit riders (Kutzbach 2009). These designated lanes will accommodate all transit modes, including the Anbessa buses, minibusses and taxis. The master plan also embraces a highly connected poly-centric model that the municipal government hopes will alleviate congestion in the Central Business District (CBD), with all major destination sub-centers aligned with planned mass transit corridors. The plan also calls for complete street design and Transit Oriented Development (TOD) principles, such as mixed use development, which should serve as effective planning methods for enhancing mobility while preserving the city's current transit and pedestrian orientation (Demdime 2012). Implementing such projects requires a strong political will and commitment to overcome numerous financial, administrative and logistic obstacles, which Addis Ababa has, as well as growing public demand for mass transportation (Jemere 2012).

ADDIS ABABA LRT

The centerpiece of the transportation master plan is the light rail transit system, which was opened to the public in 2015. Addis Ababa's LRT project is comprised of a North-South line (16.9km) and an East-West line (17.35km) that will juncture at the meticulously planned La Gare station in the Central Business District (AACPPO 2012; Jemere 2012). When completed, Addis Ababa's light rail will be able to transport 60,000 passengers per hour with an eventual 90-second headway capability (Jemere 2012). The LRT project will have ten main hubs located at important service centers and intermodal nodes. The transportation master plan integrates the LRT at these major hubs with BRT routes, regular bus services and the taxi enterprise. Additionally, pedestrian infrastructure will be upgraded to supply the major walking mode with adequate access to the LRT terminals and surrounding land uses. The LRT stations and corridors under the master plan will be integrated into public spaces in terms of urban design, landscaping and pedestrian needs. To the East and South, the LRT lines extend out of the urban core, providing peri-urban residences access to the economic and social center of Ethiopia. As well, Addis Ababa is engaging in regional planning efforts to coordinate future LRT extensions with the national rail network and the Oromia state government, granting better connectivity with the rest of the country (AACPPO 2012). The LRT will also grant improved topographic accessibility by providing transport over the steep elevations that are common to the city. Precisely, the LRT is engineered to traverse 5 percent grades, necessitated by Addis Ababa's location at 1.5 miles (2400 meters) above sea level (Jemere 2012).

TRANSPORTATION IN NORTHERN AFRICA

North African Countries include Algeria, Egypt, Libya, Morocco, Sudan, Tunisia and the Moroccan territory of Western Sahara. The literature on transportation policies of North Africa is usually meshed with the Middle East due to cultural and social resemblance. With few exceptions, the region's cities don't have well-organized transport systems and have suffered from a lack of transportation policy while transport demand is constantly increasing. Recognizing the problems and their negative impact on the economy and society, national governments, and local authorities in nearly all North African countries have now embarked on far-reaching structural reforms on the building of major infrastructure projects. Due to the lack of information available, this section will briefly discuss transportation in Algeria, Egypt and Morocco, based on discussions in a 2007 UITP (International Association of Public Transport) report.

In Algeria, each province contains a transportation department for urban transportation and land transportation (the country is divided into 48 provinces). Shortly after independence (1962), Algeria had a well-developed transport network, especially with the merging of Tramways Algeriens (TA) and the Chemins de fer sur routes d'Algerie (CFRA), now known as L'Entreprise Publique de Transport Urbain et Suburbain d'Alger (ETUSA—Algiers Public Transport Company). Algiers's first urban transport map dates back to 1908. Until 1987, urban transport services were almost entirely provided by public operators that come under the control of local authorities. The liberalization of the sector was immediately followed by the proliferation of private operators and an overall increase in supply (doubling of the number of minibuses and taxis with more than 22,000 taxis for the 6 main cities, half of which operate in Algiers). This led to a drop in the market share for public operators who lost their monopoly. In the capital Algiers, over the past few years, a major urban infrastructure construction and refurbishment program has been instituted by the provinces of Algiers. Moreover, the Algerian government has launched an ambitious five-year development plan. Accordingly, the Ministry of Transport prepared a public urban transport plan and a traffic master plan designed to resolve the problems concerning the transport sector in Algiers and meet the traveling needs of the population. This plan centers on two main ongoing projects likely to improve the services offered to passengers and ensure integration and collaboration among the different modes of transport.

In Egypt, the four main urban locations are Greater Cairo, Alexandria, Port-Saied and Suez. Urban public transport systems exist in these areas, in the main cities and the administrative capitals. Transport networks in Egypt can be divided into intercity networks and urban networks. The intercity networks include railways network, highways network and inland waterways routes along Nile River and its branches. Urban networks include local roads, subway (Metro) network, urban railways lines and some routes for ferry boat services. Passenger services in Egypt can be divided into two categories: regulated services provided or monitored by the Ministry of Transport and services provided by individuals (not planned or regulated by Ministry of Transport). According to the Ministry of Transport, Greater Cairo Region (GCR) area, as the main urban region of Egypt, will experience increasing transport problems in the future. Because of this recognition, the Strategic Urban Development Master Plan of the Greater Cairo Region, a policy and planning document produced in 2008, identified many projects that needed to be implemented, including new infrastructure projects and redevelopment projects. The master plan identified many actions, policies and projects that need special attention, such as minimizing usage of the private car, giving attention to the parking problems and developing new systems for increasing parking lots. The master plan also includes actions such as promoting park and ride, implementing traffic management solutions, applying bus priority lane and segregated lane system especially along the new planned corridors, and developing the ring roads around the main cities and communities. Introducing incentives and governmental support for the private sector to access the public transport services with coordination and integration with the existing modes, developing vehicle inspection system for assuring safety and environment friendly trips, developing comprehensive planning for both urban and rural areas, promoting demand management rather than increasing transport supply, limiting the role of the government in organizing and regulating the transport business are also among the focuses of the master plan.

In Morocco, the Ministry of Home Affairs is in charge of transportation at the national level. The Economic and Social Division manages it (for the Ministry) at the city level through various public corporations or contracts awarded by these companies to private carriers. Large segments of the region's cities have suffered from a lack of transport policy despite the fact that transport demand is constantly increasing. Information indicates that the country has agencies and departments for urban transportation that govern the transportation system, but effective transportation policy is still needed. After understanding the problems and their consequential impacts on the economy and society, governments and local authorities have now started working on structural reforms and the building of major infrastructure projects (UITP 2007).

Conclusion

For a long time, developing countries didn't have a transportation policy to guide urban transportation growth and development. For the last decade, due to an increase in urban population and its accompanying transportation problems, several countries came up with the transportation master plan and implementations are underway. Transportation in the developing world remains a subject of immense importance considering the vast increase in urban population and the emergence of large economies with increasing automobile ownership. As Europe sees population shrinkage, and the United States grows from immigration, the high birthrates among people in the developing world will continue to be the cause for the greater share of what is considered "urban life." Methods of mobility in places such as Bogotá, Curitiba and China reflect the human ingenuity and also strong government intervention. For the African continent, especially Sub-Saharan Africa, transportation is mainly shaped by The Sub-Saharan Africa Transport Policy Program (SSATP). There had been a thirty percent improvement of roads classified as good under SSATP management, but government corruption, civil unrest and poor workmanship still hindered progress. SSATP is criticized for lacking African leadership and proper management. This was somehow corrected through framework restructuring in mid–2000, which yielded a shift in donor confidence.

One additional point to note is that transportation was largely excluded from the Millennium Development Goals (MDGs). The MDGs, initiated in 2000 to alleviate poverty, do not encompass targets to lessen the transport constraints on the poor. This is a concern for many because developing countries, more than any other places, are known for their vast, sparsely populated rural areas, lack of transport infrastructure and rural poverty. The relative immobility of rural dwellers and their poor access to social and productive services and markets is especially problematic.

Review Questions

1) Why is public transportation essential in developing nations?
2) What are some of the elements of Bogotá's TransMilenio?
3) Why is Curitiba's Bus System a "Model Rapid Bus Transit" for the world?
4) What transportation challenges is China facing?
5) What impact has past colonial influence had on African transportation?
6) What are the SSATP, RMI, RTTP, UM, T&T, RR HRID and TD, and what purposes do they serve?
7) Why is Addis Ababa culturally primed for mass transportation?
8) What are the features and goals of the Addis Ababa Transportation Master Plan?
9) How does Addis Ababa's LRT promote multimodality? Why is this important for a developing city?
10) With Northern African nations in mind, why is transportation policy essential to developing nations?

Project/Paper Idea

Choose a city in the developing world. Using several Internet and library sources, conduct research on the transportation condition, the planning process, challenges and prospects of that country. What similarities and differences do you observe between the developed and developing nations' transportation? What transportation-related challenges do you see?

Videos

Brazil: Urban Planning Challenges by *Films Media Group, 2010 (27 min.)*: This program explores innovative planning, engineering, and conservation at work in the Brazilian metropolis as it transcends many of the problems plaguing other South American cities. The film spotlights fully modernized public transportation and recycling systems, a "Citizenship Street" zoning pattern that reduces high-volume traffic, an oil collection program that transforms used cooking grease into biofuel, and other successful initiatives.

A Convenient Truth: Urban Solutions from Curitiba, Brazil by *Media Group, 2014 (52 min.)*: This video is an informative, inspirational documentary aimed at sharing ideas to provoke environment-friendly and cost-effective changes in cities worldwide. The documentary focuses on innovations in transportation, recycling, social benefits including affordable housing, seasonal parks, and the processes that transformed Curitiba into one of the most livable cities in the world.

Internet Sources

- Sustainable Urban Transport Project, http://www.sutp.org/
- Institute for Transportation and Development Policy, https://www.itdp.org/

Bibliography

AACPPO. 2012. *Transportation Challenges in a Booming City; Coordination of the Mass Transit Network and Urban Development in Addis Ababa.* Addis Ababa City Planning Project Office.

Berhanu, Grima. 2004. "Models Relating Traffic Safety with Road Environment and Traffic Flows on Arterial Roads in Addis Ababa." *Accident Analysis & Prevention* 36 (5): 697–704.

Carvalho, Luís, Giuliano Mingardo, and Jeroen Van Haaren. 2012. "Green Urban Transport Policies and Cleantech Innovations: Evidence from Curitiba, Göteborg and Hamburg." *European Planning Studies* 20 (3): 375–396.

Cervero, Robert. 1998. *The Transit Metropolis: A Global Inquiry.* Washington, D.C.: Island Press.

Chandler, C. 2003. "Coping with China." *Fortune*, 66–70.

Cracknell, John. 2003. *TransMilenio Busway-based Mass Transit: Bogotá, Colombia.* The World Bank.

Darido, Georges. 2003. "Regulation of Road-Based Public Transportation and Strategies for the Developing World." *Transportation Research Record, Journal of the Transportation Research Board* 1835: 66–73.

Demdime, Fantahun. 2012. *Integrating Public Transport Networks and Built Environment: The Case of Addis Ababa and Experiences from Stockholm.* Masters Thesis in Environmental Engineering and Sustainable Infrastructure, School of Architecture and the Built Environment, KTH-Royal Institute of Technology.

Fábio, Duarte, Rodrigo Firmino, and Olga Prestes. 2011. "Learning From Failures: Avoiding Asymmetrical Views of Public Transportation Initiatives in Curitiba." *Journal of Urban Technology* 18 (3): 81–100.

Gakenheimer, Ralph. 1999. "Urban Mobility in the Developing World." *Transportation Research Part A: Policy and Practice* 33 (7–8): 671–689.

Gottman, Jean. 1983. "Third World Cities in Perspective." *Area* (The Royal Geographical Society) 15 (4): 311–313.

GTZ SUTP. 2010. "Challenges of Urban Transport in Developing Countries—A Summary." Accessed October 2010. www.sutp.org.

Haregewoin, Yared. 2010. *Impact of Vehicle Traffic Connection in Addis Ababa.* Masters Thesis, Ethiopian Civil Service College.

Herbst, Jeffrey. 2000. *States and Power in Africa.* Princeton University Press.

Jemere, Yehualaeshet. 2012. *Addis Ababa Light Rail Transit Project.* Presentation, Ethiopian Railways Corporation.

Karp, Adam. 1997. "China Must Not Wait Until the Evening: Resisting Mass Motorization's Assault on Bicycles and Mass Transit." *Pacific Rim Law & Policy Journal* 7: 717–755.

Khayesi, Meleckidzedeck, and Adjo Amekudzi. 2011. "Kingdon's Multiple Streams Model and Automobile Dependence Reversal Path: The Case of Curitiba, Brazil." *Journal of Transport Geography* 19 (6): 1547–1552.

Kutzbach, Mark. 2009. "Motorization in Developing Countries: Causes, Consequences, and Effectiveness of Policy Options." *Journal of Urban Economics* 65: 154–166.

Macedo, Joseli. 2004. "Curitiba." *Cities* 21 (6): 537–549.

Martinez, Antonio. 2001. "Road Maintenance Policies in Sub-Saharan Africa: Unsolved Problems and Acting Strategies." *Transport Policy* 8 (4): 257–265.

Miranda, Hellem de Freitas, and Antônio Nélson Rodrigues da Silva. 2012. "Benchmarking Sustainable Urban Mobility: The Case of Curitiba, Brazil." *Transport Policy* 141–151.

Mumme, Stephen, Richard Bath, and Valerie Assetto. 1988. "Political Development and Environmental Policy in Mexico." *Latin American Research Review* 23 (1): 7–34.

Mutambara, Tsitsi. 2008. *Monitoring Regional Integration in Southern Africa Yearbook: Regional Transport Challenges Within the Southern African Development Community and Their Implications for Economic Integration and Development.* Trade Law Center for Southern Africa.

Niekerk, Lolette, Emmanuel Moreira. 2002. "Regional Integration in Southern Africa: Overview of Recent Developments." World Bank Working Paper 33107.

Njoh, Ambe. 2007. "Globalization Implications of Africa's Transportation Infrastructure." *Proceedings of the Annual Transportation Research Forum.*

Pedreira, Mauricio, and Carol Goodstein. 1992. "Blueprint for an Eco-Safe City." *Americas* 44 (4): 6.

Phanikumar, C.V., and Maitra Bhargab. 2006. "Valuing Urban Bus Attributes: an Experience in Kolkata." *Journal of Public Transportation* 9 (2): 69–87.

Tafesse, Tesfaye. 1989. "The Patterns and Problems of Work Trips in Addis Ababa." *Journal of Ethiopian Studies* 22: 75–96.

Thompson, John. 2011. *1987—2011 SSATP Africa's Transport: A Promising Future.* Sub-Saharan Africa Transport Policy Program.

UITP. 2003. *Better Urban Mobility in Developing Countries: Problems, Solutions, Good Practices.* Brussels: International Association of Public Transport.

_____. 2007. *Overview of Public Transport in the Middle East and North Africa*. International Association of Public Transport. UN. 2011. *United Nations World Urbanization Data*. esa.un.org/unpd/wup/unup/index_panel2.html.

USDS. 2012. *2012 Investment Climate Statement—Ethiopia*. Bureau of Economic and Business Affairs, U.S. Department of State.

Virginia Ahalt, Virginai, Gordon Romone, Dusti Nisbet, and Lauren Vollmer. 2009. "Where Is the Third World?A Multivariate Statistical Analysis of World Development," *The Journal of the Summer Undergraduate Mathematical Science Research Institute (SUMSRI)*.

Voukas, Yorgos, and Derek Palmer. 2012. "Sustainable Transportation in East Africa the Bus Rapid Transit Evolution in Addis Ababa, Ethiopia." *CODATU XV: The Role of Urban Mobility in (Re)Shaping Cities*. Source: UC Berkeley Transportation Library.

Whitelegg, John, and Gary Haq. 2003. *The Earthscan Reader in World Transport Policy and Practice*. London: Routledge.

Wubneh, Mulatu. 2012. "Addis Ababa, Ethiopia- Africa's Diplomatic Capital." *Cities* 35: 255–269.

Yunsh, Wang, Jacob Teter, and Daniel Sperling. 2012. "Will China's Vehicle Population Grow Even Faster Than Forecasted?" *Access Magazine #41*.

Zhang, Ming, and Lanlan Wang. 2013. "The Impacts of Mass Transit on Land Development in China: The Case of Beijing." *Research in Transportation Economics* 40 (1): 124–133.

Glossary

Adapted from Federal Highway Administration, Planning Glossary http://www.fhwa.dot.gov/Planning/glossary/glossary_listing.cf m, accessed May 28, 2015

Accident

An incident involving a moving vehicle. Includes collisions with a vehicle, object, or person (except suicides) and derailment/left roadway. Occurrence in a sequence of events that produces unintended injury, death or property damage. Accident refers to the event, not the result of the event.

Allocation

An administrative distribution of funds for programs that do not have statutory distribution formulas.

Alternative Fuels

Methanol, denatured ethanol, and other alcohol; mixtures containing 85 percent or more (but not less than 70 percent) by volume of methanol, denatured ethanol, and other alcohols with gasoline or other fuels. Includes compressed natural gas, liquid petroleum gas, hydrogen, coal-derived liquid fuels, fuels other than alcohols derived from biological materials, electricity, or any other fuel the Secretary of Energy determines by rule is substantially not petroleum and would yield substantial energy security and environmental benefits.

American Association of State Highway & Transportation Officials (AASHTO)

A nonprofit, nonpartisan association representing highway and transportation departments in the 50 states, the District of Columbia and Puerto Rico. It represents all five transportation modes: air, highways, public transportation, rail and water. Its primary goal is to foster the development, operation and maintenance of an integrated national transportation system.

American Public Transportation Association (APTA)

Acting as a leading force in advancing public transportation, APTA serves and leads its diverse membership through advocacy, innovation, and information sharing to strengthen and expand public transportation.

Americans with Disabilities Act (ADA)

The legislation defining the responsibilities of and requirements for transportation providers to make transportation accessible to individuals with disabilities.

Amtrak

Operated by the National Railroad Passenger Corporation, this rail system was created by the Rail Passenger Service Act of 1970 (Public Law 91–518, 84 Stat. 1327) and given the responsibility for the operation of intercity, as distinct from suburban, passenger trains between points designated by the Secretary of Transportation.

Arterial

A class of roads serving major traffic movements (high-speed, high volume) for travel between major points.

Asphalt

A dark brown to black cement-like material containing bitumen as the predominant constituent. The definition includes crude asphalt and finished products such as cements, fluxes, the asphalt content of emulsions, and petroleum distillates blended with asphalt to make cutback asphalt. Asphalt is obtained by petroleum processing.

Attainment Area

An area considered to have air quality that meets or exceeds the U.S. Environmental Protection Agency (EPA) health standards used in the Clean Air Act. Nonattainment areas are areas considered not to have met these standards for designated pollutants. An area may be an attainment area for one pollutant and a nonattainment area for others.

Auto inspection and maintenance (IM)

Programs require the testing of motor vehicles in parts of the country with unhealthy air and the repair of those that do not meet standards.

Automobile

A privately owned and/or operated licensed motorized vehicle including cars, jeeps and station wagons. Leased and rented cars are included if they are privately operated and not used for picking up passengers in return for fare.

Average Annual Daily Traffic (AADT)

The total volume of traffic on a highway segment for one year, divided by the number of days in the year.

Bicycle

A vehicle having two tandem wheels, propelled solely by human power, upon which any person or persons may ride.

Bikeway

(1) Any road, path, or way which in some manner is specifically designated as being open to bicycle travel, regardless of whether such facilities are designated for the exclusive use of bicycles or are to be shared with other transportation modes. (2) A facility designed to accommodate bicycle travel for recreational or commuting purposes. Bikeways are not necessarily separated facilities; they may be designed and operated to be shared with other travel modes.

Blood Alcohol Concentration (BAC)

Is measured as a percentage by weight of alcohol in the blood (grams/deciliter). A positive BAC level (0.01 g/dl and higher) indicates that alcohol was consumed by the person tested. A BAC level of 0.10 g/dl or more indicates that the person was intoxicated.

Bodily Injury

Injury to the body, sickness, or disease including death resulting from any of these.

Bureau of Transportation Statistics (BTS)

The Bureau was organized pursuant to section 6006 of the Intermodal Surface Transportation Efficiency Act (ISTEA) of 1991, and was formally established by the Secretary of Transportation on December 16, 1992. BTS has an intermodal transportation focus whose missions are to compile, analyze and make accessible information on the Nation's transportation systems; to collect information on intermodal transportation and other areas; and to enhance the quality and effectiveness of DOT's statistical programs through research, the development of guidelines, and the promotion of improvements in data acquisition and use.

Bus

Large motor vehicle used to carry more than 10 passengers, including school buses, intercity buses, and transit buses.

Bus Lane

(1) A street or highway lane intended primarily for buses, either all day or during specified periods, but sometimes also used by carpools meeting requirements set out in traffic laws. (2) A lane reserved for bus use only. Sometimes also known as a "diamond lane."

Capacity

A transportation facility's ability to accommodate a moving stream of people or vehicles in a given time period.

Capital Program Funds

Financial assistance from the Capital Program. This program enables the Secretary of Transportation to make discretionary capital grants and loans to finance public transportation projects divided among fixed guideway (rail) modernization; construction of new fixed guideway systems and extensions to fixed guideway systems; and replacement, rehabilitation, and purchase of buses and rented equipment, and construction of bus-related facilities.

Carbon Dioxide (CO_2)

A colorless, odorless gas produced by burning carbon and organic compounds and by respiration. It is naturally present in air (about 0.03 percent) and is absorbed by plants in photosynthesis.

Carbon Monoxide (CO)

A colorless, odorless, highly toxic gas that is a normal by-product of incomplete fossil fuel combustion. Carbon monoxide, one of the major air pollutants, can be harmful in small amounts if breathed over a certain period of time.

Carpool

An arrangement where two or more people share the use and cost of privately owned automobiles in traveling to and from pre-arranged destinations together.

Census

The complete enumeration of a population or groups at a point in time with respect to well-defined characteristics for example, population, production, traffic on particular roads. In some connection the term is associated with the data collected rather than the extent of the collection so that the term sample census has a distinct meaning. The partial enumeration resulting from a failure to cover the whole population, as distinct from a designed sample enquiry, may be referred to as an "incomplete census."

Charter Bus

A bus transporting a group of persons who pursuant to a common purpose, and under a single contract at a fixed price, have acquired the exclusive use of a bus to travel together under an itinerary.

Clean Air Act Amendments (CAAA)

The original Clean Air Act was passed in 1963, but the national air pollution control program is actually based on the 1970 version of the law. The 1990 Clean Air Act Amendments are the most far-reaching revisions of the 1970 law. The 1990 Clean Air Act is the most recent version of the 1970 version of the law. The 1990 amendments made major changes in the Clean Air Act.

Collector

In rural areas, routes that serve intracounty rather than statewide travel. In urban areas, streets that provide direct access to neighborhoods and arterials.

Commercial Bus

Any bus used to carry passengers at rates specified in tariffs; charges may be computed per passenger (as in regular route service) or per vehicle (as in charter service).

Commute

Regular travel between home and a fixed location (e.g., work, school).

Commuter

A person who travels regularly between home and work or school.

Commuter Lane

Another name for "High-Occupancy Vehicle Lane."

Commuter Rail

Urban passenger train service for short-distance travel between a central city and adjacent suburb. Does not include rapid rail transit or light rail service.

Compressed Natural Gas (CNG)

Natural gas compressed to a volume and density that is practical as a portable fuel supply. It is used as a fuel for natural gas-powered vehicles.

Conformity

Process to assess the compliance of any transportation plan, program, or project with air quality implementation plans. The conformity process is defined by the Clean Air Act.

Congestion Management System (CMS)

Systematic process for managing congestion. Provides information on transportation system performance and finds alternative ways to alleviate congestion and enhance the mobility of people and goods, to levels that meet state and local needs.

Corporate Average Fuel Economy Standards (CAFÉ)

Originally established by Congress for new automobiles and later for light trucks, this law requires automobile manufacturers to produce vehicle fleets with a composite sales-weighted fuel economy not lower than the CAFE standards in a given year. For every vehicle that does not meet the standard, a fine is paid for every one-tenth of a mile per gallon that vehicle falls below the standard.

Corridor

A broad geographical band that follows a general directional flow connecting major sources of trips that may contain a number of streets, highways and transit route alignments.

Crash

An event that produces injury and/or property damage, involves a motor vehicle in transport, and occurs on a traffic way or while the vehicle is still in motion after running off the traffic way.

Demand-Responsive

Descriptive term for a service type, usually considered paratransit, in which a user can access transportation service that can be variably routed and timed to meet changing needs on an as-needed basis.

Demand Responsive Vehicle

A nonfixed-route, nonfixed-schedule vehicle that operates in response to calls from passengers or their agents to the transit operator or dispatcher.

Department of Energy (DOE)

The Department of Energy's overarching mission is to advance the national, economic and energy security of the United States; to promote scientific and technological innovation in support of that mission; and to ensure the environmental cleanup of the national nuclear weapons complex.

Department of Housing and Urban Development (HUD)

HUD's mission is to increase homeownership, support community development and increase access to affordable housing free from discrimination.

Department of Transportation (DOT)

Establishes the nation's overall transportation policy. Under its umbrella there are ten administrations whose jurisdictions include highway planning, development and construction; urban mass transit; railroads; aviation; and the safety of waterways, ports, highways, and oil and gas pipelines. The Department of Transportation (DOT) was established by act of October 15, 1966, "to assure the coordinated, effective administration of the transportation programs of the Federal Government" and to develop "national transportation policies and programs conducive to the provision of fast, safe, efficient, and convenient transportation at the lowest cost consistent therewith."

Deregulation

Revisions or complete elimination of economic regulations controlling transportation. For example, the Motor Carrier Act of 1980 and the Staggers Act of 1980 revised the economic controls over motor carriers and railroads.

Dial-A-Ride

Term for demand-responsive systems usually delivering door-to-door service to clients, who make request by telephone on an as-needed reservation or subscription basis.

Driver

(1) A person who operates a motorized vehicle. If more than one person drives on a single trip, the person who drives the most miles is classified as the principal driver. (2) An occupant of a vehicle who is in physical control of a motor vehicle in transport or, for an out of-control vehicle, an occupant who was in control until control was lost.

Driver's License

A license issued by a State or other jurisdiction, to an individual which authorizes the individual to operate a motor vehicle on the highways.

Driving Under the Influence (DUI)

The driving or operating of any vehicle or common carrier while drunk or under the influence of liquor or narcotics.

Emissions Budget

The part of the State Implementation Plan (SIP) that identifies the allowable emissions levels, mandated by the National Ambient Air Quality Standards (NAAQS), for certain pollutants emitted from mobile, stationary, and area sources. The emissions levels are used for meeting emission reduction milestones, attainment, or maintenance demonstrations.

Emissions Inventory

A complete list of sources and amounts of pollutant emissions within a specific area and time interval.

Energy Efficiency

The ratio of energy inputs to outputs from a process, for example, miles traveled per gallon of fuel (mpg).

Environmental Impact Statement (EIS)

Report developed as part of the National Environmental Policy Act requirements, which details any adverse economic, social, and environmental effects of a proposed transportation project for which Federal funding is being sought. Adverse effects could include air, water, or noise pollution; destruction or disruption of natural resources; adverse employment effects; injurious displacement of people or businesses; or disruption of desirable community or regional growth.

Environmental Justice (EJ)

Environmental justice assures that services and benefits allow for meaningful participation and are fairly distributed to avoid discrimination.

Environmental Protection Agency (EPA)

The federal regulatory agency responsible for administering and enforcing federal environmental laws, including the Clean Air Act, the Clean Water Act, the Endangered Species Act, and others.

Ethanol

A clear, colorless, flammable oxygenated hydrocarbon with a boiling point of 78.5 °C in the anhydrous state. It is used in the United States as a gasoline octane enhancer and oxygenate (10 percent concentration). Ethanol can be used in high concentrations in vehicles optimized for its use. Otherwise known as ethyl alcohol, alcohol, or grain-spirit.

Evaluation of alternatives

A synthesis of the information generated by an analysis in which judgments are made on the relative merits of alternative actions.

Expressway

A controlled access, divided arterial highway for through traffic, the intersections of which are usually separated from other roadways by differing grades.

Fatality

For purposes of statistical reporting on transportation safety, a fatality is considered a death due to injuries in a transportation crash, accident, or incident that occurs within 30 days of that occurrence.

Federal-Aid Highway Program (FAHP)

An umbrella term for most of the Federal programs providing highway funds to the States. This is not a term defined in law. As used in this document, FAHP is comprised of those programs authorized in Titles I and V of TEA-21 that are administered by FHWA.

Federal-Aid Highways

Those highways eligible for assistance under Title 23 U.S.C. except those functionally classified as local or rural minor collectors.

Federal Highway Administration (FHWA)

A branch of the U.S. Department of Transportation that administers the federal-aid Highway Program, providing financial assistance to states to construct and improve highways, urban and rural roads, and bridges. The FHWA also administers the Federal Lands Highway Program, including survey, design, and construction of forest highway system roads, parkways and park roads, Indian reservation roads, defense access roads, and other Federal lands roads. The Federal agency within the U.S. Department of Transportation responsible for administering the Federal-Aid Highway Program. Became a component of the Department of Transportation in 1967 pursuant to the Department of Transportation Act.

Federal Railroad Administration (FRA)

The purpose of the Federal Railroad Administration is to promulgate and enforce rail safety regulations, administer railroad financial assistance programs, conduct research and development in support of improved railroad safety and national rail transportation policy, provide for the rehabilitation of Northeast corridor rail passenger service, and consolidate government support of rail transportation activities. The FRA was created pursuant to section 3(e)(1) of the Department of Transportation Act of 1966.

Federal Transit Administration (FTA)

A branch of the U.S. Department of Transportation that is the principal source of federal financial assistance to America's communities for planning, development, and improvement of public or mass transportation systems. FTA provides leadership, technical assistance, and financial resources for safe, technologically advanced public transportation to enhance mobility and accessibility, to improve the Nation's communities and natural environment, and to strengthen the national economy.

Fixed-Route

Term applied to transit service that is regularly scheduled and operates over a set route; usually refers to bus service.

Freeway

A divided arterial highway designed for the unimpeded flow of large traffic volumes. Access to a freeway is rigorously controlled and intersection grade separations are required.

Gasoline

A complex mixture of relatively volatile hydrocarbons, with or without small quantities of additives that have been blended to produce a fuel suitable for use in spark ignition engines. Motor gasoline includes both leaded and unleaded grades of finished motor gasoline, blending components, and gasohol. Leaded gasoline is no longer used in highway motor vehicles in the United States.

Geographic Information System (GIS)

(1) Computerized data management system designed to capture, store, retrieve, analyze, and display geographically referenced information. (2) A system of hardware, software, and data for collecting, storing, analyzing, and disseminating information about areas of the Earth. For Highway Performance Monitoring System (HPMS) purposes, Geographical Information System (GIS) is defined as a highway network (spatial data which graphically represents the geometry of the highways, an electronic map) and its geographically referenced component attributes (HPMS section data, bridge data, and other data including socioeconomic data) that are integrated through GIS technology to perform analyses. From this, GIS can display attributes and analyze results electronically in map form. (FHWA2)

Grants

A federal financial assistance award making payment in cash or in kind for a specified purpose. The federal government is not expected to have substantial involvement with the state or local government or other recipient while the contemplated activity is being performed. The term "grants-in-aid" is commonly restricted to grants to states and local governments.

Heavy Rail

An electric railway with the capacity to transport a heavy volume of passenger traffic and characterized by exclusive rights-of-way, multicar trains, high speed, rapid acceleration, sophisticated signaling, and high-platform loading. Also known as: Subway, Elevated (railway), or Metropolitan railway (metro).

High Occupancy Vehicle (HOV)

Vehicles carrying two or more people. The number that constitutes an HOV for the purposes of HOV highway lanes may be designated differently by different transportation agencies.

High Occupancy Vehicle Lane

Exclusive road or traffic lane limited to buses, vanpools, carpools, and emergency vehicles.

Highway

Is any road, street, parkway, or freeway/expressway that includes rights-of-way, bridges, railroad-highway crossings, tunnels, drainage structures, signs, guardrail, and protective structures in connection with highways. The highway further includes that portion of any interstate or international bridge or tunnel and the approaches thereto.

Highway Trust Fund (HTF)

An account established by law to hold Federal highway user taxes that are dedicated for highway and transit related purposes. The HTF has two accounts: the Highway Account, and the Mass Transit Account.

Highway-User Tax

A charge levied on persons or organizations based on their use of public roads. Funds collected are usually applied toward highway construction, reconstruction, and maintenance.

Hydrocarbons (HC)

Colorless gaseous compounds originating from evaporation and the incomplete combustion of fossil fuels.

Infrastructure

(1) In transit systems, all the fixed components of the transit system, such as rights-of-way, tracks, signal equipment, stations, park-and-ride lots, but stops, maintenance facilities. (2) In transportation planning, all the relevant elements of the environment in which a transportation system operates. (3) A term connoting the physical underpinnings of society at large, including, but not limited to, roads, bridges, transit, waste systems, public housing, sidewalks, utility installations, parks, public buildings, and communications networks.

Intelligent Transportation Systems (ITS)

The application of advanced technologies to improve the efficiency and safety of transportation systems.

Intermodal

The ability to connect, and the connections between, modes of transportation.

Intermodal Surface Transportation Efficiency Act of 1991 (ISTEA)

Legislative initiative by the U.S. Congress that restructured funding for transportation programs. ISTEA authorized increased levels of highway and transportation funding from FY92–97 and increased the role of regional planning commissions/MPOs in funding decisions. The

Act also required comprehensive regional and State-wide long-term transportation plans and places an increased emphasis on public participation and transportation alternatives.

Interstate Highway

Limited access, divided highway of at least four lanes designated by the Federal Highway Administration as part of the Interstate System.

Interstate Highway System (IHS)

The system of highways that connects the principal metropolitan areas, cities, and industrial centers of the United States. Also connects the U.S. to internationally significant routes in Canada and Mexico.

Land Use

Refers to the manner in which portions of land or the structures on them are used, i.e., commercial, residential, retail, industrial, etc.

Land Use Plan

A plan which establishes strategies for the use of land to meet identified community needs.

Large Truck

Trucks over 10,000 pounds gross vehicle weight rating, including single-unit trucks and truck tractors.

Level of Service (LOS)

(1) A qualitative assessment of a road's operating conditions. For local government comprehensive planning purposes, level of service means an indicator of the extent or degree of service provided by, or proposed to be provided by, a facility based on and related to the operational characteristics of the facility. Level of service indicates the capacity per unit of demand for each public facility. (2) This term refers to a standard measurement used by transportation officials which reflects the relative ease of traffic flow on a scale of A to F, with free-flow being rated LOS-A and congested conditions rated as LOS-F.

Light Rail

A streetcar-type vehicle operated on city streets, semi-exclusive rights-of-way, or exclusive rights-of-way. Service may be provided by step-entry vehicles or by level boarding.

Local Street

A street intended solely for access to adjacent properties.

Long Range Transportation Plan (LRTP)

A document resulting from regional or statewide collaboration and consensus on a region or state's transportation system, and serving as the defining vision for the region's or state's transportation systems and services. In metropolitan areas, the plan indicates all of the transportation improvements scheduled for funding over the next 20 years.

Long Term

In transportation planning, refers to a time span of, generally, 20 years. The transportation plan for metropolitan areas and for States should include projections for land use, population, and employment for the 20-year period.

Mass Transportation

Another name for public transportation.

Mass Transportation Agency

An agency authorized to transport people by bus, rail, or other conveyance, either publicly or privately owned, and providing to the public general or special service (but not including school, charter or sightseeing service) on a regular basis.

Metropolitan Planning Area

The geographic area in which the metropolitan transportation planning process required by 23 U.S.C. 134 and section 8 of the Federal Transit Act must be carried out.

Metropolitan Planning Organization (MPO)

(1) Regional policy body, required in urbanized areas with populations over 50,000, and designated by local officials and the governor of the state. Responsible in cooperation with the state and other transportation providers for carrying out the metropolitan transportation planning requirements of federal highway and transit legislation. (2) Formed in cooperation with the state, develops transportation plans and programs for the metropolitan area. For each urbanized area, a Metropolitan Planning Organization (MPO) must be designated by agreement between the Governor and local units of government representing 75 percent of the affected population (in the metropolitan area), including the central cities or cities as defined by the Bureau of the Census, or in accordance with procedures established by applicable State or local law .

Metropolitan Statistical Area (MSA)

A Metropolitan Statistical Area (MSA) is (1) A county or a group of contiguous counties that contain at least one city of 50,000 inhabitants or more, or (2) An urbanized area of at least 50,000 inhabitants and a total MSA population of at least 100,000 (75,000 in New England). The contiguous counties are included in an MSA if, according to certain criteria, they are essentially metropolitan in character and are socially and economically integrated with the central city. In New England, MSAs consist of towns and cities rather than counties.

Metropolitan Transportation Plan (MTP)

The official intermodal transportation plan that is developed and adopted through the metropolitan transportation planning process for the metropolitan planning area.

Miles per Gallon (MPG)

A measure of vehicle fuel efficiency. Miles per Gallon (MPG) represents "Fleet Miles per Gallon." For each subgroup or "table cell," MPG is computed as the ratio of the total number of miles traveled by all vehicles in the subgroup to the total number of gallons consumed. MPGs are assigned to each vehicle using the Environmental Protection Agency (EPA) certification files and adjusted for on-road driving.

Minor Arterials

Roads linking cities and larger towns in rural areas. In urban areas, roads that link but do not penetrate neighborhoods within a community.

Mobility

The ability to move or be moved from place to place.

Mode

A specific form of transportation, such as automobile, subway, bus, rail, or air.

Motorbus

A rubber-tired, self-propelled, manually steered bus with a fuel supply onboard the vehicle. Motorbus types include intercity, school, and transit.

Motorcycle

A two- or three-wheeled motor vehicle designed to transport one or two people, including motor scooters, minibikes, and mopeds.

Motorized Vehicle

Includes all vehicles that are licensed for highway driving. Specifically excluded are snow mobiles and minibikes.

Multimodal

The availability of transportation options using different modes within a system or corridor.

Multimodal Transportation

Often used as a synonym for intermodalism. Congress and others frequently use the term intermodalism in its broadest interpretation as a synonym for multimodal transportation. Most precisely, multimodal transportation covers all modes without necessarily including a holistic or integrated approach.

National Ambient Air Quality Standards (NAAQS)

Federal standards that set allowable concentrations and exposure limits for various pollutants. The EPA developed the standards in response to a requirement of the CAA. Air quality standards have been established for the following six criteria pollutants: ozone (or smog), carbon monoxide, particulate matter, nitrogen dioxide, lead, and sulfur dioxide.

National Environmental Policy Act of 1969 (NEPA)

Established a national environmental policy requiring that any project using federal funding or requiring federal approval, including transportation projects, examine the effects of proposed and alternative choices on the environment before a federal decision is made.

National Highway Traffic Safety Administration (NHTSA)

The Administration was established by the Highway Safety Act of 1970. The Administration was established to carry out a congressional mandate to reduce the mounting number of deaths, injuries, and economic losses resulting from motor vehicle crashes on the Nation's highways and to provide motor vehicle damage susceptibility and ease of repair information, motor vehicle inspection demonstrations and protection of purchasers of motor vehicles having altered odometers, and to provide average standards for greater vehicle mileage per gallon of fuel for vehicles under 10,000 pounds (gross vehicle weight).

Natural Gas

A naturally occurring mixture of hydrocarbon and nonhydrocarbon gases found in porous geologic formations beneath the Earth's surface, often in association with petroleum. The principal constituent is methane.

Nitrogen Oxide

The term used to describe the sum of nitric oxide (NO), nitrogen dioxide (NO2) and other oxides of nitrogen, play a major role in the formation of ozone. The major sources of man-made NOx emissions are high-temperature combustion processes, such as those occurring in automobiles and power plants.

Nonattainment Area (NAA)

Any geographic area that has not met the requirements for clean air as set out in the Clean Air Act of 1990.

Objectives

Specific, measurable statements related to the attainment of goals.

Occupancy

The number of persons, including driver and passenger(s) in a vehicle. Nationwide Personal Transportation Survey (NPTS) occupancy rates are generally calculated as person miles divided by vehicle miles.

Occupant

Any person who is in or upon a motor vehicle in transport. Includes the driver, passengers, and persons riding on the exterior of a motor vehicle (e.g., a skateboard rider who is set in motion by holding onto a vehicle).

Ozone O3

Ozone is a colorless gas with a sweet odor. Ozone is not a direct emission from transportation sources. It is a secondary pollutant formed when VOCs and NOx combine in the presence of sunlight. Ozone is associated with smog or haze conditions. Although the ozone in the upper atmosphere protects us from harmful ultraviolet rays, ground-level ozone produces an unhealthy environment in which to live. Ozone is created by human and natural sources.

Paratransit

(1) Comparable transportation service required by the American Disabilities Act (ADA) for individuals with disabilities who are unable to use fixed route transportation systems. (2) A variety of smaller, often flexibly scheduled-and-routed transportation services using low-capacity vehicles, such as vans, to operate within normal urban transit corridors or rural areas. These services usually serve the needs of persons that standard mass-transit services would serve with difficulty,

or not at all. Often, the patrons include the elderly and persons with disabilities.

Parking Area

An area set aside for the parking of motor vehicles.

Parkway

A highway that has full or partial access control, is usually located within a park or a ribbon of park-like developments, and prohibits commercial vehicles. Buses are not considered commercial vehicles in this case.

Particulate Matter (PM10 and PM2.5)

Particulate matter consists of airborne solid particles and liquid droplets. Particulate matter may be in the form of fly ash, soot, dust, fog, fumes, etc. These particles are classified as "coarse" if they are smaller than 10 microns, or "fine" if they are smaller than 2.5 microns. Coarse airborne particles are produced during grinding operations, or from the physical disturbance of dust by natural air turbulence processes, such as wind. Fine particles can be a by-product of fossil fuel combustion, such as diesel and bus engines. Fine particles can easily reach remote lung areas, and their presence in the lungs is linked to serious respiratory ailments such as asthma, chronic bronchitis and aggravated coughing. Exposure to these particles may aggravate other medical conditions such as heart disease and emphysema and may cause premature death. In the environment, particulate matter contributes to diminished visibility and particle deposition (soiling).

Passenger Car

A motor vehicle designed primarily for carrying passengers on ordinary roads, includes convertibles, sedans, and stations wagons.

Pedestrian

Any person not in or on a motor vehicle or other vehicle. Excludes people in buildings or sitting at a sidewalk cafe.

Pedestrian Walkway (or Walkway)

A continuous way designated for pedestrians and separated from the through lanes for motor vehicles by space or barrier.

Person-Miles

An estimate of the aggregate distances traveled by all persons on a given trip based on the estimated transportation-network-miles traveled on that trip.

Person Trip

A trip taken by an individual. For example, if three persons from the same household travel together, the trip is counted as one household trip and three person trips.

Petroleum (Oil)

A generic term applied to oil and oil products in all forms, such as crude oil, lease condensate, unfinished oils, petroleum products, natural gas plant liquids, and nonhydrocarbon compounds blended into finished petroleum products.

Privately Owned Vehicle (POV)

(1) A privately owned vehicle or privately operated vehicle. (2) Employee's own vehicle used on official business for which the employee is reimbursed by the government on the basis of mileage.

Problem Identification

An element in the planning process which represents the gap between the desired vision, goals and objectives and the current or projected performance of the system

Public Meeting or Hearing

A public gathering for the express purpose of informing and soliciting input from interested individuals regarding transportation issues.

Public Participation

The active and meaningful involvement of the public in the development of transportation plans and programs.

Public Road

Any road under the jurisdiction of and maintained by a public authority (federal, state, county, town or township, local government, or instrumentality thereof) and open to public travel.

Public Transit

Passenger transportation services, usually local in scope, that is available to any person who pays a prescribed fare. It operates on established schedules along designated routes or lines with specific stops and is designed to move relatively large numbers of people at one time.

Public Transit Agencies

A public entity responsible for administering and managing transit activities and services. Public transit agencies can directly operate transit service or contract out for all or part of the total transit service provided.

Public Transportation

Transportation by bus, rail, or other conveyance, either publicly or privately owned, which provides to the public general or special service on a regular and continuing basis. Also known as "mass transportation", "mass transit" and "transit."

Rail

A rolled steel shape laid in two parallel lines to form a track for carrying vehicles with flanged steel wheels.

Rapid Rail Transit

Transit service using railcars driven by electricity usually drawn from a third rail, configured for passenger traffic, and usually operated on exclusive rights-of-way. It generally uses longer trains and has longer station spacing than light rail.

Regional Planning Organization (RPO)

An organization that performs planning for multi-jurisdictional areas. MPOs, regional councils, economic development associations, rural transportation associations are examples of RPOs.

Reliability

Refers to the degree of certainty and predictability in travel times on the transportation system. Reliable transportation systems offer some assurance of attaining a given destination within a reasonable range of an expected time. An unreliable transportation system is subject to unexpected delays, increasing costs for system users

Research

Investigation or experimentation aimed at the discovery of new theories or laws and the discovery and interpretation of facts or revision of accepted theories or laws in the light of new facts.

Right of Way

The land (usually a strip) acquired for or devoted to transportation purposes.

Road

An open way for the passage of vehicles, persons, or animals on land.

Road Class

The category of roads based on design, weatherability, their governmental designation, and the Department of Transportation functional classification system.

Safety Management System

A systematic process that has the goal of reducing the number and severity of transportation related accidents by ensuring that all opportunities to improve safety are identified, considered and implemented as appropriate.

Smart Growth

A set of policies and programs design to protect, preserve, and economically develop established communities and valuable natural and cultural resources.

Sprawl

Urban form that connotatively depicts the movement of people from the central city to the suburbs. Concerns associated with sprawl include loss of farmland and open space due to low-density land development, increased public service costs, and environmental degradation as well as other concerns associated with transportation.

Stakeholder

Person or goup affected by a transportation plan, program or project. Person or group believing that are affected by a transportation plan, program or project. Residents of affected geographical areas.

State Implementation Plan (SIP)

Produced by the state environmental agency, not the MPO. A plan mandated by the CAA that contains procedures to monitor, control, maintain, and enforce compliance with the NAAQS. Must be taken into account in the transportation planning process.

State Transportation Improvement Program (STIP)

A staged, multi-year, statewide, intermodal program of transportation projects, consistent with the statewide transportation plan and planning processes as well as metropolitan plans, TIPs, and processes.

Streetcars

Relatively lightweight passenger railcars operating singly or in short trains, or on fixed rails in rights-of-way that are not always separated from other traffic. Streetcars do not necessarily have the right-of-way at grade crossings with other traffic.

Surface Transportation Program (STP)

Federal-aid highway funding program that funds a broad range of surface transportation capital needs, including many roads, transit, sea and airport access, vanpool, bike, and pedestrian facilities.

Telecommuting

Communicating electronically (by telephone, computer, fax, etc.) with an office, either from home or from another site, instead of traveling to it physically.

Title VI

Title VI of the Civil Rights Act of 1964. Prohibits discrimination in any program receiving federal assistance.

Transportation Conformity

Process to assess the compliance of any transportation plan, program, or project with air quality implementation plans. The conformity process is defined by the Clean Air Act.

Transportation Demand Management (TDM)

Programs designed to reduce demand for transportation through various means, such as the use of transit and of alternative work hours.

Transportation Equity Act for the 21st Century (TEA-21)

Authorized in 1998, TEA-21 authorized federal funding for transportation investment for fiscal years 1998–2003. Approximately $217 billion in funding was authorized, which was used for highway, transit, and other surface transportation programs.

Transportation Improvement Program (TIP)

A document prepared by a metropolitan planning organization that lists projects to be funded with FHWA/FTA funds for the next one- to three-year period.

Trolley Bus

Rubber-tired electric transit vehicle, manually steered and propelled by a motor drawing current, normally through overhead wires, from a central power source.

Unlinked Passenger Trips (Transit)

The number of passengers boarding public transportation vehicles. A passenger is counted each time he/she boards a vehicle even if the boarding is part of the same journey from origin to destination.

Urbanized Area

Area that contains a city of 50,000 or more population plus incorporated surrounding areas meeting size or density criteria as defined by the U.S. Census.

Vanpool

Public-sponsored commuter service operating under prearranged schedules for previously formed groups of riders in 8- to 18-seat vehicles.

Vehicle Miles of Travel (VMT)

The number of miles traveled nationally by vehicles for a period of 1 year. VMT is either calculated using 2 odometer readings or, for vehicles with less than 2 odometer readings, imputed using a regression estimate.

Visioning

A variety of techniques that can be used to identify goals.

Volatile Organic Compounds (VOCs)

VOCs come from vehicle exhaust, paint thinners, solvents, and other petroleum-based products. A number of exhaust VOCs are also toxic, with the potential to cause cancer.

Zone

The smallest geographically designated area for analysis of transportation activity. A zone can be from one to ten square miles in area. Average zone size depends on the total size of study area.

Index